STUDIES IN IMPERIALISM

general editor John M. MacKenzie

Established in the belief that imperialism as a cultural
phenomenon had as significant an effect on the dominant
as on the subordinate societies, Studies in Imperialism
seeks to develop the new socio-cultural approach which
has emerged through cross-disciplinary work on popular
culture, media studies, art history, the study of education
and religion, sports history and children's literature.
The cultural emphasis embraces studies of migration and
race, while the older political, and constitutional,
economic and military concerns will never be far away.
It will incorporate comparative work on European and
American empire-building, with the chronological focus
primarily, though not exclusively, on the nineteenth and
twentieth centuries, when these cultural exchanges were
most powerfully at work.

STUDIES IN IMPERIALISM

Revolution and empire

ENGLISH POLITICS AND THE AMERICAN COLONIES
IN THE SEVENTEENTH CENTURY

Robert M. Bliss

MANCHESTER
UNIVERSITY PRESS
Manchester and New York

Distributed exclusively in the USA and Canada
by ST. MARTIN'S PRESS

Published by MANCHESTER UNIVERSITY PRESS
OXFORD ROAD, MANCHESTER M13 9PL, UK
and ROOM 400, 175 FIFTH AVENUE, NEW YORK, NY 10010, USA

Distributed exclusively in the USA and Canada
by ST. MARTIN'S PRESS, INC.
175 FIFTH AVENUE, NEW YORK, NY 10010, USA

British Library cataloguing in publication data
Bliss, Robert M. (Robert McKinley), 1943–
    Revolution and empire: English politics and the American
    colonies in the seventeenth century. – (Studies in imperialism)
    1. United States. Colonisation, 1607-1775 by Great Britain
    I. Title   II. Series
    973.2

Library of Congress cataloging in publication data
Bliss, Robert M. (Robert McKinley), 1943–
    Revolution and empire: English politics and the American colonies
    in the seventeenth century / Robert M. Bliss.
        p. cm. – (Studies in imperialism)
    Includes index.
    ISBN 0-7190-2383-1
    1. United States – History – Colonial period, ca. 1600-1775.
    2. Great Britain – Colonies – America – History – 17th century.
    3. Great Britain – Politics and government – 1625-1649.
    4. Great Britain – Politics and government – 1649-1660.
    5. Great Britain – Politics and government – 1660-1688.
    I. Title. II. Series: Studies in imperialism (Manchester, England)
    E191.657   1990
    973.2 – dc20   90-6462

ISBN 0-7190-2383-1 *hardback*

Typeset in Trump Mediaeval by
Koinonia Limited, Manchester
Printed in Great Britain
by Biddles Limited, Guildford and King's Lynn

CONTENTS

GENERAL INTRODUCTION

This book marks a new and welcome departure for this series. Previous volumes have concentrated on nineteenth- and twentieth-century imperialism. But this study casts our attention back to a century when the word imperialism had not even been coined, let alone acquired the wealth of meanings it has now. Even the term 'empire', which *was* in circulation, had a limited use and meaning. It implied rule or power, but was not usually employed to describe territory held under that power. Yet it has long been obvious that early modern England's expansion into the wider world did create a territorial empire, call it what we will, and Dr Bliss's study of the politics of that empire indicates that imperialism was also alive and well, thought of if not yet spoken, in England and its American colonies.

From 1625, when Charles I announced his intention to make the infant settlements part of his royal empire, to 1689, when a colonial clergyman told William III that he might, if he pleased, be emperor of America, metropolitan power and colonial dependence shaped the politics of empire. As in more modern imperialisms, colonial elites responded ambiguously to their situation, resenting imperial interference and rule while profiting from their closer ties with the centre, acting as leaders of local resistance while emulating metropolitan standards and styles. This was, to be sure, an empire of settlement rather than subjugation. Colonial populations were largely English or Creole, and the only true indigenes, the native Americans, were generally pushed aside or exterminated rather than incorporated and exploited. Yet, as in later times, England's seventeenth-century empire embodied a chain of exploitative relations which reflected metropolitan and colonial political and social structures, and linked the centre of power and wealth, the crown, to its furthest extremity in the indentured servants and African slaves of English America. Partly in order to ensure that this chain had no weak link, partly in response to the needs of economic growth and change, governments waxed in power and function. This dynamic relationship between empire and power also has a modern ring to it, not least because it was shaped by and helped to shape a century of revolution.

Robert Bliss explores the interaction of English and colonial politics in a notably original way. His book is emphatically not an essay on the origins of modern imperialism, but it is a study of imperial forces and forms influencing societies on both sides of the Atlantic. As such it not only fits the specification of the series, but may stimulate debates among historians of empire in different periods and continents.   J. M. M.

For my father, Robert,
and my mother, Clara May

PREFACE

England produced two dramatic revolutions during the seventeenth century, the Puritan upheaval of the 1640s and 1650s and the Glorious Revolution of 1688. These crises did much to shape the empire and colonies, often by provoking colonial reaction, as with the 'royalist' rebellions of 1649-51 and the mimetic uprisings of 1689, but also indirectly by bringing forth new ideas about government. But there was another revolution which profoundly affected England, the colonies, and therefore the imperial nexus which bound them together. The colonies' very existence was a manifestation of this revolution, a testament to accumulated capital and population and to a widespread desire to employ both for high and mundane ends. The growth of population and production, the rise of new and the decline of old trades, these were cardinal features of seventeenth-century American and English history, and they created a new world which was not a place on a geographer's map to which one could go or from which one could return. There was a choice, however, made thousands of times on both sides of the ocean; Englishmen who experienced this new world might react against it or embrace it. This tension, fundamentally political, between the old and the new shaped the empire and its constituent parts. Colonists, mainly English in background and attachment, met their new world in a wilderness environment, but they were not necessarily readier to change their ways on that account. The institutions of empire, including colonial governments themselves, grew from a shared experience as well as from a shared political culture.

This study covers the North American and West Indian colonies as well as England. Research on America has concentrated on the main settlements of Massachusetts, Virginia, Barbados, and Jamaica. Reference to lesser colonies, for instance New York, Carolina, and the fringe settlements of New England, arises less from a desire to be comprehensive than from the fact that the more fragile settlements have their own tales to tell about the processes of adjustment. Research on England has emphasized sources conventionally used by imperial and colonial historians, but attention has been paid to political writing and the 'non-colonial' activities of governments and politicians, among the latter concentrating on the Restoration figures of Clarendon, Shaftesbury, and Danby.

It is not possible to deal fully with politics in England and the colonies in one volume. Chapter 1 explains some of the limitations and also serves to introduce my argument and to sketch the historical background to 1625. One of the principal difficulties has been to keep my eye, and the reader's, on both England and the main American settlements, different places where similar developments often went at a different pace. Chapters 2 through 7 solve this problem, sensibly I hope, by alternating between American (2, 4, and 6) and English (3, 5, and 7) emphases. Chapters 8 and 9 are transatlantic in scope.

It is not for me to say how well I have succeeded. But readers should not blame those who have helped my research and writing. Most of the debts are acknowl-

PREFACE

edged in the endnotes, although mere notes cannot pay tribute enough to the general excellence of scholarship on seventeenth-century English and American history. I should single out for mention two areas in which I have done little research, and thus depend heavily on the work of others. These are English local history and colonial social history, rich fields indeed for any who would play the trespasser, or the poacher, and essential for a full understanding of the political history of England's empire. In acknowledging my debts to historians, endnotes partially conceal my dependence on the courtesies extended to me by librarians at the Universities of Wisconsin, Oxford, Lancaster, and Manchester, at the British Library, the Public Record Office, and the Institute for Historical Research, all in London, and at the Scottish Record Office in Edinburgh. I owe a great deal, also, to the financial generosity of three institutions. The Wisconsin Alumni Research Foundation, long ago, funded a year at Linacre College, Oxford. The University of Lancaster not only honored its generous sabbatical arrangements but also fully funded two terms' study in 1984-85. Finally, the Newberry Library, Chicago, granted me a short-term fellowship in the spring of 1981 and thus introduced me to its wonderful resources and its uniquely enjoyable scholarly environment.

Personal debts are many more than a short preface can repay. Pride of place belongs to my family, which confounds geography to act in the way we used to think colonial families behaved, extending love and money across generations and beyond nuclearity. Two family members figure in the dedication. My wife Paulette and my children Daniel and Greta, who know this book better than my father and mother, will have to rest content with love and money and wait for another book for me to express my thanks properly. Outside the family, David Lovejoy is an extra-ordinary person in many ways, notably in the tolerant patience he showed in supervising my postgraduate work at the University of Wisconsin. Not satisfied with that, David and his wife Bett have provided much hospitality and help over two decades in Madison, Wisconsin, and Stonesfield, Oxfordshire. Since 1970, the History Department at Lancaster has given me a job, better yet, a rewarding one. I am especially thankful that Austin Woolrych was my first boss, for I have learned much from him about seventeenth- (and twentieth-) century England. Other Lancaster colleagues who have read some of this book, and improved it, are Lee Beier, Michael Mullett, Michael Heale, John Gooch, and John Walton. Gordon Phillips and Marcus Merriman have *heard* the book and are, I imagine, looking forward to some other topic of conversation. Another Lancaster colleague, John MacKenzie, is the editor of the series in which this book appears, and I hope it does justice to his challenging conception of that series. A succession of students in the department have experienced bits of this book, and have made helpful suggestions. I particularly thank three veterans of my Special Subject on seventeenth-century New England, Cliff O'Neill, Joan Kind, and Matt Grunnill. Their work varied in quality, but not in enthusiasm, and in each case they pointed out areas of inquiry I had intended to leave alone. Finally, Professors Geoffrey Holmes of Lancaster and Jack Pole of Oxford gave important help when I needed fellowship support in both 1981 and 1984.

I wish also to thank two colleges. In 1969-70, Linacre College provided me with a model of how a community of tutors, staff, and students should operate

PREFACE

academically and socially. Since then, Linacre has often provided me with pleasant lodgings in Oxford. In both respects, I owe much to the first Principal, John Bamborough, and the Domestic Bursar, Peter Holloway. My experience of Linacre had much to do with my decision to play an active role in Lancaster's college system, where I have been a member of Grizedale College since its foundation in 1975 and its Principal since 1978. I cannot say that Grizedale has sped this book toward completion, but it has taught me something of the richness of university life. Among the best teachers have been a succession of very active student officers, too numerous to name; fellow senior officers, notably Henry Huddart, Jim Wood, and Michael Heale; and the college's permanent staff. I owe much thanks, especially, to two secretaries, Jayne Close and June Cross, and to the college's Manager, Betty Errington, three capable persons who have kept me honest and saved me much labor.

Robert M. Bliss
Lancaster, 1990

CHAPTER ONE

Introduction: a survey of the imperial territory and the beginnings of political empire

During the seventeenth century, England's empire grew from a publicists' dream to a precocious maturity. In 1600 there were no permanent English settlements in America; by 1700, there were seventeen jurisdictions with a population of about 400,000 spread along the North American seaboard and thickly inhabiting several Caribbean and Atlantic islands. Most of the 275,000 white settlers (mainly English) lived in rude comfort, but in most colonies appreciable numbers lived well, some very well; the planter's mansion and the merchant's town house had already made their appearance. Rude comfort and prosperity were based largely on agricultural production, which was either consumed locally or traded between colonies and across the Atlantic. Most transatlantic trade went to England, funnelled there by commercial considerations and the legal requirements of the English navigation system. England's political sovereignty in the empire was unquestioned, and although the precise implications of that sovereignty had sometimes caused conflict, the mechanisms of imperial government were well developed and well understood by 1700. Advisory councils of trade and plantations had a long history before the establishment, in 1696, of the Board of Trade, and from their creation in 1671 the Commissioners of the Customs had taken a lively interest in the colonies. Colonial governments, too, had developed mature forms. By 1700, most were royal colonies, commissioned directly by the monarch, but whether they were commissioned or chartered, American governments derived their authority from the crown and their institutional characteristics from the structure of English government. The strength of colonial government and the vitality of the colonial economies may be seen as signs of the continental colonies' eventual achievement of full independence, but this insight was denied to inhabitants of the empire in 1700. Most colonists who shared in government were happy to make use of the legitimacy conferred on them by royal grant and by the similarities between their own and English political institutions. When in 1776 colonists finally did rebel against British rule many testified to the enduring accomplishments of the seventeenth-century empire by affecting a role as defenders of an ancient and customary imperial constitution.[1]

This creation of a prosperous, stable empire was remarkable for taking place during England's 'century of revolution': or, as Lawrence Stone would have it, a century of seismic disturbance which widened fissures already opened in the sixteenth century and produced not only secondary faults but also two revolutions, the first in the 1640s. This revolution brought a republican regime, then in 1660 a restoration of monarchy, but neither political settlement established stability. In due course a second revolution, that of 1688-9, gloriously rounded off the century. Some discount these revolutions or would call them something else, but most historians – indeed, most Englishmen who lived through it – would accept Stone's metaphor; seventeenth-century England was earthquake country.[2] It is hardly surprising, then, that most students of colonial history have concluded that the empire grew rather in spite than because of the course of English politics.

Three broadly agreed views support this conclusion. The first is that imperial history turned on the tension between what Jack Greene calls 'the centrifugal forces inherent in the conditions of settlement' and England's desire to control the colonies and benefit from their growth.[3] Within this consensus, historians disagree about the sources of imperial centralization and of colonial resistance. On the English side, what might be called the mercantilist hegemony has been challenged by Stephen Webb's original, even startling, thesis that military men and attitudes informed England's approach to imperial government from the first and were dominant in the last quarter of the century. Webb would replace with garrison governors and commanders-in-chief the civilian, mercantile men and policies which previous historians such as Charles M. Andrews had seen as central to imperial development.[4] On the colonial side, agreement about the dominance of particularism dissolves into debate over whether the colonial drive for autonomy rested essentially on English political forms and traditions or was born instead of colonial social conflict and the self-seeking of nascent local elites. Thus J. M. Sosin, in developing the latter argument, criticizes David Lovejoy for taking a 'neo-whiggish' view of colonists' use of the principles of England's Glorious Revolution to thwart royal authority in America.[5] This debate, however, is not so clearly defined as some of the disputants like to think. There is indeed a crucial distinction to be made between colonists who held power and those who did not, but if it is neo-whiggish to think that colonists sought power in order to defend their interests and articulate their rights then most historians of the period are neo-whigs, including both Sosin and Lovejoy.

A second broadly held judgment is that seventeenth-century imperial history finds its major turning point during the Restoration era. During the first decades of colonization, little 'was actually accomplished either toward creating an efficient administrative machinery for governing the Empire, or toward developing a coherent system for regulating its commercial activities'. Only after 1660 were there 'serious' attempts to define and implement imperial policy.[6] The navigation system is usually accorded a vital role here, but so too is the political stability which the Restoration promised. While England still had political trauma to experience, it had forsaken the violent political divisions and religious enthusiasms of the 1640s and 1650s. Restoration England seized its chance to govern, and the colonies felt the force of new conditions and new convictions.[7] Of recent students of empire, only Webb challenges this orthodoxy by positing a non-mercantilist theme of continuity which bridges 1660. Even so, most of his *The Governor General* deals with the Restoration era and, in a more recent study, he has emphatically defined *1676* as the critical year for imperial centralization. Professor Sosin's multi-volume history of the empire begins with 1660, and his backwards glances only confirm the view that for the empire the pre-Restoration period was pre-history.[8]

A third consensus about seventeenth-century imperial history arises not from its own practitioners but from the post-1960s explosion in colonial social and economic studies. As historians delve more deeply into colonial societies and use more sophisticated methods of inquiry, the less able they have become to see a unity in seventeenth-century colonial history. Few such works touch directly on imperial history, but most reinforce the view that the colonies' main contribution to the empire was their parochialism. The result, write Professors Greene and Pole, has been a 'signal loss of overall coherence . . .in the field as a whole'. Coherence has been replaced by typology, and we seem to be faced with a colonial history based on five regions of distinctive 'socioeconomic organization and cultural orientation': New England, the middle colonies, the Chesapeake, the lower south, and the Caribbean. The empire may remain as the one unifying theme of seventeenth-century colonial history, but it looks increasingly alien to it, a graft cut into resistant root-stock.[9]

* * *

This study advances alternatives to these areas of consensus. It rests firstly on the proposition that England's empire was shaped by the course of English politics, not by the post-1660 navigation system nor by the century's mercantilist consensus nor by military men and ideas. The debate over the sources of English 'imperial policy' must be supplanted by an understanding of the 'politics of empire'. Secondly, it will argue that although imperial history was marked by tension between colonial resistance and English authority, colonial dependence – political, economic, even psychological – was the empire's underlying reality. Dependence was established early and persisted late, and although the nature of colonial dependence changed over the course of the century, the view that the Restoration marked a central turning point (or a useful starting point) for imperial history must be abandoned. Finally, although the many sharp contrasts between different colonies will not be ignored, the broad view taken here of the politics of empire aims to establish a general framework for understanding seventeenth-century colonial history.

The imperial territory we survey embodied both a community of English culture and a radical physical expansion of the English community. It was therefore shaped by both inheritance and experience. Inheritance was certainly important; their common political culture helped colonists and Englishmen early to grasp the enduring problems of American government. For instance, it has been established that assumptions born of the complex relationship between central and local government in England transferred to imperial and colonial politics.[10] For colonists bent on obtaining or retaining local power, the authority of central government could be at once a potent threat and a pressing necessity, while English politicians generally accepted that effective central government was best served by the existence of stable colonial governments. As it was also widely appreciated that stability required a degree of autonomy, the result was an imperial relationship much more complex and ambiguous than that suggested by most historians and an imperial history marked as much by continuity as by watersheds. Throughout our century, the empire and the colonies were shaped by the Englishness of their inhabitants.

However, this study does not take the naive view that a common cultural inheritance could continue to operate without a social basis or without historical reinforcement. Experience vivified inheritance. Transatlantic and intercolonial communication – complex networks of commerce, migration and remigration, official and private correspondence – sustained common understanding in multifarious ways throughout the century. Economic and social developments in most colonies maintained, perhaps even strengthened individuals' sense of Englishness; 'anglicization' is not a uniquely eighteenth-century phenomenon. Some historical episodes were particularly important both to shaping the empire and to maintaining its Englishness; here England's revolutions enjoy pride of place alongside the Restoration of 1660. Such seismic shifts forced colonists to react and made English politics acutely relevant to the colonial situation. However, such events had another significance, and this lay not so much in the drama of their immediate impact as in how they changed (and marked changes in) the ways in which Englishmen thought about government and sought to organize or benefit from the relationship between state and society.

These changes in political thought and behavior must be a concern of any study entitled *Revolution and Empire*. It should be noted, however, that the title could almost as appropriately read *Empire and Revolution*; for the imperial experience was relevant to the course of England's century of revolution. The empire represented growth and change. It was another of those reminders that nothing would ever be the same again. This suggestion is not meant to reject, even much to modify, the anglocentric perspective upon which this study rests. The American tail did not wag the English dog, but the American experience did typify some crucial problems of seventeenth-century English politics. Englishmen had embarked not only across the Atlantic but also upon that era which we now call 'modern': an era of rapid change, of population increase and mobility, of rising new and declining traditional trades and, generally, of increased production and wealth. Such conditions, encountered in England and in America, challenged existing ideas and institutions and helped to bring forth new ones in religion, politics, and economics. America, the colonies and the empire, were literally and metaphorically parts of a process of discovery which transformed England itself.

The first Earl of Shaftesbury was remarkable among seventeenth-century English politicians for the variety of his interests in America, and his career offers insights into a relationship between colonies and metropolis which was dynamic as well as mimetic. But he was not unique. Shaftesbury's adversary James, Duke of York, governed his New York colony as he would later attempt to govern England (and with similar results).[11] Shaftesbury, York, and a great many other Englishmen on both sides of the Atlantic assumed that the colonies ought to be governed as England was – or ought to be – governed. How government *ought* to operate was a pressing problem during a century of revolution, a problem addressed by such thinkers as Thomas Hobbes, James Harrington, and John Locke, and by colonists, too. They took a lively interest in it as it applied to English politics. But the colonial situation raised similar problems and tempted settlers to build perfect, or at least more effective structures than those they had known. A utopian strain operated in seventeenth-century politics, and not only amongst religious radicals in England nor only in Puritan or Quaker settlements in America. This underlines the importance of political and religious ideas as well as experience in the history of empire. Throughout, intellectual and pragmatic responses to the challenges of the century led to substantial changes in the extent and purpose of state power.

For imperial historians, the navigation system and its supporting administrative agencies are indices of the increasing power of the English state. English historians endorse this view. R. W. K. Hinton notes how, precipitated by economic and political change, the acts of trade replaced economic regulation by prerogative and private contract with devices of law and public administration. Charles Wilson aptly characterizes the navigation system as embodying the 'welfare of Leviathan'.[12] Imperial historians have seen this English Leviathan waxing at the expense of the colonies, but this is only one side of the equation. Colonial governments derived strength from the rising power of the English state. They also grew stronger as they met the challenge of providing competent government for new and rapidly expanding societies. Call it the growth of political stability or the rise of the modern state, Leviathan waxed in both England and America and was not always resisted by Englishmen or colonists.[13]

It is reasonable to characterize these changes as revolutionary, but it would be wrong to see them as invariably progressive or as signposting a clear route to political modernity. Economic and social change challenged traditional ideas about society and government and helped to provoke revolutions and the rise of the modern state, but seventeenth-century Englishmen did not easily abandon the past. A characteristic expression of English politics during the period was the desire to recapture a golden age of stability and harmony. This profound conservatism transcended several important dividing lines in English politics and crossed the Atlantic with thousands of settlers whose hopes for a better life did not always make them devotees of change, let alone revolution. Indeed, one common feature of settlers' adjustment to the New World was their resistance to it. Agricultural habits evolved in England were transplanted to America, sometimes in unconscious defiance of differing conditions, sometimes deliberately as groups of settlers sought out landscapes and soils upon which they could write familiar patterns of land use. Even where new conditions made impossible the retention of settled or habitual life patterns, colonists still clung to them. Witness Virginians' determination to preserve the family and its protective capabilities in spite of staggeringly high mortality rates. Just so, colonists responded to the 'savagism' of the Indians with savage reassertions of their own civility.[14] And it was by human device, often of very traditional English character, as well as by environmental pressure that the expansive opportunities for advancement which greeted the first settlers began to dry up in several colonies from an early date.[15]

Pace Crevecoeur and Franklin, then, America's newness did not always produce or favor new men, at least not in the seventeenth century. Nor did new men invariably thrive in England. Historians of the century have found it difficult plainly to identify progressive politicians and political forces, and most of those so identified seem to have in common their failure to come out on top or even significantly to advance their fortunes. While the century unleashed forces for radical change, we must remember that it also saw the Restoration of 1660 and ended with the Glorious Revolution of 1688. Conservative responses to new conditions as they were encountered in England and America form an important part of imperial history.

Revolutions, Restoration, Navigation Acts, administrative reforms, all demonstrated to colonists that English politics directly affected them through the imperial connection. But their experience in America often moved them in similar directions. Even in New England, where in the 1630s precious few shared the assumption that they *ought* to be governed as England was, a century's experience led many to accept that they must be governed as England was and some to suggest that it should be so. As indicated by the Puritan example and by the conjunction between Shaftesbury and York, this shared vision did not necessarily lead to peace and contentment, far less to an agreed view on imperial 'policy', but it did make of the English empire a political community of strength and vitality. To explain its vigor is to explain how, despite immense environmental differences between colonies and between America and England, Englishmen who went to America and those who 'stayed at home' could continue throughout the century to understand each other so well.[16]

A final warning against accepting too easily the siren call of progress arises from the focus on England's imperial and colonial experience. There is no doubt that this experience contributed to the growth of political stability and strength. But this was not an automatic development. Imperial possessions could as easily exhaust the state's strength or create a dangerous illusion of resource; this, arguably, was the Spanish experience between the fifteenth and eighteenth centuries. England might have gone Spain's way, and in Elizabeth's reign it often looked as if it would. In its essential outlines, the empire which publicists like Richard Hakluyt projected for Elizabeth I would have been very much like that of her arch-enemy, Philip of Spain. The failure of this vision made necessary the creation of colonies of settlement, which in turn brought new problems. Colonies of settlement had to be something more than settlements in order to survive, and as this lesson was learned colonial promoters and colonists began to think of creating societies in the new world. This momentous change requires discussion, for it made possible the existence of political empire.

* * *

Elizabethan Englishmen regarded Spain as England's premier enemy in Europe. Catholic, malevolent, and seeking universal domination, Spain drew from its American empire the sinews of power: gold and silver, valuable agricultural products, and a vast merchant marine to carry both. New Spain necessarily partook of old Spain's character, and Elizabethans made much of the Spaniard's exploitation of the native Americans. Attacking Spanish America could advance the cause of protestantism by weakening Spain in Europe and by liberating the Indians. Protestant patriotism, then, provided motivation for American adventures. However, other considerations also operated. In fleeing from Spanish dominion towards England's benign oversight, the Indians would also rush to wear English woollens. They would succor Englishmen in their midst and guide them to mineral wealth, supply them with furs, show them a passage to the South Seas. These aims were not necessarily contradictory, but they suggest a fundamental ambivalence in English attitudes towards New Spain. It was evil and deserved attack, but it was also fabulously profitable and invited emulation.[17]

Beckoned by this ambiguous vision of El Dorado, Elizabethans responded in two ways which governed their American ventures. The first was military, essentially piratical. New Spain's wealth made buccaneering attractive even while Elizabeth maintained public disapproval of such actions. After the outbreak of open war with Spain, the danger of incurring the queen's wrath diminished. Blows struck against such a foe could be both patriotic and profitable, a perfect combination. At the same time, Spain's power was to be feared, and even those Englishmen who would go in peace to the New World (if there were any such) needed prudently to look to their defences. The discovery that there were bad as well as good Indians was yet another reason that early American ventures had a pronounced military flavor. The Elizabethan experience of Irish colonization further insured that there would be no ingrained reluctance to use force in the service of Protestant civilization.[18]

Secondly, sitting incongruously with this warlike approach to America, another view made the New World into a land of peace and abundance in which Englishmen might freely share if only they approached the continent and its people with all due civility. Reports that the Indians did not work very hard but lived well led Englishmen to conclude that the wilderness might be a veritable Eden. Yet it was a primitive, uncultivated Eden. It was easy to assume that its inhabitants, already living well and enjoying it, would recognize a better life and seek its benefits. English trade goods and protestantism would bestir Indians to bring the fruits of Eden to the colonizers and perhaps even work directly for them.[19] Yet the assumed beneficence of the continent itself meant that the Indians were not vital to Elizabethans' vision of America. Thus Englishmen might introduce Mediterranean viticulture, thought appropriate for the southern latitudes of North America, by bringing with them the right root stock and skilled labor. Further north, the potential of the Newfoundland banks could be exploited by West Country fishermen almost without further ado, for fishing was fishing. With or without the Indians, on land or at sea, America was a cornucopia which required little more than tapping.[20]

From such origins arose the understandable conceit of sixteenth-century Englishmen that their society provided ample means to solve any problems which might be encountered in America. Nor is it surprising that Elizabethans perceived in America some solutions to English problems, for instance overpopulation. The surplus poor, a threat to order in England, would advance the nation's prosperity by gathering or plundering the New World's bounty. Younger sons of the gentry, a drug on the home market, might make their fortunes and recoup their morals in New World adventures, whether by overseeing the poor at work or by commanding them in battle. These ends seemed obviously to call for commercial and military means. In its various guises, America required the joint stock and the merchant investor, the military company and the soldier-statesman, the common seaman and the common laborer. Even those few who thought seriously about permanent settlement tended to see such settlement as a solution to commercial or military problems rather than as an end in itself. Edward Hayes urged settlements along the Newfoundland and New England coasts in order better to supply English fishermen and give them an advantage over their Basque and Breton rivals. Further south, Sir Walter Raleigh's famous colony at Roanoke did take on aspects of a settled society, including the presence of women and children, but its site spoke of its essentially piratical aims. A permanent settlement could only be sustained if it provided a base for successful raids on the Spanish, for the discovery of a passage to Asia, or for the exploitation of mineral wealth. Otherwise, it was thought that the problems of supply and support from England would prove insurmountable, and Raleigh's little band learned the truth of this lesson some time after 1587.[21] Hindsight tells us that the successful colonization of those parts of America which other Europeans had left fallow would require the creation of more complete social orders; but even those Elizabethans who glimpsed this failed to achieve it. Moreover, as David Quinn concludes, they did not pass their insight

[9]

on to the next major English efforts in America, the Virginia Companies of London and Plymouth, chartered by Elizabeth's successor James I in 1606.[22]

The first aims of the London and Plymouth companies, then, were essentially similar to those projected during Elizabeth's reign. Commercial factories, fishing camps, bases for further exploration, such settlements as the companies might establish would follow these familiar lines. However, there were some notable differences. Although the English still hoped that the native inhabitants might be persuaded to supply settlements with foodstuffs, it was now more generally accepted that even such limited settlements as were projected by the companies would require unprecedented levels of support from England. This required heavier investment than had earlier ventures. Some even suggested direct parliamentary subventions. James I was unlikely to countenance this, but the necessity to raise large amounts of private capital required the crown's explicit blessing for the ventures. Elizabeth's wonted coyness would no longer do. James was also more forthcoming because he wanted to insure that the companies would not wantonly hazard his peace with Spain and because he and the promoters wanted clearly to notify Spain and other European powers that the companies did have official sanction from a monarch determined to assert his historic rights to American real estate. Thus royal authority and oversight were both more apparent and more important than they had been before. This official sanction and the cumulative effect of a generation of assiduous promotion of American adventures insured that both the number of investors and the amount of their stake were greater than they had been during Elizabeth's reign.[23]

This was especially true of the London Company, more commonly called the Virginia Company, and its later offshoot the Somers Islands or Bermuda Company. The Plymouth Company was less successful in raising capital, and this, together with the bleak New England shore, kept its efforts within traditional lines for some time.[24] The Virginia Company's greater resources and ambitions centered on its settlement at Jamestown. Its heavy investments of men and material outstripped the unaided capacity of the wilderness to produce profitable returns. Meanwhile, the investments themselves proved insufficient, or were too ill-chosen, to provide sustenance for the company's employees in the colony. However serious these problems were, they at first called forth no new solutions. Instead, the company demonstrated its preference for Elizabethan ideas about the requirements of colonization. In 1611 Captains Thomas Dale and John Smith strengthened their regime with a quasi-military law code, and in 1612 a revised charter reinforced the company's commercial base.[25] However, military discipline, commercial reorganization, and further investment neither reduced stock-holders' losses nor alleviated settlers' suffering. Soon, these circum-stances conspired together to produce a momentous reformulation of the company's and England's colonizing objectives.[26]

Because the Chesapeake wilderness had proved not to be an Eden, profit and survival were now seen to require that the settlers earn their bread and produce returns to London by the sweat of their brows. Subsistence required cultivation, and the failure of manufacturing experiments meant that the search for a marketable surplus would also concentrate on what the land might produce. Thus Virginia became an agricultural settlement. Nor could Englishmen, products of a still essentially agricultural economy, fail to recognize it as such. As this recognition grew, Elizabethan assumptions about America became in-appropriate. The commercial and military characteristics of the original settlement retained a specific utility; but they no longer comprehended the necessities and aspirations of the colonists nor solved the problems of the company. A new blueprint was required. However, it was not likely to be wildly innovatory. Like its Elizabethan predecessors, the Virginia Company had first sought to solve American problems by applying conventional English commercial and military means. Now the company cast about for new solutions and found them in the broader English society. This process of recognition took clearer form in the company's promulgation of the so-called 'Great Charter' of 1618. This important step 'from organization to society' was essentially political, but not only nor even primarily because it established English America's first representative assembly. Virginia's new House of Burgesses was but a part of a broader scheme; it was included so that the colonists 'might have a hand in the governinge of themselves', but it also retained a strong prerogative element with a governor and council commissioned and instructed by the company. The Virginia Company, responsible both to the Stuart crown and to its stockholders, and intent on 'the better establishment of a Commonwealth', would not let self-government get out of hand.[27]

However, the governor and council were not there simply to check the burgesses and freemen but to conform with a range of English preconceptions about government. The aim was to create in America a 'flourishing state ...[and] a laudable form of Government by Majestracy and just laws'. Governor, council and burgesses together were to 'imi-tate and follow the policy of the form of government, laws, customs, and manner of trial, and other administration of justice, used in the realm of England'. Thus the company's political vision included a good deal more than the extension to America of the parliamentary model. It also involved more than the transfer to America of English government. The

Great Charter defined a recognizably English social order which included the free and the unfree, landlords and tenants, masters and servants, even private joint-stock ventures. Political enfranchisement was based on this English social order. In 1621, the company's General Court ruled that one Ouldsworth, 'a Justice of peace and of the Quorum' in Berkshire, should by that criterion be made one of the governor's council in Virginia. Lesser rights, including the vote, were based essentially on the right to hold private property. This right, already granted to some in 1616, was now extended, and those who held land in Virginia were in effect made freemen of the company. This seemed due to them as men whose property was involved in the Virginia venture. Meanwhile, on the Chesapeake landscape itself, the company wrote the familiar names of borough, hundred, manor, and estate. Pale imitations of England these may have been, but imitations they were. Whether the reform experiment would succeed, the company declared, would depend partly on how it was perceived, on how closely it followed the 'example of the most famous commonwealths past and present', and the prime exemplar was Jacobean England.[28]

This was sensible enough given the necessities to please public opinion and to attract settlers (not least those like Mr.Ouldsworth of 'personal merritt and worth') and investors. To the company, however, it seemed more than mere good sense. The company understood perfectly what it had done and measured the distance it had travelled from its essentially commercial and military beginnings. A promotional tract of 1620 explained the reversal of priorities; the Great Charter and other reforms had reduced the 'people and affaires in Virginia into a regular course . . . so . . . that the Colony beginneth now to have the face and fashion of an orderly State, and such as is likely to grow and prosper'.[29] As the goal of prosperity took its place beside the goal of profit, colonists gained more than the rights to hold property or vote. They won a degree of commercial freedom as the monopoly of the company magazine was broken. Nor, according to the company, could it reimpose any such monopoly; it was not a company of 'Merchaunts for the managinge of Trade but for the transportinge and setlinge of people . . . under good government and consequently for the enlargement of his Majesties Dominions'. The company could not infringe 'any liberty or freedome' possessed by the king's 'free and naturall Subjectes'.[30]

Yet with these rights came obligations, for in giving individuals land and status the company leadership never forgot what Treasurer Sir Edwin Sandys called 'the Publique'. Sandys perceived a direct link between power and freedom, company profit and colonial prosperity. In 1619, he noted that the 'Graunts and Liberties' of the Great Charter obliged colonists to keep their promise to build fortifications at their own expense. In the same year, Sandys justified regulations requiring freeholders to diversify their agricultural product: 'the maintayning of the publique in all estates being of noe less importance, even for the benefitt of the Private, then the roote and body of a Tree are to the perticular branches'.[31] Amidst increasing troubles, the company's leadership remained committed to the grand design of the Great Charter. Petitioning to the House of Commons for its survival in 1624, the company claimed that it differed fundamentally from ordinary trading companies both in its membership of 'principall noblemen, gentlemen, merchants, and others, and in the ends for which it is established, beinge not simply matter of trade, butt of a higher nature'.[32] King James was in perfect agreement with that assessment of colonization, although he would draw different conclusions as to whether the Virginia Company itself should survive.

The company's peril owed much to its internal divisions, which had not been healed despite general support for the reforms of 1618. Two main groups vied for control, one led by Sir Edwin Sandys, the other by Sir Thomas Smith. Sandys and his supporters, including the Earl of Southampton, Lord Cavendish, and the brothers John and Nicholas Ferrar, were dominant from 1619 when Sandys ousted Smith as Treasurer. Previous conduct of company affairs by Smith and his allies quickly became a point at issue, and in their defence they kept up a rearguard action within the Virginia Company while using their greater influence in the Somers Island Company and their friends at court to mount an offensive against Sandys. These internal rivalries continued to trouble both company and colony; they also made it easier for others to blame the company, or those in control of its affairs, or both, for the increasingly bad news which came from Virginia, often via the associates of Sir Thomas Smith.[33]

However these reports originated, they gained currency in London, and it was soon evident that Sandys's program for the colony had come unstuck. Company stockholders still waited to see returns on their investments, and in the colony large numbers languished and died. Now, with the company badly in debt, Sandys faced the problem of not being able to supply a colony still in desperate need of help from England. In this context, news of the so-called massacre of 1622 should perhaps be viewed as the last straw, but it was in any case a crushing blow. King James, who had already attempted to intervene in Virginia Company affairs during the treasurership elections of 1620 and 1622 (unsuccessfully, on Smith's behalf), was now bound to step in. By the summer of 1623, James had put the colony under temporary commission government and had instituted an inquiry into the affairs of company and colony.[34] Soon the crown knew enough about the colony's 'distressed estate' and the company's 'miscaryage of the govvernment' to move towards a solution. In October 1623, the king announced his intention to issue a new charter for the colony, not simply for the company.[35] An essential feature of this proposed charter was the creation of a governor and council in England, appointed by the king and directly responsible to him for conduct of the colony's affairs. This Council for Virginia would also nominate, with crown approval, and appoint a governor and council resident in the colony. As for the Virginia Company, it was not to be wound up but reconstituted, its responsibilities restricted to the regulation of the colony's trade and settlement and its operations subjected to the supervision of the governor and assistants in England.[36]

James's plan did not get very far, principally because the Virginia Company itself first delayed answering and then refused to accept it. A writ of *quo warranto* against the charter resulted; in April 1624 the charter was vacated, and Virginia came directly under crown control. James placed the colony's government under a royal commission headed by Lord President Mandeville, but this was only to be a caretaker arrangement until such time as the prescription of October 1623 could be put into effect. Indeed, one of the principal tasks of the commissioners was to make suggestions as to the terms of the 'new Charter'. That James had in mind a future role for the Virginia Company was made clear by his inclusion on the Mandeville commission of several leading figures in the company, although none who were closely identified with the Sandys group. These intentions were repeated in a second commission reconstituting government in the colony under Sir Francis Wyat.[37] Before any new charter could be agreed upon, James I died on 27 March 1625. Because Charles I would essentially endorse his father's Virginia policy,[38] the proclamation of October 1623 assumes more than ordinary importance.

Like most other English responses to the problems of colonization, James's plan of 1623 was not radically new. The Privy Council noted its similarity to the 'first Patentes of that Plantation' in 1606 which had also featured conciliar oversight of Virginia's affairs. Nor, however, was it a return to first principles, for it took into account what had happened in both Virginia and London since 1606. The deputation which the company sent to the Council Board was told that in the new charter the king[39]

> purposeth to make the like grantes as well of landes, as of franchises, and other benefites, and things, as well granted in the former charters, with declaration that for the setling and establishing of private interestes of all men, this new Companie shall continue or newly grant unto them the like interest as they enjoy, by grant, order, or allowance of the former Companie.

While colonists' privileges under the reforms of 1618 were not specifically mentioned, they were likely included in this promise. Certainly colonists' rights were prominent considerations in the negotiations between company and crown which commenced in early 1623. The company first raised the issue, arguing against a new scheme for trade regulation because it threatened to infringe the 'liberty or freedome granted by his Majestie to his Subjectes . . . in the said Plantations.' Viscount Mandeville apparently agreed that the crucial question was the 'preparation to [sic] a better forme of Government' for the colony, and James told his law officers that he aimed to preserve the rights of any who had 'been adventurers either in parson or purse'. Nathaniel Rich, a leader of the opposition faction in the company and closely involved in maneuvers at court during this period, clearly assumed that colonists' rights would be protected and advocated an assembly in order to insure 'common consent' to any new commercial policy for the colony. Thus all parties to the dispute in London accepted the central assumption of the Great Charter, that the Virginia colony ought to be considered as part of England's body politic.[40] With this consensus, we can begin the political history of England's seventeenth-century empire.

* * *

It was not only the crown and the various factions of the Virginia Company who believed that colonization was of 'a higher nature' than mere trade. By the 1620s this belief was widespread, and it extended beyond the anti-Spanish patriotism of Elizabethans' American ventures. Plantations, Francis Bacon argued in 1625, were properly the 'children of former kingdoms'. In their early years, they were to be nurtured, not exploited. In overseeing their development, England must as a good parent consider 'the good of the plantation' and forego expectations of quick gain. Governed properly, supplied with good English folk well skilled in the necessary arts of life, these children would not only grow into a profitable maturity but 'spread into generations'.[41] Bacon's views were shared by publicists for a variety of colonizing ventures, including Virginia. The new literature of colonization did not eschew mention of patriotic and religious aims, on the one hand, and profits to English-based investors, on the other. Now, however, publicists began to aim more deliberately at the prospective settler. America became less a theater for glory and adventure, more a solid bet for any who would wish to better his present and secure for his progeny a worthwhile future. Naturally America remained a veritable cornucopia (so much so that it became customary for authors to disclaim any intention of overselling the soil's fertility or the water's abundance); but it was now a place to move to, to settle in, to work hard in. With this change, emphasis shifted away from the benign physical environment towards social and political conditions which settlers would find to their liking. The laws were English, the institutions of government familiar, and most notably the means to economic prosperity were made widely accessible by human invention. The soil's fertility gave way to its availability and security of title; descriptions of abundant wildlife and fish were coupled with promises of free fowling and free access to river and sea. America's liberal political economy made its appearance as the organizers of colonization, like Sir Edwin Sandys, recognized the necessity to attract settlers of substance to the new world.[42]

Almost as quickly as such ideas took root, they bore more exotic fruit. The Pilgrim fathers' decision to leave Leyden for America was based in part on their feeling that Holland was too un-English to accommodate their vision of Christ's church; presumably America could be made, or kept, English enough. At the other end of the religious and social spectrum, Sir George Calvert, Lord Baltimore, moved from a failed commercial venture in Newfoundland to think of a refuge for English Catholics in the Chesapeake region. Similarly, the Puritans who in 1629 organized the Massachusetts Bay Company aimed not only to transfer England to America but also to continue a religious reformation which at that time seemed stymied in England. To think of the American wilderness as a sanctuary or as a 'Citty upon a hill' was, on its face, an extraordinary idea, not least because it was shared by such different folk as John Winthrop, Baron Baltimore, and the humble separatists of New Plymouth. Historians have understandably been fascinated by the utopian elements in these designs, and have noted that such ideas about America were not of themselves new.[43] But their practical application began to take concrete shape because Englishmen had come to accept the belief, as extraordinary in its way as utopianism, that America was an appropriate place to aim at the ordinary things in life, to settle and survive, to prosper, and to 'spread into generations'.

The sad history of the Virginia settlement satisfied many that the only way to survive and prosper in America was to settle in permanent and reasonably complete versions of English society. The commercial and military elements of that social order, which had so dominated Elizabethan and early Jacobean colonization, would continue to play important roles, but the vision of England in America, dimly perceived by Elizabethan promoters, now became dominant in all but a few of the ventures of the 1620s and 1630s. Because it was dominant, the settlements themselves became recognizable parts of the English political order. This guaranteed that there would be, at the very least, an attempt to govern them as such.

CHAPTER TWO

The ordered empire of Charles I, 1625–1642

Charles I has received a bad press from imperial historians. If anything, he has been blamed for the rapid growth in colonial population, much of which stemmed from religious discontent and economic dislocation for which he bore some responsibility. Those who organized colonizing ventures did so on their own initiative. Such credit as Charles has won is for allowing this to happen, whether by favor to courtiers like the Earl of Carlisle or by negligence, as in the unusual charter which allowed the Puritans of the Massachusetts Bay Company to move their government to America and beyond Charles's grasp. Although a court masque of 1634 credited Charles with converting 'several classical deities to Christianity (banishing the recalcitrant to America)', private enterprise and public negligence sum it up pretty well. Even when in the 1630s Charles asserted his imperial authority, his attempts to hamper emigration to New England and to recall the Massachusetts charter have been judged vengeful rather than statesmanlike. The outbreak of civil war in England in 1642 swept these efforts aside and left the colonies much as they had always been, neglected outposts of an accidental empire.[1]

Charles was not more successful at home. Historians who have taken some blame away from the crown for the early breakdown of relations with parliament have done so by way of criticizing parliament rather than exonerating Charles. Once parliament was out of the way after 1629, Charles used his considerable executive powers often enough to sharpen fears about arbitrary government but too fitfully to strengthen his regime in any fundamental sense. No central bureaucracy arose to take up the burdens traditionally carried by county and town oligarchs, while these local rulers naturally resented the crown's invasions of their bailiwicks. Even the Book of Orders of 1631, intended to reform county government and keep justices of the peace to the mark, arose as much from local as from central pressure. Scotland was governed even less well, and when the Scots rose in arms against royal policy, the extent to which the sinews of English government had weakened quickly became apparent.[2]

With such a domestic record, historians should not expect too much of Caroline imperial government. Nor, however, should they dismiss it lightly. While it would be wrong to credit Charles directly with the growth of empire during his reign, he did little to disturb foundations already laid, and his innate conservatism strengthened them in some ways. In particular, the emergent consensus signalled by the Virginia Company's Great Charter of 1618 remained intact. Charles forcefully endorsed it early in his reign, thus laying down principles of empire to which, on the whole, he kept. These principles were monarchical, conservative, and contractual. They were not particularly tidy, nor can they be construed as a policy, but there was a consistency in Charles's empire which will remain obscure for as long as we judge it against the inapplicable standards of the post-1651 navigation system.

It is also important that these political principles of empire proved acceptable to others, notably to those Charles favored with grants of American territory and government. To be sure, once in power colonizers used their royal grants to resist royal authority, and historians have seen this tension as central to Charles's imperial failures. Besides tension, however, there was dependence, and among several reasons for dependence emergent divisions within colonial societies were crucial. While the literature of colonization made America into a land of opportunity, in no colony were economic resources or individual rights evenly distributed. Nor were they intended to be, but colonists in government reiterated traditional English notions about the social distribution of power and privilege with a frequency which hinted at their discomfiting knowledge that their authority lacked the sanctions provided in England by a relatively stable and well-articulated social order. Throughout English America, the contractualism of Charles I's empire helped colonial governments to resist the threatening disorder of their new environment. This did not guarantee colonial loyalty to Charles when civil war broke out in England, but more significantly it clearly defined the colonies as a part of England's *ancien régime*. This was the accomplishment of Charles I and those he favored with his sovereign gifts of territory, liberty, and power in America.

* * *

Charles's most enduring contribution to the politics of empire took place at the start of his reign when he endorsed his father's solution to the Virginia problem. This was surprising, for unlike James, Charles had friendly ties with the Sandys group, and he included some of them in his first deliberations on Virginia. In Privy Council on 11 April 1625, Charles asked for advice on the tobacco trade and on 'the best course' for Virginia's government. He appointed a committee of three, including two supporters of Sandys, the Earl of Dorset and Lord Cavendish, to sound out the views of the old company. Encouraged by these circumstances, Sandys – with the help of John and Nicholas Ferrar – wrote a reply which exuded confidence.[3] Part apologia for Sandys's conduct of affairs, part attack on the opposing Smith faction within the company, the 'Discourse of the Old Company' did not mince words in analyzing the colony's past development and present troubles.

Sandys and the Ferrars continued in this blunt vein when they made proposals for Virginia's future. They were not above flattery, of course. The great work of colonization was 'fitter for the power & purse of a Great Prince & State, then of private Adventurers.' Should the crown 'undertake' the colony, there could be no better government than that already suggested by King James. However, investment was essential and could only come from private men who would not venture 'any great matter in thos Actions, in the ordering of which they have no voice or interest.' If the king would govern Virginia, the 'Discourse' seemed to say, he should first invest in it; otherwise, the colony government should be 'incorporated as before into a Legall Companie.' In a perfunctory bow to James's scheme, the 'Discourse' conceded that the company might be 'assisted and advised' by a royal council, but this concession was more than balanced by two further suggestions. The *quo warranto* had created a 'jealousy' amongst planters and traders which could only be removed by parliamentary confirmation of the charter. Adventurers would like it even better if Virginia 'might be annexed to the Imperiall Crowne of this Realme' by act of parliament.[4]

Charles's proclamation of 13 May 1625 'for setling the Plantation of Virginia', disabused Sandys and the Ferrars of any notion that they had made him an offer he could not refuse. Charles rejected their proposals wholesale. Parliament had no standing. Virginia and all of English America were 'part of Our Royall Empire, descended upon Us and undoubtedly belonging and appertaining unto Us'. Nor could the company retain a governing capacity, not so much for the wrong it had done as because it could not do right. The company was a 'multitude of persons of severall dispositions, amongst whom the affaires of greatest moment were, and must be ruled by the greater number of Votes and Voyces'. This 'popular government' had no place in King Charles's empire:

> Our full resolution is, to the end that there may be one uniforme course of
> Government, in, and through Our whole Monarchie, that the Government of
> the Colonie of Virginia shall immediately depend upon Our Selfe, and not be

committed to any Companie or Corporation, to whom it may be proper to trust
matters of Trade and Commerce, but cannot bee fit or safe to communicate the
ordering of State-affaires, be they of never so meane consequence.

For good measure, Charles announced that he would take control of the
tobacco trade. It seemed that the Old Company had no place in the
colony's government, nor in its trade.[5]

While that was the way things turned out, it would be wrong to treat
the proclamation as a bench mark for an imperial policy. Besides the
general question of whether Charles's government was interested in or
capable of formulating and executing 'policy' even at home, Charles's
subsequent imperial record would not sustain such a reading. Even
trading company government was not entirely ruled out, although
clearly it was not much liked. Bermudans would continue to suffer
under it for another sixty years, and Charles would soon confer corporate
charters on other colonial ventures. Moreover, he would make repeated
attempts to devise a regulatory role for the Virginia Company in the
tobacco trade, thus dispensing with the 1625 proclamation's hint at
direct royal regulation; and of course a navigation system imposed
generally on all colonial trade lay some decades and a revolution in the
future. Nor can we regard the decision to govern Virginia directly by
commissioned government as a policy marker, for Virginia was both the
first and last royal colony of Charles I's empire.[6] Finally, the king's
response was governed partly by mere bad temper. Sandys and the
Ferrars had misjudged their monarch; their 'Discourse' both rejected his
father's plan for Virginia and continued to stress those 'former personall
differences' which, Charles thought, had already done so much damage
to the colony. With right royal dudgeon he put them firmly in their place.
Charles's was a monarchical empire in which the king's mere grace and
motion were sufficient reasons for decision.

However, neither regal ire nor the infelicities of Caroline government
should conceal the important fact that both Charles and the authors of
the 'Discourse' endorsed the consensus on colonization which had
emerged late in King James's reign. Central to Charles's reasoning was
the distinction between matters of state and 'mere' commerce. From
this Charles concluded that the Virginia Company had no business in
governing the colony. The 'Discourse' did not agree with the conclusion, but its authors accepted, even gloried in the premise. It was a theme
they had played on for years, and in 1625 they returned to it to argue that
it was just this which distinguished their government of Virginia from
the earlier rule of Sir Thomas Smith. Then, they asserted, colonists had
'lived or rather suffered under Martial lawe ... Without assurance of
wives or servants ... Without assurance of their estates ... Without
assurance of their Libties.' Before 1618, the aims of the 'people in

Virginia, were no wayes to settle ... but to gett a little wealth by Tobacco, then in price, and to return to Englande'. 'Of a merchantlike Trade there was some probabillitie ... but of a Plantation there was none at all'. Under Sandys, the company had silenced the 'bloudy Lawes' and settled the colony's government 'like to that of this Kingdome'.[7] The exchanges of April and May 1625 between Charles and the Virginia Company demonstrated that by becoming a society, Virginia had moved up the scale of English values from commercial factories, fishing camps, and military outposts.[8] Therefore, as Francis Bacon argued, its inhabitants deserved better treatment than they had received from the Virginia Company. John Winthrop, the first governor of the Massachusetts Bay Colony, made a similar point in different fashion when he argued that infant societies in America deserved better colonists than the 'scomme' the Company had sent to Virginia.[9]

Yet the nagging questions about 'burden & charge' raised by Sandys's "Discourse" would not go away. Colonies remained commercial ventures, and the Jacobean consensus led few to conclude that these infant Englands should be governed only for their own benefit. Even Bacon predicted future gain for the parent society. Others, less philosophical, noted that new, brisk trades had risen to supplant the alchemical dream that English woollens might be exchanged for American gold. Colonists' need for servants, supply, and the credit to pay for them was complemented by English interest in plantation profits. Charles was alive to the opportunities presented by the American trades and was unlikely to ignore the precept of early modern statecraft that to regulate trade was both an essential mark of sovereignty and vital to the common weal. His government, however, lacked the bureaucratic resource for direct control over commerce. Its reflex solution was to license regulation out through commission or charter, as his father had done in chartering the Virginia Company in the first place. Charles's subsequent attempts to revive the company in a purely regulatory role showed that he had no intention of breaking this mould.[10]

In this context, the old company's disagreements with the king have a special significance. Sandys agreed that colonization involved matters both of state and commerce, but without a share in colonial government he would reject responsibility for trade regulation. He based his refusal partly on grounds laid down in the 'Discourse'. Virginia needed investors and settlers of substance; such men required security and therefore power. This was not a new position for Sandys. As Virginia Company Treasurer, Sandys's support for the reforms of 1618 and his efforts to give them effect had demonstrated his belief in an ideal congruence between private interests and the common weal, a congruence defined by reference not to tradition but to right reason, natural law, and experience.

[21]

Sandys followed the same rationale in parliament, where during the 1620s he persistently warned that if parliament were to share in government MPs would have to pay as much attention to supplying the crown's needs as to defining them. Just so, the policy of devolving power to Virginia's local government aimed to create a powerful community of interest between the company and colonists whose estates in Virginia gave them legitimate political status.[11] But Sandys knew, too, what Edmund Morgan has demonstrated, that the results had been disastrous, not only in terms of the company's bankruptcy. Colonists empowered by his reforms had used that power to advance their own interests against both the company and other colonists. The Great Charter's 'laudable form of Government' had become a nasty system of forced labor as lawmakers and magistrates used their power to procure and keep servile labor on their own land. Meanwhile, their power to regulate trade, intended to shore up the company and promote the colony's welfare, furnished some of them a licence to produce artificial famine for private profit.[12]

It was not surprising that Sandys refused to undertake trade regulation without a share in colonial government, nor that his successors in the company continued to seek repayment for Virginians' peculations.[13] By the same token colonists learned to value highly the reforms of 1618. Through them, colonists enjoyed not only property but also power, and power was something to cherish in Virginia's death-prone and unstable environment. It was also something to use, and the colony government did so as soon as Governor Yeardley arrived in 1619. John Pory, the speaker of America's first representative assembly, apologized to Sir Dudley Carleton for the 'errours & imperfections' of its laws yet boasted that in them Carleton could 'observe the very principle and rudiments of our Infant-Commonwealth'.[14] Quite so; thus in 1623 Virginia's colonial rulers feared that the *quo warranto* against the company might endanger the privileges they enjoyed under company rule. Yet they might gain from the company's demise if the crown would secure those privileges, and by 1625 those who now held the king's commission were invoking the company's Great Charter to distribute company assets and dues among themselves. We shall see Virginians opposing the revival of the company after they had become accustomed to their new dispensation under the crown.[15] By such steps, the colony government came to regulate Virginia's trade, to distribute its land, and to control its labor. In these functions it effectively replaced the Virginia Company, and the use of the term 'freemen' to describe its enfranchised citizens was entirely appropriate.

Similar lessons were learned elsewhere. In 1622, Bermudans seized the opportunity presented by the Virginia Company's troubles to protest against their own Somers Islands Company. In a petition to King James, islanders lamented that company control caused the 'people to sighe and some of them to say, Wee are the kings subjects and freemen wee will serve the king and obay and honor him[.] The marchants slaves wee will not bee. It will never bee well with us until wee bee given up unto the King'. In attacking their company Bermudans were not aiming at freedom from regulation but, as they stated in 1626 during a later conflict with the company, at the liberty 'to make the best we can of our tobaccos, and to dispose it at our pleasure; we always humbly submitting ourselves to [the king's] Customs and rights every way'.[16] 'Given up unto the King' Bermudans would gain the power formerly held by the company to regulate their trade and other aspects of the islands' life. Like Virginians, Bermudans who aspired to hold the king's government were seventeenth-century Englishmen who knew well the double-edged utility of such franchises. Through devices like charters, the crown gave liberty to some men, made them 'free', and in doing so gave them considerable powers over others.

Only the king could give such powers to his subjects. Sandys's 'Discourse' had accepted this, although in proposing an act of parliament to confirm a new royal charter, Sandys had suggested an alternative which Charles, following his father, utterly rejected.[17] Thus the prerogative rather than the king-in-parliament remained the sole source of colonial government; this was the 'one uniforme course of Government' which, Charles insisted, must prevail 'in, and through all Our whole Monarchie'. Nor should a colony's government be in the gift of a trading company whose membership was defined merely by the purchase of stock: a 'multitude of persons of severall dispositions' which could establish a colonial government 'by the greater number of Votes and Voyces'.[18] Charles condemned this as 'popular government', but this attack on the Virginia Company was not a direct threat to fledgling local governments or their assemblies. Bermudans sensed this when they sought from the king the privileges of self-government, among which was the right to regulate their trade as the king directed. Charles confirmed it in 1628 when he commanded his royal governor of Virginia to call an assembly in order to determine the best way to regulate the tobacco trade. Autonomous local governments, much like that set up under the Virginia Company's Great Charter, would be part of Charles I's 'royall empire' in America.[19] This would be confirmed by the new colonial charters of Charles's reign.

* * *

From the 1620s, more Englishmen than before came forward to seek royal authority for colonial ventures. The results demonstrated that both crown and colonizers had learned much from Virginia, and while the idea of trading company government was not wholly disqualified, it was under a cloud. To Charles's objections against placing the gift of English government in the hands of an investor majority, Bacon added that trading companies by their nature were likely to produce tragedy, in Virginia's case the tobacco mania and the 'blood of many commiserable persons'. Yet it remained necessary to regulate colonial economies for England's benefit. Charles responded with several devices already used or forecast late in his father's reign, most notably the proprietary charters, the Massachusetts Bay charter, and royal councils for overseeing colonial ventures.

The proprietary charter emerged as the chief means of making new colonial grants. The proprietary nicely married the realities of colonization with the political prejudices of the era, avoided the faults of trading companies, and confirmed the belief that colonization was something 'of a higher nature' than mere commerce. Proprietors might venture to trade with their possessions, but the Earl of Carlisle's first patent for the Caribbee Islands was unusual in granting special trading privileges to the proprietor. Otherwise, proprietors had power to regulate but not to monopolize the trade of their provinces; all English subjects inhabiting the colony were equally bound by these regulations and thus enjoyed 'free trade' as this term was understood in the seventeenth century. Other clauses echoing the Jacobean consensus included those which guaranteed to colonists English law and familiar institutions of government, including representative assemblies.[21]

However, one feature of these proprietary charters seemed to hark back to an earlier age, for proprietors were given the powers of the medieval Bishops of Durham. Thus they might become princes palatine in the unlikely setting of the American wilderness. No doubt this archaism appealed to Charles, whose court was addicted to elaborate masques (many on medieval themes), and to the courtiers who received these charters. Much the same might be said for the forms of tribute proprietors were to make to their monarch: for example a white horse to ride whenever the king should visit Barbados! These are best regarded as matters of style, ceremonial statements that a proprietor's power in America was subject to his allegiance to the crown. The substance of the charters makes it apparent that contemporary England, not medieval Durham, was the model for the proprietary. This was best demonstrated by the proprietor's income, which was to come chiefly from his roles as landlord and head of government, from sales or rents of land granted by charter and imposts on trade granted to him by his assembly. He would thus, as a good landlord, take a long-term view of the development of his property; and as his chief interest in trade came from the impost, he would as any good monarch seek a general increase in trade rather than push particular ventures.[22] Proprietary charters recognized that the English colonies could prosper only by the production and trade of many hands and sought to govern them as such. Who in early seventeenth-century England would say that the landed proprietor was not a better governor than the trading company? Not many: and we would not find among them the monarch or the courtiers whose influence with him was sufficient to gain such generous grants of land and power. The proprietary was a sensible application of contemporary English values to the problems of colonization.[23] It was also a progressive one; well might Charles have followed its precepts in his realm of England.

The conventional wisdom on colonization also informed the Massachusetts Bay venture of 1629. In the first place, the Puritan organizers proved their intention to learn from and avoid the implications of the Virginia disaster. While Virginia's translation from commercial outpost to society was governed much by events, Massachusetts was designed with polity in mind. This design was undertaken deliberately, and in some respects was completed before settlement began in earnest. That this process had religious or utopian aims is well known, but the Massachusetts design represented also the pragmatic application of lessons learned. Virginia must have been near to the puritan vision of hell, but it (and England's threatened Egyptian apostasy) helped the Puritans to plan for their American zion.[24] In their preparations for the early voyages of 1628 and 1630, in their intention to select as settlers only 'fit instruments' for the work, even in their apparent aim to settle in one great 'city', the members of the Bay Company showed that theirs was to be no ordinary trading corporation. Here the decision of August 1629 to transfer both government and charter to New England assumes special significance.[25] There was to be no directorate in England with powers to translate its financial stake into decisions which would bind, even impoverish or corrupt the settlement. It was also important to the Puritans' social vision (as to other English colonizers) to encourage men of quality to settle in New England. The transfer of government was thought likely to conduce to that end. Indeed, the men who led the migration made it a necessary condition of their venturing, thus signalling their endorsement of Charles's dim view of trading company colonization.[26]

The question remains how, only four years after he had denounced company government as unfit in principle for his empire, Charles I came to give a group of Puritan colonizers a company charter. Here it is possible to charge the crown with ignorance, crown lawyers with carelessness or venality, and the Puritans with subterfuge or bribery. Historians have not been slow to do so. The likelihood that the Bay

Company later suppressed some documents adds weight to these charges; doubtless some fast footwork was involved.[27] But another explanation is that while Charles I was not about to endorse the Puritans' social and religious aims for England, he took seriously their claim to a higher purpose than mere commerce for their American errand. Thus he gave the company a charter, but one which paid unusually close heed to the ends and means of the settlement and of its government, and unlike most trading company charters, including those of Virginia and Bermuda, laid down no rules linking investment to the freemanship. Another unusual omission was that the charter failed to specify *any* location for the company's governing body to meet to conduct its business.

In early modern England, the rules of entry and the seat of government for trading corporations were vital matters – the very stuff of conflict within companies and of debates over free trade between crown and parliament.[28] It is, therefore, plausible to suggest that the Massachusetts charter's silence on these points was deliberate. By asking for a charter on these terms, the organizers signalled that the Massachusetts Bay was to be no ordinary trading company. In granting the charter the crown accepted and endorsed that intention. That the charter allowed the seat of government to be moved to America was an inadvertency owing to the decision not to specify where in England the General Court should meet. John Winthrop's speech to the company's court in December 1629 makes clear that removal was not an original intention of the organizers, and it seems certain that the liberty of removal out of England would have been disallowed by the crown had it been explicitly proposed.[29] The Massachusetts charter of 1629 was a contract by which both crown and colonizers hoped to translate a working social order to America and to avoid the cruel fate which, they believed, had overtaken Virginia while (and because) that colony had been under the rule of a trading company.

Thus the proprietary and corporate charters of the reign adhered to the general principles laid down in Charles's Virginia proclamation of 1625. They made clear, too, that the king did not intend to apply outside of Virginia's special case the expedient of direct royal government. For the crown, the charter remained a useful mechanism for legitimating colonial ventures and by no means denied the objective that there should be a 'uniforme course of government' throughout the monarchy. These were contracts whereby the king wrote or approved the ground rules but left expense, risk, and trouble to his subjects. Moreover, the king retained latent powers over the undertakers. They might find their charter deficient and apply to the crown for amendment of the charter terms, a traditional mechanism in the case of trading company and municipal borough charters which the Providence Island Company took advantage of when it absorbed a secondary settlement on Dry Tortuga in 1631.[30] In case the undertakers defaulted on their side of the bargain, Charles could always take the charter to court. These may appear cumbersome procedures, but they made sense enough for a government whose legislative competence in organizing foreign trade was centered in the prerogative, not parliament, and whose bureaucratic competence was limited.

It would seem, however, that the crown did not regard the charters as sufficient in themselves. Perhaps it was unwilling to depend entirely on those latent powers which had brought the Virginia Company to heel; more likely it made unthinking use of a device it used heavily enough within the realm, not least in the far corners of the land. For whatever reason, royal councils, commissioned by the king and based in London, were also used to oversee colonization. None of these were very successful, and the failures of Archbishop Laud's Plantations Council in the late 1630s are well known. More interesting were the 'regional' supervisory councils for New England, Virginia, and the West Indies, the first two James's, the last Charles I's creation.[31] Both the Maryland and Massachusetts charters were granted in the context of developing plans for conciliar direction of American ventures. The Maryland proprietary, carved out of the old Virginia grant, was apparently to be subject in some respects to the Council for Virginia. During the lengthy gestation of the Maryland charter, the Council for Virginia was still engaged in efforts to turn over the regulation of Virginia's trade to the old Virginia Company. Indeed, the Council for Virginia consulted the old company about the Maryland grant. The company's principal objection (based on its claims to undistributed land within the old patent) was rejected; but the old company was instrumental in retaining for Virginia the southern tip of the eastern shore, perhaps on the ground that a future general regulation of the tobacco trade would be eased by keeping the jaws of the Chesapeake under one political jurisdiction.[32] It is more certain that the public rationale for the Massachusetts charter of 1629 was to confer royal sanction upon grants already made by the Council for New England. In 1622, the Council had issued a patent for colonization to the Earl of Warwick, its president, and in 1628 Warwick assigned to the New England Company some of his patent rights to territory and government. The Massachusetts charter superseded both. The later disappearance of the Warwick patent and the New England Company charter complicates the historian's task, but crown lawyers doubtless accepted that all had proceeded in accordance with James I's injunction to the Council for New England to 'freely give way' to any merchants or planters who would agree to submit to the council's orders and regulations.[33]

The colonial charters of Charles I's reign offer evidence of court intrigue, antiquarian frivolity, and sheer carelessness. But there was design, too. The creation of competent governments in America was part of that design, an important element of the Virginia Company's Great Charter, of James I's proposed replacement for the company, and of the proprietary and corporate charters issued by Charles I. And, although the Virginia Company refused royal offers to take on trade regulation, although the councils for Virginia, New England and the West Indies soon became moribund, they were rational attempts to provide royal oversight for activities which clearly involved matters both of state and of trade. In order fully to understand Charles I's empire, however, it is necessary to examine how English artifice actually worked in America.

* * *

By granting powers of government and trade regulation to the English overseas, the crown made manifest its sovereignty. In seeking these powers, colonial undertakers demonstrated their dependence upon the only source of legitimate authority in America. Yet the usefulness of authority depended on more than its mere possession. Colonial governments had to wield effective power, by command or by consent, in the wilderness. Their distance from England, the desultory ways of Charles I's rule, and American instability sometimes visited upon colonial governments all the disadvantages of being in limbo without benefit of its security of tenure. Even so, they learned to exploit their perilous position in the web of imperial politics. In the process, they acquired a range of powers greater than those held by trading companies and further secured their claim to be recognizable parts of the English polity.

Virginia's case is instructive because of its direct dependence on the crown. Central to Virginia politics for much of Charles's reign was the king's failure to define the effect on colonists' rights of the 1624 *quo warranto* against the Virginia Company. To be sure, in 1623 Virginians were promised all that they held of the company, including the right to trade freely from any power 'to force contracts upon them for their commodities'. Repeated assurances followed, as in 1634 when Charles told colonists that 'it is not intended that the interestes which men had settled when you were a Corporation should be impeached, that for the present they may enjoy their estates and trades with the same freedomes and privileges as they did before the recalling of the Patentes'. Oddly enough, these promises were kept, not only in respect of settlers' rights; company stockholders were able for some time to convert their equity into landholdings.[34] However, royal action and inaction gave such assurances a hollow ring. Insecurity about land titles arose from the crown's failure until 1638 explicitly to sanction the headright system and was intensified when the king granted much of the old Virginia patent to Lord Baltimore and Sir Robert Heath. The colony government's power to regulate trade was at risk for as long as Charles schemed to turn that task back to the Virginia Company. Even colonists' right to be governed by laws of their own making lacked clear sanction until the royal commission and instructions of 1638 gave a degree of permanence to the assembly. Uncertainty on these imperial questions was compounded by local instability consequent on falling tobacco prices, rapid immigration, and high death rates.[35]

Given all this, it was no miracle that Virginia's representative assembly survived. These prototypical American whigs were concerned as much with securing their wealth as with preserving their liberties,[36] and they happily used their local institutions to protect their privileges against external threats from all quarters, old company, the king's governor, or the king himself. The 'thrusting out' of Governor John Harvey, engineered by members of the Virginia Council with support from the burgesses, was a case in point, and the rebels celebrated with a rash of headright patents.[37] Dissident councillors joined burgesses to oppose the king's grant to Lord Baltimore, which Virginians viewed as destructive of their own proprietorial rights descended from the company. Neither failure to deny Baltimore his charter nor the crown's orders to aid the fledgling colony discouraged the same 'faction' from using its power in Virginia government to harass the colony's new northern neighbor.[38]

These episodes demonstrate not so much a precocious spirit of independence as the ambiguity of the relationship between colonial government and English authority. The Virginia assembly, for example, owed its survival as much to occasional royal orders to call it into session as to colonists' devotion to the representative principle. Colonists took advantage of Governor Harvey's removal to reinstitute headright grants, but no doubt they were reassured by a royal warrant endorsing the practice. Colonial reactions to royal efforts to regulate the tobacco trade were also ambiguous. As we have seen, the crown favored the revival of company regulation; colonists opposed this because it would render them vulnerable to monopolist machinations of 'pryvate men in *England*'. However, some monopolies were better than others, the more so if colonists could have a hand in them. In March 1628, the governor, council, and burgesses announced their willingness to supply 500,000 weight of tobacco annually to the crown at 3s 6d per pound. In anticipation of the burgesses' agreement, the governor and council had already ordered 'the shipps . . . now ready to depart. . . to give in securitie' to ship their tobacco only to London.[39] Later, Governor Harvey illustrated his own ambivalent approach when, in one letter, he pressed the crown both for the planters' freedom to seek the best market for their tobacco and for a new tobacco monopoly headed by the London merchant Maurice Thompson. For Harvey and his partners these may not have been mutually exclusive aims; colonists outside the monopoly would have seen the matter differently. Had Harvey's proposal succeeded, his 'thrusting out' might have occurred sooner than it did. It is some credit to Stuart colonial policy that Harvey's suggestion qualified for a forceful rejection by Privy Council warrant.[40]

In the politics of empire, the crucial question was not whether trade was to be regulated but who was to regulate it. Virginians generally opposed schemes to vest regulatory powers over their trade in an external authority, whether the Virginia Company or some other device. However, they had other privileges to worry about than 'free trade', especially land titles. As long as they remained uncertain about their rights under the settlement of 1624-25, the company's Great Charter of 1618 served usefully to defend those rights and made revival of company government a plausible alternative.[41] However, royal commissions and instructions to Governors Wyat (1638) and Sir William Berkeley (1642) secured land tenures and the reinstatement of the headright system; these instructions also confirmed various regulatory powers and perquisites to the colonial government and gave official sanction to the continuance of the colonial assembly. Virginia, once the fief of a London corporation, now assumed full corporate status in its own right. Once this happened, company control in any form was vigorously opposed, most notably in the colony's eloquent 1642 'Act against the Company'. The Assembly celebrated its self-deliverance from the 'designs of monopolizers contractors and preemptors' by voting new taxes to Governor Berkeley.[42]

The Virginia government's defense of colonial rights against outside interference was a story repeated in other colonies during Charles's reign, and it bears close attention lest we mistake its roots. Impatience of external controls was woven into English political tradition, but it also answered colonial necessities. Given the nature of English public policy at this time, external regulation implied monopoly and thus limitations on trade or production. However, it had become increasingly apparent that colonies' economic success depended upon the freest possible flow of trade goods, credit, and labor. This fact had sustained Sir Edwin Sandys in his efforts, through sheer weight of investment and by extending much commercial freedom to colonists, to transform Virginia from a failed trading venture into a flourishing commonwealth. Colonists repeatedly endorsed the insight. Chesapeake colonists thus pursued declining tobacco prices with increasing production. This gave them insatiable appetites for land and labor and made them increasingly impatient of all efforts to regulate the tobacco trade through limitation, whether 'stints' or monopolies. Such restrictions, Virginia's burgesses declared in 1638, would limit the colony's growth and therefore endanger its very survival. Much better a 'free use and benefitt of the trade of our comodity', which would bring people of quality into the colony and vastly increase trade with England.[43] What Virginians knew, Antiguans learned; a tobacco stint in 1641-42 brought only misery and political strife. Increased production of cotton and tobacco, then sugar, resolved Antigua's version of the colonial economic dilemma. Meanwhile, in New England, the lack of a staple commodity of sufficient value in Europe made the economy at first dependent upon feeding and housing a continued flow of immigrants and then, when this virtually ceased after 1640, pursuing trade in provisions with the tobacco and sugar colonies. The goods produced may have been different, but New England's dependence upon expanded production and trade was not.[44]

In recognition of these necessities, colonies sought to attract settlers of substance and others who had only labor to offer with promises of a bounteous environment which individuals might freely exploit. Public promoters and private correspondents made the same points. Even Puritan New Englanders thought Zion was also Canaan, and should flow with milk and honey. Rich and poor could live in New England 'as well for soul and body as anywhere in the world', a guarantee underwritten by the liberty for 'any man' to 'employ his stock in what merchandises he please'.[45] Thus it was recognized that the economic problems of America required what we might call today a liberal political economy. Virginians' increasing hostility to the traditional means of trade regulation by restriction underlined the point. Chasing expensive manufactured goods with cheap primary products, colonists saw no alternative to economic expansion.

Colonists' suspicion of outside interference did not make them into advocates of *laissez faire*. Even as they used their governments to resist external regulation, they deployed public power within colonial societies to enhance expansion, to promote immigration, to discover new trades, and to increase acreage under cultivation. The headright systems, guaranteed freeholds by which the Chesapeake and West Indian colonies sought to attract both men of wealth and laborers, were perhaps the best examples of this, but everywhere public power was used to promote growth. In Massachusetts' first settlement at Salem in 1629, the wide distribution of land gave even poor folk 'more wood for Timber and Fire . . . then many Noble men in England can afford', and the colony's 1641 law code, published in London, made it clear to prospective migrants that all admitted householders would be made 'free

Inhabitants . . . and accordingly shall enjoy freedome of Commerce and Inheritance.'[46] Very early in America's history of economic expansion, law and boosterism functioned together to paint a picture of open opportunity.

However, circumstances conspired to produce a somewhat different reality. The emergent elites which controlled colonial governments lived in a local as well as in an imperial context, were subject to political as well as economic necessities, and these facts tempered their enthusiasm for expansion and liberality. The market was not yet supreme in America, for colonists played a dangerous game with stakes higher than mere economic success and with aims often at variance with the free trade and open opportunities they mentioned in disputes with English authority and in their promotional literature. This was demonstrated in the Chesapeake and West Indian colonies by the exploitation of servants and poor freemen. Here was more than a predictably distressing story of human greed, more even than 'the fleeting ugliness of private enterprise operating temporarily without check'.[47] For it was public enterprise – legislatures, governors and their councils, the law courts, and the headright system – which was mobilized to serve private men and dominant elites. In 1638, Virginia's burgesses feared more than external regulation; they suspected the governor and council of favoring a stint for their own ends, and not without reason. In the West Indies, attempts to regulate production fell with particular force on the poor and brought a characteristic complaint from men out of power that government should guarantee to each man the freedom to make the best of his lands and goods. The economic uses of power were more starkly illustrated in the plantation colonies than in New England, but the Puritans were no strangers either to the virtues of servitude and subordination or to the dangers of liberty. From England the Reverend John White warned eloquently against the excesses which might accompany too much liberty of conscience and liberty of trade.[48]

Public power was a dear prize in the colonies, and its value was not lessened because it derived ultimately from an external, often wayward authority, the Stuart crown. The right to govern, granted by royal charter or commission, served elites well in maintaining control over the poor. But the possession of power could also be a point of contention between those who had more to lose than just their freedom. In Virginia, Sir John Harvey was by 1640 out of power and down on his luck, but he retained enough influence to preserve eight cows and a life interest in lands ordered sold to cover his debts. Meanwhile, in Massachusetts, it was suggested that because John Winthrop had lost much of his estate, he should not continue in high office. Besides colonists who were or had been wealthy, English investors found it difficult to protect their economic interests without a share in political authority. The Puritan merchants and gentlemen who gave up control of the Massachusetts Bay Company to those who went to America never recovered their original investment. Nor did those who invested in the Saugus ironworks. English merchants trading to America found it hard to collect their debts. Complaints about colonial justice were common, and even those who thought themselves good friends to the colonists threatened to call in English authority to redress their grievances. Resentment would eventually result in English merchants attempting to forge for themselves a place in English imperial administration.[49] Such outside interference obviously threatened those who held colonial authority; but the threat was the more serious when it came from within as well as without the colonial polity.

This was made clear by the trials of Peter and John Hay, sent out to the Caribbees in 1637 to secure the rights of the first Earl of Carlisle's creditors. Despite assurances that the second earl would honor his father's assignment of proprietary revenues to the creditors,[50] Carlisle's governor at Barbados proved to be totally uncooperative, an attitude which enjoyed, as it was allegedly designed to win, the support of the chief planters. The Hays soon concluded that nothing could be won without an unambiguous commission of authority to collect their dues.[51] With the help of their courtier kinsmen Sir James and Archibald Hay, the agents obtained fuller authority from Carlisle and the king. This proved insufficient for effective revenue collection, but enough to worry the island's governing elite. Once frustrated by their impotence, Peter and John Hay now encountered the dangers of power. In the ensuing political strife, the new governor, Henry Huncks, made common cause with members of his council to promise a reduction in colonists' rents and to threaten to make Peter Hay 'shorter by the heade'. In retaliation, the Hays curried favor with the colonists by promising to seek from the crown duty-free trade for Barbadian products and meanwhile urged their London principals to secure Huncks's removal from office. In the end, Huncks was recalled, but not before he and his council imprisoned 'untill further order' the 'body of Mr Peter Hay'. Peter Hay's letters during this period betray a certain alarm; perhaps he knew how previous losers in Barbadian politics had fared.[52] After their years in Barbados, the Hays understood the old Virginia Company's refusal to undertake trade regulation without a share in colonial government.

Such episodes demonstrated the importance of colonial governments' economic powers. These powers, granted by royal charter and commission, were no longer merely the consequences of the crown's desire to regulate colonial economies for England's sake. Had this been the case, such regulations might have been uniformly resisted by colonial governments, for they did restrict colonists' economic freedom. But the regulations also conferred powers which colonists in government were intent on using and retaining, sometimes at the expense of their fellows. In the Caribbees, the Hays' power to collect proprietary revenues threatened all colonists, but threatened island governments in a particular way. If proprietary dues were to be collected, Governor Huncks and his Council wanted to collect them; they were Carlisle's government, and in taking their perquisites, the Hays threatened their power, indeed their survival. While ordinary islanders worried about the prospects for continued rent evasion, Carlisle's government competed with Carlisle's creditors for the proprietary dues much as later politicians would compete for votes; as with later politicians, their ultimate aim was power.

As the Hays found, the crown's desire to regulate colonial economic life did not always coincide with the interests of colonists in government. But more than occasionally there was a congruence. The power given to Virginia's governor and council to enter and clear all ships only at Jamestown, for instance, facilitated regulation of the tobacco trade and thus served the king's interest. But it was also important to the private and public purposes of those Virginians who held royal authority. By entering and clearing ships at Jamestown, Virginia's rulers helped to insure their own prosperity as planters, for the ability to get first crack at incoming cargo and outgoing space was no small advantage in Virginia's economy. Moreover, the process produced fees and was a visible exercise of power. This political dimension was recognized by Governor Wyat and his councillors when in 1639 they accused colonists who had petitioned the king against this restriction of plotting 'an alteration in the government' of the colony.[53] In 1643 Massachusetts's Governor Winthrop made much the same point when Essex County leaders challenged his decision to allow the French adventurer Charles LaTour to trade at Boston. Not only had he taken advantage of a 'meere liberty of commerce' which was within his authority under the 1629 charter, but by publicly objecting to his decision the Essex men had committed 'an act of exorbitant nature, out of rule, out of season, and of dangerous consequence'. That the dissenters were colony magistrates only made their offence worse. Because they had divided legitimate authority, their opposition verged on rebellion. It was equally clear that whatever the justice of his arguments, biblical and otherwise, Winthrop had used his authority under the royal charter to drive a sharp bargain to the benefit of the Boston area, where he and most of the magistrates lived, at the expense of Essex County.[54]

* * *

The conditions which cried out for colonists' economic freedom and made them resentful of interference from England, then, were muted in their effect by colonial governments' pressing needs to retain and use the powers conferred upon them by English authority. This not only made colonial rulers sharply aware of their dependence upon England, but it also inhibited what some have seen as the ineluctable progress of 'the liberal tradition' in early America: Another obstacle was the social and cultural conservatism of the settlers. Countless ordinary folk adjusted reluctantly to new American conditions, clinging to old habits even when these were clearly inappropriate.[55] Conservative political values also survived the Atlantic crossing and retained an attraction as settlers confronted the wilderness. This conservatism was doubtless wide-spread, but it was particularly useful to colonists in government, especially when new settlement, expanding production, and growing population brought forth new individuals and groups claiming power, or a share in it, or merely a slice of freedom. The challengers were not necessarily 'radical', but those who would retain power inevitably took on a conservative role, whether as upholders of constituted authority, as defenders of religious orthodoxy, or as advocates of property, law and order. In these guises, colonists in government did not aim to share the liberty and power they enjoyed.

It was hardly surprising, therefore, that the common English belief that masterless men represented a fundamental threat to the masters was universal in America. However, it achieved a particular intensity of political meaning in the Chesapeake and West Indian colonies, where planter elites' vulnerability was increased by patterns of recruitment into the elite which paid scant respect to traditional criteria of social status and social quality. On the other hand, the ease with which Governor Winthrop turned aside the Essex leaders' challenge over the LaTour affair reminds us that in most of the New England colonies elites governed relatively securely, thanks in part to widely shared religious and social values. To be sure, not all were sanguine: note the dismay felt by a humble settler at the death of Nathaniel Johnson, kin to the Earl of Lincoln and the 'chiefest stud in the land . . . the chiefest man of estate in the land and one that would have done most good'. However, despite Johnson's death and the departures of other notables, members of New England elites generally governed longer than their peers in the plantation colonies who, if they survived long enough, were likely to return to England to enjoy their profits in a healthier climate. New England's 'greatest success', its 'century of social cohesion', began quickly and offers an apparently sharp contrast to the more turbulent social and political early history of the Chesapeake and West Indian colonies.[56]

A notable element of this contrast was the Puritans' strong desire to compose their differences by agreement, a desire often gratified by explicit covenants. Such covenants, written into the beginning of town and church records, were of solemn moment for these new wilderness settlements. Under them, land was distributed to all or most heads of household, not in the first instance as a commercial commodity but as the freely available basis of community. Initially, churches were gathered by covenant and were governed congregationally rather than clerically, locally rather than by central institutions. Such practices were conspicuously absent from the nativity of the Chesapeake and West Indian colonies. No doubt religious differences between New England and the rest of English America do much to explain these contrasts, but the matter deserves a closer look. After all, in early Stuart England covenant ideas enjoyed a wide currency by no means restricted to those we call Puritans. Nor was it a Puritan monopoly to think that social harmony was a desirable goal.[57] Given their turbulent early history, surely the leaders of Virginia, Barbados, and the other plantation colonies might have used the covenant or social compact, if only to exhort their servants to pursue the ways of peace. However, to make the distribution of power and property subject to forms of compact or covenant requires not only the inclination to do so but also a social or political rationale. Before the 1640s, both were absent in the plantation colonies. These societies were characterized by marked divisions in population between older, wealthier men who owned land and generally younger and poorer inhabitants who were typically servants. Shipping lists from the 1630s suggest that in Barbados the ratio of servants to freeholders might have been as high as 19 to 1. That ratio probably never actually obtained in the island, and was lower in Virginia. It was further lessened by a reasonable degree of upwards mobility out of the servant class. On the other hand, it signified a small, narrowly based elite, a social order whose hard lines of division were not softened by strong family or community ties, and a mode of production which emphasized the direction of servile labor. In Maryland, Virginia, Barbados, and the Leewards the most important, and in terms of sheer numbers the prevalent social relationship was that between master and servant. When disorder threatened, as it seemed often to do, the natural response of these narrow elites was to use their power to suppress. The charters and commissions granted by Charles I, whatever their other defects, met well enough their function to convey legitimate public authority to those who would use it, whether against unruly servants or ambitious challengers for power.[58]

Early New England presents a striking contrast. Migrants came mainly from the middle reaches of English society.[59] Moreover, most adult male migrants moved to New England as heads of families, and many families moved in groups, as if to recreate in America the community they had left behind them in England. However well they succeeded at that, they did make the family farm the common denominator of the New England economy. This created some problems. While it is reasonable to suppose that most New Englanders agreed with John Winthrop's view that in every society there should be some eminent in power and dignity and others low and mean and in subjection, his famous lay sermon on board the *Arbella* was a better 'Modell' of the society they left astern than of the one they were about to establish. In comparison to old England and the rest of English America, there were in Massachusetts fewer masters and therefore fewer servants, fewer employers and therefore fewer wage laborers, fewer landlords and therefore fewer tenants. Early decisions to grant freedom of commerce and inheritance to all admitted inhabitants meant, too, that there were in the traditional economic senses of the terms none free of the corporation, none barred from its freedom.[60] This society did not easily yield up governing distinctions between superior and inferior. Seen in this context, Massachusetts's early decision to restrict the colony suffrage to members of the churches assumes a practical function, indeed. But there were other adjustments to make. In an age which assumed that government ought to embody or replicate social relationships, the covenant emerged as an acceptable basis for authoritative rule amongst men whose relationships one to another were, if not those of equals, then such as to render awkward or unavailable many of the customary mechanisms of English government.

They were also responses to the problem of guaranteeing order amongst men who were strangers to one another: increasingly so, as settlement spread along the coast and inland and as the pace of migration picked up in the mid-1630s. Towns like Dedham and Dorchester were gatherings up from all over England, and even where, as in Hingham and Rowley, a nucleus of settlers came from one English locality, they often needed to make up their numbers in order to provide a viable basis for settlement. On such matters as religious doctrine or land distribution, agreement was highly desirable, and it made sense to include as many as possible in positive assent. Here New England puritanism and capitalism do come together, for if we accept the thesis that the common law of contract arose to regularize commercial relationships between men who were otherwise free of one another, then contract rather than covenant might better describe New Englanders' frenetic consensus building. Of course, New Englanders invested their covenants with religious meaning. It was not surprising that people schooled in England's reformed tradition used covenants and found biblical warrant for them. It is safe to say, however, that experience recommended the use

[37]

of covenants for sacred and secular ends. And as the flood of immigrants mounted, it was no longer enough for admission to the church covenant to demonstrate one's orthodoxy and good behavior. From early 1636, the device of a relation of spiritual experience was used to insure the *bona fides* of strangers to the religious brotherhood of both church and state.[61]

Neither the theory nor the practice of the covenant came to New England fully articulated but developed, in Winthrop's words, as we 'come to clearer light and more Libertye'. Just as Virginian masters modified English law and custom to turn indentured servitude to the requirements of the tobacco economy, so New England's covenanting met American necessities. Church covenants grew in elaboration as time passed. Boston's 1630 church covenant was apparently the work of an afternoon and required only 135 words. By 1636 it was found wanting, and the church made a new covenant in 'large explanation of that which they had first entered into'. The new covenant was not only literally larger but also more precise. Its first paragraph ran an exact line between legalism and free grace, thus testifying to problems already raised by Mistress Anne Hutchinson's antinomian tendencies. New churches gathered during and after the period of heavy immigration and the antinomian crisis often labored long to produce covenants which now required the approval of the colony government and neighboring ministers. The process took several months at Dorchester, in 1637, while the covenant for Dedham was two years in the building.[62]

New England covenants did not aim for equality, but were attempts to deal with the facts of rough social equality and the implications of soul equality. In town and church covenants, order was a primary objective. In the churches, a well-educated clergy expounded doctrine to and expected deference from the laity, saints and sinners. Most towns distributed land widely, but almost never equally. All admitted inhabitants might qualify for a house lot, but only the town proprietors could share by right in the division of larger acreages, and even among proprietors the size of the division depended on the status of the recipient. New England covenants, then, were as much exclusive and hierarchical as inclusive and egalitarian in their operation, and had a conservative function which might have been appreciated by other English colonists in government.

However, what may be most interesting about the covenant is how dangerous it seemed. Viewed from England, it looked virtually incomprehensible even to Puritan friends of the migrants. The Reverend John Cotton, who in 1630 had preached the farewell sermon to Winthrop's fleet, wrote reprovingly from Boston in Lincolnshire about the church covenants and their implications of separatism and anarchy. Other prominent Puritans, including Viscount Saye and Sele, were even less pleased. Perhaps they heard from men like Sir Richard Saltonstall who had returned from Massachusetts disillusioned by the difficulty of maintaining traditional social, political, and economic relationships there. No wonder men of this class who thought of migration wrote ahead to seek guarantees that Massachusetts had not gone too far down the road to democracy. The reply, ironically penned by John Cotton, now in New England's Boston and a partaker of light, did not satisfy them, and they stuck to their other American ventures. At Saybrook and Springfield in New England and Providence Island in the West Indies, these class-conscious puritans, most of whom remained in England, used such devices as tenancy, indentured service, and even slavery to define colonial social structure, maintain order, and to produce profits.[63] A touchy correspondence ensued, which led Viscount Saye and Sele to observe, in 1640, that Massachusetts seemed a good place to stay away from.

Saye and Sele objected partly because he wanted settlers from New England for his Providence Island Company. Massachusetts survived economically by the 'spending of estates'; good men should go where a cash crop might be raised. But there was a social and political critique behind his observations. The spending of estates only accelerated that process of levelling which Saye and Sele had espied in Massachusetts. 'I say agayne noe wise man shoud be soe folish as to live whear every man is a master, and masters must not correct their servants; where wise men propounde and fooles determine'. Far better a political economy that would enhance wealth, secure authority and aristocracy, and preserve a social order which also included 'those that are poor'. Saye and Sele discounted Winthrop's objection that such a government, based on hereditary principles, would 'enthrale' others.

> Not at all . . .This constitution doth not abridge power in those that give it, though they injoy it not themselves . . .Thear is noe danger in such different degrees . . .soe long as they are allwayes accomptable to parliaments consisting of all estates united yearly and having in that union supremam potestatem.

To all of which Winthrop added a sour note referring to the losses of the Providence Island Company: 'what has become of their £120,000'?[64]

Applied in the Long Parliament, Saye and Sele's logic was to have momentous results, but in the meanwhile John Winthrop was no stranger to the problem of applying 'supremam potestatem' to the covenanted communities of Massachusetts. Defending the colony against criticism from its English friends or attack from its enemies Winthrop and other leaders celebrated Puritans' ability to covenant together to provide orderly government in church and state. Within the colony, they were never quite so sure. In 1639 Nathaniel Ward was neither first nor alone in warning that 'the spirits of the people runne high, and what they gett they hould'. Ward cared for the 'proper and lawfull liberties' of the people, but he would not refer his projected law code to the freemen for their judgment. That was a matter for government, not people, nor even for saints. Massachusetts' rulers gladly deployed the authority provided by the royal charter of 1629 and traditional English law to restrain some of the tendencies which their critics feared. It is noteworthy, indeed, that in the 1630s their use of the charter's power was characterized by less covenanting and more imposing than went on in Massachusetts towns and churches. The colony government's achievements during this period were typically legislative and institutional, or involved the imposition on localities of prescriptive and proscriptive justice. Possession of legitimate power had been vital in isolating the separatist Roger Williams from his Salem congregation; the General Court denied Salem some land it needed, and the church saw the error of its ways and dissolved its covenant with the stormy pastor. Similarly, effective action against the antinomians had failed within the confines of Boston church despite its revised covenant of 1636. Success awaited the dislodging of Henry Vane from the colony governorship and the crucial election meeting of 1637 in the friendlier air of Cambridge. Such episodes typified the General Court's tendency to intervene in local disputes which overstrained the covenanted authority of towns and churches. Individuals, too, often turned to the colony's courts for adversarial justice in preference to local arbitration. Closed Christian peasant communes the Massachusetts towns may have been, but in cases where peasants would not accept communal authority the charter government was called in, or stepped in uninvited, often to impose traditional, English solutions.[65]

Covenants notwithstanding, then, Massachusetts's charter government played a crucial role throughout the Bay patent during the 1630s. Its use of coercive power produced little of the violence and strife which characterized the early years of Virginian and West Indian government, but Puritans in government were as aware as any colonial or English politician of the intimate connections between political power, social stability, and economic prosperity. In aiming at these desirable goals, Puritan leaders were often drawn in different directions. As we have seen, much of Puritan publicity and law seemed to aim in the direction of economic liberalism. Yet order and authority were also vital to the Puritan blueprint. From Ipswich, in December 1635, Nathaniel Ward argued that the town's need for immigrants had now to give way to the necessities of social peace and religious orthodoxy. Ipswich town meeting had already conceded the point in an ordinance limiting the distribution of land to those of proven worth, but Ward believed that the authority of the colony government was necessary to make the restriction stick. Earlier, the Reverend John Eliot noticed the tension between social order and the dream of prosperity when he advised an English friend on the practicalities of immigration. Skilled labor was necessary, but 'bring not many servants, for they be a sure charge and trouble and an uncertain gain'. Servants brought 'for your comfortable attendance', Eliot continued, should be 'but poor and such as cannot work, and then you shall keep them'. The 'workful', Eliot explained, 'will desire freedom'. As in Virginia, so in Massachusetts; even traditional English household government was endangered by the expansive possibilities of American commonwealths. Massachusetts may not have treated its servants so badly as Virginia, but the social fears implicit in Eliot's and Ward's observations were backed up by laws which restrained wages and prices, told the poor what they might wear, placed unattached individuals firmly under family government, and sought to insure that towns would obey and enforce the same laws.[66]

The same dynamic tension was apparent in the efforts of early town covenants and ordinances to balance the goals of prosperity and order, for instance by limiting the number of inhabitants for a frankly stated mixture of practical and religious aims. In practice, however, the balance was difficult to maintain. Free and absolute title to property was vital to farming folk, especially to those who might wish to sell up and move on. Yet towns typically passed ordinances limiting freedom of sale, for who could say what stranger might be able to afford the purchase price?[67] If Salem wished to begin a shipbuilding enterprise, how could it restrain townsmen from free use of common woodlands without seeking the help of higher authority? Salem's ambition to create a port trade which would rival Boston's not only recommended investment in shipbuilding but also led the town to invite fishermen to settle. Concerned to insure both that these traditionally wayward folk would not disrupt the Christian community and that they should fish rather than farm, Salem denied them rights to common land and required them to settle some distance away, at Marblehead; but Salem needed fishermen, profane or otherwise. Other towns bowed to the same kind of necessities when they virtually advertised on the open market for sufficient numbers to make up a viable settlement, or for men possessed of particular skills like leather tanners or clergymen, or for gentlemen of status. Given these needs, how relevant was the spiritual estate of such desirable new inhabitants?[68] Neither individuals nor towns could refrain from acting in ways which threatened order and purity and thus vitiated the towns' organic covenants.

New England's covenants may have been unique,[69] but along with ordinances and laws throughout the colonies they operated as species of traditional English mechanisms imported to the colonies by English migrants and used for traditional ends. They remind us that the 'liberty' sought by those who dominated colonial governments retained its traditional, exclusive characteristics. It did so although the same people often recognized that the American environment encouraged, even required, a more inclusive or positive application of liberty. They sought these kinds of liberties themselves, for instance by making land easily available and by rejecting the monopoly principle in organizing trade and commerce, but deliberately restricted the liberty of others in ways which were sometimes more savage and repressive than would have been acceptable or necessary in old England. Change enveloped the colonists, but still they kept it at arm's length.

In all these cases, we sense the vital importance to colonial governments of their grasp on power and legitimacy. It is clear, too, that the sources of power and legitimacy varied from colony to colony according to local conditions. Some colony governments were blessed by a population which generally supported the aims of the colonizers; other governments had to use more force more often to insure peace and good order. In the rapidly changing environment of America, however, neither deference nor coercion was sufficient. Power depended also and perhaps ultimately on the nature of each government's tie to English authority. Royal charters underlined the fact that the colonies were politically creatures of the English state and particularly of the English crown. They were species of local government, parts of an imperium. Without that tie, they would have been – or believed they would be – in a great deal of trouble.

Even the Massachusetts General Court gave notice of this fact. When in the late 1630s the colony's charter was challenged by Archbishop William Laud's plantations committee, the General Court warned him against persisting in his challenge. Should he carry on,[70]

> the common people here will conseive that his Majesty hath cast them off, and that, heereby, they are freed from their allegiance and subjection, and . . .will be ready to confederate themselves under a new government, for their necessary safety and subsistence, which will be a dangerous example to other plantations.

The implication that Puritans, of all people, might safely cast off from England must have infuriated Archbishop Laud. But that 'dangerous example' was also a threat to Massachusetts's social order. The General Court admitted that should the Massachusetts common people set up their own government, it would be 'perillous to ourselves of incurring his Majestyes displeasure', and that was a more than ritual obeisance to the authority by which the Court ruled. Massachusetts leaders' concern to stay on the right side of English authority had been demonstrated frequently during the 1630s, and they feared the crown because they feared losing their right to rule, feared being cast off with the common people. By 1638, they had more experience than they wanted of disputes which called their authority into question, warm memories indeed, for they had only just stilled a conflict over the nature of salvation which brought with it fears of revolution and social chaos. In meeting these and other threats,[71] as well as in providing a backstop to the covenanted power of local towns and churches, the authority of the royal charter proved a useful asset. For the plantation colonies, lacking popular adherence to a set of publicly articulated social and religious aims, and additionally threatened by generic social instability, the English connection was more vital, the threat of intervention from England more serious.

* * *

It was clear that Adam Smith's world of freedom, if implicit in the American environment, still waited to be given its full political effect. 'Modern' political conceptions of individualism and democracy lay even further in the future, even though they may be seen in embryo in some aspects of colonial government and politics. But there was more strength to Charles I's empire than its inertia in the face of 'modernizing forces'. The concept of modernization has some serious limitations, not least the requirement that we give analytical weight to old-fashionedness. Perhaps Charles I's world was old-fashioned, but it fitted the American environment as perceived by colonial elites. The legitimate authority he conferred upon colonial governments was vital to their survival in a world which did not widely accept the idea that sovereignty inhered in the people. The contractualism of his charters was admirably suited to provide the necessary liberty for those able to profit from it. In return, Charles required colonial governments to regulate their individual trades and to give English law to Englishmen in America. Autonomy and dependence were already inextricably woven into the fabric of England's empire, just as they characterized the relationships between the crown and England's local governments.

Historians have generally dismissed the imperial accomplishments of Charles I for a variety of reasons, most notably his failure to devise and impose a general administrative and commercial policy of empire. Had Charles's personal rule continued unchallenged, he might have transformed the imperial relationship in such a direction. The 1635 decision to send Sir Ferdinando Gorges as New England's Governor-General might support this view, but this was rather an attack on the Puritan colony of Massachusetts than a new departure in imperial policy.[72] The contractualism which inhered in Charles's charters and commissions made new departures in policy unlikely anyway, and the solid accomplishments of crown and colonizers between 1625 and 1642 recommend instead George Chalmers' evaluation of two centuries ago:73

> In his colonial administration, he copied the practice of his father, because he inherited his principles. . .he regarded the plantations as a patrimony, which he might give away or govern, according to his will; though he seemed proud to acknowledge to the world, that he considered these transatlantic settlements as territories of the English empire. The charters of his reign were dictated by a knowledge of the law . . . establishing regulations, as he was supposed to possess legislative authority, and granting exemptions, as he actually possessed the power of taxation. To him England owes the original policy of the acts of navigation . . .though he has been robbed of the merit of invention and the praise of consistency.

What Charles and, to give them their due, the organizers and executors of colonization had accomplished was to make the colonies clearly and indisputably parts of England's existing political order, recognizable extensions of English thought and practice in society and politics. This would determine their fate during the revolutions to come.

CHAPTER THREE

The English revolution and the empire, 1642–1660

Whether they thought Charles I a tyrant or a martyr, Englishmen everywhere agreed that his execution in January 1649 was an awesome and terrible event. It was made more momentous still by the abolition of monarchy and the proclamation of a parliamentary republic. Although the army which had brought Charles to justice still waited in the wings, parliament thus claimed total victory in the constitutional struggle. This did not necessarily entail change in the empire, but change was implied; all colony governments recognized that a supreme legislature threatened their position as creations of a monarchical prerogative. The Commonwealth's commercial and colonial legislation of 1650 and 1651 explored some of this potential and made it clear that more was involved than a change of masters or procedures or constitutional structures. This legislation tells us and warned colonists of the radical, transforming potential of the English Revolution. The acts provide evidence for new conceptions of government and society which threatened the old order in both realm and empire. These conceptions were first widely explored in the political debates and pamphleteering which flowered during the civil war years. The context established by these debates will help us to understand why colonists saw the Plantations Act of 1650 as far more intrusive and threatening than the more famous Navigation Act of 1651.

However, there were countervailing forces at work. Colonies, as parts of the *ancien régime*, enjoyed some protection, and not merely because revolutionary England became, soon enough, Restoration England. There were strongly conservative elements in English politics during the Interregnum, by no means all of them in the crown's camp. Many fought against the crown not to transform England but to preserve its 'ancient constitution', and at some point most of these found that they wanted to stop short, to restrain or even to destroy the forces of radical change. This ideological conservatism was reinforced by the sheer administrative and legislative detail for which parliament undertook responsibility; whether the king was 'absent', as a necessary legal fiction declared during the civil wars, or dead, parliaments without kings had much more to do than parliaments with kings. Just how much more can be graphically if roughly gauged by weighing the *Acts and Ordinances of the Interregnum*, 1642-1660, against the *Statutes of the Realm* for the eighteen-year period of Charles II's Cavalier Parliament. Much of parliament's massive production was pure routine. For instance, new oaths had to be imposed; provision had to be made to administer them and to replace men who refused the oaths. Such business would seem hardly to be stuff of which revolutions are made, but it underlines the point that there was a constitutional conservatism or legalism in inter-regnum regimes which existed alongside conflicting tendencies towards pragmatic innovation and radical restructuring.

These countervailing forces were understood by colonists at the out-set of England's domestic strife, but their effects on colonial politics became clearer as time passed. Occasionally colonial governments were reduced to confusion or chaos as they struggled to keep an even course amidst the storms of civil war, the hurricane winds of change potentially represented by the Commonwealth's legislation of 1650 and 1651, and the fitful breezes of Cromwell's rule. There was also a good deal of more purposeful adjustment. Explanations for these colonial reactions belong mainly to the next chapter. Here we need to consider how far and why England's mid-century revolution changed the context of imperial poli-tics. That it would do so seemed obvious, for the view that there should be a uniform course of government throughout England's empire be-came more than ever a point of contention as Englishmen struggled with one another over the proper course of government for the nation itself.

* * *

While the crown and its cause played an important role in imperial affairs during the 1640s, and indeed throughout the Interregnum, our main concern must be with parliament, both because it was the ultimate victor in the civil war and because its claim to exercise a governing capacity was a new element in England's political equation. Certainly in imperial matters there had been no effective challenge to Secretary of State Sir George Calvert's view, stated in 1621, that the monarch's American possessions were his by right and 'therefore not subject to the laws' of parliament.[1]

The Short Parliament of 1640 and, in its initial sittings of 1641, the Long Parliament seemed to have set for themselves conservative goals. Thus, initially, MPs like Sir Edward Hyde could act as leaders of a constitutional opposition. This conservative strain was to remain an important factor in English politics for the rest of the century, but increasingly direct attacks upon the prerogative destroyed conservative harmony by forcing men like Hyde to declare for the king even before he raised his standard at Nottingham in early 1642. Even so, the parliamentary cause continued for some time to operate under conservative leadership. This was not too surprising, for although actually doing battle against their monarch was a momentous step, most of the nobility and gentry who adhered to the parliamentary cause believed that they were righting a series of imbalances, between crown and parliament and also between central government and the localities from which they sprang. They were sustained in their stand by the support of their neighbors in their county and borough communities, men of substance who had long experience of working together as Justices of the Peace, aldermen, lords and deputies lieutenant, and also as men who, in parish vestries or as manorial lords, had dominated local religious affairs. They felt that Charles's government and his bishops had intruded too much and too often on their bailiwicks.

Although the necessities of civil war would make parliament itself an intruder,[2] parliament's initial responses to colonial questions were governed by such considerations. Striving rather to limit than to abolish the prerogative, parliament was disposed to respect the crown's legitimate creations. Not all of Charles I's creations (in England or America) automatically qualified as legitimate, but the colony governments' claims were strong ones. English county and town governments had traditionally depended upon royal commissions and charters, and the colonies fitted easily into this picture as species of local government, legitimate at least until proven otherwise and therefore to be sustained rather than attacked by a parliament which claimed to have a care for the maintenance of lawful government. To be sure, this very claim led parliament to assume administrative and quasi-judicial responsibilities which might before have been left mainly to the crown, and acting as a court to which Englishmen, including colonists, might make petition, parliament was more active than it had been before. From 1640 to 1643, however, parliament generally respected the crown's prior dispensations in colonial matters even where, as in the Caribbee proprietary, these had produced much confusion. Parliament did feel it necessary to consider Charles's commission to William Berkeley as governor of Virginia, but its decision not to interfere was a mark of its constitutional caution in prerogative matters.[3]

However, parliament's legislative capacity made it by nature a good deal more than a court. Its transforming potential was exercised early, in 1641, when the Long Parliament resolved that parliament's power to establish customs rates was an 'ancient right' and proceeded to enact a new Book of Rates. This constitutional position was not to be relinquished even in 1660; but from early 1642 the absence of the king and the outbreak of civil war required another advance, that parliament pass and give effect to laws without the king's assent. In these legislative and executive claims lay the essence of parliament's power to transform England and the empire. Yet in its capacity as an imperial legislature, parliament proceeded cautiously. Parliament's first direct legislative incursion into colonial affairs was an ordinance of March 1643 granting duty-free status to the New England trades. This, however, was little more than an extension of the privileges granted by Charles I to the Massachusetts Bay Company and was modelled after the relevant provisions of the 1629 charter. We may well doubt whether King Charles would have granted this favor had Massachusetts taken the trouble to ask him, but the mechanism of petition and response was a familiar enough way to confirm or extend previously granted charter privileges. Of course the king would have made any such grant by proclamation or charter amendment, while parliament framed it as a legislative act. There is no evidence that parliament thought it was doing anything portentous; it simply conferred a benefit on colonists it presumed to be ideological allies, and it did so in the only way it could, by legislative enactment. In New England there was a sharper perception of the importance of the precedent; what one legislative majority might give, another could take away, and more. The Massachusetts General Court took care to enact its own version before taking advantage of such a dangerous gift. In 1646, John Winthrop drew the moral still more clearly in arguing against proposals to seek parliamentary confirmation of the charter of 1629. As we shall see, all colonists looked askance at a supreme legislative power in the empire.[4]

Parliament was less generous to Chesapeake and West Indian colonists than to Puritan New Englanders. Some in parliament suspected the southern and island colonies of royalist sympathies, but it may be doubted whether there was much political significance to parliament's decisions to raise tobacco duties and to deny customs advantages to English colonial sugar, now beginning to trickle into London. With a war on, parliament needed money as well as friends; there was a lot more money in the tobacco and sugar trades than in the commerce with New England. Parliament had already taken the important step of claiming authority over setting customs rates, and colonial tobacco had already proven its capacity to generate revenue. Meanwhile, parliamentary leaders like the Earl of Warwick were as aware as anyone of the potential for sugar to fuel the sinews of war.[5] These revenues and the control of the port of London were to be crucial to parliament's survival and success in the civil wars, a good deal more important than the precise political sympathies of colonists.

Parliament's first notable exercise of its power to intrude in colonial affairs in an executive capacity did not come until November 1643, when it commissioned the Earl of Warwick and others to oversee the colonies' governments. Parliament accorded the commissioners power to 'order, and dispose, all things . . . fit and advantageous to the well-governing, securing, strengthening, and preserving of the said planta-tions', including powers to appoint and remove governors and other officers.[6] These were sweeping powers indeed, in theory greater than the crown possessed over any colony but Virginia. During the committee's four-year tenure, however, these powers were generally exercised with restraint. Even in Virginia, where Governor Berkeley's notorious roy-alism obliged the committee to take some initiative, it acted cautiously. The inhabitants were authorized to select their own governor but 'left at libertie to choose the present Governor if you shall see cause'. In explanations for the Warwick committee's moderation, historians have stressed the variety of personal opinions and colonial contacts of the membership and the shifting strength of various elements in the parliamentary coalition throughout the years of the committee's activi-ties. While these were undoubtedly important, and were thought to be so at the time, it was equally important that the committee normally acted rather in response to colonial petitions than to establish new positions and policies on its own initiative. Given that the committee had to come to decisions when petitions came before it, the charter and commission rights of existing colonial governments offered a conven-ient and plausible basis for agreement. Most of the committee's major decisions followed this common thread whatever its members' ideologi-cal and religious sympathies or the shifting strength of their support in and outside of parliament. This was certainly the case in the decisions reached concerning New England and Maryland. In New England, Samuel Gorton and Roger Williams received parliamentary charters for their Rhode Island settlements upon their satisfying the Warwick com-mittee that their lands lay outside the bounds of the crown's previous grant to Massachusetts. However, those who, like the Child petitioners, challenged Massachusetts's authority from within the charter's bounds got short shrift from the committee and from parliament. Nor was Gorton successful in his efforts to prosecute the Bay Colony for its treatment of him while he had been within Massachusetts's jurisdic-tion. Of course, all the New England parties to these disputes could call for support on ideological allies within the parliamentary coalition; it was more remarkable, therefore, that the Roman Catholic Lord Balti-more won endorsement of his right to govern his Maryland proprietary under the royal charter of 1632. In doing so, Warwick rejected the pretensions of Maryland protestants who had rebelled against Baltimore and for parliament.[7]

It was only in the Caribbees where the committee intervened consistently in internal colonial politics, and here it did not initiate but reacted to King Charles's own meddling with the *status quo ante*. There was no concerted effort to disturb local elites in favor of parliamentary stalking horses. Both the proprietor, the Earl of Carlisle, and his creditors soon abandoned the view that the whole thing was a ploy designed to help Warwick achieve his old ambition to take over the proprietary. They believed that the Warwick committee's very existence arose directly out of Charles's attempt, in 1643, to place new governors in the islands.[8] The language parliament used to establish the committee supports this view.[9] Once established, the committee's most sustained intervention in West Indian affairs took place in 1645 and 1646. This time the committee acted in response to the king's grant of the Carlisle proprietary to the Earl of Marlborough.[10] It was as if the committee's function was to preserve the colonial establishments as created by the prerogative before the king took up arms against parliament. Royal intervention after 1642, especially to change an earlier dispensation, could not be allowed to pass unchallenged, but by the same token the committee would not encourage colonial insurgency against legitimate local authority, either in New England or elsewhere. As late as February 1644, Warwick deprecated reports of royalist sentiment in the colonies, and even after parliament voiced its strong concern about Virginia the committee did little to disturb local government. The considerable number of Puritans in Virginia had better luck appealing to their coreligionists in New England than to those in old England, and some were finally taken in by the Catholic Lord Baltimore.[11]

The Warwick committee's respect for established colonial authority owed in part to its members' instinctive fellow feeling for Englishmen charged with the responsibilities of local government in troubled times. However, parliament itself had enjoined regard for the status quo of 1642 in its initial legislation establishing the committee. In this ordinance, parliament proved to be thoroughly conversant with the early seventeenth-century consensus about the political necessities of colonization. The sweeping powers given to the committee, in effect a generous definition of the king's prerogative powers over the colonies, were, as the prerogative had been, limited by the recognition that colonial rights and necessities had to be respected if order were to be maintained in English America.

[F]or the better government and security of the said plantations . . . and the owners and inhabitants thereof, there may be just and fit occasion to assign over some part of the power and authority (granted in this ordinance to [Warwick's committee]) unto the said owners, inhabitants, and others.

The committee was authorized to assign its authority to fit persons 'for the better governing and preserving the said plantations and islands from open violence and private disturbance and distractions'.[12] Doubtless some colonial 'owners and inhabitants' took more comfort from this than did others, but it was clear that in parliament's eyes, colonies continued to be polities worthy of protection both in their own right and as legitimate creations of the sovereign English state.

As long as parliament maintained the fiction that it governed in the physical absence of Charles I, it would have been difficult to justify an invasion of colonial powers and privileges held by previous prerogative grants. Warwick himself urged Virginians to declare for parliament because it was 'the great Councell of the kingdome, whence his Majesties commands are dispenst with most life, and whose resolutions are bounded with most loyaltie & dutie to his Majestie'.[13] Parliament and the Warwick committee acted decisively to stymie royal efforts to change the status quo of 1642, but in general found it more congenial to work with colonial governments as they had been established at the outbreak of hostilities in England. Even the royal government of Virginia survived, despite the fact that its governor, William Berkeley, actually returned to England to fight for the crown. Only in Maryland was the government of 1642 overthrown in favor of parliament, and that was done not by the Warwick committee but by colonists themselves. As we have seen, the proprietor regained his government with the help of the Warwick committee and despite the rebels' plausible claims to religious and ideological sympathy with the parliamentary cause. We can imagine that the Maryland rebels' chagrin was of the same species and grew from the same circumstances as the disappointments suffered by the Child petitioners.

It would be wrong to say that cordial relations existed between parliament and established colonial authorities. Colonists of all ideological and religious opinions had reason to be wary of a parliament which claimed an extensive legislative competence, and for its part parliament desired and occasionally demanded support or explicit recognition of its authority from colonial governments. It would certainly not do to have any colony openly challenge the legitimacy of parliament's cause. But parliament's very claim to legitimacy, grounded as it was on England's ancient constitution, safeguarded the existing order in the empire. Under the oversight of the Earl of Warwick's committee for plantations, then, the empire continued to work in familiar ways. Whether this would last was another question which would be raised in stark outline when parliament tried and executed King Charles I and then proclaimed the English republic. But the question was examined before the drama of the regicide. During the 1640s, open civil strife encouraged Englishmen to think radically about the proper organization of government and society, and the colonies, as parts of the *ancien régime*, could not expect to escape attention, or criticism.

* * *

The civil war brought forth attacks on the English hierarchy of liberty and privilege.[14] Some aspects of the old order, such as patents for industrial and retail monopolies, were especially unpopular; they had come under attack during James's reign and now were said to epitomize the rottenness of Charles I's regime. Obviously, too, the king's powers over parliament and the church became burning issues. However, these more egregious vices of Caroline government soon called others to mind. Seventeenth-century England was as privilege-ridden as it was class-ridden, and in the political heat and light generated by civil war it was inevitable that strictures against monopoly patents and court privilege would be applied more widely than even many parliamentarians, themselves elected by exclusive franchise, would have liked. In this whirligig of politics, grievances against one sort of privilege formed grounds of principle which could be used, in turn, to attack other privileges. Much later, Sir Edward Hyde would speak for many conservatives when he likened this chain reaction of circumstance to 'so many atoms contributing jointly to this mass of confusion now before us'.[15]

It was an apt metaphor which would have been understood by governing elites on both sides of the ocean. The changed economic climate which Englishmen encountered in America had already begun to thaw some of the glacial characteristics of England's traditional systems for regulating production and trade, and with similar effects. While it would be too much to suggest that English society had become atomized, long-term economic change had put great strain on traditional mechanisms of government and social control. Declining old trades and rapidly expanding new ones had cast many loose from their traditional social moorings and on to an increasingly open market. Thus individuals reacted to market forces, but the trouble was that by doing so they were brought into conflict with settled ways of organizing and conducting economic exchanges of goods and labor and with traditional social structures and mores. Interloping merchants invaded the rights and liberties of trading corporations and corporate towns and cities. Improving landlords strained traditional rural social orders through enclosures of common land and by putting pressure on tenants and copyholders. Humbler folk driven to search for work in areas far from home were likely to be identified as vagabonds, arousing fear in those charged with keeping the peace, and resentment amongst both the settled poor and the rate payers of their new parish.[16] The result was that grievances multiplied.

Both grievances and ideas for redress came from many quarters. Not all were inherently hostile to the traditional system. Some, and they were on both sides of the civil war, aimed to reassert traditional institutions and values as best calculated to revive England's moral and political economy. Others sought redress for specific grievances in the traditional way by securing their own entry into the liberties and privileges which had previously been denied to them. However, such traditional mechanisms could not be a universal solution. They were inherently restrictive and, as we have seen in the colonies, they were therefore ill-suited to cope with the rapidly changing conditions which actually obtained in the domestic and international economies. As men confronted the limitations of tradition and as the contagion of liberty spread, the system was brought into disrepute and came under attack. Many, perhaps most, of these attacks came from the radical fringes of the parliamentary party and army, but the pattern of thought and action was pervasive. From the beginning of his reign, Charles I struck a comfortable pose as the defender of legitimacy and guarantor of order only to find that the necessities of government in peace and war required him to invade traditional liberties and privileges. During the civil wars, parliament itself encountered similar gaps between pretence and practice. Ultimately, Oliver Cromwell (who took to himself the significant title of Lord Protector) joined with the ghost of Charles Stuart by dispersing the Long Parliament, at the center the last vestige of continuous legitimacy, and then, later, by imposing on English counties the rule of the major-generals. It was as if neither king nor protector could govern effectively without invading a system to which both professed their allegiance.

Meanwhile, the ferment of the 1640s produced more trenchant and more deliberate attacks on the system. Often these came from humbler men who did not share their masters' reluctance to do away with the old forms. The process of attacking tradition led to the construction of new ways to legitimate the social and economic order, or disorder, which characterized England at mid-century.[17] In religion, men and women were moved to seek grace after their own lights and, having found it, to insist on their right to organize their spiritual life as they found fit, free from the interference of either bishop or presbyter, 'freer than they had ever been', as Christopher Hill puts it, 'free from prosecution for "sin",free to assemble and discuss in their own congregations' and to tell the world about it. Independency and a veritable cacophony of more radical variants found voice in the 1640s, not only to construct a rationale for religious toleration but also to enforce it on the parliamentary coalition. Many such folk came to value religious freedom enough to explore some of its wider implications. Thus John Milton and others brought leading economic and political issues into service to argue that a state church should form no part of the new order of things. Intolerance and erastianism in religion denied freedom of commerce in ideas and equal rights for men's consciences.[18] The course of argument flowed the other way, as well; when religious radicals took their grievances into more secular areas, they were often joined by others of less saintly hue in attacks on England's restricted markets of liberty and privilege. The Levellers and Thomas Hobbes may be taken as representative of the men and the ideas which began seriously to challenge the conservatism of the age, whether they found it amongst royalists or roundheads.[19]

Although their influence on events proved finally to be slight and their ideas were in some crucial respects contradictory, Hobbes and the Levellers shared enough in common to mount similar attacks on the ways in which Englishmen had been governed and by which they had governed one another. Distrusting hierarchies of power, they agreed that the relationship between the state and the individual should be direct and unimpeded by intermediary, autonomous authority. Government ought to relate to a society composed of individuals who were in some essential respect equal. Such distinctions as might be drawn between individuals should not be those of the traditional order; instead, wealth, or the price men could command in the market for their skills and strengths, would determine their place and power. All other distinctions were, to Hobbes, mere window dressing for the ego and, to the Levellers, anathema.[20]

The Stuart state was riddled with such distinctions, which were especially undesirable where they were bound up in corporate and monopoly rights. Hobbes and the Levellers argued that corporations' economic privileges harmed the common weal, Hobbes believing that certain kinds especially were economically harmful. However, their political objections to such privilege were probably more important than their economic objections; certainly this was so for Hobbes, given his views on the unlimited authority of the sovereign to do good or evil. To Hobbes, the chief danger of corporations lay in their tendency to arrogate sovereign power to themselves. He warns against this in a general discussion of subordinate bodies politic, and returns to the fray later while considering 'those things that weaken, or tend to the dissolution of a Common-wealth'. Corporations 'are as it were many lesser Common-wealths in the bowels of a greater, like wormes in the entrayles of a naturall man'. There they sapped the state's strength.[21] Leveller objections to corporate government and privilege would seem at first sight to be based on grounds antithetical to those used by Hobbes. These kinds of 'liberties', Levellers charged, were in truth chains which denied to freeborn Englishmen their natural rights: not only the right to vote, but also the rights to produce, sell, and buy both goods and ideas on the open market. These chains should be broken. Thus Levellers sought to enhance the individual's power, not the state's. Moreover, as if to distance themselves still further from Hobbes, they argued that the state should be denied the power ever again to restrict the people's liberties and freedoms.[22]

However, the distance between Hobbes and the Levellers was not so great. Given the situation as it existed in the 1640s, the Levellers' demands required, even assumed, the existence of Hobbes's strong and totally sovereign government. Levellers demanded that the government should take away privileges which, as the civil wars showed, a good number of Englishmen viewed as sacrosanct rights of property. Even the Levellers' demand for widening the suffrage was viewed as grand theft by gentlemen who regarded that franchise as an exclusive right. Levellers did not naively think that their goals might be attained easily. Powerful obstacles required powerful remedies, as Richard Overton argued in 1646 when he stated that only a House of Commons which derived its authority from all the people could be powerful enough to conquer the king and establish justice. Within the constitutional limits they would place upon the state, men of Overton's kind expected it to respond directly and effectively to the wishes of the electorate, in many cases invading the bastions of privilege against which they fought. For instance, they demanded the legislative invasion of the common law; parliament should tell judges by statute what laws to enforce and how to interpret them. The conception of government as a steward of the existing social and economic order, shared by conservatives on both sides of the civil war, was foreign to Leveller thinking. The best of all possible worlds was too far away to allow them that particular luxury. 'The end of Parliaments', said John Wildman during the Putney debates of 1647, is 'not to constitute what is already [established, but to act] according to the just rules of government'.[23] Further to the left, the Digger, Gerrard Winstanley, sensed the intimate connection between universal liberty and power when he wrote that 'wheresoever there is a people . . .united by common community of livelihood into oneness, it will become the strongest land in the world; for then they will be as one man to defend their inheritance'. Those who pleaded the case for property and privilege divided the people and weakened the nation.[24]

Arguments that greater liberty, for instance in trade or religion, might enhance the power of the state were by no means the monopoly of the Puritan left in seventeenth-century England, but what a Leveller parliament might actually do frightened a good many people in the 1640s. Such thoughts drove some parliamentarians into the king's arms; others, the 'presbyterians', became more willing to pay a good price for peace. Levellers' ideas caused concern even among their superior officers in the army. In the debates at Putney, conservatives voiced these fears and underlined the radical potential of the Leveller position. Oliver Cromwell may not have been the best of the debaters at Putney, but he knew what bound man to man in England and saw clearly that the Levellers' justifications for widening the suffrage and for renouncing the Engagement called into question all such covenants.[25] Cromwell's clearest statement came before the suffrage had become the center of attention. Cromwell's son-in-law Henry Ireton conceded that covenants should not be 'sinful' in God's sight, but insisted that justice was more concerned with relations between man and man who, having made covenant together, must keep it. If lawfully made human covenants were put to the tests of natural right and divine justice, Ireton 'would very fain know what you gentlemen, or any others, do account the right to anything you have in England – anything in estate, land, or goods . . . what ground, what right you have to it'. Ireton's honesty was disarming, a realist's confession that society and history were flawed vessels. Yet his was also an explicitly conservative plea to preserve what the Levellers' test of natural law would destroy: 'those that were fixed men, and settled men, that had the interest of this kingdom'. To protect themselves and that which was lawfully theirs, 'persons in whom all land lies, and those in corporations in whom all trading lies' possessed the traditional rights of freeholders, including the suffrage, and enjoyed the liberties of chartered corporations.[26]

Although at Putney the extent of the suffrage became the major point at issue, it is important to note both sides' appreciation that their views on the vote were tied inextricably to equally contrasting ideas about the functions of government and its relationship to society. Ireton and Cromwell wanted government to protect and defend those fixed and settled interests upon which much besides the right to vote depended. Theirs was a defence of some essential lineaments of the old order. The Levellers may not have wanted manhood suffrage, but they wanted a greatly enlarged electorate which alone could justly empower government to change what was already constituted, to break unjust covenants, and to force an opening through which a wider constituency might gain access to the kingdom of equal opportunity in economics and politics.[27]

This was not to be, at least not for those for whom Levellers claimed to speak. However, their arguments and those of Hobbes show that during the civil war period ideas were in the air which were fundamentally opposed to the established system of government and economic regulation by privilege, franchise, and exclusion. 'Freedom', 'liberty', and 'right' were all terms which were in danger of losing their sense of exclusiveness as marks of propriety, or property, which derived from tradition or precedent and set those who enjoyed them above the common rank of men. While few argued for doing away entirely with these social, political, and economic distinctions, it became more common to hear that their possession was in some degree common to all or most men, whether by birthright, or natural law, or divine decree. It was common, too, for listeners to be moved by such arguments. Thus conservatives on both sides of the civil war and on both sides of the Atlantic hastened to remind the new citizenry that there were higher forms of liberty than that called natural, forms by which alone man could be both secured and distinguished from brute nature and human society delivered from a state of war.[28] We must remember, however, that these exclusive franchises and liberties, as defended by Oliver Cromwell and Henry Ireton at Putney, also insulated those who held them from the power of the state. For Ireton, the laws of the land were sufficient to guarantee security and safety, if only King Charles would adhere to them. For the Leveller John Wildman, however, this was not enough; he was 'but a single man', a lesser breed without the law, and for his safety he would have to 'venture myself and [my] share in the common bottom'.[29]

* * *

These arguments about power and liberty are essential to our understanding of modern history, of the rise of the state and, latterly, the concurrent expansion of democracy. They also underline some common points of development between seventeenth-century England and her colonies. In America, as we have seen, circumstances seemed to call for greater economic liberty, yet they also called forth strong conservative impulses; if anything, this tension would be heightened by the unsettling effects of England's Interregnum. In England, of course, the relatively advanced or radical position taken by the Levellers was not to win through, but it was to retain a significance throughout their own century and particularly during their own decade. It was a time of war and political upheaval, and events often seemed to favor the prophets of a new order and to encourage those who found the established liberties of some Englishmen to restrict their own, natural or otherwise. Their success depended very much on the power they were able to command.

While humble folk known as Diggers gathered wood and sewed seeds where the Surrey gentry said they should not, interloping merchants defied the rules and ignored the privileges of the Eastland Company, and traded to the Baltic as they pleased. These actions were not different in kind. Both were exercises in outlawry, invasions of settled rights of property and of government, and both derived ideological justification from the ferment of ideas of the 1640s.[30] These were significant similarities, but the results were different. The Diggers took on the fixed and settled interests of England's dominant landowning class in the name of liberty and equality; this, to say nothing of their poverty and obscurity, effectively placed them beyond the pale. They faded as stability returned, robbing them of time and space. Interlopers and their kind, however, were better favored. They attacked monopolies, trading companies, and municipal corporations in the name of liberty and property; they often were and spoke for men of substance; and they argued that the prosperity and power of the commonwealth depended upon their efforts. Correspondingly they enjoyed more success than their ideological 'allies', the Diggers. The Navigation Act of 1651 may be viewed partly as a measure of that success.

The Navigation Act was a good deal more, and less, than a charter for interloping merchants. While some historians have seen the Act in those terms, others have argued that it was the companies themselves who urged the passage of the Act and benefited from it. Still others have seen the Act of 1651 as anti-Dutch, aimed at England's great trade rivals and thus a prelude to the first Anglo-Dutch war.[31] These disagreements over the exact provenance of the Navigation Act are unlikely to disappear, for the evidence is insufficient to clinch any one line of argument. Moreover, the debate rests on the unlikely assumption that it was *the* Act of 1651, as finally passed, which competing groups and individuals had in mind when, between 1649 and 1651, they urged the Commonwealth to do something to rescue the nation's trade from the confused and depressed state into which it had fallen. The Act's provisions might best be regarded as a general response to this general agitation. If it is to be considered as interest-group legislation, the most one can say about it is that it suffered the usual fate of horses designed by committees. There was something in it for everyone, and arguments over which group had the upper hand in politics or the more powerful allies in parliament or in the Councils of State and Trade are unlikely to be fruitful.[32]

It was of more importance that now these competitors for state favor appealed to a sovereign legislature and in a much altered ideological climate. S.R.Gardiner was right to include the Navigation Act, albeit as an appendix, in his *Constitutional Documents of the Puritan Revolu-*

tion, for in this legislation parliament took in the whole sea-borne commerce of Britain – foreign, colonial, and coasting. Furthermore, parliament applied its regulations to and on behalf of 'the nation' and 'the people of this Commonwealth'. The Act of 1651 'nationalized' England's trade, not in the sense of state ownership but because it was blanket legislation which on its face applied to all trades and equally to all Englishmen. Thus parliament moved away from the idea of regulating particular trades which had heretofore characterized royal policy. To be sure, the traditional means of trade regulation, the chartered companies, were not abolished by the Act, and indeed their rights to carry on their trades in the traditional way were implied by several exemptions written into the Act; but their powers of regulation were nowhere mentioned, far less confirmed. As the companies had asked for such confirmation in their petitions, we must assume their disappointment.[33] Nor was this an oversight; the Council of State, to which most company petitions had been directed, had either taken no action or referred them to parliament, conceiving that if granted they might tend to a diminution of the liberty of trade against which parliament had specifically warned the council. Parliament then repeated the warning when in August 1650 it created the Council of Trade and instructed it in ways which betrayed considerable hostility towards monopoly regulation.[34] The trading companies had run into revolutionary prejudice against privileged limitations on trade; but it was their powers and not their rights which had been put at risk.[35]

Simply but crucially, the Act of Navigation reduced the companies' status to that of any other legal individual; the Act applied to and comprehended the companies; the companies did not comprehend the Act. The companies continued to exist; their interests *vis-à-vis* foreigners were upheld and asserted; the special nature of their established trades was recognized; but the Act applied to the companies as it applied to all Englishmen. The trading companies stood in danger of ceasing to exist as licensed agencies of state power and were placed on an equal footing with others before a transcendent state authority. As with the Levellers' proposals for the domestic economy, the Navigation Act bypassed the powers of corporations and monopolies and enhanced the economic rights of the individual citizen. As it also increased the power of the state, it well deserves Charles Wilson's description as the 'welfare of Leviathan'.[36] Certainly there was a taste of Hobbes about it, and even something of the Levellers; given the Act's revolutionary redefinition and augmentation of state power and individual liberty, it was entirely appropriate, if fortuitously so, that the Rump Parliament waited to pass finally on the legislation until it had heard of Cromwell's victory over Charles Stuart and the Scots at Worcester. That 'crowning glory' insured

[59]

the republic's survival, while the Navigation Act testified to the potential of its sovereignty over Englishmen at home and in America..

* * *

In previous chapters, we have seen that colony governments, like trading companies, had developed vested interests in the means, if not necessarily in the ends, of Stuart trade policies. The regulations the crown imposed on colonial trade may have restricted economic freedom, but the regulatory powers conveyed to colonial governments had proven valuable considerations in themselves, vital to the authority and prosperity of those in power.[37] While it generally reaffirmed the ends of Stuart colonial policy, and thus threatened all colonists by restricting their freedom of trade, the functional similarities between colonial governments and the chartered trading companies of Stuart England meant that the Act of 1651 and its successors also had a political incidence. Precisely because the Act legislated for all the colonies and for the whole of their trade, it threatened the franchises by which the Stuarts had granted liberty and power to regulate the trade of each colony. Corporate embodiments of the trade policies of the early Stuarts, the colony governments looked like becoming mere instruments of, or obstructions to, the national trade policy of the English republic.

However, colonial rulers had not needed to wait for the Navigation Act to learn of their peril, for the Commonwealth had already taken a sharply different view of the empire from that with which colonists in government had grown comfortable. The regicide itself struck at the very source of the charters and commissions by which colonies had been contractually governed, and arguably made it inevitable that the Commonwealth would challenge the old ways of imperial and colonial government. Indeed, in establishing the Commonwealth, on 19 May 1649, the Rump had asserted that all the 'dominions and territories' previously belonging to the crown were now under the authority of the 'people of England', an authority which inhered in parliament.[38] Soon parliament was challenged to define more exactly what this meant as news trickled back to England that, upon hearing of the execution of Charles I, several colonies had declared their loyalty to Charles II.

The colonial proclamations of the English royal succession, which took place in Virginia, Maryland, Antigua, Barbados, and Bermuda, had complex causes and aims which will be discussed in Chapter 4. Here we are concerned with parliament's view that these proclamations were traitorous acts which by the law of nations rendered their perpetrators outlaws and rebels. These colonies might serve as redoubts for royalist exiles and royalist privateers; worse, their example might encourage rebellion nearer home.[39] The proclamations of loyalty to Charles II were by far the most open colonial rejections of parliamentary authority since the outbreak of the civil war, and they would have to be reversed. This was the main business of the Act of 3 October 1650: to 'reduce . . . all . . . parts and places belonging to the Commonwealth of England'. To this end, all merchants, English, colonial, and foreign, were barred from trade with the rebel colonies unless they had first obtained licence from parliament or the Council of State. Finally, the council was authorized to commission a force of ships and men to subdue the rebels and to set up new governments in the colonies, 'Any Letters Patents, or other Authority formerly granted or given to the contrary notwithstanding'.[40]

There was, however, more to the Act of 1650 than parliament's voiding of the charters and commissions of the rebel colonies. Its commercial provisions not only interdicted the trade of rebel colonies but also required foreign merchants to obtain licences for trade with all English settlements. This at once invaded the regulatory powers which colonial governments had come to value and limited freedom of trade for individual colonists. It was a sweeping assertion of a new legislative supremacy over all colonies, and its potential was not lost on the Rump Parliament. In the preamble, parliament nullified the contractual basis of the early colonial charters. Explicitly in the charters and implicitly in the facts of early settlement, the crown had granted powers of government in return for the undertakers' promise to follow the rules of the charters, but also in recognition of the expense, risk, and trouble of colonization. The Act of 1650 declared, on the contrary, that as the colonies had been 'planted at the Cost, and setled by the People, and by Authority of this Nation', they were subject to the laws of the nation in parliament. The far-reaching implications of this doctrine were made clear later on the same day when, by mere parliamentary order, the letters patents of the rebel colonies were required to be brought to the House 'to be disposed of as the Parliament shall think fit'. Thus the Commonwealth Parliament achieved what Charles I had set his face against when in 1625 he had attacked the Virginia Company charter for placing the disposal of colonial government in the power of 'the greater number of Votes and Voyces'. The analogy was not lost on Virginians, who had lived for a generation with the issue of company control and who now were told by Governor Berkeley that to surrender to the Act of 1650 would be 'to yield to whosoever possesse themselves of Westminster Hall'.[41]

We might expect that royalists like Berkeley would be none too pleased by the Act of 1650. It is more significant, therefore, that the Massachusetts General Court reacted similarly to parliament's commercial and political view of empire. Massachusetts's Puritan rulers naturally disliked the Act's restrictions on their trade with the rebels. New England had found economic salvation in supplying the plantation colonies, and the interruption of trade would be of 'great losse and prejudice'. Defiance on this point was not carried too far, however. The General Court recognized the trade boycott, but once again insisted on enacting itself before it would obey a parliamentary statute. Thus the Massachusetts authorities retained their chartered powers (as they saw the case) over their own trade regulations, but they were more worried about parliament's general assertion of supremacy over the colonies. This, coming together with news that parliament expected the Bay Colony to take out a new patent and to conduct its business in the name of the English Commonwealth, struck the General Court as distinctly sinister, and it responded on two main points, law and equity. Parliament's assertion of its rights to settle new governments and governors on colonies could not stand with the Charter of 1629, by which 'the late King, who then ruled all' had granted colonists the right 'to live under the government . . . of our owne chusing, and under laws of our owne making (not being repugnant to the laws of England)'.

The General Court had in 1638 responded in much the same way to Archbishop Laud's attack on their charter, but parliament's assertion of its authority in America had raised a second and weightier problem. Laud had challenged the legality of the charter in the courts; the Rump Parliament went beyond that to assert an immediate supremacy over the colonies, based on its own unchecked legislative power and on the view that the colonies had been settled at the cost and by the authority of the nation. This clause convinced the Massachusetts General Court that the Act of 1650 encompassed all the colonies and impelled the Court to go beyond a legal defence of its rights. The time, expense, and hardship of colonization had been incurred by the settlers 'without the help of the state' and their 'posterity should reape the fruit of our labours, and enjoy the liberties and privileges we had obteined for them, and for which we have payd soe dear and run soe great hazards'.[42] Often called the first navigation act, the legislation of October 1650 might with equal accuracy be called the first Intolerable Act, for it bears more resemblance to the coercive legislation of 1774 than to any of the commercial legislation of the seventeenth century.

* * *

Like the civil war, and for similar reasons, the regicide divided 'cavalier' from 'puritan' in America. Yet it brought them common problems, too, striking at the roots of their governing authority by subjecting them to an imperial legislature. Accordingly, colonial elites united in defence of what the Massachusetts General Court called the 'liberty and power' which the Stuarts had conveyed to them, whether by prerogative charters or, in Virginia's case, by the accretion of precedent and custom. The rebel declarations of Virginia and Barbados were more extravagantly worded than Massachusetts's politely stubborn defence of the charter of 1629, but they came to much the same thing. Planters themselves, not 'those that stay[ed] at home', had borne the costs and suffered the hardships of settlement. They had not usurped their governments, which had been 'given to us by the same power and authority' by which Massachusetts was governed. Once given and paid for, the rights of government could not be taken away by 'a Parliament in which we have no Representatives'. If colonial privileges and powers could be taken away from those who paid for them, they could be given away to others. In New England, radical puritans who had already challenged the authority of the Massachusetts charter were heard to say 'that if the Parlyament doe take displeasure against Massachusitt . . . as they have done against Barbadas and other places, then this will serve as an inroade to lett in forces to over-runne the whole country'.[43] As seventeenth-century Englishmen, colonists understood the connection between liberty and power. The Act of 1650 threatened more than their autonomy from England; it endangered their capacity to rule in America.

Given fears such as these, it is likely that the Navigation Act of 1651 came as something of a relief to some colonists. For, while it placed restrictions on their trade, it certainly did not turn American commerce over to old-fashioned monopoly regulation as Virginians and Barbadians had feared. Moreover, the Navigation Act left open the question how it was to be enforced and by whom. Thus, whatever its long-range political implications, it nowhere made the open threat to the survival of colonial government which had permeated the Act of 1650. As with the trading companies, so with colonial governments, the Act of 1651 ignored rather than killed them. As we shall see, the powers to enforce and interpret the Act of 1651 were not negligible considerations, and colonial authorities made use of them.[44]

In any case, the colonies survived the Commonwealth with their institutions generally intact. Massachusetts was quickly assured that the Act of 1650 meant it no harm, and although it has to be said that the colony did not take such assurances at their face value, they proved to be accurate enough. As for the royalist rebels of 1649, they were able to negotiate favorable terms with the commissioners who had been sent out to subdue them. So generous were these articles of 'surrender' that colonists came to view and use them as virtual charters.[45] Nor were the colonies to be much disturbed or, for that matter, much helped by English governments for the remainder of the Interregnum. In New England, Lord Protector Cromwell's support for Rhode Island's tolerationist experiment helped that colony to survive the attentions of its more orthodox neighbors, but otherwise the region was left alone. The Protector's wish to recruit godly New England settlers for his imperial designs in the Caribbean proved an irritant rather than a threat. In the next chapter, we shall see that Interregnum England's benign neglect had the capacity to unsettle the colonies, but the Acts of 1650 and 1651 had much greater potential than that. The Commonwealth's legislation might have provoked the most sweeping alterations in the empire since Charles I's reorganization of Virginia's government in 1625. That they did not may be laid in part to the failure to match them with purposeful changes in administration.

That much is obvious, but it requires explanation. Among possible reasons, ignorance and indifference must be rejected. Many men in power during the Interregnum, including Oliver Cromwell himself, had long been interested and often personally involved in colonies and colonization. To their interest they added a growing awareness of the importance to the English state of revenues derived from the colonial trades. Both Commonwealth and Protectorate erected advisory councils on trade and plantations in order to add to the available stock of information and advice on these vital matters. Nor were England's governors blind to the value of reforms in administration; indeed, the period saw important changes in such areas as customs collection, potentially vital to effective enforcement of navigation policy. English diplomacy and warfare, although centrally concerned with Europe, won from several European powers formal recognition of England's monopoly of her colonial trades and, in the shape of Cromwell's 'Western Design' of 1655-56, made of the Americas an important strategic theater. Neither Cromwell's protestant obsession with the aim of dealing a fatal blow to Spain nor the Western Design's failure to do much real harm to Spanish America should obscure the scheme's solid roots in more than a generation of English colonizing. Although the Western Design failed to achieve any of its main aims, it was more 'imperialist' in motivation than any other single act of the seventeenth-century English state. Moreover, during its visit to Barbados, Cromwell's fleet, like the expeditions of 1651, showed that the state suffered no uncertainty about its ultimate sovereignty over established colonial communities.[46]

* * *

In view of all this activity, some of it quite constructive, the failure to extend effective control over the colonies becomes a curiosity not to be explained by the government's preoccupations with war in Europe and unrest at home, nor as a function of the insulating qualities of salt water.

These were constant problems which at other times English government surmounted with respect to the colonies and which interregnum
regimes proved impatient of in confronting other issues. It becomes
necessary, then, to consider the possibility that the 'neglect' of the
colonies during the 1650s was in some sense deliberate, or inherent to
the nature of Interregnum politics, and certainly not a failure or a story
of lost opportunities.

The answer lies in the ambivalent nature of the English revolution.
In some respects, the Acts of 1650 and 1651 characterized the revolution's radicalism. In their hostility or indifference to the established
ways and means of colonial government and trade regulation they were
fitting accompaniments to the extirpation of monarchy. Moreover, they
confirmed in statute form beliefs in the transforming power of the state
– beliefs such as those which had been expressed by army radicals and
by Thomas Hobbes. However, such ideas were not universally popular
even within the parliamentary coalition. Nor was the Commonwealth's
commercial and colonial legislation necessarily the best test of its
radicalism. Here it was significant that these Acts dealt largely with
matters outside the direct political experience and economic interests
of most Englishmen. Even after the purges of 1648 and 1649, landowners
dominated the Rump Parliament, and they did not show much interest
in limiting their own economic freedom by invading the privileges
traditionally associated with land ownership. Nor, tests of personal
loyalty aside, were the privileges of borough governments much altered
by Commonwealth legislation. When it came to giving effect in America to the Commonwealth's commercial and colonial legislation, the
radical tide broke not only on colonial resistance but also on the
underlying reefs of a revolutionary conservatism which had been called
into being to protect the fixed and settled interests of Englishmen from
the depredations of an arbitrary prerogative. Thus it was that in the fears
they expressed after the regicide, in their objections to the Act of 1650,
and in their negotiations with the parliamentary commissioners colonists did not speak in a strange, outlandish tongue nor in language
unduly tainted by royalism, but as participants in a common political
universe, as purveyors of a line of argument which would at least be
understood by men who presumed to call themselves Keepers of the
Liberties of England.

Powerfully rooted in English history and social structure, this line of
argument enshrined a conservative conception of politics which denied
absolute power to the state, guaranteed subjects' liberties and properties, and, crucially, confirmed considerable powers of positive government and proscriptive privilege to some Englishmen over others. Thus,
when members of the Barbadian Assembly declared their intention to

protect their 'Comon Libertie Freedomes and Imunities', they struck a responsive chord. Of course such rhetoric must have bemused servants and those small farmers who were beginning to be pushed off the island by the economics of sugar production, but then it was not the language of the Levellers.[47] The ideology protected those it was supposed to protect. It promised liberty and power to those who governed (or aspired to govern) locally by virtue of their wealth, their standing, their prior rights. It was a language colonial elites had already learned to use in the 1620s and 1630s, and parliament's acceptance of the Barbadian and Virginian articles of surrender showed that colonists still enjoyed the protective coloration provided by similarity between their own and English local governments. This would continue through the Protectorate, but not only because of Cromwell's legendary sympathy for society's natural rulers. When necessity forced Cromwell to overcome that sympathy, Englishmen who considered themselves to be natural rulers resisted his innovations. The rule of Cromwell's major-generals in English localities proved no more popular nor more sustainable than the nearly contemporary 'government' of Barbados by the commissioners of the Jamaica fleet, and it is worth noting that the commissioners were especially resented in Barbados for upsetting local social structures. They had spirited servants away from masters, allowed debtors to escape creditors, and had enticed small planters to try their luck wherever England's power might provide more liberty and space than they had found in Barbados. It is worth noting that many of those who left were making a second attempt to level English society by emigrating away from it.[48]

* * *

The ambiguous impact of England's revolution on the politics of empire can be deduced from contemporary debates about the proper relationships between state and society and demonstrated by what happened in the colonies and in England during the 1640s and 1650s. Whether it was understood by contemporaries is another question. We shall be examining that question with regard to the colonies in the next chapter, but what of English perceptions of the relationship between revolution and empire? That question has a long answer, extending, for instance, through the colonial careers of such men as Benjamin Worsley, who claimed authorship of the Navigation Act of 1651 and in the early 1670s was still launching imperial ideas which savored more of Interregnum than of Restoration politics. Anthony Ashley Cooper, in the 1640s already an investor in Barbados, was another whose revolutionary perceptions would shape a long career in English and colonial politics.[49] But for close observation of the state of the empire at the end of the

Interregnum, we are fortunate to have the papers of Thomas Povey, placeman, merchant, and imperial schemer.

The Povey family's involvement with colonial affairs dated from the late 1630s, when Charles I named Povey's father Justinian to a commission to settle disputes in Barbados. That interest continued, commercially, through 1654, when Thomas Povey helped to outfit the Western Design fleet. His brothers Richard and William accompanied the fleet and in due course took up offices in Jamaica and Barbados. In the next year, 1655, Thomas Povey entered the state's service as a member and probably the original proponent of advisory councils for trade and plantations. Despite Povey's commercial interests in the West Indies, and although merchants and colonizers dominated the Protectorate's plantations committee, it would be dangerous to identify this as a mercantile supremacy. Povey certainly knew better than to do so. He capitalized on own gentlemanly background in seeking influence in the politics of empire, and in his original proposals for a council to advise the Protectorate on its commercial and colonial decisions, he sought to insure that the council would be and remain subordinate to the Protector and the Council of State. At one point he suggested that only one of the seven members should be a merchant currently involved in trade. Povey's patron, the London merchant-capitalist Martin Noell, recognized the problem, too. He recommended Povey to the Virginia Assembly as fit to represent the colony at Whitehall because Povey was a gentleman and not tarnished with that reputation for partiality and bias which went with being a merchant.[50]

All this owed partly to a general prejudice that merchants were not capable of offering disinterested service to the state, but it was more than that. Povey's 1655 proposals were in significant respects post-revolutionary. Povey made this clear when he insisted that the committee must be thought of as a council, not a corporation. As if announcing a new era, Povey declared that 'A Corporation' was not suitable, it 'being usually a body of Subjects empowered to advise, regulate, and controll certain things within themselves without account, pursuing and affecting therein privat interests and mysteries, and so farr only the Publick'. Only a council could adequately serve the state's wider responsibilities and powers, for a council would be 'a collection of so many persons, qualifyed and adequat to the severall parts intrusted to them accountable from time to time of their proceedings, and receiving from the Prince or Supreame, farther powers and Instructions as Emergencies doe arise'.[51] Thomas Hobbes could not have put it better. Here in an administrative detail we find the logical impact of the revolution and the Act of Navigation and a clear statement of the differences between the old and new ways of making and enforcing commercial policy. Merchants might still serve the state, but only as individuals. The state would remain the master; even to propose corporate trade regulation was not in tune with the times. Or so it would seem. However, English politics was too much in flux to give consistent guidance on such points, and within a short time Povey himself virtually abandoned his original view of things and urged that the nation's West Indian trade and its colonies could be properly governed only by a chartered corporation.

Povey's ideas changed partly out of sheer frustration, the product of the Protectorate's failure to take the empire in hand and of Povey's difficulties in maintaining his position in imperial politics. Povey had a particular interest in Jamaica, and his repeated assertions of the value of the island to the state and the need for supplying it fell almost unerringly on deaf ears. Meanwhile, in Jamaica, the soldier-planters fell prey to malnutrition and disease. In Barbados, Povey's client, Governor Daniel Searle, found his power slipping partly because neither Povey nor Noell could counter the influence Searle's Barbadian adversaries had cultivated at Cromwell's court. There were other disappointments, as well. Povey could collect neither the debts nor the gratitude owed to him and Martin Noell by his brother William, still a government officer in Barbados. Povey and his fellows on the plantations council discovered their lack of muscle in 1657 when they failed to induce the Protector even to commission a new government for Virginia, let alone name their client and colleague Edward Digges as governor. This insult was rendered injurious when, in Virginia, Digges's ally and pro-tempore Governor Samuel Mathews seized the cargo of one of Povey's ships and then held on to it.[52]

These difficulties would be intensified by the uncertainties which followed Oliver Cromwell's death in September 1658. Oliver's son and chosen political heir Richard ruled ineffectively, and the Protectorate fell in April 1659. All this depressed Povey, but he kept his balance, and his imperial ideas kept pace with England's political changes. Late in the Protectorate, Povey put to Oliver or Richard Cromwell – probably to both – his idea for a new West India Company, chartered by the Protector, which would solve the problems of supplying Jamaica and securing the cooperation of the other island colonies. Alternatively, the plantations council itself might act as a corporation if only it could be endowed with greater powers and a revenue of 'from Tenn to Twenty Thousand pounds' for organizing the Jamaica trade and supplying the infant colony. Clearly the Protectorate's inaction had caused Povey to conclude that when the state failed to act, a company or even a council of merchants might do so.[53] Some of these proposals survived to be put to Charles II in 1660, but before then English politics was to take yet another turn. The rebirth of the Commonwealth in May 1659 brought a radical transformation of Povey's colonial schemes.

Povey had just asked the Lord Protector for a chartered monopoly for his West India Company, but now England was again a Commonwealth, and Povey again conceded that legislative supremacy precluded the grant of a trade monopoly by letters patent under the Great Seal of England. He had used similar arguments in putting his original proposals for an advisory council to Oliver in 1655, but in 1659 Povey showed little interest in councils. Councils required someone else to act on their advice, and Povey had too strong a grip on reality to expect that the restored Commonwealth might accomplish much in this way. Yet it was during this period that Povey produced his most extreme proposal for the empire and colonies. He went far beyond his last proposals to the Protectorate to ask for much more than a trade monopoly. Povey's new company was to have heavy state support: from fifteen to twenty-five ships of the line, fully armed and rigged. It was also to have a good deal of state power, not least powers to command the established colonies to aid in the settlement and supply of Jamaica. The company would make war and conclude peace in the name of the Commonwealth, and it would have complete economic and political monopoly over any of its conquests. Among still other powers, including admiralty and martial law jurisdiction in America, the West India Company would be empowered to 'take and detaine [in its] service, the Bodies of Englishmen against their Wills, and carry them from their native Country, and dispose and keepe them as servants in [the company's] or in other Plantations for certain yeares'. To be sure, these dragooned servants would be persons whose absence from England would give 'no offense or inconvenience to the Lawes or the good People of this Commonwealth'; they would be beggars, vagabonds, pardoned capital offenders, and there is a hint that disaffected sons of the gentry (thought in 1659 to be a major source of royalist conspiracy) might also be drafted.[54]

Trade monopoly, the state's military might in private hands, dictatorial powers over the 'bodies of Englishmen': doubtless such powers seemed necessary at a time of political confusion in England and near-disaster in Jamaica. Yet they demand our attention for other reasons, for they tell us something of revolutionary politics. In several respects, notably the request for a trade monopoly for a private company, Povey's 'Act for incorporating a Company for the Trade of America' turned on its head the logic of the Navigation Act of 1651. On the other hand, Povey fully accepted the constitutional logic of parliamentary supremacy as embodied in that act and also in the Act of 1650. A supreme parliament could do what it willed in America, even to establishing a chartered leviathan with powers of command not only over the bodies and against the wills of individual Englishmen but also over established colonial governments. Povey recognized the problem precisely. Indeed, he acknowledged that the proposed company's powers were 'expressly against the Freedom and Libertie of the people, of any commonwealth (if not done by a Lawe)'.[55]

'If not done by a Lawe': colonists' nightmares of 1649 and 1650 would have been amply realized in the shape of this West India Company Act. Although there is no direct evidence that colonists knew of Povey's last Interregnum scheme, its nature and its timing help us to understand colonists' fears about parliamentary supremacy and their relief at the restoration of monarchy in 1660. As for Povey, he was, as ever, quick to perceive a connection between politics and empire. The Restoration required another change in his imperial schemes. His radical proposals of 1659 were almost certainly not put before the crown; instead, Povey revived the more moderate ideas he had put to the Protectorate, taking care only to alter certain telltale terms like 'his highnesse'. Truly Povey sensed that there was a sharp difference, for both England and its empire, between government by a supreme parliament and government 'by a single person'.

* * *

But in 1659 a restoration of monarchy hardly seemed inevitable. As England slipped towards political chaos, Povey's good political sense did not desert him, and thus he grew more pessimistic about accomplishing anything at all. Jamaica, he acknowledged, was in a sorry state, and he would have advised his brother Richard to return home had not the desperate conditions in England 'made me rather wishe my selfe in some Forreigne and more Secure [land], than to drawe you hither to mee'. It seems he was willing to leave William, his bad brother, to whatever fate Barbados had in store. Still, Povey struggled on. By April 1660 he was probably chairman, secretary, and sole member of the committee for plantations, which had promised so much and accomplished so little. His perceptions, however, remained clear. He wrote to Thomas Temple, one of his colonial clients, that not much progress had been made in advancing Temple's claims to Nova Scotia, nor should Temple expect more for the time being. 'Things are now heere in such a Condition that nothing but the grand and Supreame Settlement is now to be attended from which all inferior settlements may bee the better derived'.[56]

Povey's voluminous papers raise the vexed question of his actual influence. Its difficulties are well illustrated by Charles M. Andrews who, after making much of Povey, concluded that the papers 'form a remarkable series of unofficial papers which formulate foundation principles of empire that England never applied'.[57] Even this judgment, however, requires qualification. Povey himself once confessed that his success in colonial business depended on whether his 'words bee soe luckily placed, as to be able to please'. Povey never forgot that he sought influence and favor from a position on the fringes of power. His proposals never aimed to be new, far less controversial, but to please the powers that were. Whether his words pleased authorities depended partly on their substance, partly in their style; he advised one of his clients that representations to the Lord Protector should be 'dextrously insinuated', not bluntly stated.[58] Because Povey was concerned with putting forward proposals in words that would please, he never questioned the 'foundation principles' of mercantilism, never doubted that England was sovereign in the empire and that the colonies should be governed in ways calculated to benefit the English state and economy. However, his schemes varied considerably in the means which he would apply to those ends. He had learned that the shape of English politics had a determining effect on the structure of empire. Precisely because he did aim to please the powers that were, Thomas Povey's various proposals may be read as a commentary on, and as evidence of, the ambiguous effect of the English revolution on imperial politics.[59]

This ambiguity arose in large part out of the divided nature of the revolution itself, but it also owed to the failure of any one constellation of ideas and interests to achieve clear supremacy for a sufficiently long period. Thus the conservative leadership of the civil wars gave way to the more radical Commonwealth, which in turn was replaced by the Protectorate, during which an increasingly conservative political climate favored the retention, or even the restoration, of old forms. Cromwell, after all, was offered a crown, and although he refused that, he did restore rule by a single person and attempted to establish the dynastic principle for the succession of sovereignty. Whether or not the English revolution was revolutionary is a question which has spawned an immense and rewarding literature, from which it seems sensible to draw the conclusion that it was, and it was not. As we shall see in the next chapter, the colonies were deeply affected by this ambiguity, but it must be noted here that they also illustrated it. The colonies 'fitted' both revolutionary and conservative trends in English politics. Their economic development, particularly the newness and rapid expansion of their trades, made them natural objects for centralized definition and control of commercial policy, while their political characteristics as local governments reinforced their claim to constitutional status within a recognized English tradition. The resulting paradox was difficult to deal with, and not only for colonists who had a clear interest in keeping their heads above the political tide whichever way it flowed. How to govern America was not easy for those who seized power through a revolution yet called themselves Keepers of the Liberties of England or

Lords Protector. In 1660, of course, the English conservative tradition was revivified in monarchy, but when Restoration parliaments took up and extended the Commonwealth's doctrine of parliamentary supremacy in commercial regulations, Charles II would be lumbered with the same ambiguity and similar dilemmas.

CHAPTER FOUR

'A time of soe greate uncertaintie': the colonies during the interregnum, 1642-1660

England's mid-century revolution failed to transform the empire. In Chapter 3, I suggested that this owed to the workings of English politics, to the revolution's ideological ambiguity and the colonies' status within the English political tradition. This anglocentric view begs the question of how far colonists may be credited with a successful evasion of English rule. It does not directly address the historical consensus that colonists capitalized on England's turmoil to strike independent poses and win positions from which they enjoyed formative experiences of self-government and free trade with all comers, notably the Dutch. This consensus requires examination. In defending their trade with the Dutch, for instance, colonists spoke as much of necessity as of preference. Interregnum England rarely enjoyed peace both at home and in Europe, and the coincidence between expanded colonial production and wartime disruptions of English shipping often made a Dutch vessel a very welcome sight. However, the Dutch could neither supply all colonists' needs nor free them from their fundamental dependence upon English commercial partners. For these reasons, and because colonial governments were also defending regulatory powers conveyed to them by the crown, their complaints about the Commonwealth's colonial legislation had complex roots and are not to be interpreted solely, or even mainly, as expressions of a desire to secure commercial freedom from England.[1]

Much of colonial politics during the Interregnum does suggest the growth of an independent spirit, not least those most spectacular expressions of colonial defiance, the royalist declarations of West Indian and Chesapeake colonies following the regicide. There was an aura of self-government, too, around the forging of local consensuses, often crowned by the adoption of formal political compacts even in such unlikely settings as Barbados and Maine. Another important development was colonial governments' growth in competence, especially in the older settlements. In Virginia and Massachusetts, legislators extended and gave fuller definition to county and town governments, and both colonies achieved major law codifications during the 1640s. The West Indies were not as quick off the mark, but did much catching up before 1660. Barbados's fledgling assembly survived and in 1654 emulated its elders with a codification of law and local government. Thus colonial governments demonstrated their usefulness, and those who benefited grew more wedded to their own local power.[2]

These were important phenomena of the Interregnum empire, but not all of them were new. Several were already in train before 1642 and therefore cannot be seen merely as opportunistic exploitation of England's trauma. Indeed, throughout the period colonists expressed their desires for the resumption of 'free trade' with England and for the return of political stability to the mother country. To take these pleas seriously is to recognize that colonists' solutions to their problems were often shifts and scrapes which demonstrated dependence as much as the stirrings of a sturdy colonial autonomy and, ultimately, American independence. The newness and fragility of colonial polities seemed to conspire with England's turmoil to produce too little authority and too much liberty. In this context, colonists' Interregnum political covenants were designed more as an antidote to disorder than as a basis for self-government. If anything, these compacts articulated Hobbesian rather than Lockean political principles. It is perhaps more sensible to see them as endorsements of the basic structure of Charles I's empire and to argue that they owed something to the survival through the Interregnum of the Caroline consensus that both English authority and local autonomy were needed to insure stability in America. Either way, they offer us the salutary reminder that the eighteenth century did not begin in 1642, either in England or in America..

* * *

From the outset, few doubted that England's crisis would unsettle the colonies. 'It concerneth us deeply', wrote Edward Winslow of Plymouth, 'to be affected with them as a people that must share with them in weale and woe'. Woe seemed the more likely harvest to John Winthrop's English friend Benjamin Gostlin. The stormy close of the Short Parliament roused his fear that the colonial 'Dawghter' might be burdened by maternal ills. On the other hand, fear could breed hope. In July 1642 Virginia's assembly welcomed its new royal governor, William Berkeley, and the good news he brought of the Long Parliament. The assembly seized upon 'the gracious inclination of his majesty . . . now more particularly assured to us with the concurrence of a happy parliament in *England*' to enact a barrage of legislation in part aimed at approaching more closely the laws and customs of the mother country.[3] Thus on the eve of England's civil war, Virginians reiterated the credo of the Great Charter of 1618 that their happiness depended on their ability to replicate the example of England's polity.

That belief had shaped colonists' adjustments to American realities. Virginians testified to its continuing importance by whistling its message of faith into the gathering darkness, although (or perhaps because) they knew that the meeting between Charles and the Long Parliament was no longer 'happy'. As that breach widened, the idea of England in America, designed to bring order to the wilderness, threatened chaos instead. On St. Christopher, already riven by political and economic discontent, news of English events in 1642 encouraged rebels to cry 'now there is noe Lawes in England, and therefore wee will have noe Lawes here'. Governor Warner executed some 'runaways' and proposed to send the leading rebel home for trial, but he can have had little assurance that the trial would take place, let alone that its outcome would justify his government. Thus colonial disputants mimed roles cast for them by crown and parliament in England. The prospects depressed Antigua's governor, Henry Ashton, who saw little hope for government anywhere 'soe universally . . . doeth this Run-away planett raigne amongst us'. William Johnson observed that until peace returned to England 'there is little hope to have any settled government in these remote parts'. This unsettling effect of England's strife was compounded when crown and parliament interfered in local colonial politics to force adherence to their respective causes.

Colonial ability to ride out these storms depended upon a number of local factors. The gloomy outlook of governors Warner and Ashton owed much to the facts that both St.Christopher and Antigua were small, poor, and had a history of political strife. Eastwards in the West Indies, Barbados had known both poverty and discord since its settlement in 1627, but now the sugar boom helped some Barbadians to attain wealth far beyond the dreams of Antiguans who, Ashton reported, 'beare theire wants, and suffer Government' with 'desparate impatience'.[4] Virginia's size, climate, and fertility meant that its dependence on tobacco was not as severe a handicap as it was for the Leewards. Massachusetts reminds us of another important local variable, the degree of consensus between colonial populations and governing elites. Even so, there were patterns of political response which transcended these local differences.

The most obvious of these patterns emerged as soon as civil war in England had become an unavoidable reality. As with many English county and borough communities, colonial governments typically attempted to maintain neutrality even where, as in New England, ideological sympathy lay clearly with one side. In September 1642 Massachusetts's magistrates and clergy declined an invitation to contribute to the projected reordering of England's church at the Westminster Assembly. Among several reasons, they noted that the 'breach between king and parliament' rendered hazardous any taking of sides by the colony. This caution slackened, but even when the Bay made it an offense to declare openly for the king it based the act on the Long Parliament's legal fiction that it fought to rescue Charles I from his 'malignant' advisers. Along with most colonies, Massachusetts also made it clear that trade was too vital a consideration to be made hostage to politics; the Bay would be loyal to its customers whether royalist or parliamentarian.[5] In the Chesapeake, it was royalism which was tempered by prudence. Damning either 'Rundheads' or 'Rattleheads' could bring one before Virginia's local courts, and while Governor Berkeley briefly returned to England to fight for the king he kept on his council parliament men like William Claiborne and Richard Bennett. In its law revision of 1642-43, Virginia's assembly required churches to use the Book of Common Prayer but imparted a Puritan flavor to accompanying acts on moral behavior, sabbath observance, and church government. Until 1648 Berkeley tolerated a Puritan congregation at Nansemond and its pastor Thomas Harrison.[6] The spirit of accommodation extended to Maryland, where Governor Leonard Calvert neglected to exercise a commission to intercept parliamentary shipping. Meanwhile, in England, Lord Proprietor Baltimore preserved a neutral face towards the English disputants and any potential American surrogates. He broadened his government to include protestants and (incautiously) invited Puritans to settle in Maryland where they might share in the benefits of religious freedom and staple crop agriculture.[7]

Clearly the policy of neutrality encouraged Chesapeake governments to pursue the politics of consensus. This may have been the case, too, in St.Christopher, where Governor Warner conceded demands which had led to rebellion in 1642 and granted colonists an assembly.[8] But it was Barbados where the connections between neutrality and consensus were most fully explored. Barbadians' sympathies between crown and parliament were perhaps more evenly divided than elsewhere, and the island suffered more than other colonies from the efforts of the English protagonists to secure loyalty from colonial governments.[9] Another complicating factor was the interest in Barbados of leading figures in English politics, notably the proprietor, Lord Carlisle (who vacillated between crown and parliament), Carlisle's creditors Sir James and Archibald Hay (loyal household officers to Charles I), and the parliamentarian Earl of Warwick.[10] Neutrality, the only sensible course, was followed resolutely. Through the early 1640s, Barbadians continued to haggle with Carlisle and the Hays over rents and tenures while begging both crown and parliament for an English monopoly or a reduction of duties on their new staple. Governor Philip Bell played a similar game, 'humbly' accepting a commission from parliament while insisting that this did not compromise his allegiance either to Charles I or Carlisle. The creditors agreed, advising Bell that his acceptance might 'strengthen that authoritie you have' from the proprietor![11]

Soon, however, new measures were required. In late 1644, acting on the false belief that Carlisle had sold his patent to Warwick, Charles I gave the islands to the Earl of Marlborough. Although Bell and his council had before rejected Marlborough's royal warrant to intercept parliamentary shipping, this new patent put them in a more difficult position. Their government, based on a royal charter, now faced a royal warrant dissolving it. They might have stood on their parliamentary commission, but that would have compromised their much advertised neutrality. In the crisis, governor and council felt unable to act alone or even in concert with the island's assembly. Instead, it was decided to obtain 'the vote & consent of the whole countrey'. The freeholders of 'every severall parish', wrote Bell, met and

> declared themselves resolutely for the maintenance of their peace & present Government; & to admitt of no alterationes or new Commissions from eyther side, untill it pleased Go[d] to send a happy peace & unity betwixt them: for if we should pertake or declare ourselves on eyther side we wer undone: for against the kinge we are resolved never to be, & without the freinshipe of the perliament & free trade of London ships we are not able to subsist.

Bell later used the same vote to fend off Warwick's demand that Barbados declare for parliament: thus the later jibe that Barbados's 'subtil Statesmen' 'temporized with al new Commissions, came they either from the Parliament or . . . King.'[12] However, the declaration of 1645 went beyond both neutrality towards the English disputants and the 'treaty of the shoat and turkey' by which leading planters agreed not to reflect on each other's loyalties to crown or parliament. Unable to base its authority securely on crown, parliament, or proprietor, the government offered a deal to all freeholders; and the freeholders, caught up in the sugar boom, rising land prices, and the introduction of mass servile labor, closed the bargain. Barbadians had made a political covenant, an act we usually associate with New England's more temperate latitudes. But historians' views that Barbados had thus achieved independence from England are wide of the mark even if independence is qualified as 'virtual' or 'precarious'.[13] Barbadians covenanted together in order to salvage a universe made chaotic by the 'runaway Planett' of civil war in England.

Because Governor Bell wanted a firmer basis for government than the compact of 1645, he looked forward to the day when 'God shalbe so

Mercifull unto us as to unite the King & Parliament'. Nor could the island's rising sugar barons count on the traditional local ties which sustained some English county communities in their efforts to mini-mize the disruptive potential of civil war by maintaining local neutral-ity. There was little security for them in the 'treaty of the shoat and turkey'. They agreed to tolerate one another but suppressed sectarian conventicles and punished obstreperous servants. Meanwhile, the sugar boom marginalized smallholders. A New Englander recently arrived in Barbados shared their worries about the island's stability. 'I am afrayde when I consider off the profaness of the place, and the divisions that are here and are like to be'.[14] Barbadian society provided a fragile basis for either neutrality or consensus; as we shall see, both failed in the face of the regicide, which also destroyed consensus politics in Virginia and Maryland. Perhaps in these divided societies no local consensus could have survived for long. What is interesting is that Englishmen in the plantation colonies nevertheless made the attempt. It may be more significant that in New England the tribulations of the Interregnum exposed both the necessity and the fragility of consensus politics.

* * *

The New England settlements enjoyed some insulation from the prob-lems besetting other colonies during the civil war period. The region's failure to produce a cash crop made it less important to contesting Englishmen and tended to sustain the colonies' social and economic homogeneity. Puritanism may have had a similar effect, rendering New Englanders' loyalty less of an issue during the civil war and making it easier for them to adjust to its ultimate result. During this time, too, moral and material support began to flow from England to help ministers like John Eliot in the mission to the Indians. This last may not have been entirely welcome,[15] but at least New England was spared the sort of interference which so troubled Barbados.

In other ways, the importance of the religious issue in old England increased New England's vulnerability and sapped its leaders' confi-dence. During the 1640s, discord in the parliamentary coalition between Presbyterians, Independents, and sectaries made the New England Way an example in debate and an object of criticism. The attack came first from Presbyterians and was couched in terms similar to those earlier used by Viscount Saye and Sele to criticize New England's social order. The early responses of New England clerics affected regret but were apologetic only in the classic sense. 'Irenic' best describes the tone of John Cotton's *Keyes to the Kingdom*, John Norton's *Answer to Appolo-nius*, and Peter Bulkeley's *Gospel Covenant*. These men saw no middle ground between a church governed by bishops and a congregational church governed by the consent of the saints. Norton explained the superiority of lay consent with a biblical type which was also a parable of New England's social history. Once the church abandoned 'primo-geniture' or 'natural succession within one tribe', there was 'no system left except that of mutual consent'. Men free in Christ must be free with one another. Norton preferred a show of saintly hands to mitre, scepter, or synod in matters of church government.[16] Cotton's defence of congre-gationalism also drew on ideas common to contemporary secular debates in old and New England. He aimed to define the 'right and due settling . . . of the holy *power* of the *privileges* and *liberties* of the brethren, and the ministerial authority of the elders' so as to prevent 'tyranny and oligarchy'. Of these, power was fundamental and rested rightly with the brethren.[17]

Thus Norton and Cotton saw virtue in what Presbyterian critics thought the worst vice of New England churches, their covenanted independency. But even in praising mutual consent they insisted that the New England churches were still made up of 'men in office and men in the ranks . . . there must be . . . those who are governed'.[18] New England's officer corps, veterans of 1630s campaigns against separatism and antinomianism, already had much experience in resisting dissent from 'those who are governed'. The 1640s gave them more. Their intolerant response, notably in Massachusetts, provoked attack from a new quarter, as English radicals identified New England as another part of the world which needed turning upside down. New England's defend-ers could live with these attacks. Criticism from the Presbyterian right and sectarian left confirmed their belief that theirs was a middle way and helped them to demonstrate its truth. They cannot have expected, however, that they would come under fire from their nearest English friends, the Independents. Owing partly to the exigencies of civil war politics, the Independents embraced toleration, and Massachusetts's intolerance became an embarrassment to them. Some, like the ex-colonist Hugh Peter, delivered mild, private reproofs. Others openly disowned the New England Israel. The sense of isolation was difficult to bear for men who liked to think that their move to America had placed them on the cutting edge of Christian history.[19] Some argue that this led New England Puritans to identify their 'errand into the wilderness' more closely with their own patch of real estate. However, the counter-vailing tendency among New Englanders to return to the mother country during the Interregnum suggests that the American Zion had some ways to go before it could convince a solid merchant like Samuel Sewall that its human and natural resources and rhythms contained a millennial promise.[20]

In the meanwhile, being forced back on their own resources proved a discouraging exercise. New England's orthodox apologists became less irenic, some downright defensive. Nathaniel Ward, the 'simple cobler of Aggawam', and Thomas Shepard went beyond defense to lecture Englishmen on the dangers of toleration,[21] but such efforts did not conceal waning confidence in New England's good example. With Rhode Island on their doorstep and Plymouth nearly succumbing to 'full and free tollerance of religion', orthodox spokesmen began to concede points to the Presbyterians, to accept that to vest church power in the brethren was to strike the chain at its weakest link. From Ipswich, the Simple Cobler sailed for England to take up the Presbyterian cause. At Newbury, James Noyes was 'not satisfied touching the Charter of the Churches' of New England, and Thomas Parker saw virtue even in episcopacy. Peter Bulkeley of Concord never abandoned the gospel covenant, but writing privately to John Cotton in 1650 he reflected darkly on the consequences of moving from old to New England.[22]

> Remember the former days you had in old Boston, where though . . . there was an increase daily added to your church, yet the number of professors is far more here, than it was there. But answer me, which place was better governed? . . . swayed there by your wisdom and counsel, matters went on with strength and power for good. But here, where the heady or headless multitude have gotten the power into their hands, there is insolency and confusion. And I know not how it can be avoided . . . unless we should make the doors of the church narrower than we have warrant for in the Word.

Even Cotton moved towards Presbyterian points of view in some aspects of church government and theology, as Norton observed with approval in his sermon at Cotton's funeral in 1654.[23]

Uncertain at what they had wrought in New England and unhappy with the course of events in England, Massachusetts conservatives entered the 1650s in pessimistic mood. Little happened during the decade to cheer them up. An intractable church dispute in Hartford, Connecticut, drew a typical response from Massachusetts ministers in 1656: 'Alas! Alas!' They could admonish, but they were impotent to 'put out this wildfire'. 'Better it had beene for us to fall by persecution then by division; by the praelate's power, then by our own handes'.[24] This sense of weakness was sharpened by the Quaker invasion of New England, beginning in 1655, not least because of the sympathy Massachusetts people showed for Quakers' sufferings and opposition even in the General Court to the harshest of the anti-Quaker laws.[25] The need for propaganda led to the General Court's request that John Norton compose a tract defending the colony's persecution. Norton's *Heart of New-England Rent*, first published in Boston in 1659, admirably met its sponsors' brief,[26] but it also spoke to their unease.

For Norton, Quakers were more than heretical invaders of Israel.

Characters in a familiar plot, they reminded him of the tragedy of Munster, of Massachusetts's early religious crises, of the excesses of England's Puritan revolution. Massachusetts' problem was not merely one of stamping out heresy, but of stopping the process which had so often run Protestant societies right from *'prelacie* to *attoxie'*. The gathered church was part of the problem. Until the world ended, the church would contain a human plurality, not only because hypocrites and liars might worm their way into fellowship, but also because of the 'darkness and obscurity in the hearts of all the children of light'. Church order could not be secured by the justness of the saints but only by properly ordained 'Church-Officers, Church-worship and administrations'. Norton attacked more than Quakerism when he declared that 'the Rule of Doctrine, Discipline, and Order is the *Center of Christianity'*. The saints, too, had to be reminded that 'by Order, plurality is formed into, and subsists in unity" and warned that without order 'plurality is but an heap'. 'An heap' was what Quakerism would bring, for it challenged the *'divine disposall . . . of Superiour and inferiour relations'*. Quakers would destroy society by 'changing places with their Superiours, and possessing themselves with their power, honour and estates'. In church and state, Norton looked for a 'compleat Polity' which would possess sufficient means 'for the defense of the Law, and of all those that are loyal Subjects thereunto'.[27]

In an appendix prepared for a London edition of his tract, Norton pursued this social point and, turning his *Answer to Appolonius* on its head, concluded that Massachusetts could not form such a complete polity. A plantation of religion and not of trade, Massachusetts had neither attracted nor kept many men of substance and quality. Those who had come had 'bought the truth with Realities' at a cost measured by the 'Relations, Estates, Opportunities' they had left behind. Now Norton feared that they had brought themselves so low that they would 'sell [truth] *for that which is not bread'*. Too many of those who stayed were 'perrilously disposed to receive [Quaker] Doctrine, being already too much disaffected, if not enemies unto Order, and affecting to live according to their own spirits, and the dictate of every mans Conscience'. Norton reckoned that England would survive the Quaker menace, but Massachusetts lacked the social wherewithal of the metropolis. As Norton reminded Englishmen, 'that quantity of water sinks a little Boat, which a lusty Ship doth not feel'. The language is important. Both Puritan doctrine and American experience had had a levelling effect, and Norton could no longer find his ideal social whole in Massachusetts.[28]

Norton reminds us that Massachusetts Puritanism, though reined in by the federal covenants, could still drive saints to kick over the traces.

Congregationalism encouraged the laity to challenge attempts to set up a special role for the ministry. Made freemen by virtue of divine election, they did not always heed magisterial direction. In their towns, the laity had vaulted into positions from whence they exercised some mastery over their material and spiritual lives. Their experience of the liberty and power once so persuasively outlined by Norton and Cotton made them loath to retreat to the ranks and suspicious of those who claimed to be their commanders. The depth of feeling such suspicions could produce was indicated by the rumor of 1643 that the magistrates plotted to poison Richard Saltonstall, tribune of the people. Thus the saints confirmed the warnings of New England's critics. What was worse, internal dissidents accurately exploited these tensions. The Child petitioners made much of the rights and liberties of Englishmen and the overweening authority of the magistracy. Radicals like Samuel Gorton and the Anabaptists appealed to the priesthood of all believers to defend the individual's right to determine truth and to attack clergymen who set up synods and demanded salaries for preaching the Word as would-be papists and hirelings for Christ. Most of these dissenters were disappointed in their quest for help from England, but that was only part of the problem. Their appeal for support from within New England made more urgent the tasks to define orthodoxy, to extirpate heresy, and to secure good order in the state.[29]

Confidence in mutual consent as the right means to deal with such problems had never been complete, but as it waned in the 1640s and 1650s an ironic contrast became apparent. While Barbados and Virginia were driven to experiment with consensus, Massachusetts relied increasingly on law and coercion. It is significant that when Robert Child accused the General Court of governing by mere 'civil covenants', the Court sternly replied that it ruled solely on the authority of its royal charter.[30] History confirmed the point. Ably led by John Winthrop and other magistrates, Massachusetts's government ruled authoritatively. The Hingham militia affair of 1644-45 was typical. Not only did a covenanted town deny the authority of the General Court to intervene locally, but within the court the affair raised again the dispute over the relative authority of magistrates and deputies. Both were turned aside, and the magistrates' power was further secured. Winthrop's famous victory speech on the matter might have served as a text for Ireton's homilies on order at Putney two years later. Hingham also preferred a Presbyterian church discipline, and thus symbolized the difficulties of establishing an agreed religious orthodoxy in New England. Here the climax came in 1648 with the Cambridge Platform, a statement of church discipline by a synod whose very calling marked a triumph for authority. Afterwards, armed with the Westminster Confession, the

1648 platform, and its royal charter, Massachusetts's government embarked on a 'decade of reaction'. To judge by the complaints of those who suffered, the government was successful.

New England's fringe settlements, Puritan and otherwise, had an even less happy time of it during the Interregnum. Less populous and poorer than the Bay, most of these settlements faced an additional problem, for few possessed a legitimate title to government and territory. In such places, settlers 'mutually promised' to govern themselves by compact. That most tried to improve their title is significant: some by recourse to dubious patents issued by the old Council for New England, others by private purchase of such patents. Several towns, including Dover in New Hampshire and Newport in Rhode Island, wrote 'his Excellent Majestie' Charles I into their covenants, presumably to give them a bit more weight, but these were unhappy expedients. Such claims to legitimacy begged the question. Where a covenant proved insuf-ficient to settle local disputes, to what higher authority might towns appeal? This problem of legitimacy, already recognized by fringe settlements in the 1630s, became more pressing during the Interregnum.

Solutions varied, but in most of them Massachusetts's charter government played an important role, most quickly in the four New Hampshire towns. In 1639, Hampton, already settled by licence from Massachusetts, was fully integrated into the Bay's legal system and given representation on the general court. The other towns, isolated from their English sponsors and riven by inter- and intra-town conflicts over land and religion, were soon drawn into the same orbit. Dover and Strawberry Bank had been settled under grant from the Council for New England, but the death of the council and the disinterest of the towns' English backers left them 'without legitimate authority'; they succumbed in 1641. Exeter proved more reluctant to come in from the cold, but in 1643 the town submitted, specially requesting from the Bay a commission to judge several disputes between citizens whose obligations to the town covenant did not extend to obeying it. Thus the need for legitimate authority (without which 'we shall not be able to subsist to be a Towne') triumphed over forces which had rent Boston itself, for Exeter had been settled by the Reverend John Wheelwright and other antinomian exiles from Massachusetts.[31]

Exeter's surrender was eased by Wheelwright's removal to Wells, in Maine. Sir Ferdinando Gorges' proprietary patent gave Maine the best legal title of any New England fringe settlement, but the confusions in England weakened Sir Ferdinando's hold, and Wheelwright's 'submission' to Massachusetts in 1644 may have signified his appreciation that Wells was not beyond Boston's reach. Indeed it was not; by the mid-

1640s, Deputy Governor Thomas Gorges's authority was so fragile that he had to seek the Bay's forbearance before dealing with local malcontents. In 1646 he accepted a final trial of the dispute before the Massachusetts General Court. Ironically, Massachusetts hesitated because of Gorges' royal patent. 'Having no jurisdiction, we had no coercion', John Winthrop reflected, and the Massachusetts magistrates 'persuaded the parties to live in peace, etc., till the matter might be determined by authority out of England'.[32] However, England was not interested, and only a year later Edward Godfrey of Maine concluded that calling in Massachusetts was 'the safest waie to quallify these broyles'. A government already so compromised could not survive the double shock, in 1649, of the regicide and the proprietor's death. Maine settlers attempted to establish their own government on the basis of their 'one free and unius animus consent', but this was a desperate independence. The inevitable annexation of Maine came in 1652.[33]

Rhode Island's towns had also to reckon with Massachusetts, but with different results. Given the fiercely independent nature of such leaders as Roger Williams, Samuel Gorton, and William Coddington, it is not surprising that conflicts within and between towns were common features of Narragansett politics. As in New Hampshire, their town covenants better expressed their need for harmony than their success in finding it even if, as at Portsmouth, they had covenanted in God's presence and added the imprimatur of 'King Charles . . . [and] his lawes'.[34] As problems grew beyond the reach of their town covenants, Rhode Islanders frequently appealed to higher authority, temporal and divine. An approach to Massachusetts was a possibility which men already exiled from the Bay were reluctant to follow; but both Williams and Coddington appealed to Massachusetts for justice against local men who would not accept Rhode Island's version.[35] Faced with the fiery presence of Samuel Gorton, the residents of Pawtuxent went further and in September 1642 asked to be brought under the Bay's charter.

William Arnold, Gorton's chief foe in Pawtuxent, remained a friend of the Bay's,[36] but Gorton proved more typical of most of his neighbors when, in 1643, he appealed to England both for protection from Boston and for a grant of government and land in Rhode Island. Roger Williams went to London the same year and, like Gorton, was successful in receiving a patent from Warwick's parliamentary committee. Williams's charter spoke directly to the main needs of Rhode Islanders. Its professed aims were to empower the Narragansett towns to establish justice amongst themselves and towards their neighbors. Warwick's committee supplied the defects of Rhode Island's covenants and followed its mandate to give government to those who needed it in America. Its safe conduct passes to both Williams and Gorton warned

Massachusetts against interposing its authority over Rhode Island. Instead, all the New England colonies were to use their 'utmost endeavours of nearer closing' with one another.[37]

That was an ironic request, for in 1643 Massachusetts had already joined its more orthodox southern neighbors – Plymouth, New Haven, and Connecticut – in a 'nearer closing' which meant Rhode Island no good. The Bay was senior partner of the United Colonies of New England, and among its aims were to establish its seniority and to quarantine Rhode Island. At the same time, the junior partners gained some benefits, not least Massachusetts's recognition of their separate existence. Rhode Island applied for membership three times for just such a reason, and recognition was an especially important objective for Plymouth and Connecticut, who had suffered from Massachusetts's interventionism.

Connecticut's Fundamental Orders of 1639 had expressed the river towns' 'shyness of coming under [Massachusetts] government', for in part it was a reaction to the Bay's meddling in their affairs by defending the secession of one of them, Springfield.[38] Now membership in the confederation helped Connecticut (and New Haven) to absorb nearby towns on the mainland and Long Island. Although Connecticut, New Haven, and Plymouth all attempted to secure charters from Interregnum regimes, it would seem that until the Restoration membership in the United Colonies served the three junior partners well enough. Each colony sent two delegates, and the requirement that positive action needed the assent of six of the eight delegates underlined its federal nature, protecting the interests of the smaller colonies.[39]

To be sure, the confederation, like Massachusetts's annexation of New Hampshire and Maine and its attempts on Rhode Island, also expressed the Bay Colony's own brand of imperialism. Yet, while most Rhode Islanders would have demurred from the judgment, Boston's authority did impart stability to New England during the Interregnum. After the Restoration, Massachusetts defended its annexations of New Hampshire and Maine as a proper extension of its chartered authority which 'concurr[ed]' with its 'abillity to proove wee could protect them'. This was only a little disingenuous. As we have seen, many northerners said much the same thing at the time of the annexations.[40] Maine men put it best when in 1657 they petitioned Oliver Cromwell in defence of Massachusetts's annexation of their settlements.[41]

> Wee have but smale power to carry on government, being a people but few in Number & those not competent persons to manage such weightie affaires, our weakness occasioning distraction, our paucity division, our meanness contempt, as our owne former experience hath fully evinced.

Massachusetts had effectively taken the place of the crown in giving government to New England. This ironic twist in imperial history would be unravelled after 1660, when the restored monarchy proved that for most New Englanders the Bay had been but a temporary haven from the storms of the Interregnum. In the meanwhile, it either protected the unseaworthy or drove them to seek refuge under parliament's protection. The Bay Colony's possession of a royal charter, held in unbroken succession since 1629, was an important factor here, note Massachusetts's awkward but stoutly maintained claim that the patent bounds included the northern settlements. Everywhere, the Massachusetts charter either supplied the deficiencies of local covenants or forced settlers to seek better grounds for government from English authority. Within its own bounds, Massachusetts used its charter both to secure internal stability and to resist parliament's claims to supremacy. However, it was Barbados, Bermuda, Antigua, Maryland, and Virginia which most emphatically rejected the Commonwealth, for upon receiving news of the execution of Charles I, these colonies proclaimed his son to be King Charles II.

* * *

These royalist proclamations might be laid to cavalier sentiment or to fears that London merchants ('whose sickle hath bin ever long in our harvest') enjoyed undue influence in parliament.[42] However, such views had not deflected these colonies from neutralism during the civil wars. Planters' defiance came too late to be regarded as unalloyed cavalierism and was too perverse to qualify as rational economic self-interest. Nor were the rebellions declarations of independence. They were more in the nature of *coups d'état* in which dominant factions abandoned the politics of compact and consensus in a hazardous quest for political survival. Political survival was at issue for several reasons. In comparison to most New England settlements, the plantation colonies enjoyed few advantages in 1649. Each had had a turbulent early history, and their extraordinary attempts at consensus politics during the 1640s lacked the religious and social bases of the New England covenants. Worse, the loyalties of those who held authority rendered most of them suspect in the eyes of England's new rulers. Maryland was the proprietary of an Anglo-Irish Catholic peer. In 1647 the Earl of Carlisle had leased his Caribbee proprietary to Francis, Lord Willoughby, a Presbyterian turned royalist, and the lease carried the additional liability of confirmation by the then Prince Charles on his father's orders. Virginia was governed not only by royal commission but by a royalist governor, William Berkeley. Furthermore, all of them produced goods which were in great demand in Europe and of great fiscal importance to the English state. Given their situation, these colonies were perhaps unwise to proclaim Charles II, but in fact they had little choice.

Political desperation ruled in Maryland, where Deputy Governor Thomas Greene and his council declared that the 'undoubted right' of Charles II to the throne of England was inseparable from their right to govern Maryland. Although their decision put Lord Baltimore, still in England, in a difficult and perhaps dangerous situation, they were probably right. In November 1649 the proprietor's safety was the least of Greene's worries. News of the regicide coincided with Governor William Stone's absence to compromise the authority of Greene and his council. Against them stood a Puritan faction which had already shown willing to use English events as a pretext to rebel against a Catholic proprietor whose power rested upon a royal charter.[43] The logic of the situation was clear even to Baltimore; he thought Greene's action imprudent enough to justify dismissal yet he ordered new oaths taken which pledged colonists to accept his rights as granted by 'the late King of England'. Those who refused were to be punished in ways suitable to their station and their offense.[44]

Elsewhere, royalist rebels went further in rejecting consensus politics. For Bermuda's Puritan congregations, the colony's royalist proclamation of 1649 marked an intensification of persecution.[45] Virginia's assembly actually proclaimed Charles II in a treason act (October 1649) which noted that those same 'cursed and destructive principles' which were used to justify the execution of Charles I and to deny his son's right to the throne would also render 'void & null' Virginia's royal 'commission . . . and all magistracy and office thereon depending'. To justify regicide, to deny Charles II's kingship, to propose a change of government in Virginia, all were equally treason. This was 'no mere expression of outraged royalist sentiment, but the voice of men who feared for their lives and their property". And they feared for their power; Virginia's government proclaimed Charles II to justify its existence, not to declare its independence. There is a legend that when news of the regicide reached Virginia, Colonel Richard Lee sailed to Amsterdam to obtain from Charles II a new commission for the colony government.[46] If the legend is true, one hopes that the outlawed monarch and the colonist searching for lawful authority gave each other comfort.

Barbados's royalist coup produced a complicated variation on these patterns. Its proclamation of Charles II, on 3 May 1650, was instigated by recently arrived refugees from England led by Humphrey and Edward Walrond. In the vacuum left by the regicide, these men exploited local cavalier sentiment to reduce Governor Philip Bell to the status of figurehead, to punish parliamentarian planters through fines and confiscations, and to establish their own wealth and power.[47] They then faced an embarrassment: the freshest grant of royal authority extant in America, Charles II's sign manual on Francis Lord Willoughby's proprietary lease. This arrived, with Willoughby himself, only two days after the proclamation of 3 May. Inconsistently but predictably the Walronds opposed Willoughby's right and forced him to endure a three-month political quarantine. When the quarantine was over, Willoughby supplanted the Walronds with apparent ease.[48]

Islanders had to recognize Willoughby's claim despite their dislike of the proprietary. Their rebellion and his right both rested on the kingship of Charles II. However, there was an important change as Barbadians faced the implications of having proclaimed the king. As concern shifted from asserting the legitimacy of government to assuring its survival, consensus politics of a sort came back into fashion. Taking into his confidence moderate royalists like Thomas Modyford and Thomas Middleton, Willoughby repealed the Walronds' persecuting legislation and, through an act of indemnity, reestablished parliamentarian planters who had remained on the island. Willoughby also changed his approach to the other islands in the proprietary. In the summer of 1650, St.Christopher and Nevis had rebuffed Willoughby's uncompromisingly royalist assertion of his rights. In December, having learned moderation in Barbados, Willoughby tried a more conciliatory approach. He protested that the governor and assembly of St.Christopher had 'mistaken my intentions and meaninge . . . as if I had delighted more in Divisions then in Unitie, more in Warre & differrences then in quietnesse & peace'. He had not aimed to force the islands into 'Part taking'; rather he would send an 'agent into England to satisfie the whole Nation of the Proceedings before my coming hither, but allsoe of what hath been done since, and to prevent all misunderstandinge & to settle a perfect & free trade with them'.

Neither St.Christopher nor Nevis were impressed.[49] More to the point, the agent Willoughby sent to England, George Martin, did not arrive early enough to counter the news of Barbados's proclamation of Charles II and its harassment of parliamentarians. Parliament's response, the Act of 3 October 1650, gave all colonial governments ample reason to fear an unchecked parliament's imperial supremacy. Even Massachusetts joined the chorus of protest, but news of the Act and of the naval expedition being sent to enforce it required rebel governments actually to provide for their defence. Cavalier enthusiasm waxed again in Virginia and Barbados, no doubt encouraged by news of Charles II's 'strength with the Scots' but also impelled by the necessity to identify and punish any dissidents who might seize the occasion to defy local authority.[50] However, the cavaliers did not ride so high as to forget other political necessities. Maybe the 'hot cavaliers' intended to die in defence of their 'ould liberties and privileges', but for public consumption they stressed more palatable ends. Willoughby's professed desire for friendly correspondence with London merchants and 'our country' did not breathe of martyrdom, and doubtless many less enthusiastic rebels were relieved to learn that the parliamentary fleets carried trade goods as well as powder and shot. Willoughby clearly promised to seek favorable terms for Barbados, and in Virginia it seems likely that Berkeley had similar ends in mind.[51] By tying military preparedness together with readiness to negotiate, colonial leaders appealed not only to cavaliers but also to a widespread appreciation, already woven into the colonial mentality, of the benefits of autonomy.

As we have seen in Chapter 3, the Act of 1650 provided them with excellent propaganda. Colonists protested that they deserved something better than the Act, which was bad enough but could be made even worse by a different majority in a legislature where, Barbadians added, 'we have no Representatives'. Equally pointed was Barbadians' response to parliamentary commissioner Sir George Ayscue's initial demand for their surrender, that their 'Comon Libertie Freedomes and Immunities' rested absolutely on the right and title to the island of both Charles II and Lord Willoughby. This was neither intransigent royalism nor a precocious spirit of independence; rather it was an accurate comment on the island's predicament in the face of the Act of 1650. It was also a bargaining position. If their freedoms and liberties could be made secure on some other basis, colonists might talk turkey.[52] In the end, few shots were fired in anger. Ayscue, who had been empowered not only to reduce Barbados to loyalty but also to give it government on such terms as seemed reasonable, found that opposition within the island crumbled in the face of such terms, negotiated as 'Articles of Surrender'. The Virginia commissioners, who had witnessed some of the proceedings at Barbados, sailed on to the Chesapeake, where they and their adversaries ran a repeat performance. By the autumn of 1652, the rebel colonies were restored to England's empire.

The generous terms of these 'articles of surrender' owed much to circumstance, to the commissioners' wisdom and to colonial resolve.[53] They owed more, however, to imperial and colonial history, for in meeting the concerns expressed by the rebel colonists, they confirmed the political principles of empire laid down in the 1620s. The articles established autonomous colonial governments fully empowered to tax, legislate, and adjudicate. The representative principle was confirmed, too, and the attention given to indemnity clauses in effect endorsed the 1640s politics of consensus.[54] Yet it was made clear that these governments did not exist by virtue of local mandates. Their legitimacy derived from the 'authoritie of the Parliament of England', and tradition was also served by the requirement that colonial law should be congruent with and subordinate to English law.

Imperial history gave particular point to the articles which guaranteed both colonies 'free trade' with English ports and with all nations in amity with England. The immediate context of these articles and of the whole negotiating process was not the Navigation Act of 1651 but the Act of October 1650. That Act's commercial restrictions and its assertion of parliament's sovereignty in America looked especially sinister to colonists who feared the influence on parliament of London merchants. Virginians knew all about the dangers of company government. Crown rule had protected Virginia from these evils and had conferred on the colony government the regulatory powers of a company. In time, Virginians came to view themselves as a body corporate, a local government with sufficient powers to secure both law and order and the material interests of masters and freeholders. In different manner Barbadians had arrived at the same self-regard. The Carlisle charter had made them tenants of a lord proprietor but had also conferred upon them important political rights. They had used these, particularly their powers of consent in matters of taxation and trade regulation, as bait to secure their land tenures. This, indeed, was the essence of the bargains Barbadians drove with Lord Willoughby in 1650 and King Charles II in 1663; both accepted their claims to unencumbered land tenures in return for revenues on the island's trade. But by 1650, Barbadians had already found the proprietary charter, although troublesome, to be midwife to a serviceable definition of their political being.[55]

It was therefore not surprising that Virginians and Barbadians contrived to see in the Act of 1650 the creation of a private company in England that would regulate their trade and over which they would have no power. This device would 'perfect and accomplish our intended slavery'; under the Act, Barbados's assembly declared, 'no inhabitants ... may send home upon their own account any Island goods of this place, but shall be as slaves to the Companie ... and submit to them the whole advantage of our labor and industry'. Governor Berkeley invoked the same sense of colonial history to warn that by the Act of 1650 Virginians 'are forsooth their worships slaves, bought with their money and by consequence ought not to buy, or sell, but with those they shall Authorize with a few trifles to Coszen us of all for which we toil and labour'.[56] These remarks were not mere propaganda, although the language chosen was vivid enough for men whose fortunes depended on their mastery over servants and slaves. In negotiating the 'free trade' articles, colonists aimed to preserve those powers which had heretofore depended upon royal licence, powers which they had used to forge an intimate link between their corporate identity and their own well-being.

Naturally colonists wished also to retain the liberty of direct access to foreign markets and merchants which the dislocations of civil war and the expansion of colonial production had brought. It seems unlikely, how-ever, that they expected to escape entirely from English regulation of their trade. The meaning they accorded to 'free trade' was governed by their historic fears, not their prescient knowledge of England's future navigation system. In granting 'free trade' and considerable powers of self-government to the rebel colonies, the articles of surrender guaranteed immunity from the perils of monopoly regulation by a 'Companie'.[57] It was in this sense that the Navigation Act of 1651 must have come as something of a relief to colonists, for whatever else it was, manifestly it was not a licence for trading company exploitation of the colonies.

After 1652, the governments of the once rebel colonies used their powers to their commercial advantage, even to using the Act of 1650 to infringe the Navigation Act of 1651. This was the peculiar achievement of Daniel Searle, Commonwealth Governor of Barbados, who employed the strategy to allow Dutchmen to trade at the island. When attacked for his legerdemain by the commissioners sent in 1655 with the Western Design fleet, he replied that he had signed the articles of surrender and did not propose to go back on them. Virginia's government accomplished similar ends through legislation. The point of the negotiated settlements was not that they freed colonists from English trade regulations, but that they empowered colonial governments to evade, interpret, even occasionally to enforce those regulations. Searle's 'licences' drove the point home by warning foreigners that, licenses or none, they risked all if they 'trade[d] against the Laws of England'.[58] It is interesting to note that in 1659, Barbados's petition to the restored Rump Parliament asked for confirmation of the articles of surrender, the grant of a charter, and the repeal of the Act of 1650 but did not complain about the Navigation Act.[59] The articles of surrender were in truth ersatz charters which secured the authority of colonial governments and reestablished their corporate identities vis-a-vis a newly assertive English state. Thus the Virginia treaty included provision for a charter, while the 1654 *Acts and Statutes of Barbados* unilaterally defined the articles of surrender as the colony's 'charter'. It is also easy to understand colonists' view that the articles had effectively negated the Act of 1650. After the uncertainties of the civil war period and the trauma of the regicide, the rebel colonies once again enjoyed governments whose power was based on a 'contract' with the English state. Nevertheless, fears that the articles did not provide a sufficient basis for local authority and autonomy were intensified by the Rump's failure explicitly to confirm the articles. During the 1650s, Virginia suffered particularly from this uncertainty.

* * *

Virginia lived through exciting times in the 1650s. Given leave by the articles of surrender to make laws and to appoint their own governor, councillors, and other officers, Virginia's burgesses needed for their political happiness only a primer in republican government and the reassurance of a stable social order. As they had neither, they asked England to confirm by charter their rights and powers. In the meanwhile, Virginia's government put into effect the terms of the settlement. In 1652, the burgesses named their governor and council, laid down the structure of government, and proceeded to yet another revision of the laws.[60] This represented neither an internal revolution nor an act of independence. Most of the councillors of 1652, including Governor Richard Bennett and Secretary William Claiborne, had previously served in Berkeley's councils, some as long ago as 1642. Those councillors who would not serve the Commonwealth had to be replaced, but the new councillors were past burgesses, which continued the pattern of recruitment used by Berkeley himself.[61] The election of Bennett and Claiborne signified colonists' wish to be governed by old Virginians with the colony's interests at heart, but both men were also parliamentary commissioners, and the assembly also deferred to English authority by noting that its elections were valid only until the pleasure of parliament were known.[62]

However, despite assurances from the commissioners that parliament was bound 'in honour' to a full performance of the articles, parliament dealt haphazardly with the matter, and the article concerning a new charter for the colony was referred to the Navy Committee where it disappeared.[63] Meanwhile, the colonial assembly continued to recognize in its annual elections the contingency of its authority.[64] In October 1656, perhaps hoping for better things from the Protectorate, Virginia's assembly sought to end this insecure state of affairs by sending agents to England to obtain a legal settlement, to make representations to Cromwell about the colony's troubled relationship with Maryland, and to secure better trading conditions for tobacco. The agents chosen were the incumbent governor, Edward Digges, ex-governor Bennett, now of the council, and councillor Samuel Mathews. In Digges's absence, the Assembly appointed Samuel Mathews, Jr., as governor.[65]

While they had been left in limbo, Virginians had reverted to the consensus politics of the 1640s. Now, with a settlement in the offing, disagreement surfaced. The assembly almost certainly directed the agents to seek a charter based on the 1652 articles of surrender. Once in England, however, the agents asked Cromwell to appoint Digges as governor under 'a Commission . . . whereby the Governor and Council may more warrantably and effectually proceed in their Duty'. Clearly expecting opposition from the colony, the agents advised Cromwell that the news should be broken gently.[66] No doubt they had enjoined even greater caution on the acting governor, but young Mathews, not yet thirty, was made of sterner stuff. Only a month after the agents' departure, Mathews denied a burgesses' petition for an assembly. By March 1658, when finally the assembly did meet, Mathews had received a promise from Cromwell's plantations committee that the desired commission would be forthcoming. Thus fortified, Mathews and his council adopted a pugnacious attitude and, meeting some opposition, dissolved the assembly. Since by the articles of 1652 the governor and council were the assembly's creatures, this was bluff, and when the burgesses called it Mathews backed down and agreed to continue the session. Now convinced that Mathews was up to no good, the burgesses would not even allow him to refer to the Lord Protector the question of whether he and the council had legal powers of dissolution, and to make sure, they ordered Secretary Claiborne to surrender to them his records and the colony seal and then proceeded to a new election. They reelected Mathews and his whole council, although they added three new members, burgesses who had been prominent in drawing up the constitutional case against the governor's powers of dissolution.[67]

The burgesses based this practical demonstration of their power on the negotiated agreements of 1652. To this the burgesses added that they were the 'representatives of the people', but we may doubt whether this implied an endorsement of popular sovereignty. Rather the burgesses stated a fact which reminded the governor and council that they were elected by nobody; by the terms of 1652 they were the assembly's creatures. 'Untill the next Assembly or untill the further pleasure of the supreame power in England shall be knowne', the assembly was 'not dissolvable by any power yet extant in Virginia but [the assembly's] owne'. Governor Mathews and his councillors were compelled to accept their reelection as their sole commission of authority, with what grace we can only guess.[68] Mathews and the burgesses had fallen out over the sort of government the colony should seek from the supreme authority of England and over the way in which Virginia's government should be conducted in the meanwhile. But there was fundamental agreement that the colony needed and would accept effective directions from England on both questions. Safety and stability required sovereign authority, preferably from a source higher than the 'people'.

The assembly next met in March 1659, over two years since the colony had sent agents to London to seek that settlement. The agency had produced nothing except Cromwell's promises which, unfulfilled, had only provoked divisions between council and burgesses. Now news had arrived that Oliver had died and power had passed to his son Richard. Henry Lawrence, Lord President of the Council, wrote to the governor and council ordering them to proclaim Richard and promising that the new Protector intended to honor his father's pledge to settle Virginia's government. The climate of uncertainty moved Governor Mathews and the burgesses towards a local *modus vivendi*. Governor and council did not, as in the previous year, use a letter from England to secure their authority in Virginia, but instead referred Lord President Lawrence's message to the burgesses. They voted to accept their duty of obedience to Richard Cromwell and to acknowledge Lawrence's letter as an 'authentique manifestation' of Richard's intention to settle Virginia's government: 'wee owne the power and the whole contents thereof'. The burgesses could have done little else, for to have challenged the order would have called their own power into question, but they were still unhappy. Pointedly ignoring the agents already in England, the burgesses resolved to petition Richard directly for a confirmation of the colony's rights. Further, they asked Governor Mathews to affirm by his 'owne expressions' that he regarded this as their privilege and that he would join them in the petition. Mathews agreed, and although it must be said that his affirmation was not ironclad,[69] the burgesses returned the compliment by re-electing Mathews to the governorship. Then, somewhat surprisingly, they proposed that councillors should serve for life after being nominated by the governor and confirmed by the burgesses. More surprisingly, the burgesses acquiesced in a dissolution by the governor and council, who did not wish to accept lifetime office on the burgesses' sole authority. Wherever authority was located in Virginia, the Assembly of March 1659 was not inclined to tamper with the balance of it in the absence of clear directions from England.[70]

No such directions came; instead, England's troubles insured that when the assembly next sat, in March 1660, Virginians did not know who, if anyone, exercised authority in England. Meanwhile, in January 1660, discontinuity had been made complete by Governor Mathews's death. These events forced Virginians to make their own settlement. The council nominated Sir William Berkeley and called for an assembly so that Berkeley's government might enjoy the sanction of conforming to the only settlement that the colony had received from any Interregnum regime – the articles of 1652. It was the best they could do, even though as Berkeley pointed out the articles had never been secure, for the authority under which they had been negotiated had 'continued not long ... but another supreame power outed them, whoe remained not long neither, nor his sonne after him ... And now my intelligence is not enough to tell me what ... power there is' in England.[71]

Virginians' election of the royalist Berkeley qualified them neither as political seers nor as true cavaliers; the burgesses' accompanying assertion of their supremacy in Virginia did not make them republicans, far less prophets of American independence (even though it was agreed that for the time being the colony secretary should issue writs *ex officio*). It simply stated the fact that the assembly was the only extant authority in the colony. Berkeley's election was by legislative act, and so were his powers defined by law. While this recalled the disputes with Governor Mathews, it is doubtful that the precise location of power in Virginia was any longer a point of serious contention. In 1660 burgesses and councillors laid aside the suspicion which had provoked conflict over the agency of 1657 in order to provide government, law, and order. The Assembly drove this point home by enacting a flurry of laws including one for 'the peace of this Collony under the present Government'. Its preamble is worth quoting.[72]

> WHEREAS by reason of the late frequent distractions in England there is no absolute generall confessed power, And necessitie forceth us (during these distractions) to declare some power, Under which the collonie may be settled, It hath been thought necessary and convenient by the present Burgesses of this Assembly, the representatives of the people, during the time of these distractions, to take the government into their owne power with the conduct of the ancient lawes of England, till such lawfull commissions appear to us as wee may dutifully submit to . . . Bee it ordained and enacted . . .

Any persons who questioned the assembly's power should be proceeded against as traitors, 'enemies of the peace of this collonie'.

Berkeley was the perfect candidate to stand on this platform. It was not only that Berkeley declined to accept the governorship on any other authority than that of the burgesses; this old cavalier would be committed in principle to lay down his commission should monarchy be restored and to do the same should England move towards a republican settlement. He added that he would then continue to live, as he had for the past eight years, in submission to whatever power God might place over him. In the meanwhile, he would exercise the powers the burgesses could confer upon him. In accepting his role as constitutional custodian, Berkeley accepted a political task, too. He nominated a council of no clear ideological color, containing (like his 1640s councils) parliamentarians like Bennett and Claiborne (who continued as secretary) and royalists like Francis Moryson. Here also were the men who in 1657-59 had sought to subvert the burgesses' *de facto* supremacy through an appeal to the Lord Protector. The burgesses understood their part well enough to confirm these nominations.

Whatever the effect of Interregnum commercial legislation on Virginia's economy, the colony had not thrived politically. In 1649, Virginia proclaimed Charles II partly because its own legal foundation was a royal commission. The 1652 articles of surrender provided an alternative basis for government but never received official English sanction. Thus, in 1660, with England in chaos, councillors and burgesses had to 'declare some power', an expressive phrase which admitted that they governed in Virginia without a legal commission. Apologizing to Charles II in October 1660 for accepting such an authority, Governor Berkeley stated that it had been necessary to preserve the colony from internal war.[73] If there was truth in his claim, did he mean the skirmishes between councillors and burgesses which had preceded his election? Or perhaps he spoke to a more fundamental fear, implicit in the legislation of March 1660, that Virginia's would-be rulers could only survive their independence from English authority by learning to hang together and lord it over the rest. In any case, what finally ended Virginia's uncertainty was the king's commission of July 1660 which, carrying the seals of the English state, arrived in Virginia in September to give the colony legal government for the first time since January 1649.[74] Such a gift had been in the power of successive Interregnum regimes, but they had never given it.

During the 1650s, Maryland closely replicated Virginia's experience. Deputy Governor Greene's untimely proclamation of Charles II allowed parliament's commissioners for Virginia to have the whole Chesapeake included in their commission,[75] and in due course Maryland, like Virginia, entered upon a period of government by virtue of the parliamentary commission of 1652. However, Lord Baltimore succeeded where Virginians had failed; in 1657 Cromwell recognized his rights of government, and in 1658 Marylanders got together to construct a local settlement based on a watered down version of the proprietary and with a governor, Josias Fendall, acceptable to protestant settlers.[76] No doubt Marylanders were glad to follow a command from the Lord Protector which kept them free of Virginia and restrained them from killing one another, as pro- and anti-proprietary forces had done on a small scale at the Battle of the Severn in 1655.

Marylanders avoided another round of battle when the fall of the Protectorate again exposed the colony's divisions between north and south, Puritan and Catholic, assembly and proprietary. During the session of February – March 1660, the anti-proprietary faction in the assembly offered terms to the governor and council. Would they sit in an 'Assembly of Burgesses judging themselves to be a lawfull Assembly without dependence on any other Power in the Province'? Secretary Philip Calvert, Baltimore's half-brother, asked whether the assembly meant to cut itself completely from the proprietor's power. The assembly did not have to answer this embarrassing question; after all, Governor Fendall and his council sat in power as much by Oliver Cromwell's order as by Baltimore's charter, and the dissolution of the Protectorate weakened their power at its source. However, desiring continuity in government, the burgesses not only asked Fendall and his council to sit in the assembly but also allowed Fendall a casting vote as Baltimore's representative. Secretary Calvert and Councillor Baker Brooks announced that they could not accept this without compromising their oaths to Baltimore, but they were in no personal danger. Having asked leave, they entered their dissent in the journal and departed peacefully.[77]

After the Restoration, Lord Baltimore charged Fendall with treason, but another observer more precisely judged Fendall's 'rebellion' as 'a small fit'. It was not rebellion at all but a local settlement whose makers understood it to be conditional on the outcome of events in England. In both context and result, Maryland's own settlement was nearly identical to Virginia's – deliberately so; frequent adjournments from 29 February to 12 March gave Maryland's assembly time to observe what Virginia had accomplished. Many Marylanders, perhaps the majority, did not like the proprietary, yet they accepted it on orders from England in 1658 and, in March 1660, had to realize that it might be imposed upon them again. Their request to Fendall to sit with them as Baltimore's representative suggests a wish to preserve some continuity with proprietary rule and to avoid a return of the violence of the mid-1650s. By agreeing to the request, Fendall helped to avoid that. Fendall's defence of his actions to Lord Baltimore does not survive, but we may suppose that it read similarly to the apologia Sir William Berkeley addressed to Charles II.[78]

* * *

The West Indies had similar experiences in the 1650s but did not fare so well in 1660. In 1652, Sir George Ayscue used the authority vested in him by parliament to dissolve the Carlisle proprietary, to commission governors, and to devise frames of government for Barbados and the other islands by negotiations with colonists. However, as with Virginia, the English state failed to ratify these agreements, and considerable confusion resulted. In Antigua, for example, in the late summer of 1655, disputes over Indian policy led to wrangles between Ayscue's governor, Christopher Kaynell, and a majority of the council and assembly. Kaynell left the island under a deputy and sailed for England, perhaps to seek a clearer commission of authority. Incensed over the Indian problem and fearful of Kaynell's purpose, islanders seized power from his deputy. They argued that by Ayscue's commission Kaynell could neither leave the island without permission nor appoint a deputy governor. Kaynell's abandonment of government meant that

> the visible power, government and Authority remaining and being upon this Island and which is to continue till other order or settlement therein from his Highness the lord Protector or his Immediate substitutes for that purpose is in the council and freeholders, or deputies of the severall divisions chosen for them . . . which was and is so to be by the agreement and assent of Sir George Ayscue and the whole body of this Collonie.

Antiguans claimed that the "law of nations nature and reason" required them to take government upon themselves, but what law of nature required the rebels to reappoint the councillors named in Ayscue's original commission? Or to proceed against inhabitants who refused to 'yeild present obedience' as 'enemies to his highness the Lord protector the Commonwealth of England, and this colonie'? Clearly legitimacy required better validation than the laws of nature or Antiguans' local compact could offer, so they cited also their 'obedient care towards his highness' and voted to obtain the judgment of Barbadian Governor Daniel Searle, recently commissioned by Cromwell as 'Lieutenant Generall' of all the islands. When Kaynell, who had gotten no further than Nevis, returned to reassert his authority, the rebels were forced to beg Searle's intervention on rather different grounds.[79] Antigua's was another of that series of colonial attempts to 'declare some power' by which government and order might be maintained in lieu of directions from England. Their decision to appeal to Searle also demonstrated their need for a higher authority than the island could provide.

Searle's Cromwellian commission was important for another reason. It marked a turning point in West Indian affairs and a divergence from the experience of the Chesapeake colonies, for under the Protectorate English involvement in West Indian affairs became more direct and more persistent than in the Chesapeake. Cromwell's dream of displacing Spain in the Caribbean required him to pay attention to the islands, while his advisers on colonial affairs like Martin Noell and Thomas Povey were directly interested in West Indian trade and government. As we have seen, Povey himself was finally to feel that little had been accomplished during the 1650s, but islanders might have put the case differently. It was not so much the lack of English intervention as its fitfulness which reduced Barbadian politics to confusion.

The commissioners of 1652 had left Searle as governor of Barbados in much the same position as Kaynell at Antigua. The Commonwealth did not respond to Barbadian desires to use the articles of surrender as a charter, but in contrast to Bennett in Virginia Searle did receive from the Commonwealth a direct commission as governor.[80] This helped Searle to survive the transition from Commonwealth to Protectorate, but soon he found that commission government could be a perversely insecure arrangement. Commissions and instructions, like laws, could be changed with ease, and could also be superseded. This was demonstrated by the commissioners who accompanied the 1655 Penn – Venables expedition on Cromwell's Western Design. During their brief sojourn in Barbados, the commissioners used their more recent authority from the Protectorate to invade Searle's Commonwealth commission, to upset the island militia's chain of command, and to offend local sensibilities by advertising for settlers to leave Barbados to populate the fleet's conquests. They also took it upon themselves to enforce the Commonwealth's trade legislation. Governor Searle and his assembly found common cause in opposing these high-handed measures, but acted cautiously. Indeed, they scarcely acted at all while faced with the fleet's overwhelming presence and the commissioners' authority from Cromwell. Searle and his Council waited to reverse the damage until the fleet sailed, and even then they found it politic to use a recently arrived commission for Searle from the Lord Protector, and not their sense of grievance, to reassume authority over the revenue and the island's militia.[81]

Thus these remote colonists complained against the same sort of invasion of local government that characterized the rule of Cromwell's major-generals in England. Hardly yet, if ever, a traditional ruling class in the way of the English gentry, Barbadian planters knew the language and shared the aspirations of England's county communities. Events during the 1650s confirmed their view that commission government encouraged the appointment to vital local offices of parvenus whose lack of connection in Barbados meant that they could have only a venal interest in the office.[82] To lay themselves open to rule by outsiders was to deny that they had interests worth protecting. However, the problem was more complex than that. As in Virginia, as in Kent and Somerset, so in Barbados the capacity of central government to intervene in local affairs through the use of commissioned authority encouraged more than the migration of carpetbaggers.[83] Ambitious locals were also tempted by the rewards which might come through cooperation with central power. Digges and his fellow agents played this role in Virginia, while in Barbados Thomas Modyford, once a moderate cavalier, now assumed the guise of an enthusiastic Cromwellian. Modyford's chameleon-like loyalty has given him a bad press, but a man who defended the actions of the commissioners *after* the Penn-Venables fleet had left Barbados was not without courage.[84] By the same token, he cannot have aimed for power through cultivating local popularity. Rather he joined with John Colleton, a planter with close London ties, to seek Cromwell's support in displacing Searle. Their actions produced bitterness and division in the island. Soon, Searle was advised by Povey and Noell, his English agents, to accommodate matters with his local dissidents lest the noise of faction encourage Cromwell to take too close an interest in

Barbadian affairs. Searle described this local accommodation, effected in the spring of 1658, as intended to 'prevent further trouble to my friends, to prevent Clamours at home raised on plausible pretences . . . to draw some factious spirits amongst us into a unison' and, in general, as 'Christian like good pollicies'.[85]

No doubt Modyford accepted it for similar reasons, but whatever its virtues, the settlement of 1658 lasted for only a year. Both it and Searle's commission depended upon the Protectorate, and Richard Cromwell's fall threw all into confusion. To maintain his government, Searle was advised to use a letter from some of the new councillors of state which purported to validate his great seal, 'it being a tender thing for one in your place, to keep up a Reverence, and enforce an Authoritie, without a Commission'.[86] This accurate comment was an insufficient remedy for Searle's problem. Indeed, the letter did not satisfy the Barbadian assembly, which decided to seek from the restored Rump a colonial charter by 'lawe or commission'.[87] Given the very different charter 'by lawe' for the West Indies that Thomas Povey was seeking from the Rump, there was a nice irony in this, but Barbadians were probably more worried about Modyford and Colleton. Those two proved equal to the changed climate and constitution of 1659, accusing the assembly of seeking to 'shake off and Renounce the Authority of the Nation'. Searle, under fire from all directions, joined with the assembly to rebut this slur on the loyalty of colonists who 'now are, and at all times for the future shall Continue to bee in all one submission and obedience to the supreame Authority of the Nation of England'. They spoke truthfully enough, for they had already experienced the inadequacy of both laws and commissions as the fundament of government, and to ask for a charter based upon either alternative was rather evidence of desperation than of an opportunistic maneuver to secure colonial independence. It also signified Barbadian awareness of England's constitutional confusion. In January 1660, to which 'Authority' could colonists declare their allegiance? Not knowing, they declared their loyalty to 'England successively as it now is or shall for the future be fixed or settled' and hoped for the best.[88]

* * *

Thomas Modyford and John Colleton succeeded in their individual quest for power, receiving a commission for government from the caretaker Council of State in March 1660. The restoration of monarchy was to show that they had been guilty of bad timing;[89] meanwhile, their attempt had again made strange bedfellows of Searle and his assembly who worked together to frustrate Modyford's ambition. Yet, when Modyford arrived with his commission in the summer of 1660, Barbadians accepted it. After their feverish and febrile behavior of 1659,

Barbadians had tired of politics and were ready to settle for government. In this, they shared much in common with Virginians and Marylanders, whose political settlements had been made necessary by the 'miserable distractions of England' and would last only until 'God shall be pleased in his mercy to take away and dissipate the unnatural divisions' which had reduced English and colonial government to chaos. Likewise, Benjamin Langham, Joseph Lee, and Robert Smithers, the leaders of the Antiguan 'rebellion' of 1655, had protested that a full settlement of their affairs required the decision of a 'higher & Legall Court', or, as Virginia's assembly put it, a 'resident absolute and generall confessed power'.[90] As during the civil war, uncertainty at the center of the empire had forced local, consensual settlements; but the conditional and temporary nature of these settlements was everywhere recognized, and for these colonists the restoration of stability in England would come as a relief. They would have agreed with Thomas Povey's advice that 'nothing but the grand and Supreame Settlement is now to be attended from which all inferior settlements may bee the better derived'.[91]

However, colonists had also developed a strong sense of corporate identity. English tradition and their own experience confirmed colonists' regard for local autonomy, and nothing happened during the Interregnum to diminish it. Colonists in government, whatever their religious or ideological sympathies, drew from history a preference for the contractual empire of Charles I and distrust of the legislative empire presaged by the notorious Act of 1650. Barbadians complained that they were not represented in the imperial legislature, but we may doubt whether they would have welcomed the dispensations of an English parliament in which they had been represented. Together with Virginians they sought charter status in their negotiations of 1652, for they wished to share the benefits which Massachusetts derived from its chartered autonomy.

In 1660, autonomy and dependence remained the twin poles of imperial politics. Massachusetts' Nathaniel Ward, trained in both law and divinity, put the point well when, in 1647, he urged crown and parliament to recognize that the course of public wisdom was 'rather to compose, than tolerate difference in Religion'. For government, too, the middle way was best: 'over-risen Kings, have been the next evils to the World, unto fallen Angels:and ... over-franchised people, are devils with smooth snaffles in their mouths'. 'He is a good King that undoes not his Subjects by any one of his unlimited Prerogatives: and they are a good People, that undoe not their Prince, by any one of their unbounded liberties'. In England and America, politically aware Englishmen would have understood Ward's meaning perfectly. With these conventional political moralisms, Ward wished a peaceful end to England's turmoil

[101]

and idealized the constitution of both realm and empire.[92] As idealizations go, it was reasonably accurate, but it concealed a problem which was central to England's century of revolution. An unlimited sovereignty did not mix well with franchised liberties. That problem was to be highlighted by the Restoration settlement of 1660.

CHAPTER FIVE

The Restoration in England, 1660–1667

The Restoration has seemed to historians to call more clearly than the Commonwealth had for new imperial policies, for a half-century's experience of empire and the restored regime's needs both recommended closer central control over the colonies. This traditional view is made more plausible by the advice Charles II received early in his reign from his merchant-dominated councils of trade and plantations to establish a more effective imperial administration. Parliamentary legislation reinforced the councils' advice. In September 1660, the Convention Parliament passed a Navigation Act which affirmed the principles of earlier legislation and added features to insure that the bulk of the colonial trades would not only be carried in English ships but also flow through the English entrepot. Parliament drove the point home by fashioning a financial settlement which made the crown heavily dependent upon customs revenue. Truly the winds of change seemed to set a clear course towards imperial centralization.

During the 1660s, however, the crown steered a different course. Most existing colonies were restored to their old, autonomous governments, while of the new settlements only Jamaica, a Cromwellian conquest, became a royal colony. The new colonies of Carolina, New York, and the Bahamas were given proprietary charters. New York, formerly New Netherlands and conquered from the Dutch in 1664, was made the personal fief of the king's younger brother James, Duke of York, who then proceeded to balkanize the colony by giving bits of it away. The leaders of the New Netherlands expedition were also commissioned to investigate the New England colonies and bring them to better order, but this went awry. Meanwhile, in London, the councils of trade and plantations atrophied. Judged against its apparent potential, the Restoration's imperial accomplishments seem anachronistic. Among several reasons for this perversity was a certain nonchalance which produced a casual distribution of colonial patronage, territory and rights of self-government. Furthermore, the 1660s decade brought the second Dutch War, the plague, the Great Fire of London, and an increasingly evident public penury, all of which would have tested any government trying to implement any policy.

Of course, these circumstances influenced colonial administration, not least because in 1667 they brought down the chief architect of the Restoration settlement, Sir Edward Hyde, Charles's Lord Chancellor and created Earl of Clarendon in 1661. But they have been accorded too much importance by an explanatory strategy which virtually assumes failure.[1] This strategy arises from historians' focus on Restoration commercial legislation: the Navigation Act of 1660 and its supporting legislation of 1662 and 1663. But Clarendon's imperial administration, indeed the Navigation Acts themselves, must be judged in the context which produced them: the restoration settlement of 1660. In the empire, as in the realm, the moving force behind politics was the crown's perception of what had to be done in order to secure and then sustain its power. In its proper context Clarendon's imperial policy assumes its true character as an imperial settlement: comprehensible, deliberate, and in some of its aspects a conspicuous success.

* * *

Well over a century ago, W. W. Hening ridiculed the idea that Virginians' "election" of Sir William Berkeley marked their anticipation of the restoration of monarchy in England. Virginians could not have known and were unlikely to have guessed the outcome of England's chaos.[2] Englishmen at home were not much wiser, for the confusions of 1659 made it seem that anything could happen. Finally, in January 1660, General George Monck moved his troops south from Coldstream to London in order, so he said, to bring stable, civilian rule. This did not insure the return of monarchy, but it made finite the 'endless series of possibilities'.[3] The range narrowed further as Monck secured the return to the Rump Parliament of the old "secluded" members, victims of Pride's Purge in 1648 and not lovers of republican experiment. With republican elements in disarray, the Long Parliament dissolved itself and called for elections to a 'free' parliament. By mid-March 1660, the return of Charles II was likely.

What sort of restoration it would be remained an open question. Those who had paved the way for a restoration, men like Monck, the Earl of Manchester, and members of the interim Council of State such as Arthur Annesley and Sir Anthony Ashley Cooper, thought in terms of a restoration which would secure parliamentary government, prevent the return of episcopacy, and protect the lives and property of most of those who, like themselves, had done battle against the royal cause in the civil wars or had served in Interregnum regimes. With these 'Presbyterians' making the running, a conditional settlement was a likely outcome. Nor did it seem that cavaliers could do much to change that. Royalist conspiracy had been quiescent in England since the disastrous rising of summer 1659, while the king himself was still in exile, still uninvited, and in danger of being detained by the Spanish authorities in Flanders. Charles bettered his chances by moving to Breda, in Holland, but had to do so under cover of darkness and disguise. This must inauspiciously have reminded him of his flight from Worcester nine years earlier, yet at the end of May, only nine weeks after his flight to Breda, Charles and a swollen retinue dined splendidly in London's Guildhall. The pomp of the occasion underlined the fact that Charles II was king by right, for already, on 8 May, lords and commons had formally proclaimed that the full power of the crown belonged to Charles II 'by inherent birth-right' at the death of his father; it was the twelfth year of Charles II.[4]

After eighteen years of what we now call an interregnum, this sudden restoration of the monarchy produced a spate of providential and astrological explanations. These glosses shared in common the grain of truth that as late as March 1660 no one had felt sufficiently in command of the situation to impose a solution. Like Virginians, Englishmen awaited events, but were soon caught up in enthusiasm for monarchy. Charles II cynically remarked that this 'royalism' proved him a fool for staying away so long, but whatever its sources it led to the election of perhaps one hundred known cavaliers to the Convention Parliament despite prohibitions against cavalier candidatures. This dished the Presbyterians. Their goal of a conditional restoration required a united House of Commons, for they feared the army and loathed radicalism too much to mount an appeal to the Good Old Cause. Meanwhile, early election returns encouraged Charles II, still in Breda, to take a moderate stance, to think that parliament 'would not exact more from him than he was willing to consent to'.[5]

This astute judgment, confirmed by Monck's advice from London, led Charles to offer generous political conditions within the framework of a fully restored constitution. The Declaration of Breda, dated 4 April 1660 and sent along with letters to Monck and the Council of State, the army and navy, the two houses of parliament, and the City of London,[6] erected a platform upon which parliament willingly stood. Charles set the tone by offering a general pardon from which only parliament might except individuals. He also promised toleration for peaceable religious dissent, leaving the details to parliament, while committing himself generally to an erastian and protestant church settlement. Most aspects of the land settlement, a contentious issue given Interregnum fines and confiscations, were also reserved to parliament's judgment. Charles reassured parliament by giving it much to do. From Breda, he asserted that as parliament's 'authority is most necessary for the government of the kingdom, so . . . the preservation of the king's authority is as necessary for the preservation of Parliaments'. Not to be outdone, the Commons replied that the regicide, that ultimate invasion of royal authority, could not have happened without the prior invasion of parliament by Colonel Pride and his troops. So appealing was this balance, it was difficult to see how the civil war could have happened but through 'mistakes and misunderstandings'.[7]

That the wheel was to be reinvented was made clearer by Charles's letter to the City of London, which pointed beyond the return of parliament and crown towards a restoration of government by licence, patent and prerogative grant. In this sense, the rash of corporate and proprietary charters which characterized Clarendon's colonial policy was no more retrograde than the Restoration settlement itself. These successful applications in America of the principles of Breda suggest a strong line of continuity between the empire of Charles I and the empire of Charles II. Whether Clarendon's colonial policies should be seen as swimming against the centralizing tide of the Restoration's commercial legislation is another question, which requires us to examine parliament's role in making the Restoration settlement.

* * *

In the Declaration of Breda, Charles outlined his goal of a restoration of monarchy, but left the fine details – and much of the difficulty – to parliament. This was important business, but the crucial function of parliament, as the Duke of Ormonde told the Irish Commons in 1662, was to provide 'the foundations upon which monarchy is built, the strength wherewith it is guarded, and the wealth whereby it is sustayned, inricht, and beautifyed'.[8] England's parliament, though less supine than Ireland's, endorsed the general sentiment. Once the pressing matters of indemnity and the land settlement had been dealt with, and that of religion deferred, parliament turned to the problem of providing money for a regime to which it was inextricably committed. The revenue settlement was to be a critical factor in English politics for nearly three decades; it also shaped the politics of empire, initially by providing context for the Navigation Act of 1660 and for the trade legislation of 1662 and 1663.

Although both the Convention and its successor the Cavalier Parliament contributed to the revenue settlement, the main outlines of the crown's income were clearly defined before Charles dissolved the

Convention in December 1660. The revenue settlement had two major features. Firstly, the Convention drew a sharp line between ordinary and extraordinary revenues. Ordinary revenues were set aside as Charles's permanent income, some for his life and some for the crown in perpetuity. Extraordinary revenues were for extraordinary purposes which would require legislation by the king in parliament. Secondly, the Convention calculated that the ordinary revenue should amount to £1,200,000 per annum. Although the king and his advisers early agreed that this was not enough, their more immediate problem was that the revenues actually conferred upon the crown were not coming even to that figure. Thus they tried to get parliament to make it up to £1,200,000, and parliament responded with an addition to the excise in December 1660 and the Hearth Tax in 1662.[9]

In 1660, the annual amount of ordinary revenue was not intended as the fulcrum of a constitutional balance between crown and parliament. If a balance was being aimed at in setting the revenue at £1,200,000, it was thought to lie between the penury that had forced Charles I to resort to Ship Money and the high taxes which had allowed Commonwealth and Protector to maintain standing armies and govern without the consent of England's natural rulers. It was a fiscal poultice applied to the wounds which had disabled the ancient constitution.[10] King and commons were not eyeing each other warily across a £1,200,000 barrier; for both, the real wolf at the door was the fear that the Restoration itself would not survive. For much the same reason, sheer stinginess can also be ruled out as a reason for parliament's calculation of a suitable annual supply. Members of parliament and those they represented had been restored, too, and they paid heavily for the privilege through grants of extraordinary revenue. The most effective device parliament used was the assessment, an Interregnum innovation which was for all practical purposes a direct tax on land. It was first employed by the Convention to pay off and disband the Cromwellian army, an urgent task beyond the crown's ordinary revenue. The Cavalier Parliament was less happy about the assessment, but even so by the end of the decade about £8,000,000 had been raised via assessment acts.[11]

Parliament's generosity was, however, tempered in two respects. Firstly, efforts were made to shift part of the burden of direct taxation from the land to other sources. Members correctly believed that commercial and financial assets escaped lightly from the assessments. Other expedients were sought, but with little success; the Cavalier Parliament's outlawing of the assessment in a 1661 Act granting an eighteen months' assessment symbolized the uncomfortable fact that the land tax was the most reliable way to raise a stated amount of money.[12] Secondly, the openhandedness of the landed gentry did not extend to a willingness to underwrite the ordinary expenses of government with land taxes. The estimate of £1,200,000 for the ordinary revenue may have been guesswork of no intrinsic importance, but there was a sharply drawn line between the permanent and occasional revenues. It followed an exact political calculus which not only hoped that the king could 'live of his own' but also changed the nature of the king's own. The revenue settlement of 1660 shifted the basis of ordinary public finance from the land to trade by confirming the Long Parliament's abolition of the Court of Wards and purveyances. Of course, this transition had been going on since medieval times, and one should not casually accord great significance to the removal of these last fiscal remnants of the crown's rights over subjects' lands. Nor can this be passed off as mere tax evasion by a dominant landed class. The annual value of the Court of Wards and purveyance was about £200,000, only a sixth of the proposed annual revenue and, spread over the 1660s, only a quarter of the amount raised by land assessments during the decade. Moreover, the compensatory tax voted by the Convention, the excise, was adopted by only the narrowest of votes, and that under heavy court pressure. Professor Chandaman seizes upon these points to argue that the 'abolition of the feudal incidents' was used as a 'convenient lever' to preserve for royal use a productive Interregnum fiscal device. Insofar as the excise did shift ordinary revenue from land to trade, it was politically insignificant and may even have been unintentional.[13]

Chandaman's analysis, however, concentrates too closely on the putative connection between the lost revenues and the excise *per se*. What does require explanation is that no land taxes contributed to the ordinary revenues of the restored monarchy, while customs and excise alone were reckoned to make up well over half the required sum. This was undoubtedly a matter of power and politics. The feudal incidents were disliked because they subjected estates to occasional, heavy, and therefore apparently arbitrary royal levies. As hereditary rights of the crown, they remained vulnerable to abuse from a still largely unchecked prerogative. These fears were emphasized by those who said that they would accept retention of the Court of Wards if it could be placed under statutory regulation.[14] Yet a statutory land tax should have been even less objectionable than a regulated Court of Wards. As the debate over the compensatory excise showed, many felt strongly the political and moral point that a land tax should replace a land tax; and the assessments laid by 1660s parliaments demonstrated their willingness to pay heavy land taxes for the strength and safety of the regime. Given that despite all this no land tax contributed to Charles II's ordinary revenues, we must conclude that reluctance to impose the excise did not constitute eagerness to confer upon the crown a hereditary right to land revenues.

Any reluctance there was soon passed; in December 1660 the Convention voted without a division to double the excise in order to make up a shortfall in the ordinary revenue. Once the deed was done, it was easier to do it again.[15] It remains reasonable to regard the changed basis of ordinary taxation as the intention, as well as the clear result, of the revenue settlement.

The point assumes direct relevance to imperial history when we look beyond the excise to consider customs revenue, which, in turn, brings into view the commercial legislation of the Restoration, the Navigation Act (1660), the Statute of Frauds (1662) and the so-called Staple Act (1663). Considered together with customs, excise, and the direct assessments on land, these laws drew even more sharply the lines between ordinary and extraordinary revenues and between trade and land as sources of public finance and subjects of public administration. That customs revenue depended both upon the state of trade and upon the government's ability to regulate trade had long been apparent, for instance, in trading company and colonial charters, and was reinforced by Interregnum experience. The political attractions of trade revenues had been enhanced by the expense of Cromwellian government and the efficiency of the land assessments which had been its main support. By 1657, Oliver's second parliament hoped that the £1,300,000 it offered him as an annual ordinary revenue could be raised mainly from the nation's trade and not at all from its land. Similar hopes lay behind the Interregnum wars against Holland and Spain, both of which were supposed to pay for themselves, not only through prizes but also through capturing for England a larger share of the world's trade.[16] The revenue settlement of 1660, which aimed to supply one-third of the crown's ordinary income from customs alone, showed that Charles II and his parliaments inherited from their predecessors the belief that trade policy and public finance were inextricably linked.

The fiscal implications of the Navigation Act were undoubtedly in the minds of those who guided it through the House of Commons, for instance, Sir George Downing, Teller of the Exchequer, and Sir John Shaw, a customs commissioner soon to resume his role as customs farmer. Both men served on the Commons' committee to investigate the revenue, which made its crucial report on 4 September 1660. On the same day, Downing successfully moved the inclusion in the Navigation Act of the clause requiring that the most important colonial products, including sugar and tobacco, be shipped directly to England.[17] The fiscal implications of this 'enumeration' cannot have been lost on parliament. Certainly they were known to Sir Anthony Ashley Cooper, MP for Dorset, ex-investor in Barbados, and Chancellor of the Exchequer. In December 1660 he calculated the revenue value of the Navigation Act to be £100,000 per annum. Six months later, Cooper (now Baron Ashley) and his uncle, Lord Treasurer Southampton, confirmed the Navigation Act's fiscal importance when they recommended on revenue grounds that the colonial trades should be excluded from a proposed grant to Dover of free port status.[18] This connection between revenue and trade legislation bore further fruit in the Convention Parliament's prohibition of tobacco planting in England, which Ashley considered to be an act for the revenue,[19] and in the Cavalier Parliament's Statute of Frauds and Staple Act. The Statute of Frauds had a long gestation. It was twice discussed by the Convention, first during deliberations on the Navigation Act and again in November 1660. In 1661, Lord Ashley sat on a committee of both houses which discussed a statute of frauds. When the act finally passed in 1662, it was occasioned by concern at the continued shortfall in customs revenue below the promised £400,000 per annum.[20] The 1663 Staple Act was more clearly a piece of trade legislation, but its utility to the revenue was clear to all, not least to Charles.[21] There is enough evidence to call unnecessarily cautious Chandaman's conclusion that parliament 'took serious account' of the fiscal implications of trade regulation 'only on the broad assumption that trade and revenue went hand in hand'.[22]

As the debates over the feudal incidents had shown there were also important political calculations to be made, such as those the Speaker had in mind when he presented the Navigation Act for the royal assent. Such measures, said Sir Harbottle Grimston, were designed to bring trade into English hands; and 'when it is ours your majesty cannot want it'.[23] Few parliament men would have said the same thing about their landed estates. The excise Acts of 1660, presented at the same time, gave further emphasis to this point. So, too, had the Book of Rates (revised by parliament in the summer of 1660) and the Staple Act, for both helped agricultural exports, the former by reducing duties, the latter by removing several prohibitions.[24] These Acts accorded with mercantilist ideas, but also, as surely as abolition of the Court of Wards, they lessened the financial obligations of landed proprietors to the crown's ordinary revenue. The settlement of 1660 not only freed land from perpetual liability to taxation (insofar as this was in parliament's power) but also left landowners freer to exploit their estates than they had been before. The 'strict settlement' Act of 1647 was confirmed, thus opening to large landowners the general facilities of entail, while the rights of tenants and copyholders were reduced. It was appropriate, then, that the land assessments would be collected by local men appointed by parliament:'while taxes on trade or consumption might safely be entrusted to royal nominees, the sacrosanct sphere of property should be invaded only by independent property-owners'. Lesser folk were less well protected, and in 1663 and 1664 parliament legislated to plug loopholes in the collection of excise and hearth money, both notoriously regressive taxes. It would seem that Sir Edward Seymour was but one of many members of parliament who wished to increase the king's revenue by trade while welcoming 'all propositions that have a tendency to ease Lands'.[25]

The navigation Acts endorsed conventional economic wisdom and undergirded the revenue settlement. Both taken together may be regarded as statesmanlike. On the other hand, the powers of trade regulation and revenue collection conferred on the crown contrasted starkly with the immunities conferred upon landed property. The attitude of Restoration parliaments towards England's domestic, foreign and colonial trades was thus at least partly predatory. Politically we find little evidence that parliament's landed gentlemen loved or trusted merchants. Merchants were, the Convention's speaker said, the 'labourious bees that bring in honey into your majesty's hive', but in 1661 his successor apologized for parliament's delay in perfecting 'the coercive power' necessary to sharpen merchants' homing instinct and invited Lord Treasurer Southampton to authorize MPs from port towns to act as agents against fraudulent traders. Merchants, unlike country gentlemen, were interested parties; considered as individuals, along with brewers, distillers, and humble hearth owners, they stood before the Restoration's revenue legislation as before Leviathan.[26]

The revenue settlement and the acts of trade did more than remove vestiges of the crown's feudal past. Historically deriving much of its settled revenue and much of its symbolic power from its role as the nation's landlord, the crown now stood *rentier* of the nation's wealth by trade. This role was imposed on Charles by landed men who well understood that their wealth would be enhanced by England's trade, and indeed were given to invest their own surpluses in trading ventures as well as in estate improvement. Yet in the context of Restoration conservatism it was a fittingly archaic solution and should be called commercial feudalism. Navigation Act in hand, Lord Chancellor Clarendon thanked a landowners' parliament in its own language. He hoped that England would 'flourish to that degree that the land of Canaan did, when Esau found it necessary to part from his brother; for their riches were more, than that they might dwell together; and the land wherein they were could not bear them, because of their cattle'. (To make sure whose cattle was meant, parliament soon passed an act excluding Irish cattle from England, over Clarendon's objections.) Whether the 'motions of these last twenty years' owed, as Clarendon told the Convention, to the 'evil motions of a malignant star' or, as he put it to the Cavalier Parliament, to the 'extreme poverty of the crown', he hoped that now all would be well. The evil star was 'now expired', and parliaments had provided the king with a 'constant growing revenue' which would repair that fatal want of money which had brought down Charles I and laid waste to the nation. The navigation system furnished the small print for the Restoration political contract by which, Clarendon hoped, England would be returned to 'its old good manners, its old good humour, its old good nature'.[27]

It is more difficult to determine parliamentary attitudes towards the actual ways and means of regulating trade and of overseeing colonial government. The Presbyterian element in the Convention House of Commons might have favored the old trading companies, but Sir George Downing was hostile to them, and the Navigation Act he helped to draft shows little sign of the companies' influence despite their petitions for direct confirmation of their rights.[28] In 1660 the old trading companies failed to win recognition of their rights and powers *vis-à-vis* English interlopers; thus they remained in the legal limbo into which they had been cast by the Commonwealth's Navigation Act. Certainly the Council of Trade thought so. In 1663, it recommended incorporating the fisheries but advised that outside the king's waters the only legal way to do so would be by parliamentary enactment. Charles, however, rejected this advice, chartering the Royal Fisheries Company in 1664, just as he chartered more substantial ventures like the Royal African Company in 1663 and the Hudson's Bay Company in 1670.[29] Restoration legislation laid down commercial regulations for the king's subjects and for foreigners, but it does not appear to have bound the king to any particular governing mechanism.

Parliament now legislated for a monarchy, not a republic. All who possessed or sought powers of government over their fellow subjects needed to remember that, too. An unconditional Restoration meant that the prerogative was the center and source of government. Charles's letter from Breda to the City of London emphasized this by promising the capital not only a restoration of its old privileges and powers but also 'any new favors which may advance the trade, wealth, and honour of that our native city'. That was a broad promise, and its importance lay only partly in the fact that the king honored it in 1663 with a new charter for the city.[30] The promises to London could have been extended through the king's 'mere grace and motion' to every municipal borough in the realm, to trading companies and to chartered colonies. Direct relationships between royal and local authority found equally traditional expression in royal commissions to lords lieutenant, county justices and royal governors of castles, garrisons, and the colony of Virginia. Finally, the king ordered his own household and government, appointing servants and officers from cooks to privy councillors. Thus was restored a personal government, and the ease with which great and humble approached Charles to ask for his favor testified not only to the king's affability but also to his use of these historic powers.[31] The navigation laws' silences on how colonies should be governed followed this drift by leaving intact the crown's prerogative powers over trade and empire. Charles I's view that the colonies were his by birthright again came into its own, as Charles II signified when he slapped down efforts by parliament to annex Jamaica to the imperial crown by legislation.[32] How to use these powers remained an open question. In the long run, the crown would answer the question by attacking colonial autonomy, but in the short run, the crown had different aims. These aims were rooted in English domestic politics during the ministry of the Earl of Clarendon.

* * *

During the early 1660s, Clarendon was at the center of power. He was to fall from power and into disgrace in 1667, and chinks in his armor appeared earlier than that, but his temperament and ideas indelibly marked the settlement of 1660 and much of what followed. His constitutional and political views, essentially those laid down in the Breda letters, were old-fashioned, perhaps unrealistic, but they had strong appeal in 1660. For him, England's ancient constitution was strong not because it balanced crown and parliament but because it placed both within an organic whole. As a spokesman for the constitutional opposition to Charles I in the early sessions of the Long Parliament, he had as much right as any to take this position, and his right was further strengthened when, as adviser to Charles I and then the exiled Charles II, he had consistently opposed the schemes of extreme royalists. He believed that the Restoration confirmed his views, and he stuck to them with a doggedness which rendered him politically diffident.[33]

Clarendon's reluctance to abandon the settlement of 1660 showed in his relatively relaxed view of the regime's rapidly mounting revenue problems. Like Sir Harbottle Grimston, the Lord Chancellor believed that there was an organic connection between Englishmen's hearts and purses; he did not wish to break the former by making too heavy demands on the latter. Clarendon thus resisted the advice of fiscal hawks like Sir Henry Bennett who wished to manage parliament into greater generosity. Bennett, said Clarendon, knew more of China than of the English constitution. Later, Viscount Bolingbroke was to praise Clarendon for thus preserving the constitutional balance, but that was an eighteenth-century concept. Such jobbery as Bennett proposed would have jarred the Lord Chancellor's sensibilities but not his regard for parliaments. To beg or bully for money would lessen the constitutional distance between superior and inferior and carry the risk of political confrontation. Thus Clarendon would later praise Charles for his conduct in opening the parliamentary session of 1664, when assuredly the government's need for money was very great:[34]

> It was very happy for his majesty that he did cut out their work to their hands, and asked no money of them. . . . It made their counsels very unanimous: and though they raised no new taxes, they made what they had before raised much more valuable, by passing other acts and declarations for the explaining many things, and the better collecting the money that had formerly been given, which much added to his majesty's profit without grieving the people.

Clarendon's diffidence over the money question reflected also his belief that eventually the revenue settlement would be made good. Eventually, in the 1680s, he would be proved right about that, but in the meanwhile his inaction in the face of financial crisis strengthened his critics and weakened him. His conduct of government calls to mind the modern aphorism that in a state of bliss there is no need for a ministry of bliss.[35] In a well ordered constitution, the king would govern wisely and parliament would give generously. Clarendon's belief that both parliament and king were responsible for failing to maintain bliss contributed not only to the sanctimonious air of his memoirs but also to his post-1667 exile which gave him the leisure to write.

In the meanwhile, Clarendon' conservatism both defined the purpose and limited the influence of the councils of trade and plantations established in late 1660. Clarendon told parliament that these bodies owed their creation to the king's awareness of the 'infinite importance' of trade. It was also the case that the new regime was inexperienced in trade and colonial affairs. The long exile had given the court plenty of training in plots, but little in government, and advice was needed on the 'mysteries of trade' and the state of the colonies. Thus men like Thomas Povey and the Barbadian planter-merchant James Drax moved easily from their advisory roles in Interregnum regimes to take up membership on Charles II's council for plantations. Members of the council worked hard enough, but as A.P.Thornton points out they often found themselves discussing bad debts in Barbados while important matters were settled by the Privy Council. One reason for the councils' limited influence may be found in Clarendon's assurances to parliament that they would not only contain men well versed in commerce and colonies but would also depend for advice and honor upon gentlemen of quality and some of the Lords of the Privy Council. In his memoirs he more frankly dismissed the councils as a 'crowd of commissioners' and referred to their merchant members as 'inferior persons'.[36] Given Clarendon's attitudes towards the councils, to say that their ineffectiveness owed to their structural distance from the center of power is to mistake (as Povey himself did) a symptom for a cause.[37] The case was much the same for the surplus of even humbler men who rushed to advise the regime on trade and colonies. That these volunteer counsellors also sought personal preferment did not necessarily disqualify their opinions, but it certainly multiplied them, and there is evidence that Clarendon himself regarded such advice with caution if not with disdain.

Although the colonies benefited from Clarendon's social snobbery, his political views were more important. Both Clarendon and Charles believed that the moderation of the Breda letters had contributed to the speed and ease of the restoration process. Their desire for a moderate settlement was, however, soon placed at risk. Early in the summer of 1660, the House of Lords bayed for more sweeping vengeance against adherents of republicanism. Charles chided the peers for blocking the promises of indemnity he had made from Breda, promises 'which, if I had not made . . . neither you nor I had been here'. The Presbyterians in the Convention Commons obstructed the king's promise to establish a measure of toleration, although they were happier with his apparent intention to secure a broad religious settlement within the establishment. The Cavalier House of Commons, which began its long life in May 1661, proved a different matter altogether. It bluntly rejected Clarendon's advice to be patient with those weak brethren who dissented loyally. It was 'not reasonable to imagine that the distemper of 20 years can be rectified and subdued in 12 months. There must be a natural time, and natural applications, allowed for it'. Parliament responded with the Corporations Act of 1661, which aimed to purge borough governments of political and religious radicals. Then, over a three-year period beginning with the 1662 Act of Uniformity, the Cavalier Parliament enacted the intolerant religious legislation which unfairly bears the Lord Chancellor's name, the Clarendon Code.[38] Through these laws, parliament endorsed Anglican purity within the national church and made worship outside its doors virtually illegal.

The Corporations Act has particular significance for imperial history, especially for relationships between the restored monarchy and the Puritan colonies of New England. With some reason, cavaliers believed that boroughs had been centers of rebel strength during the civil wars and now sheltered Presbyterians and other dissenters. True to its name and nature, the Cavalier Commons resolved that 'the whole Regulation of Corporations doth consist in placing the Government in right hands'. Amongst the touchstones of the cavalier definition of 'right hands' was service to the royal cause, but that category now included many Presbyterians, so the Act went on to require a thoroughly orthodox Anglicanism and a renunciation of the principles that had seemed in the early 1640s to justify taking up arms against a bad or badly advised king.

These tests, written into the Act of 1661, aimed to exclude from corporation affairs not only those who still adhered to the good old cause but also many otherwise conservative supporters of monarchy. Even if a Presbyterian burgher could attest the prescribed oaths and partake of an Anglican communion, he might not survive a further test. The Act empowered commissioners to exclude individuals from corporations on grounds of suspicion 'if expedient for the public safety'.[39]

Given all this, it was little wonder that New Englanders were alarmed to hear in 1664 that Charles had sent commissioners to examine their own corporations. Yet they were to find that this alarm was not fully justified. New England's chartered colonies emerged from the commission's inquiries essentially unscathed for a number of reasons, including the crown's increasing preoccupation with other matters.[40] Even so, the threat to the colonies implied by the Corporations Act and the Clarendon Code was not as clear as it might have seemed from Boston. The king's aims *vis-à-vis* England's chartered governments were not necessarily those of the House of Commons, nor even of the House of Lords, although Charles is generally credited with inspiring the upper house's amendments to the commons bill. These amendments proposed to give the crown a number of direct powers over corporation governments. All charters were to be surrendered to the crown or to become forfeit. In all new charters, the crown would have the power to appoint the crucial local officers of town clerk and recorder, and after naming the first mayor the crown would 'prick' each town's subsequent mayors from lists of nominees submitted by the town. Moreover, county justices were to be installed in the towns, while in county boroughs the crown would appoint all justices. The commons rejected all of these amendments *nem con* and thus ruled out the Lords' project of continuous crown control over borough affairs. More loyalist than royalist, most of them sitting for chartered boroughs, cavalier MPs aimed to impose a special political and religious orthodoxy on corporations, not to change the nature of their relationship with central authority. Indeed, following the Corporations Act, it was easier for a Presbyterian to sit on the Privy Council than to be a member of the corporation in such places as Bewdley, Lancaster, or Bodmin.

The membership of the Privy Council suggests that Charles's definition of political loyalty differed from that of the cavaliers. Charles could be amused by dissenters as individuals, even appoint them to high office, and it is clear that both he and Clarendon accepted that loyal dissent in religion was possible. On the other hand, neither king nor Lord Chancellor had much love for dissent in the abstract, and like the House of Commons they preferred to have local government in 'right hands'. In the negotiations which led to the issue of a new charter for the City of

London, for instance, the king insisted upon his preference for safe, loyal men on the aldermanic council. Other towns understood this well enough to remove from power prominent dissenters both before and during the issuance of new or confirmation of old charters.[41] Thus Charles used criteria similar to those used by commissioners under the Corporations Act. On the other hand, Charles also used some of the devices proposed in the Lords' amendments. In some charters issued during this period, the king not only designated the first mayor and aldermen but also reserved powers over future elections, and court influence was apparent, too, in the naming of prominent politicians to such borough offices as high steward and recorder. In other words, neither the act nor the Lords' failed amendments defined crown policy.[42] Even after the passage of the Corporations Act, as Sir Thomas Clifford reminded the Commons in 1664, the business of modifying or granting charters remained wholly within the prerogative. Before and after the Corporations Act the crown pursued its own policy towards corporations. Its central objective was to force or entice corporations to resubmit their charters and to take out new ones in exchange. The crown might secure patronage powers similar to those aimed for by the House of Lords or a purge of dissenters as preferred by the Commons, but neither was essential, and insistence upon both could provoke resistance from the corporation and its local sponsors. Resistance was not the objective; the process was an end in itself for crown and corporations who both had too much to gain or lose to be governed entirely by an Act of parliament.[43]

Whatever its specific provisions, a new charter emphasized that once again local political power derived from the crown. Politically, the point was demonstrated in actions which carried symbolic significance. The crown might receive a delegation of corporation members which pledged fealty and gave gifts. Sureties might be offered by neighboring gentry sponsors. If the corporation had not already done so, the return to the crown of the old fee farm rents further widened the concentric circles of favor and obligation. In granting the charter, the crown re-established local government and also customarily named the first mayor and officers of the corporation, men whose faces the king and his officers of state had looked upon. The king and his authority were thus visibly restored to the corporation, a valuable consideration after a period of usurpation, especially for those corporations which had accepted a Cromwellian charter. To this important gift might be added new privileges for the corporation or royal confirmation of rights which had previously been only customary. Finally, new charters often put the king's seal on the local dominance of groups and individuals. Thus, in a way strikingly reminiscent of but distinct from the restoration settlement between crown and parliament, resubmission formed a political contract which included the exchange of valuable considerations. By so much the precise religious or partisan complexion of a borough became a matter of lesser importance to the crown than it was to the local county gentry who, through the Corporations Act, had imposed their own political scrutiny on this traditional process. Certainly the act of resubmission seemed to satisfy Charles, who soon neglected the tiresome business of deciding which burgher should be mayor, which recorder, which town clerk, in those cases where new charters had given him these powers.[44]

The king's impatience with cavaliers' narrow definition of loyalty was underlined by his efforts to fulfil the promise of toleration contained in the Breda letters. This was not an easy road to follow. Fear of religious radicalism was pervasive, and in at least two instances, the first of which was Samuel Venner's rising in London in the winter of 1660-61, the crown was itself frightened.[45] The temptation to pursue a politically popular course of repression was not lessened by the king's need for money. The Quakers suffered from this sort of calculation during the early 1660s. Yet both king and Lord Chancellor generally resisted temptation; for instance in May 1661, court influence thwarted a cavalier attempt to subvert the Act of Indemnity and Oblivion.[46] Crown resistance to cavalier intolerance continued without sharp focus until December 1662, when Charles took a dramatic step which was to echo throughout his reign. Speculating publicly that repression might actually produce rebellion, Charles urged parliament to turn its attention back to Breda and to make a place in the religious settlement for those who 'through scruple and tenderness of misguided conscience, but modestly and without scandal' could not conform to the Church of England.[47]

One of the more extraordinary features of this royal 'declaration of indulgence' was that Charles asked parliament to pass an act to enable him to use a dispensing power 'which we conceive to be inherent in us'. This apparent inconsistency needs to be judged in its proper context. From Breda, Charles had made clear his preference for an inclusive and tolerant religious settlement, but he left inclusion to the established church and toleration to parliament. As politic as this may have been in April 1660, it compromised both the king's supremacy in the church and his power to dispense with or suspend parliamentary legislation on religious matters. Charles further weakened his case when he failed in an attempt to have his dispensing power written into the Act of Uniformity, an act to which he nevertheless gave the royal assent. Then, in June 1662, his own judges advised him against a wholesale suspension of the act.[48] All this had narrowed the king's options, and thus it was with perfect political logic that he asked parliament legislatively to confirm his inherent powers. Through the 1662 Declaration he aimed at securing the promises of Breda, at satisfying dissenters of royal good faith while making some room for Roman Catholics, and at reasserting with parliament's consent the royal supremacy in religion.

We shall see that in its dealings with New England dissenters the crown's freedom of action was not so hindered by its commitments to parliament.[49] In England, however, the crown's aims were at once dictated and limited by the Declaration of Breda and the Restoration settlement. Thus parliament's stout resistance to toleration in its spring 1663 session could not be overcome, and Charles proved cynical enough, Clarendon Anglican enough, to acquiesce. Later in 1663, a foiled rising of northern radicals pointed the way towards a reversal of government policy and an intensified program of persecution under the Conventicles Act, passed in the Spring session of 1664. Once again Quakers were the chief sufferers, while as Clarendon's recollection of the session made clear the crown benefitted from cavalier gratitude at Charles's apparently new mood. Not least, a new Triennial Act denied its name by removing the legal obligation, imposed by the legislation of 1641, to call a session of parliament at least once every three years.[50] Charles's anger at Clarendon's lukewarm support for the declaration of December 1662 soon dissipated in this climate, but courtiers knew that Charles's dissatisfaction with Clarendon had a number of sources besides tension over religious issues. The Chancellor disapproved of Whitehall morals, of the king's social friends and habits, and particularly of Charles's mistress Barbara Palmer, Countess Castlemaine. The king also grew impatient with Clarendon's avuncular style of guidance. In a courtly system of politics, these personal differences were important, and they were exploited by Clarendon's enemies who wished to displace him and by court wits who wished merely to amuse the king. The former found additional ammunition in what we would today regard as more substantive issues, issues which certainly had more direct bearing on imperial history. Chief amongst these was the financial problem, which may be regarded as symptomatic of others.

It was quickly apparent that the crown's ordinary revenues had fallen short of the promised £1,200,000 per annum, and Charles compounded the problem by overspending. In 1662, Ashley reckoned the annual deficit at £120,900 on a revenue of £965,000. Parliament returned a more optimistic report in 1663, but the real picture was worse than Ashley's calculation, which left aside the accumulated deficit.[51] From this base, Charles was unlikely to be able to bluff parliament into accepting toleration even had his constitutional promises and political maneuvering not given so many hostages to fortune. Once parliament had turned aside the projected toleration, it turned to the revenue problem in a somewhat less generous spirit than before. The efficient assessment was rejected in favor of a subsidy, an easily evaded form of direct taxation, while in the 1663 and 1664 sessions enforcement legislation aimed at improving the yield of hearth money, excise, and (through the Staple Act) customs. No new ordinary revenues were added. The government had little choice but to thank parliament and to announce a retrenchment by which Charles was expected to do without his cormorant keeper, his 'musique', his thirteen falconers, and to reduce his gentlemen pensioners to thirty as they 'dye off'. Charles must have chafed at these demeaning economies which reduced his household but had little impact on the underlying problem. They were public relations exercises, aimed to counter the court's reputation for extravagance and to incline parliament to greater generosity. Even Clarendon found them distasteful.[52]

That parliament increasingly restricted its revenue measures to enforcement legislation testified as much to doubts about government efficiency as to resentment of government extravagance. Meanwhile, at court, ambitious politicians like the Earl of Bristol told Charles that he could get additional permanent revenues if only parliament were better managed. Bristol overplayed his hand and suffered disgrace, but Clarendon was ill-equipped to meet either challenge. His reluctance to press parliament for additional revenues has already been noted, and the political and constitutional conservatism which informed this attitude contributed also to an antiquated administration which was not responsive to the financial crisis. Clarendon, however, was not the only hidebound conservative at court. In financial administration, the Earl of Southampton proved the limitations of Clarendon's dictum that only a great magnate could properly secure the dignity of the Lord Treasurer's 'ancient office'. Efficiency was not an aim, either, of the Duke of Ormonde, whose prescriptions for ruling Ireland would have pleased many a colonial governor, so intent was the duke on preserving the authority of the king's Irish government from the authority of the king's English government. To be sure, Clarendon's administration did include such men as Downing and Ashley, both of whom had experience of and useful ideas about revenue, administration, trade and plantations. Yet they owed their places to their political nimbleness and their connections, not their progressive ideas, and their greatest successes in reforming government awaited the period after Clarendon's fall.[53]

In the meanwhile, government returned to many of its traditional courses. A government committed to restore legitimate right to those to whom it belonged not only brought old cavaliers back into service but also favored a return to government by contract or licence. Many, perhaps most new and old officers of government enjoyed their place by patent rather than commission and thus 'owned' their office as a species of property. In this way many Cromwellian reforms were apparently lost, and bureaucratic weakness became an inevitable feature of Clarendon's regime. Undermining all was the government's steadily mounting debt. Reversion to the old method of farming the customs provides a good example of how necessity and inclination conspired together to produce problems and block solutions. Charles I had farmed his customs, and in 1660 the attractions of tradition were reinforced by the fact that most of the old king's farmers still lived and still remembered his debts to them, amounting to £250,000. Their legitimate rights, like those of other adherents to the royal cause, were to be recognized. Although practical problems delayed the restoration of farming as such, the old farmers and their new partners soon became customs commissioners at annual salaries of £2,000. When in 1662 the government's increasing debts added to the attractions of the Great Farm its capacity for raising money on credit, it was inevitable that the farm should be restored. The excise, an Interregnum innovation, could not be 'restored' to traditional methods of collection, but after a brief period under commission, it, too, was farmed from 1662.[54]

Professor Chandaman convinces us that farming was not necessarily an inefficient mode of tax collection, but it certainly confessed to both the government's bureaucratic weakness and its need for credit. Nor was the system much liked at the time. That parliament required the excise farm to be parcelled out by county and to farmers approved by parliament suggests something of the unpopularity of farming and the suspicion that the system was open to abuse: a 'dismal necessity', as Sir William Coventry called it. The farmers were private collectors of public revenue who profited when actual collections ran ahead of their contract payments to the crown. This rendered them suspect, and their reputation was not enhanced by their tendency to sue the king for 'defalcations' when the balance sheet worked out the other way for reasons which might, *prima facie*, be blamed on government. Suspicion of farming allowed parliament to suggest that the crown's financial problems owed rather to inefficiency or corruption than to the insufficiency of parliamentary grants. The Statute of Frauds was an expression of this view.[55] Dislike of the farmers may have enhanced the traditional attractions of tax evasion, and certainly added to problems of enforcement. When farmers' deputies encountered problems in revenue collection, this was often because they could not depend on the help and often faced the opposition of local authorities, notably county justices, despite their direct commissions from the king.[56]

To some extent, this reflected nothing more than JPs' local loyalties and their suspicion of outsiders. Such localism was a significant feature of English (and colonial) politics, but other royal officers without strong local ties could also be depended upon to make life difficult for the king's revenue men. In July 1665, when customs officers dared to accuse the royal governor of Carisbrooke Castle, Isle of Wight, of holding contraband tobacco, the governor 'caned them with twenty or thirty blowes, and broke the head of one of them in severall places', then threw them into the castle dungeon. The injured officers appealed to the Privy Council for relief and restitution, but unsuccessfully.[57] That the governor in question was Thomas Lord Culpeper and one of the damaged collectors was Nicholas Badcocke gives the episode particular piquancy for the colonial historian, for Badcocke was later to experience similar troubles as collector in Maryland, when he chose not to ask for help from the neighboring governor of Virginia, by then Lord Culpeper.[58]

There was, however, more to it than coincidence. In the early 1660s, English military governors, county justices, and garrison commanders in the Channel Islands were not the only royal officers suspected of subverting the king's revenue. Colonial governors, too, were believed to be negligent enforcers of the acts of trade. The customs farmers proposed to rectify this problem by appointing their own officers to enforce the acts in the colonies. The Council for Foreign Plantations endorsed the idea and in 1663 asked the farmers to draw up a 'modell' for such an office. But the council probed the heart of the matter by asking the farmers to specify how such officers would gain the cooperation of colonial governors. However, the farmers got little help. The Privy Council invited the farmers to appoint, send, and pay for the requisite under-officers, but did not even send out the letter to each governor, recommended by the plantations council, enjoining their support for these officers. Rather, the officers themselves were to 'apply . . . to the respective governors for their allowance, advice, and care herein'. No doubt wisely, the farmers did nothing; had the under-officers been appointed and sent to America, their authority would have approximately equalled the warmth of their colleagues' welcome at Carisbrooke.[59]

It was a significant comment on Restoration government that customs farmers could not lay down the law to royal governors either in America or in England. Lines of authority flowed from one agency of government to another not directly but through the Privy Council. This was as Clarendon intended, but as a system of government it did not work very well. Quite apart from the question of whether the Privy Council could have coped with the mass of detail, its authority to enforce its decisions had been considerably circumscribed through the loss of the prerogative courts. Nor, by the same token, could it enjoin its decisions on local magistrates as precedent or policy, save by the cumbersome process of removing or replacing the recalcitrant. This was a pervasive problem, extending to far more than revenue matters: witness the fine disregard shown by local courts for the crown's wishes in the matters of whether, when and how far to enforce the penal laws in religion against Protestant dissenters and Catholic recusants. Local authorities, it seemed, were secure enough to obey royal commands when they wished to do so.[60] This suggests that we are dealing with a political as well as an administrative problem.

This problem was of crucial importance to the empire, and to understand why we must return to the fact that the 1660 settlement involved more than the return of king and parliament. Through the prerogative was restored a host of local institutions and a system of office-holding which made of power a right, in some cases a form of property. For a political nation which had suffered too much the intervention of central government and armies in its local bailiwicks, this seemed right almost beyond question. There can be little doubt that Clarendon was committed to this view. By design, King-in-Council governed England not directly but through the county lieutenancies, justices of the peace, municipal and trading corporations, patent officers, garrison governors, and customs farmers. That these disparate organs of government often proved resistant to command might exasperate Clarendon but can hardly have surprised him. Thus Presbyterians, even Puritans, might find their way into the lieutenancies, the commissions of the peace, and, despite the operations of the Corporations Act, into municipal boroughs. Once there, they enjoyed all the protection that the tradition of local autonomy could provide. Many of the king's party did not like it, and even after all the purges complaints flooded back to the secretaries of state and to the Lord Chancellor. Norfolk, Sir Robert Hyde wrote to his cousin Clarendon in 1664, was like 'linsey woolsy, mixed with Good, and Badde . . . but the Comfort is, that the greatest part of the Better sort stand well Affected'. Distant Massachusetts may have been worse, but then so was Suffolk,[61] a county which, nevertheless, like the others, had been restored to the old ways of local government, its boroughs governed by chartered corporations, its country districts under the care of a lord lieutenant and the justices of the peace.

The Restoration itself owed something to the residual strength of the system, and the imperial restoration carried out by Clarendon was to prove, too, that English local government in America still shared the same presumptive right to corporate identity and autonomy. The next chapter will deal in detail with Clarendon's imperial restoration; here it is important to point out some immediate similarities between domestic and colonial rule. The colonies of Clarendon's empire were, like

England's counties and towns, autonomous, subsidiary agencies of the English crown licensed to carry on the business of governing Englishmen in America. They owned no other authority than that of the crown, and as Governor Culpeper had proven on the Isle of Wight that did not necessarily extend to obeying others who served the crown in a different capacity. Chartered colonies exploited this autonomy more readily than royal colonies, but all proved adept at it. As during the Interregnum, however, colonists in Clarendon's empire could find that autonomy had its drawbacks. It was not only customs farmers who had cause to complain of the unresponsiveness of central government to the problems of governing America.

Cries for help came particularly thick and fast during the second Dutch War. Virginians found the response not only stingy but downright troublesome. The king's commands for the defence of the tobacco colony strained its finances and also displayed lamentable ignorance of Chesapeake geography, apparently assuming that a fort at Point Comfort could command the entrance to the Chesapeake. Whoever was to blame, the Dutch sailed in unhindered to make mincemeat of the tobacco fleet in 1667, and Virginia's elite worried that a poor, discontented and armed populace might seek to solve the resulting problems in its own way. Meanwhile, Jamaica's Governor Sir Thomas Modyford found English aid so meager that he was forced back into dependence on the privateers for the island's defence, or so he claimed. This hazarded the declared aim of both Charles II and Modyford to establish civilian, planter supremacy on the island.[62] Lack of military support thus undermined colonial governments' political as well as their strategic security.

This was the experience of the royal governor of Barbados, Francis Lord Willoughby, whose assembly refused to give a supply for arms and fortifications without attaching conditions which Willoughby believed damaged the prerogative. Willoughby charged the Assembly with dancing to the tune of the Long Parliament (a familiar refrain) and sent the chief miscreant, Speaker Samuel Farmer, to be tried in England on a charge of high treason. Farmer was allowed to cool his heels in Oxford jail, which cannot have been pleasant but was healthier than plague-ridden London, and then was brought before the Privy Council in March 1666. Clarendon would later find his treatment of Farmer included in the articles of impeachment brought against him, probably because the Lord Chancellor had insisted that Farmer had 'no tytle to any other Lawes than what are constituted' in Barbados. If that doctrine made Clarendon's government arbitrary, it also left Willoughby's government without the aid it needed. Clarendon worried that a man like Farmer could have made himself so popular, but, satisfied that the Speaker was 'much mortified', sent him back to the island unpunished. The only comfort Clarendon offered to his friend Willoughby were musings on the ungovernableness of Englishmen and his regrets that Willoughby had 'no Fort or Castle there of strength to resort to in case of suddaine danger [of] Invasion and Insurrection'. It was an ironic reply to make to Willoughby's request for military aid.[63] There is more to say of Clarendon's government of the colonies, but the Farmer episode suggests that colonial dissidents had little to fear from the way in which the Lord Chancellor might use his power to invade local liberties. As significantly, colonial loyalists had little to gain.

Restoration government reverted to tradition by regarding colonies as corporate entities in the economic as well as in the political sense, again with corresponding advantages and disadvantages for local governments. Thus Clarendon and Charles offered Massachusetts the reward of further economic privileges should the General Court agree to resubmit its charter; probably they did not know that the Bay Colony had long since opened economic privileges to non-freemen.[64] Clarendon also responded to the economic problems of the plantation colonies by treating the colonies as if they were trading companies capable of entering into contracts in order to regulate the sugar and tobacco trades. Colonists demanded reforms; sugar prices had fallen to the point where even Barbadians were complaining, and Virginia, utterly dependent upon the cheaper tobacco staple, was in a sorry state. Pressure for reform also found some support from London sugar and tobacco merchants. In 1663, Lord Willoughby gained royal approval for a scheme to regulate the sugar trade by contract between colonists and merchants. The scheme came to nothing, but it clearly assumed that island governments possessed corporate economic powers and encouraged their use towards an end which combined Stuart paternalism with self-interest. A guaranteed price for sugar would help colonial producers, while assurances that the whole crop would be purchased and returned to England held obvious benefits for the royal exchequer.[65]

Similar considerations governed restoration England's first approach to the tobacco problem. Colonial self-sufficiency and prosperity was the aim, and Charles II obligingly wrote into Governor Berkeley's 1662 instructions several of Berkeley's ideas as to how these good things might be secured. A year later the Carolina proprietors endorsed similar propositions for their new colony, and the exalted status of the proprietors (who included Clarendon, Albemarle, and Ashley, as well as Berkeley) suggested a general commitment at court to these aims. Tobacco production was to be stinted, agriculture diversified, urbanization encouraged, and in this colonial governments were to play a major and essentially contractual role. Significantly, both tobacco and sugar schemes bore striking resemblance to Charles I's efforts to regulate the tobacco trade in the 1630s. Despite the navigation acts and the apparently clear dictates of the Restoration revenue settlement, despite the inherently open and expansive nature of the sugar and tobacco trades, conservative habits of thought about the colonies had clearly persisted into the 1660s and were reinforced by the cast of mind which characterized the Clarendonian restoration.

The Virginia proposals ran aground principally because Charles II's deepening financial plight rendered unacceptable any scheme likely to limit the total tonnage of tobacco flowing through his customs houses.[66] There were also important colonial obstacles to contractual schemes for both sugar and tobacco. Difficulties experienced in Virginia and the islands underlined once again the fact that the preferred solution was to increase production; it seems likely that only well-established producers favored stints or other forms of limitation. We hear no more of limitations from Barbados, unless limitations of sugar production on the other English islands. Virginians, however, persisted in their efforts, and learned a further lesson. Tobacco was produced in more than one colony, and even should the crown give positive help to Virginia, neighboring Maryland stood ready to take up the slack and drain Virginia of energy and resources. Virginia's London agent put it clearly to Clarendon: 'By not bringing both Countryes [Virginia and Maryland] under one Standard, wee cannot have benefitt of any Act of Grace'. The agent disclaimed, probably disingenuously, any desire to make Maryland subordinate to Virginia, but begged that both colonies might be made equally subordinate to the crown. Clarendon, as a Carolina proprietor, was willing to participate in a stint, but he would not infringe on proprietorial rights in Maryland by forcing the acquiescence of Lord Baltimore's government.[67]

Baltimore's revenues depended on the volume of trade leaving St. Marys, so the outcome demonstrated that in England's empire local autonomy could benefit one colony while frustrating another. Jamaica's Governor Modyford, not at all averse to exploiting autonomy when it suited, also learned of its drawbacks. Modyford and the crown knew that the island colony needed planters and support if it were to survive the dangers represented by Spain on the one hand and its own privateers on the other. Royal revenues arising in Barbados were to provide the help, and before Modyford went to Jamaica he asked that his own instructions bind Governor Willoughby to pay up. This request was explicitly denied by the Privy Council. Clarendon preferred gentle persuasion and 'hoped' that Lord Willoughby would follow orders to pay £1,000 towards the settlement of Jamaica. Two years later, Modyford despaired of ever getting the money from the sovereign colony of Barbados. By Cromwell's design, endorsed by Charles II, Barbados was to have been the parent, or at least the guardian, of Jamaica, and Jamaica's public seal read in part 'Indus Uterque Serviet Uni'[68] It is difficult to think of a motto more inappropriate to the Restoration empire, marked as it was by the corporateness of each petty government.

* * *

In the empire as at home, then, Restoration government operated according to other necessities than the Navigation Act and the revenue settlement. However, it was the nagging question of the revenue which more than any other factor brought Clarendon down and opened the way for new departures in the politics of empire. As we have already seen, indebtedness made the Lord Chancellor vulnerable to criticism; the Earl of Bristol's impeachment scheme had included a promise via Bristol's commons ally Sir Richard Temple to increase the annual revenue to £2,000,000 per annum through better parliamentary management. In 1663, Charles had sense enough only to listen, but get-rich-quick schemes were in the air, and as sober a politician as Ashley lent some support to Bristol's rash plan.[69] Bristol's timing was amiss, but he judged his royal audience correctly, for Charles was susceptible to the attractions of quick, dramatic solutions to his financial problems.

Many leading politicians shared Charles's eye for windfall profits. The Royal African Company, its 1663 charter a revived variant of the old Guinea Company, was one result. To be sure, the African Company looked towards long-term benefits: securing for the plantations good supplies of cheap labor, increasing colonial production and trade, and breaking into the Spanish slave trade, an historic goal of the English in the Caribbean. Charles endorsed these goals not only by giving the company its charter but also by issuing appropriate instructions to colonial governors.[70] However, the charter cost Charles nothing. Just so, these potential gains did little to relieve his immediate needs. The tedious business of supplying slaves on credit to debt-ridden planters was undoubtedly less attractive than the Royal African Company's plans to plunder West Africa for gold and ivory. Such schemes, which also included giving the Dutch a knock, promised quick profits and glory and may help to explain why company stock proved such a popular investment at court. Charles himself pledged £6,000, and the Duke of York (named governor in the first charter) and Prince Rupert headed up a distinguished list of courtier-promoters. Investors' motives doubtless varied, but circumstances suggest that the speculative flutter for gold and ivory, cargoes which were to be returned directly to England, outweighed the slave trade. Certainly both Charles and James had already tried their hands at similar short-term and semi-private ventures to West Africa, and several of the noble proprietors of Carolina invested more in African Company stock than they did in their infant American venture.[71]

The African Company's attempt at a Gold Coast coup failed, but was prelude to a more dramatic effort to improve crown finance, the second Dutch War of 1665-67. Of course it will not do to treat this war simply as a result of Charles II's penury. England fought Holland three times during the third quarter of the century, and the commercial rivalry which was a fundamental condition of all three wars encompassed far more than concern with the desperate state of English public finance.[72] Yet in the early 1660s, the fiscal motive assumed particular importance. Not only might a successful war lead to increased trade revenues, but a popular one might get more money out of parliament. Young men like Charles and James chafed at their poverty and the inaction it enjoined upon them, and such royal impatience was played on by others. The financial imperative figured in justification for the 1664 expedition against New Netherlands in America. Too much colonial tobacco and thus too much royal revenue was being siphoned out of the navigation system by the Dutch colony. Those who favored the expedition overestimated the amount of revenue lost through Manhattan, and even their guess (£10,000 per annum) was small in relation to Charles's overall revenue problem. However, their arguments attracted a king who had been forced to contemplate economies in his household and diet, economies no less demeaning for being small ones.[73]

It is possible that Charles endorsed the New Netherlands caper because he thought he might get away with it. A general war against the Dutch was another matter, suggesting more caution and a better rationale. Charles turned away from caution and towards enthusiasm for various reasons. Caution was Clarendon's policy, and Charles was attracted to the war hawks at court in this as in other matters. Furthermore, the Dutch had offended national sensibilities, and for a king already being unfavorably compared to the late Oliver foreign militancy had its attractions. The logic of short-term fiscal benefits from war was raised again, as in Oliver's day, in arguments that maritime prizes might themselves pay for the war. London's Lord Mayor noted hopefully that the last war with the Dutch had produced nearly a million this way. Charles was perhaps too sensible for all this, but he did aim to get substantial prize monies, while the Duke of York's naval operations during the war have justly been called piratical. Meanwhile, the king noticed a great appetite for war 'in both this town and country, especially in the Parliament men', and suddenly the claims of the war hawks, notably Sir Henry Bennett, that they could manage parliament better than could Clarendon, began to hold promise. In November 1664 parliament voted a war subsidy of £2,500,000, larger than Bennett (now

Earl of Arlington) had thought prudent to ask for and, indeed, the largest ever given an English king.[74]

That the enemy was Holland helps explain parliament's generosity. Whatever had been the case under the Commonwealth, Dutch protestantism was now no bar to war. The Cavalier Parliament had already made abundantly clear its view that presbyterianism and republicanism had much to answer for, and had not the Dutch Republic snubbed the king's nephew, the Prince of Orange? To this and other insults, the Dutch added the injury of being prosperous while England languished. A successful war would bring more trade to England and reduce the dependence of English producers upon Dutch middlemen. This, many felt, would increase landowners' rents as well as the king's revenue. Charles accurately played on these hopes and fears when he explained to parliament the reasons for Anglo-Dutch hostility.[75]

The level of rents was an understandable obsession for landed parliament men, but the king's revenue was also important. We have seen that parliament believed the king ought to have enough and had voted some additional revenues while concentrating heavily on enabling and enforcement legislation. Still the ordinary revenue had failed to reach the desired level of £1,200,000, and the Cavalier Parliament had already laid four separate direct taxes to meet resultant needs. If direct taxes were not to become a permanent part of England's public revenue, something had to be done to bring trade revenues up to expectations. By 1664, an increase in the level of customs duties remained about the only legislative solution still unexplored, and this ran against the conventional wisdom that such duties might reduce the level of trade and might do so to such an extent as to reduce revenues. Indeed, it was a settled belief that Dutch prosperity owed much to low customs duties.[76] In part then, parliament's enthusiasm for war was a direct extension of the logic which in 1660 had led the Convention's Speaker to say of the benefits of the Navigation Act that when overseas trade 'is ours, your majesty cannot want it', to which Lord General Albemarle now added the codicil, 'what we want is more of their [Dutch] trade'. Parliament's willingness to invest still more and greater assessments in the war effort owed to hopes that when Dutch trade were England's, the king would no longer need land taxes.

The hopes which moved king and parliament to make war on Holland were soon dashed. After initial successes, the war went badly; worse, it went on, reaching its nadir when the Dutch raided the English fleet at anchor in the Medway. Trade was disrupted for too long, and then the plague and the fire of London did further economic damage. Parliament perforce added to its original subsidy, mainly through land taxes. As demands grew for a new form of direct taxation which fell less heavily on land, parliament increasingly suspected that the vast sums raised for the war had been misspent or embezzled. Soon enough the constitutional nightmare that had informed Clarendon's original diffidence over the revenue question was realized. The claims of Clarendon's enemies that they could manage parliament into a greater generosity became rearguard actions to fend off demands for a parliamentary committee of account.[77]

The king had little choice but to acquiesce, with consequences to be discussed in Chapter 7, but it was clear that ill humor had crept back into English politics. Parliament's willingness to sustain the government through direct taxation waned and, with it, commitment to the settlement of 1660. Clarendon was the chief individual casualty of these changes in political temper, not least because the style and substance of his government was widely thought to have contributed to the disasters of the mid-1660s. This was of course unfair. The whole nation had celebrated the restoration of the old constitution and the sometimes archaic forms that went with it. That the restored monarchy had survived at all, after so many false settlements in the 1650s, was tribute to the Lord Chancellor's success and one with which he had to rest content in his exile.

★ ★ ★

The financial and commercial aspects of Clarendon's Restoration settlement may logically have recommended a centralized administration of trade and plantations. Here lay the king's own estate; the navigation laws gave him ample powers to govern it, while the fiscal settlement gave him a pressing motive to use these powers. By the end of the reign, considerable centralization had occurred, but it is historians' guesswork to say that Charles's early parliaments intended such developments to proceed from their legislation. Except for a few enforcement provisions imposed on colonial governors, the colonies were not mentioned in the laws and trading company governments were not mentioned at all. Parliament's clearest invasion of corporate government came in the form of the Corporations' Act of 1661, and the House of Commons' rejection of the Lords' amendments reminds us that it was an equivocal invasion. In the end, the Corporations Act proposed only to oust disloyal persons from corporations, not to change the method of corporation government. Nor did parliament want centralized control of members' own county domains, far less of their own lands. Certainly noble lords, gentry commoners, Lords Lieutenant, and JPs reckoned to combine loyalty with local autonomy.

The Restoration settlement was constitutionally unconditional, and sovereignty was restored to Charles by right. Imperial history must give that point due weight, but beneath the pleasing rhetoric Charles II exchanged with the nation in 1660 there were important implied conditions. Englishmen may have felt that they had lived through a facsimile of Hobbes's state of nature; they may have accepted the Restoration in order to escape chaos; but the Breda letters rejected Hobbesian ideas about sovereignty to posit an organic affinity between the prerogative and subjects' liberties and rights. As we have seen, this was not a new departure in English political thought or practice. Recognizing its wide appeal, the exiled court had from the mid-1650s solicited support from moderates in such terms. In 1655, Charles II wrote to Sir Anthony Ashley Cooper that men like him could not rest easy in their own estates 'till I am restored to that which belongs to me'. In 1660, Charles promised the House of Lords that 'We shall be all happy in each other'. Thus Englishmen were reminded that liberty and privilege derived from the prerogative, depended upon it, and had been placed at risk by an unchecked legislature, a usurper's power, and an ungovernable army. The king's assurance from Breda that he did not 'desire more to enjoy what is ours, than that all our subjects may enjoy what by law is theirs',[78] was an auspicious omen for all Englishmen who felt within themselves the habit of command, the rights of property, and the privilege to govern.

No one imposed a Hobbesian solution on the empire, either; indeed Clarendon's regime continued the Cromwellian retreat from the centralizing potential of the Commonwealth's commercial and colonial legislation. Insofar as it did concern itself with trade and the colonies, the new regime was anyway inclined by poverty and inexperience to revert to old forms. Clarendon's conservative views offered another reason to do so, for these old forms did, after all, constitute the traditional liberties and privileges of many Englishmen. The conduct of colonial affairs in the early 1660s would demonstrate that the crown sought the implementation of this political vision. The progress, successes and failures of the Restoration settlement in England, from its roots in the Declaration of Breda, offer a better perspective than do the navigation Acts for those who would explain the early colonial policies of the restored monarchy.

CHAPTER SIX

The Restoration in America

Charles II inherited the English colonies by right, and Restoration parliaments did little to direct or to lessen his powers over his American patrimony. The Navigation Act had limited impact on the crown's colonial decisions, and proposals to annex Jamaica and New England to the crown by legislation came to nothing.[1] Thus, while the crown was forced to adapt to cavalier politics in England, it was free to apply in America the principles of Breda, or any other principles or expedients it cared to follow. How the king would rule his American inheritance was, however, no easy question, and made no easier by the fact that most colonial governments had no extant legal connection with the crown. In 1660, with the ironic exception of Massachusetts, the English colonies were governed by local makeshifts or a usurper's dispensation. Thomas Povey, the aspiring midwife of empire, surveyed the scene and despaired.

Empire there was, however. Its reality would be demonstrated by the success of a multiform colonial restoration. The Earl of Clarendon was unconcerned by the rich variegation in form and structure which his imperial restoration recreated. His determination to restore made him no man for Leviathan; but he who would govern Massachusetts as if it were a corporation 'at Kent or Yorkshire' and Barbados by way of saving a lessee's legal rights had a clear enough sense of empire, and it ill becomes historians to cavil if he based his vision on the prerogative rather than on the Navigation Act. Indeed, the flexibility of the prerogative was an asset for an inexperienced regime which confronted colonies as different from one another as Barbados and Massachusetts.

Such differences insured varied colonial responses to the Restoration. But there were common patterns, too, and to understand these we must recall some pre-1660 colonial history. Colonists' position in the Atlantic economy required them to expand production and population and to regard as essential free access to trade. In England such ideas had coalesced into the beginnings of an economic liberalism which had helped to energize revolutionary radicalism in the 1640s. However, with the possible exception of Rhode Island, colonial elites did not rush to embrace such dangerous thoughts. Instead, they discovered an organic connection between their social survival and their ability to use public power to restrict the freedom, economic and otherwise, of their neighbors, white, red, and black.[2] Some colonial elites succeeded better than others, but disorders of the Interregnum inclined most colonial rulers to welcome a conservative restoration in England. Their positive responses eased Clarendon's work and help to explain an interesting contrast between Clarendonian purposiveness and Cromwellian diffidence in imperial affairs. Within three years, the great work of restoration in America was completed; every English colony was ruled by new or renewed royal grant. Furthermore, Clarendon's ministry saw the creation of new colonies, so that by 1665 the North American coastline was solidly English, at least as men draw maps, from Nova Scotia to Carolina. Only in Massachusetts did the crown fail to win full acknowledgment of its sovereign power. We need to study Clarendon's successes and, more closely, this single apparent setback to explain the politics of the early Restoration empire.

* * *

Seen merely as a change of regime, the Restoration discomfited many in America. Thomas Modyford's commission to govern Barbados in the name of the Council of State now became downright dangerous, while in Virginia and Maryland William Berkeley and Josias Fendall prepared their apologies for accepting authority from their local 'parliaments', now a discredited basis for government. Alarm was, however, most widespread in Puritan New England. Roger Williams saw the Restoration as another defeat for world protestantism, a cosmic event presaging worse to come: 'The bloody whore [of Rome] is not yet drunk enough with the blood of the saints and witnesses of Jesus'. More prosaic souls feared that the king would send a governor-general to invade their civil liberties and destroy their churches. Some counselled defiance, such as one Joseph Jenks, who vowed that 'if he had the king heire he would cutt off his head & make a foot ball of it'.

However, Jenks's sporting proposition brought him only trouble from the Massachusetts authorities, who also thought it best to call in and condemn a book by the Reverend John Eliot which 'too manifestly scandalized the government of England, by King, Lords, & Commons'.[3] There was more to this than mere prudence. For one thing, Puritans' anxiety about the Restoration was tempered by disillusionment with

England's republican experiments and with the religious radicalism which seemed to have reduced the mother country to chaos. John Davenport of New Haven reported a story that some Fifth Monarchists, seeing Christ had not yet come, had *per interim* anointed Sir Henry Vane with oil and proclaimed him king of Jerusalem. Davenport was sickened at the heresy but wryly concluded that 'men, it seemes, are serious about setting up Kings'. On 30 May 1660, ignorant of the day's events in London, the Massachusetts General Court proclaimed a day of humiliation primarily for the sake of old England, threatened as she was by 'those horrid blasphemies & wickednesses that there abound'. Puritans usually reserved that sort of language for their own lunatic fringe and rarely applied it to the Presbyterians who, New Englanders believed, might be preparing the ground for monarchy.[4] News that England's troubles might be over inspired some relief; even a Stuart might be a lesser evil than a blasphemous king of Jerusalem.

There were also many in New England who positively preferred a Stuart's dispensation to continued dependence on Interregnum expedients of government. They quickly concluded that the imperial role played in New England since 1640 by Massachusetts and its royal charter was now at an end. For twenty years, the Bay had provided a point of reference for colonial government, absorbing New Hampshire and Maine, threatening Rhode Island, and leading New Haven, Connecticut, and Plymouth in the United Colonies of New England. In 1659, the land speculators of the Atherton Company understood the region's political geography well enough to appeal to the United Colonies to approve their purchases in the Narragansett region, also claimed by Rhode Island. The United Colonies were glad to confound Rhode Island's claims and to help a company which included such prominent citizens as Connecticut's Governor, John Winthrop, Jr. In earlier disputes Rhode Islanders had sought help from the Earl of Warwick and then from Cromwell, but who would hear them in England in the troubled winter of 1659-60?[5]

The Restoration provided the answer, and not only for Rhode Islanders who quickly proclaimed Charles II and petitioned for his protection.[6] Predictably, the Atherton Company was not far behind, for the United Colonies' sanctions were now not enough to legitimate its land claims. Governor Winthrop surveyed the expedients upon which Connecticut's government rested and also made plans to carry his colony's case to the throne. New Haven's Governor William Leete wished him well and, naively as it turned out, hoped that Winthrop might gain for New Haven privileges similar to those he sought for Connecticut. For twenty years colonists had recognized the authority of the Massachusetts charter. Now, whatever they thought of Charles II, they knew what the restored prerogative might do for them. By their own acts New Englanders shifted the hub of their political universe away from Boston and towards London. And Charles responded. In 1663, upon receipt of their new royal charter, Rhode Islanders reported the event to Massachusetts in a letter which, with transparent satisfaction, spoke of their own 'General Court' and of the king's grace to them.[7]

Such royal interventions affected intra- as well as inter-colonial politics. Rhode Island had suffered much from internal dissension, and the new General Court aimed to use its charter to bring that to an end. Although many of these colonists in government were Quakers, they proved to be adepts at political ceremonial. They ordered that the

> box in which the Kings gratious letters were enclosed be opened, and the letters with the broad seale therto affixed, be taken forth and read . . . in audience and view of all the people . . . and the sayd letters with his Majestyes Royall Stampe, and the broad seale, with much becomming gravity held up on high, and presented to the perfect view of the people.

thus was authority crowned in Providence,[8] and we are reminded, as were onlookers, that the power of the king's charter was not equally shared by all colonists. Likewise, Connecticut's royal charter of 1662, with its liberal definition of citizenship, promised much to those who wished to ease access to church privileges. Thus emboldened, the General Court asked, not altogether politely, 'whither it be not the duty of the Court to *order* the Churches' to adopt broader admission policies.[9] Such episodes demonstrated that the restoration carried threats and promises which were differently perceived by different colonists. In Maine and New Hampshire, some held power under Massachusetts authority while others petitioned the crown for release from the Bay's yoke.[10] New Haven was divided, too. The colony briefly played host to the regicides Goffe and Whalley, and Governor Leete's tentative approach to Winthrop suggests a desire to keep a distance from the monarchy. In May 1661, one magistrate took his oath on condition that he might be excused from office 'in case any business from without should present', and not until August could New Haven's General Court bring itself to proclaim Charles II. However, other New Havenites seized upon the promise of the Restoration to complain that John Davenport's Christian Commonwealth had denied them their 'just priviledges and liberties'.[11]

Poor New Haven: while Rhode Island's charter helped to protect that colony from its neighbors, New Haven, a full member of the United Colonies, was swallowed up by Connecticut's new charter. No doubt the inhabitants of New Haven who had complained about their loss of liberty were now among those who quickly applied to be taken under the more liberal Connecticut charter. New Haven complained to its confederates, but without effect. Its last, despairing protest of March 1664 recited all the colony's touchstones of legitimacy; it included a letter from the Warwick Committee recognizing its existence and signed, New Haven lamely added, by two who were now members of Charles II's Privy Council. However, the Restoration made redundant these old expedients, as New Haven's rulers acknowledged when they fell back on a peculiar reading of the Connecticut charter to justify their independence: 'in a just Grammaticall construction . . . this Colony. . . may be Mathematically demonstrated to be' outside the charter bounds. A year later, however, faced with possible absorption into another royal creation, proprietary New York, New Haven 'Mathematically' preferred to be within Connecticut's patent.[12] The United Colonies continued to exist, and in 1675 would perform fairly well in King Philip's War, but it could not reconstitute New Haven colony. Its function as an ersatz imperium had passed to Charles II.

Outside New England, in the Chesapeake, the Restoration quickly transformed and, for a time, quietened politics. In Virginia, the king's commission to Governor Berkeley rendered irrelevant the debates of the 1650s over the proper basis of public authority. The governor and council were restored to their old pre-eminence and even given limited powers of taxation. Charles was joyfully proclaimed, and the anniversaries of his nativity and his fathers' execution were given their appropriate symbolic functions. Over the next two years Virginia's laws underwent substantial revision, with a noticeable emphasis on insuring conformity between the colony and the restored monarchy.[13] Meanwhile, on 3 July 1660, Charles had ordered Virginia's governor and council to assist Lord Baltimore in recovering Maryland from Josias Fendall. Supremely confident that the king's return would secure his rights in Maryland, Baltimore had already revoked Fendall's commission as governor, appointed his brother Philip Calvert in Fendall's stead, and directed Calvert to declare a general pardon. Unlike King Charles, Baltimore named Fendall and several others as traitors who should be excepted from this indemnity, but he gave Calvert enough leeway to achieve a bloodless restoration in Maryland. Fendall gamely attempted to govern in the king's name, but by December 1660 Maryland was again Lord Baltimore's. Calvert tactfully thanked Governor Berkeley for his undoubted willingness to help restore the proprietary, but that help had not been necessary. Fendall's stout party of 'Mutiners' collapsed on sight of the royal letter. As they and Governor Calvert understood, the reimposition of the Maryland proprietary was part and parcel of 'his Majesties reinthronement, and [Berkeley's] restauration to the Government of Virginia'.[14]

This widespread perception established significant patterns in imperial and colonial politics. In America, local settlements were not forced by the crown or resisted by colonists. Instead, ambitious local leaders sought royal legitimation, and when they were successful a new charter, commission, or royal letter proved sufficient to establish them in authority even where there were deep local divisions. The Restoration offered them a chance they could not refuse to achieve political legitimacy, to establish law and order within or to resist pressures from without their bounds. Clearly, for Englishmen in America, monarchical tradition had considerable pulling power; and, as in England, the restoration in America pulled some into power and pushed others out. In practical terms, the settlement in the Chesapeake confirmed the ascendancy of a new elite in Virginia, while in Maryland Baltimore saw to it that the upstarts of the 1650s should no longer share in the political process. Rhode Island's 1663 charter enthroned quakers and anabaptists, an irony given events that same year in northern England, while in Connecticut the charter of 1662 not only destroyed New Haven's separate existence but, as John Davenport saw, weakened the cause of strict congregationalism throughout the region.[15]

In each settlement, the crown demonstrated its preference for traditional forms of colonial government and, in Virginia and Maryland, for the actual persons who had enjoyed Charles I's trust. Despite the fears which the restoration instilled in men like John Winthrop, Jr, and Roger Williams, it is hard to see what the crown might have done other than to grant their colonies' requests for charters. Clarendon's aims of continuity and legitimacy insured success for Winthrop and Rhode Island's agent John Clarke. Written by the agents themselves, the charters confirmed existing governments and privileges, but also (like the proprietary charters granted during the 1660s for the new colonies of Carolina, New York, and the Bahamas) marked a return to the old means of governing the empire; they granted privilege and power to colonists in return for the time, energy and money they had invested in the enterprise. The only major change from the substance of Charles I's charters was the absence of exclusive commercial privileges.[16] If the new charters thus implicitly recognized the Navigation Act, they more clearly rejected the logic of the Commonwealth's plantations act of 1650 and demonstrated to colonists the advantages of a monarchical empire based on contract between crown and subject.[17]

But in concentrating on the fringe settlements of New England, Maryland, and Virginia, we have followed the line of least resistance. Elsewhere in America, restoration was to prove more difficult, the necessity for direct political intervention more pressing. In the cases of Jamaica, the Caribbees, and Massachusetts, choices were not easy or automatic for either the crown or colonists.

* * *

The West Indian islands draw our attention because they occupy so much space in Restoration state papers. This was partly because most of those who advised the crown on colonial affairs had interests in the West Indies: among them Thomas Povey, Martin Noell, James Drax and Thomas Kendall, all members of the committee on trade and plantations created in December 1660. Povey's proposal to establish this council was entitled 'Overtures touching the West Indies', and this more accurately reflected his and his colleagues' interests than the amended version which spoke of all the 'Forreigne Plantations'.[18] This West Indian lobby publicized the great value of the islands, sometimes in terms which strained credulity. Povey, for instance, reported that Jamaica's sheep were mercantilists, producing good mutton but poor wool.[19] Doubtless Charles II was amused by some of these details, but he accepted that the islands were economically important. West Indian wealth and the eagerness of many to tell of it were not, however, the only reasons for dealing urgently with the islands. Also important was the state of island governments. Of all English America, only Maryland in 1660 presented such a picture of political uncertainty. Whatever their commercial prospects, the West Indian islands were politically poverty-stricken, and Jamaica was in a sorry state. Its garrison was in disarray and desperately needed supplies. Moreover, as its commander Edward D'Oyley and others chorused, it required government. This Charles provided. In October 1660 it was decided to commission D'Oyley, and in February 1661 Jamaica became a royal colony.

This was in some respects the most singular of all the Restoration settlements. The royal colony, commonplace in the eighteenth-century empire, was not the preferred form in the 1660s. Jamaica was only the second royal colony after Virginia and, were it not for the Caribbees, would have been the only new royal government before New Hampshire in 1679. Following both precedent and Restoration conservatism, all other colonial grants of the 1660s were made by charter.[20] Why make Jamaica a royal colony? Jamaica's vulnerability to attack and its status as a colony of conquest do not suffice to explain the decision, as New York and New Jersey shared both characteristics yet became proprietaries. Another plausible explanation is that the crown followed the plantations council's advice to reduce all colonies to an orderly and common frame of government, but as the crown failed to follow this advice in all other cases during the 1660s, we may doubt that it was crucial in regard to Jamaica.[21]

There are better explanations for Jamaica's royal status. First, the island was a counter in European diplomacy. In 1656, Charles II had promised to return Jamaica and Dunkirk to Philip IV of Spain upon regaining his throne. Charles did not agonize over this promise, not least because Philip utterly failed to honor his word to help with Charles's restoration; but until Charles had secured his diplomatic and dynastic position in Europe Jamaica's status remained undecided, and it would not do to grant the island to English subjects by charter. Nor, as we have seen, could parliament be allowed a say. Jamaica's English future became more secure when on 23 June 1661 Charles consummated a treaty with Portugal. The treaty not only brought Charles a queen and a rich dowry but also gave European diplomatic recognition to English possession of Jamaica and Dunkirk.[22] Meanwhile, the place had to be governed, and for this Charles commissioned the existing regime under Colonel D'Oyley.[23] Once it was decided to keep the island this interim decision became permanent. Secondly, the common courses taken with other colonies were simply unavailable with regard to Jamaica, where Charles II could not restore the *status quo ante*. Moreover, no one offered to take the colony off his hands via a charter.

This lack of interest in undertaking Jamaica's government was remarkable. While other colonists jockeyed for power in America and sent agents to London to seek charters, Jamaicans only appealed for help.[24] Such schemes for Jamaica as surfaced in London have mainly a curiosity value, notably John Lord Berkeley's bizarre plan for military government by contract and a no less striking idea to establish the Earl of Craven in Jamaica as the largest landlord and cattle baron in the West Indies. The Earl of Lauderdale was interested in a Jamaica scheme which promised the 'inlargeing of his majesties dominions and multiplieing his subjects . . . in a Christian and Heroike way', but his correspondent gave no details.[25] If Lauderdale's idea had to do with the slave trade, it was the only one of the three to be carried further. Even Thomas Povey's interest declined, for he knew too much about Jamaica's present needs to think that a company or a proprietor might take up the burden of government.[26] Povey and his friends were happier to volunteer as provision merchants to the relief expedition they urged the king to send to Jamaica. Drax offered to supply £1,000 worth of brandy, despite advice that liquor killed more men in the island than did disease.[27] One thing all these schemes had in common was that the king was to foot the bill.

Having received no compelling offers from his own subjects or from his royal cousins of Europe, Charles II became master of Jamaica. In the later 1670s, Jamaica's status as a colony of conquest would be used to justify an attack on islanders' privileges,[28] but now Restoration politics ruled even the treatment of Jamaica's Cromwellian soldiers. This was probably not because of Thomas Povey's claim that the garrison contained many loyal men who had been 'forced by their sufferings . . . in his Majesties cause to engage in that designe' and others who had 'cherefully' attacked the island because in 1655 the Spanish king had been Charles II's 'capitall Enimie'. Povey's was a pleasing conceit, possibly drawn from Clarendon's witty observation on the necessity to disband Cromwell's English army: 'the only sure way never to part with them is to disband them'. In England, soldiers would be better employed as 'good husbandmen in the country, and good citizens in the city'.[29] In the same spirit it was decided to pay off most of Jamaica's troopers. The loyalty of soldiers turned sugar planters was something to bank on, and if in Jamaica there was not, as in England, an established gentry class willing and able to pay for disbandment, there was plenty of land to finance it. A different problem was presented by those who had already acquired land on the island, but again Restoration principles applied. Just as the king had promised from Breda to respect rights to English property lawfully acquired during the usurpation, so Jamaican land titles were confirmed to civilians and soldiers alike. To say the least it would have been troublesome to do otherwise, but Charles went beyond this to confirm Cromwell's political promises to Jamaicans. They and their progeny would be English subjects governed by English law; they would have all other rights and privileges of Englishmen at home; and the headright system already in use was confirmed. These guarantees, written into governors' commissions and instructions throughout the 1660s, were in 1661 given the added force of a royal proclamation. As the Earl of Lauderdale observed, the king found his Jamaican subjects in possession and saw no reason to put them out.[30]

Jamaica's potential wealth influenced these decisions. Even those who did not like the place believed that it would eventually benefit the crown. Edward D'Oyley judged Jamaica a killer of Englishmen but 'wonderfull healthfull' for blacks; it would soon return £100,000 per annum to the exchequer. Another lobbyist predicted a healthy future in trade with Spanish America. Charles and Clarendon agreed,[31] but in the meanwhile Jamaica's dilapidated condition meant that it would soak up royal resources. It was therefore significant that few short-term expedients were devised for defraying these expenses out of the island's economy. The three governors who followed D'Oyley, Lord Windsor, his deputy Sir Charles Lyttelton, and Sir Thomas Modyford, were all financed from England. Besides the governors' annual stipend of £2,000, costs arose from disbandment of over half the garrison, fortifications and supply. Reliable sources estimated these at from £20,000 to £50,000. Windsor was sent with £21,200 and promised more if needed, and although Modyford's expenses were reduced as the work of disbandment was finished, he was still allowed £1,500 annually over and above his salary for the maintenance of his government.[32] The crown did expect governors to look to Jamaica for some revenue, for instance from the 400,000-acre royal demesne Charles established in 1661, and Modyford's instructions empowered him to raise a revenue with only his council's consent. However, these were expected to be marginal sources, at least in the early years, and they had other than fiscal functions. The royal demesne was 'a marke of Our soveranity', and Modyford's taxing power was restricted to alcohol and justified as a police and public health measure.[33] More significantly, when Povey's council recommended that all Jamaican goods save those enumerated by the Navigation Act should enter England duty free for seven years, the king improved the advice by granting exemption from English customs on all Jamaican produce and added that there should be no trade duties in Jamaica for twenty-one years.[34] This extended to Jamaica Clarendon's politic acceptance of the English revenue settlement. As Jamaica prospered it would contribute to what the Lord Chancellor called the 'constant growing revenue' which parliament had based on England's overseas and colonial trade.[35]

The principle that conquests fell under the conqueror's absolute power had little impact on the Jamaican settlement. Of course the crown did not slight military matters. The island was open to attack from Spain, which had not yet abandoned its *de jure* claim, and then from the Dutch and French during the war of 1665-67. But to view the decisions which gave Jamaica's governors great powers and the leeway to use them as militarist in inspiration is to make the cart draw the horse.[36] The island's volatile mixture of army riff-raff and pirates required powerful government, but it also possessed the core of what Restoration London regarded as a solid citizenry. Governors were to do nothing to cause these planters 'any unnecessary impediment' or to 'discourage the acces of new planters'. Towards this end, Charles ordered Modyford to release the royal demesne to freehold settlers.[37] Jamaica was to be part of the English polity, and Jamaica's governors got the message. Edward D'Oyley, who ruled the garrison with a rod of iron when he could, returned to London and sensed what his audience wished to hear; what was vital, he assured Clarendon, was to insure civilian government and settlement. Lord Windsor boasted that he had found Jamaica with no civil government and left it 'regulated by the laws and government of England'. Sir Charles Lyttelton strove harder to make a civilian colony, enjoyed a good session with Jamaica's first elected assembly, and made an alliance with its Speaker, Samuel Long. He told Clarendon that islanders were 'apter to be lead than driven', a judgment Long would bear out in his political career. Sir Thomas Modyford was less enamored of Long and of assemblies, more friendly with Jamaica's privateers, but he boasted of his success in attracting planters and understood that he was expected to bring the privateers 'to more humanity and good order'.[38] For Jamaicans, secure land titles, generous trade policies, the settling of an English legal system and royal guarantees of their rights as Englishmen seem to have compensated for the lack of assemblies.[39] For the crown and its governors, the need for an assembly was limited by the sheer impossibility of raising significant revenues locally. Perhaps Jamaica was fortunate in its poverty.

* * *

Charles II might dispense with Acts of parliament for Jamaica's benefit, but in Barbados he required the strict enforcement of those same acts. Barbadians' attempts to escape from the rigors of the Book of Rates and the Navigation Act were doomed.[40] The only trade concession in the instructions to the governor of the Caribbees, Francis Lord Willoughby, was that, as at Jamaica, Spaniards were to be allowed to trade for slaves. Willoughby's instructions also varied from those of Jamaica's governors in the attention given to the collection and accounting of local revenues. Charles might lose money on Jamaica, but the government of the established island colonies was to be profitable.[41] Thus the islands' wealth affected their political settlement. However, it would be wrong to say that Barbadians were too wealthy for their own good, for their wealth helped to make unworkable the crown's preferred solution to the problem of Restoration.

The king acted swiftly to restore his authority in the Caribbees. On 23 June 1660, shortly after his return to England and before he had settled the government of any other colony, the king confirmed Lord Willoughby's leasehold of the Caribbees and ordered colonists to conduct themselves accordingly. The king could not easily ignore Willoughby's title. It derived from a Charles I charter which the Restoration automatically revived, and Willoughby's lease of the charter had been confirmed in 1648 by both Charles II and his father.[42] That Willoughby had been exiled from Barbados by the Commonwealth reinforced his case, and it helped, too, that he was personally known to the king and Clarendon, that he was in London in early 1660, and that those working for a Restoration thought enough of Willoughby to invite him to take his seat in the House of Peers in May.[43]

In spite of all this, Willoughby was in for a rough ride. The Caribbees' history had been long enough to produce a faction-ridden politics, and no faction wanted a reimposition of the proprietary. If no one wanted Jamaica, quite a few were interested in Barbados, so the lease aroused opposition in London, too: 'from the Exchange', from the Carlisle creditors, and from the plantations council. As befitted its sources, this opposition was divided within itself, deeply enough in Barbados that had the king not interceded there might have been a hanging or two. Besides these colonial rivalries, which included inter-island jealousies, no love was lost between islanders and London merchants; and the Carlisle creditors, although they knew that the survival of the proprietary was their sole hope of collecting their decades-old dues, were suspicious of Willoughby. The way in which Willoughby and the crown negotiated a path through this minefield tells us much about the politics of the Restoration empire.

Willoughby's first obstacle was Thomas Modyford, the resourceful incumbent governor of Barbados. His commission was redundant, but he used it to proclaim Charles II and to replace the Commonwealth's with the king's arms in the council chamber. He repealed a law disarming Irishmen and, miraculously, took an oath to enforce the Navigation Act before it was passed in London.[44] Modyford was also well-connected. The Council of State which had commissioned him contained several who became Privy Councillors upon the king's return, including George Monck who soon added to the distinction of being Modyford's cousin the dukedom of Albemarle. Modyford also had ties with London planter-merchants like his brother-in-law Thomas Kendall and John Colleton, soon to be members of the plantations council. Thus fortified, Modyford gambled for place in the Restoration empire by making common cause with colonists who, according to their petition of 2 August 1660, wished for nothing more than to come under Charles II's protection and to return to the freedom of trade they had enjoyed under Charles I. Such blessings would 'make every day to us a Coronation day'.[45] Modyford's quest for power was a significant one. He made much of the fact that he was the first Barbadian governor who could address members of the island's assembly as 'Deare Freinds and fellow Planters'. He opposed the proprietary because of its impact on land tenures; a more direct dependence upon the crown would disencumber titles. He also, disingenuously given his links with Colleton and Kendall, argued that only by securing a charter could the island stop London merchants from establishing their own company and making 'us as poor and comfortless as the unfortunate Bermodians at this day are'.[46] These potent appeals testified to Modyford's long experience of island politics and help to explain sugar planters' opposition to the proprietary.

However, unanimity broke down on how to secure Charles II's 'Imediate protection'. Modyford asked the assembly to raise a revenue in order to obtain a charter 'with such Libertyes and freedomes . . . as New England and Virginia have'. Late in the Interregnum Modyford had condemned just such a petition from Barbados because it demonstrated a desire to cut away from England.[47] But now, operating under different necessities, Modyford argued perceptively that government by charter was more in the style of a monarchical than a republican empire. However, the assembly disagreed with Modyford's program, perhaps because it distrusted him, certainly because it preferred to await events.

The island's petition had yet to be heard, and if it were granted, there would be no need for expense; the king, the assembly thought, would not charge much for a charter. This apparent naivete left Modyford and the Council with little choice but to enter their dissent in the records and to send the agreed petition to London with their agent, Peter Watson.[48] Thus rebuffed, Modyford eked out his tenure until the arrival in December 1660 of the king's letter confirming Willoughby's leasehold and of Willoughby's order to Modyford's old adversary, Humphrey Walrond, to assume power as President of the Council. On 20 December, Walrond and his council proclaimed their authority and took care to proclaim the king, too, even though Modyford had already done that in July.[49] Modyford was committed for trial on treason charges, one of which was that he had accepted authority from a usurped power. Within three years, Modyford's English connections were to gain him a knighthood and the Jamaica governorship, but now they had more desperate work to do. Albemarle interceded with the king, who sent peremptory orders that the Act of Indemnity applied to Barbados as well as to the realm.[50]

Despite Modyford's difficulties, colonial opposition to the proprietary was strong, and here at least there was agreement between the islanders and London merchants, who continued their sniping and widened their range of fire to take in Willoughby's claims to Surinam. They even revived the Courteen claims to the Caribbees and threatened to challenge the Carlisle patent in the courts. The death of the Earl of Carlisle added further uncertainty, for the Earl of Kinnoul, both as legatee and creditor, was interested only in selling his rights to the highest bidder. The defence of the patent would be expensive, and even success would not bring sure rewards for it would make Willoughby, as lessee, directly responsible to the creditors.[51] By March 1661 it had been decided to commission Willoughby royal governor of the Caribbees. However, the king's straitened finances did not recommend a direct resumption of the proprietary charter, which would have transferred to the crown the obligations to the creditors and the inevitable pension to Kinnoul.[52]

Ironically, the means of extinguishing the patent while securing Willoughby's rights was suggested by the London merchants, who offered the crown a permanent income from the islands as the purchase price for ending the proprietary. The merchants' ulterior motive was to make Modyford royal governor of the Caribbees,[53] which may have been why colonists disavowed the offer. Still, the merchants' claim to be acting on colonists' behalf was plausible. Even the Walronds, who had tried to hang Modyford, accepted that the extinction of the proprietary would cost money; compensation would have to be paid in order to secure land titles. What islanders could not agree on was how much, to whom, and who should be governor.[54] In any case, the price they ultimately paid was very near to the 5 per cent duty on exports proposed by the merchants, while the benefit they received was virtually identical to what they had achieved in their bargain with Willoughby in 1650-51. For that bargain, too, had tied security of land titles to the revenue obligations of colonists. Already in 1660 Willoughby had been thinking along the same lines, promising that a new settlement would secure land titles if colonists would make appropriate acknowledgement of the Carlisle patent.[55]

In 1663, the crown imposed a settlement by making an offer colonists could not refuse. Through his commission and instructions to Governor Lord Willoughby, Charles II ordered islanders to ay in perpetuity a 4^1/$_2$ per cent export duty on all dead produce. During the remaining years of Willoughby's lease half of the duty would go to him for support of his government. The other half would go via the crown to the Carlisle creditors. In return, the proprietary was extinguished as were, of course, all tenurial obligations to the proprietary. Each island's assembly followed the royal instructions closely, and St. Christopher, Nevis, Antigua and Montserrat unambiguously accepted the bargain.[56] Barbados's assembly, however, added a clause which tried to insure that all revenue from the 4^1/$_2$ per cent would be spent on the island's government. That much is beyond dispute, as is the fact that neither Charles II nor his successors regarded the clause as binding. Disagreement soon arose (and has persisted) over whether Charles's assent to the act bound him to spend the revenue on island government.

However, the Barbadian assembly did nothing more than to advance towards a position it could neither occupy nor defend. In the first place, no other assembly attempted to appropriate the 4^1/$_2$ per cent, which was a hereditary revenue of the crown as lord of the islands. Secondly, Barbados's 'appropriation' clause was vague and loosely worded. In contrast to the clauses concerning land tenure and the extinction of former rents and arrears, which (as in the Leewards' Acts) were quite explicit and prefaced by the phrase 'be it enacted', Barbados's 'appropriation' clause began with 'and forasmuch', declared it desirable that the revenue should be 'in some measure proportioned to the publique charges' and then listed ways in which public money might be spent. This only paraphrased the king's pious promise (in his instructions) to use the revenue 'towards the support of the Government of the said islands, and to such other uses as his Majestie shall please to assigne the same'.[57] Had Barbadians gone much further, Charles would have vetoed it, for he read the Act carefully enough to veto a clause exempting from the duty a single 10,000-acre estate. One can see why Barbadians would later read the Act differently, but while the Assembly may be credited with a game attempt to tell Charles how to spend his birthright, it did so cautiously as befitted its case.

Until the 1670s, Charles II's half of the $4^1/_2$ per cent came to nil. Thus the Carlisle creditors gained nothing from the settlement of 1663.[58] Otherwise, it was the London merchants who came off least well. Their pleasure at the end of the proprietary was spoiled by Willoughby's success in retaining his perquisites. Moreover, he kept both his proprietary claim to Surinam and the right to annex new islands to his Caribbean domain, despite the claims of merchants and the plantations council that these would divert trade from the established settlements and from Jamaica.[59] However the merchants did enjoy one important success: the king's appointment of one of their number, Francis Cradocke, as Provost Marshal of Barbados. This suggested divisions in the mercantile community, for Cradocke replaced Thomas Povey's brother, but it testified to an original and consistent basis for merchant interest in imperial affairs. Time and again through the 1640s and 1650s it had been reported that the islands were 'scandalously defective' in the 'distribution of publick justice'. This concern deepened when in 1661 the Barbadian President and Council stopped all executions for debt, a high-handed executive act opposed by the assembly, which now made Thomas Modyford its speaker.[60] No wonder that when they recommended Modyford as governor London merchants had told the king that Modyford was a lawyer 'full of justice and ability'; purposeful words, but the merchants had to rest satisfied with Cradocke in post as the island's chief law officer.[61]

Thus, in A. P. Thornton's pithy view, the merchants of the plantations council discussed 'bad debts in Barbados' while colonial governments were settled by the crown.[62] The crown controlled the process and result of the settlement in the Caribbees, which was in the end an assertion of royal sovereignty, not an expression of a specifically imperial policy. Later disputes over the $4^1/_2$ per cent should not hide from us the confusions which were removed. The crown absorbed the proprietary and all creditors' claims and freed island estates from tenurial ties. This ended thirty years of haggling while leaving intact the institutions of government which had evolved under the proprietary. In return, islanders gave the king what he required, a hereditary revenue which, Barbadians hoped, would be 'in some measure proportioned' to the public expense. Neither the Convention nor the Cavalier Parliaments had wished Charles a better gift, nor had they imposed any stiffer conditions on it, nor had they received in return considerations of greater value: the preservation of property and privilege and the restoration of settled government. Meanwhile the king secured the one right he had originally aimed to secure in his orders of June 1660. Francis Lord Willoughby took up the unusual position of royal governor by right for the remaining seven years of his lease, and when he was lost at sea in 1667 his brother William succeeded to both the title and the governorship. All other claimants on the Carlisle proprietary were cast from Charles's thin exchequer on to a no more certain but, crucially, separate revenue which itself had historic roots in the islands.[63] Had it not taken three years, it would have been a display of considerable virtuosity.

* * *

Restoration imperialism faced its most difficult test in Puritan Massachusetts. This was the view of most observers in London in 1660 and early 1661. Had not the regicides Goffe and Whalley fled to Boston? Had not 'diabolical Venner' come from Massachusetts to hatch his rising against the king? The colony's reputation was not helped by its ties with Sir Henry Vane and the Reverend Hugh Peter, the former eventually and the latter immediately excluded from the benefits of indemnity and oblivion, and the wily George Downing had blamed his misdeeds on his New England upbringing in order to obtain safety and favor with the monarchy. Besides dubious old friends, there were plenty of old enemies. The Mason and Gorges families came forward to claim that Massachusetts had robbed them of New Hampshire and Maine. Quakers detailed their sufferings in Massachusetts and asked for royal protection, while the ex-New Englander Samuel Maverick and the Boston merchant Thomas Breedon sought a mixture of revenge and advantage by urging quick action to reduce colonial Puritans to obedience lest they rebel. Nor did Massachusetts help its reputation by waiting until December 1660 to acknowledge the Restoration with a letter to the king. Collecting its reports from such sources, the Council for Plantations urged drastic measures and even asked Charles to consider the sins of New England's sheep, which (unlike Jamaica's) produced wool to compete with the English product.[64]

However, the crown neither implemented nor seriously contemplated any extreme measures. No governor-general was sent, no trade embargo declared, no *quo warranto* entered against the Massachusetts charter. No one in power displayed any great enthusiasm for bringing Goffe and Whalley to justice, and Whitehall was apparently unconcerned about how New England's sheep spent their energy. Sensing this climate, the plantations council moderated its memorandum and then was 'ledd by Instructions' to write to Massachusetts in a sweetly reasonable tone.[65] Even Samuel Maverick learned moderation. The author of several extreme proposals, by early 1662 Maverick was enough on the defensive to collect testimonials from New England merchants and to cultivate or renew friendships with New Englanders in London like John Winthrop, Jr. All this paid off; Maverick became one of the commissioners sent to New England in 1664, while Thomas Breedon, who did not change his tune, lost favor and had to surrender his Nova Scotia claims to Sir Thomas Temple, identified at court as Massachusetts' friend.[66] If Massachusetts's enemies ever possessed the initiative, they lost it in February 1661. On the 11th, the colony's curious but loyal address arrived at court. The next day, an unclear passage in the Navigation Act was interpreted in New England's favor, and on the 15th Charles wrote to Massachusetts in conciliatory mode. Whatever Charles made of the General Court's biblical trope on their shared problems of exile, his reply caught its tone by agreeing that his exile had ended when God touched the hearts of 'our people . . . with a just sense of Our Right'.[67] In May, as if to confirm his friendly overture, Charles put New England business in the hands of a Privy Council committee, again denying to the plantations council a role in settling colonial governments. Moreover, a committee which included conservative royalists like Clarendon as well as Presbyterians like the earls of Anglesey and Manchester and Temple's father-in-law Viscount Saye and Sele would be inclined to favor traditional modes of government and disinclined to punish Massachusetts for its religion.[68]

However, the crown had not made clear its good intentions. Few in Massachusetts could have known that the king's aims did not rest on the whispers of their enemies or the persecuting spirit of parliament. What information they had led many to fear the worst.[69] The royal letter of February 1661 was friendly enough, but it contained a sting in its tail which soon brought a new letter ordering the colony to moderate its persecution of the Quakers and to send them to England where they would be tried 'according to our laws and their demerits'.[70] The General Court obeyed, but this second letter caused consternation and led to the decision to send agents to London to put the colony's case directly to the crown. Ominously, this decision provoked discord, more than had been evident in December 1660. Deputy Governor Thomas Danforth refused to have anything to do with it, and rumor had it that Governor John Endecott felt the same way. The General Court required its agents to promise not to concede or negotiate on any point in their instructions and refused to offer financial or other sureties should things go wrong. Not surprisingly, the agents, the Reverend John Norton and magistrate Simon Bradstreet, nearly refused to go; in the end they went, helped on their way when a few prominent men subscribed £425 to their agency.[71] Already, by late 1661, lack of clarity in the crown's approach and deep divisions among colonists had begun to determine the course of the Restoration in Massachusetts.

Some clarification came in 1662 when Rhode Island and Connecticut won new charters with apparent ease. Agents Winthrop and Clarke found that the king who was even then trying to soften the Bill for Uniformity would deal kindly with dissenters whose governments came under his unchallenged prerogative, and that the Lord Chancellor whose main aim was to restore the king's government to Englishmen would do so by traditional means. They would use neither the letter nor the spirit of the Corporations Act in their dealings with New England colonies. The new charters were part of that process, promised at Breda, of restoring customary links between the prerogative and local governments, between the crown and the rights of Englishmen.[72] If the process were to be extended to Massachusetts, the Bay Colony had to be encouraged to seek a renewal of its charter. This objective would not be advanced by refusing charters to Rhode Island and Connecticut. Equally clearly, Massachusetts presented a different problem and stiffer challenge than had its southern neighbors. The Bay already had a charter which had given it power and prominence within New England, and it was less likely to come to the crown hat in hand.

If Clarendon wanted a voluntary resubmission, he had to convince the Governor and Company that Charles II intended them no harm. Virtually every letter sent to the colony during Clarendon's oversight of New England affairs oozes reassurance. Such long-distance courtship was reinforced by the effusive welcome New England's friends received at court. Besides winning Connecticut's charter, Governor Winthrop received the signal honor of membership in the new Royal Society. Sir Thomas Temple got similar treatment when he accompanied Winthrop to court. Later, in a London pub, while Samuel Maverick fumed in a corner, Temple regaled New England merchants with talk of the king's disregard for 'all those affidavits and oathes that ar given in against the Countrey' and his intention to maintain Massachusetts's 'libertye contrary to expectation'. Temple's news moved one merchant to give good odds (6 to 1) that the Bay's charter was safe, and Temple wrote that 'the King & Chancellor & all the Lords are as zealous for New Englands good as Mr.Wilson is'. No doubt Boston's eldest clergyman was also glad to hear of Clarendon's promise that Massachusetts's 'priviledges charter Government or church discipline' were all safe in his care. To this good news, Temple added that the king, upon hearing that the colony had freed Quakers in obedience to his earlier letter, 'clapt his hand on his breast [and] sayed he intended not soe, but that [you] should not hang them, until further order'.[73]

In June 1662, Charles greeted agents Norton and Bradstreet. The fears which had delayed their departure from Boston proved nearly groundless. The king professed his delight to see them and his pleasure with their addresses. These, if again curiously worded, were clear on two points: Charles II was lord of Massachusetts, and the colony desired from him his 'gracious confirmation of our pattent graunted by your royal predecessor of famous memory'. The king wished that the agents had been given leave to discuss outstanding matters, but so had the agents themselves. In any case, Norton and Bradstreet were sent packing with a royal letter which granted their main request, confirmation of the charter, as amply as any Bay Puritan could have desired. Charles also declared an indemnity for any misdeeds committed by Massachusetts or its inhabitants 'during the late troubles'and withdrew royal protection from the Quakers, which must have pleased John Norton. The king also allowed the colony to reduce the number of magistrates required by the charter from eighteen to ten. This may have been in response to Norton's view that the colony possessed too few gentlemen, and it gave a taste of the new privileges which the colony might gain should it accept the king's invitation to submit its charter for renewal under the great seal of Charles II.[74] However, a charter was a contract as well as a licence, and the king expected Massachusetts to honor its side of the bargain. Any laws derogatory to monarchy were to be repealed; charter rules enjoining the oath of allegiance were to be followed; writs were to run in the king's name. Charles, then trying to convince Anglicans to give toleration to loyal protestant dissenters, insisted on his reading of the charter's provisions for liberty of conscience. Common Prayer was to be allowed to any who wished it, all orthodox protestants were to have access to communion and baptism, and those of competent estate were to have the right to vote. Charles's letter was to be published in the colony, so 'that all our loving subjects . . . may know our grace and favour to them'. Moreover, the king was ready to grant new favors to the colony, 'presuming that they will still meritt the same by theire duty and obedience'.[75]

Not all this was universally welcome in Massachusetts. The king's commands respecting religion and the suffrage raised issues which were already dividing the colony. A major synod had just completed its deliberations as Charles's letter arrived, and its decision to widen the baptismal covenant roused fears about the changes demanded by Charles II. Opponents of the new baptismal rule played on this connection. Some of these 'commonwealthmen' charged that popery was the ultimate objective of all who wished to change the New England way. Such charges were easier to believe because one of the agents had been John Norton himself, a strong supporter of the Half-Way Covenant. To be sure, Norton had in 1661 urged submission to the 'present, and ancient Government of our nation' in order better to preserve Massachusetts's charter and church order, but his loyalty to both was called into question by his warning that without such a submission Massachusetts might become known as 'Sion the Outcast', 'a dry, withered, hapless thing; a barren, and forsaken, and undesirable place and society'. Commonwealthmen would have been surprised at historians' later characterization of men like Norton as 'moderates'. Indeed, we can recognize them as conservatives, men who had drawn little comfort from the direction of New England history and were ready to think, with the Reverend Thomas Parker of Newbury, that Charles II might 'fill the sails of our hopes with the blasts of [his] noble achievements'. Men like Parker, Norton, and Norton's colleague John Wilson were disposed to see some good in the royal letter and to note a connection between those who would deny the king and the sons of Corah who condemned clerical authority in the church and threatened to sink New England in a slough of Morellianism. It is difficult to read such tracts without concluding that some 'moderates' would have preferred sinners of substance to the saints of light as voters.[76]

The king's letter strained the imperial relationship and tested the strength of local consensus. The General Court was plunged into debate, even over the royal command to publish the letter. However, it was agreed that the letter should be published,[77] and the court declared a day of thanksgiving for the king's promise to preserve the colony's civil and religious liberties. The restive inhabitants of Maine were told that they owed obedience to the charter until 'his Majesties pleasure be further knowne', and the court re-enacted one of its less harsh laws against Quakers. As for the royalist Thomas Breedon, he, too, was to feel the sting of His Majesty's chartered authority in Massachusetts. In a reflexive spasm of spitefulness, the General Court fined Breedon £200 and bound him to good behavior for his 'insolencies & contempt ... of the government here established by his Majesties letters patents'. Clearly it made good sense not only to publish but also to use the king's letter, and it is likely that this good sense united commonwealthmen and moderates. There were other agreements, too. The General Court decided to administer an oath of allegiance (of sorts), to expunge antimonarchical laws from its books, and to order that henceforth all writs should run in the king's name. This was neither the first nor the last time that a colony government used a letter from English authority to shore up its own.[78]

The religious issues raised by the king proved more difficult. Discussion began in October 1662, was deferred to May 1663, and then referred to a committee which, if it met, produced no surviving recommendations. Perhaps it was unable to agree on any, for the committee's membership probably reflected the divisions within the colony on these issues. All that the General Court managed in response to the king's more controversial commands was an extremely modest extension of the franchise which pleased no one.[79] Meanwhile, in November 1662, Governor Endecott wrote a temporizing letter to the king which was a minor masterpiece of fiction, but perhaps the best the colony could do without falling apart at the seams.[80] The Bay sought a solution which would be 'sattisfactory and safe': satisfactory to the king and safe for the colony. The General Court could not agree on what was safe, and Endecott's effort to strike the balance did not satisfy the king. Upon reading the letter in April 1663, Charles announced that he would undertake 'to preserve the Charter of that Plantation and to send some Commissioners thither speedily to see how the Charter is maintayned on their part'.[81] This was not a complete surprise, for in 1662 the New England agents had been told that commissioners would be sent to settle inter-colonial disputes, mainly over boundaries, which could not be properly determined in London.[82] However, the king's declaration made it clear that by April 1663 the crown's aims and objectives extended well beyond boundaries. Massachusetts's perverse use of the king's letter of July 1662 guaranteed that political objectives would be central to the Commission of 1664.

* * *

Clarendon's instructions to the commissioners show, however, that the main end of Restoration policy remained unchanged. 'The ground . . . of your employment is the exact observation of the Charters and reduceing to that rule whatsoever hath swerved from it'. The Lord Chancellor was a stickler for form, but he had in mind more than legal punctilio. The commissioners' 'maine end and drift' was,[83]

> to informe yourselves and us of the true and whole state of those several Colonies and by insinuating yourselves by all kind and dextrous carriage into the good opinion of the principall persons there, that soe you may (after a full observation of the humour and interest both of those in government and those of the best quality out of government and, generally, of the people themselves) lead and dispose them to desire to renew their Charters and to make such alterations as will appear necessary for their owne benefit.

A Royal Commission seems a lot of trouble to take in order to convince Massachusetts that it should take out a new charter. This apparent discrepancy has led some to suggest that the commission's real aim was the attack on Dutch New Netherlands, and after a brief stop at Boston, the commissioners did make conquest their first business. Clarendon, however, had the last word, and he told the commissioners that while they might say that their chief business was the conquest of New Netherlands, their true purpose lay in New England.[84] Another possibility is that the commission aimed at a radical centralization of imperial authority, perhaps by entrapping Massachusetts into some indiscretion which might lead to a *quo warranto* and the establishment of royal government.[85] There is no evidence for this view and much against it, including the instructions themselves.

What best explains Clarendon's limited objectives is the English political context. The instructions recall nothing better than the crown's impatience with the Cavalier Parliament's partisan definitions of political and religious loyalty in the Corporations Act and other legislation. The commissioners were not to exploit the 'very great factions and animosityes' within and between colonies. Indeed, they were to beware especially of discontented persons (including any New England cavaliers) they might meet. Colonists' religious preferences were to be respected. Should Massachusetts wish to rejoin the Anglican communion, the king would 'looke upon it as the greatest blessing God Almighty can conferre upon us in this world', but to expect it would not be 'rationall'. Instead, the commissioners were to encourage a more tolerant religious order in New England.[86] We are also reminded of the English Restoration settlement by the instructions concerning the possibility of raising a revenue in Massachusetts. This was not originally the crown's suggestion; agents Norton and Bradstreet had suggested that the colony might make an annual tribute to the crown, 'as masts, corne, and fish'. This would of course please the king, but the commissioners were to countenance no proposals which did not come from the General Court, for no royal revenue could be raised 'by our owne imediate power and authority, without manifest violation of their Charter which wee resolve to keep observe and maintaine'. Nor was any such scheme to 'obstructe the more necessary designe upon [colonists'] obedience and loyalty'. The private instructions bluntly called schemes for a regular royal revenue 'ayrey imaginations'.[87]

The instructions were also cautious in their direct commands. The commissioners were to press the colony to perform the duties expected of it by the king's letter of June 1662, but were given positive powers to insist only upon those matters already conceded, or apparently conceded, in Governor Endecott's reply: the repeal of laws derogatory to monarchy, the imposition of the oath of allegiance, and legal process in the king's name. The commissioners were not directly to challenge the authority of the colony government unless there were a *prima facie* case that the magistrates were proceeding in ways expressly contrary to the charter. The Navigation Act was to be enforced, but the crown had already been assured that Massachusetts was doing this. In all other matters the commissioners were to aim for agreement with the corporation. Even in those difficult religious issues still outstanding from the royal letter of 1662, the commissioners were instructed to wait for a 'due season . . . when you are well acquainted with them' and then 'dexter-ously take notice, and presse the execution and observation' of those royal orders. Even boundary disputes were not to be decided unless the decision either won the consent of the relevant colonies or was mani-festly required by the language of the charters.[88]

Of course the crown had important ulterior motives, as it had in its dealing with English local government. In any new charter, the crown would want to prick the colony governor from a list of nominees submitted by the colony and to appoint the major-general of the colony militia.[89] But these were secondary ('to be wished' and 'wee could heartily wish', as the instructions put it) to that 'more necessary designe' on Massachusetts's 'obedience and loyalty', the 'generall disposeing that people to an entyre submission and obedience to our government . . . leading them to a desire to renew their Charters'. To this end, the commissioners were instructed to discover what new privileges the Bay might wish to have in a new charter.[90] The objectives enjoined on the commissioners, then, were not those of mercantilism or of the cavalier spirit. Rather they drew on the king's promises from Breda to the greatest chartered corporation in the empire, the City of London, to hold out the reward of a new charter and express the hope that

> wee shall looke hereafter upon our Colony of the Massachusetts as within the same limitts of affection duty and obedience to our person & government as if it were as near us a[s] Kent or Yorkshire, and they againe with the same confidence of our care and protection as the other doe.[91]

This was Restoration politics, advancing not a new imperialism nor yet a careless or hapless policy, but an old conception of the king's royal empire. It was one which would have been understood perfectly by the founders of Massachusetts and by Charles I himself.

Clarendon understood that he could not achieve his goals without the support of the existing corporation and other 'principall persons'. He knew that there were ill-affected persons in Massachusetts, but his fundamental assumption was that a loyal party could be raised. This may have been wishful thinking, but Clarendon had been told that a loyal party existed by virtually everyone he had consulted. Samuel Maverick, Thomas Breedon, Sir Thomas Temple, John Winthrop, Jr, Simon Bradstreet, and John Norton disagreed on the location, strength, and nature of Massachusetts loyalism, but they all said it was there.[92] Even so, the commission failed; Massachusetts never applied for a new charter; not only that, but despite its modest objectives the commission was met by virtually unanimous hostility on its arrival in Boston in August 1664. This initial reaction surprised the king and Clarendon, and ought to surprise us, for it raises the question of where the Massachusetts 'moderates' were in the late summer of 1664. Between the August session of the General Court, called to greet the commissioners, and the regular October session, hard-line opposition seemed universal. We might expect that the commonwealthman, Assistant William Hathorne, would spread rumors about the commission with the intention of rousing resistance, but we need to know why he was successful. One of the stronger petitions of this period came from Captain Edward Johnson, who although later identified with the moderates now indignantly rehearsed the colony's successes and the sacrifices which had obtained them, and stated (as became the author of *Wonder-Working Providence*) that all would be lost without the charter and churches which had 'turn'd this wilderness . . . into townes'. Johnson warned the king that 'more compleatness cannot be expected by any inovation'. Petitions came in from the towns urging a hard line, and in October a sort of opinion poll produced over 400 supporters of an intransigent attitude. Even the magistrates ominously proclaimed that those who from within or without denied the power of the charter government were liable to be charged with insurrection. The General Court's petition to the king mixed passion with insolence and even suggested that the commission had been fraudulently obtained. The petition was drawn up by the Reverend Jonathan Mitchell, a leading advocate of the Half-way covenant, and commonwealthmen John Leverett and Francis Willoughby.[93]

That petition brought from the king a sharp reply which is said to have been a reason for the moderates' success in the 1665 elections. The idea has merit, for the General Court did show more tact in its May 1665 session with the Commission, and there was a greater than average turnover in the spring elections. The king's letter, however, did not arrive in Boston until after the election of magistrates, and most towns' deputies were elected before this.[94] What is certain is that by April 1665 colonists knew more than they had known in August 1664, and the most important new information was Clarendon's instructions to the commissioners. In August, the commissioners had shown only their commission and the article of their instructions which ordered an attack on New Netherlands.[95] In the commission, the king gave 'full power . . . to examine and determine all complaints and appeals in all cases and matters as well military as criminall and civill, and proceed in all things' for settling the government of the New England colonies. These powers were limited by the king's instructions and the commissioners' 'good and sound discretion', but in August the commissioners had shown only the second article of their instructions and, Richard Nicolls aside, they did not behave discreetly. Samuel Maverick was an old enemy whose discretion would have sold cheaply at Boston's wharf and not at all in the First Church. The merchant John Hull could scarcely believe what was

happening, for the commission seemed to contradict the king's promises to uphold the charter of 1629 and to threaten the colony with worse
treatment than that experienced by English towns and dissenters under
the sting of cavalier legislation. Conservatives and moderates who had
chosen to believe the king's assurances found it especially easy to hope
that the commission was a forgery or a fraud, for otherwise their position
was discredited. As Hull later noted, the autumn of 1664 was a time
when fear led many 'honest-minded' men to sign commonwealth
petitions which, had they known more, they might have refused.[96]

In its 1665 apologia to the king, the General Court criticized the
commissioners for withholding those instructions which 'direct[ed] and
limit[ed] them in the exercise of their commission in this colony'.
Together with the swaggering behavior of two commissioners, this
'occasioned in the hearts and minds of the people a deep sense of the sad
events threatening the colony, in case the commissioners should improve their power . . . as they feared they would'.[97] These fears were
allayed by the commissioners' unruffled progress through their business
with Connecticut and Rhode Island during the winter, and by February,
some in Massachusetts had seen the instructions; Maverick reported
that 'I am undeceived if . . . I did not undeceive both Majestrates,
Ministers and other considerable persons'. Maverick hoped he had not
been 'over sociable'. Doubtless he had not (he claimed only £10 in
expenses), but it is clear that by 7 April 1665, well before receipt of the
king's February letter, magistrates and ministers had begun serious
preparations for serious negotiations.[98] Having seen the instructions,
many in Massachusetts decided that their first reactions had been
impolitic.

It seems unlikely, however, that this turned the electorate against the
commonwealthmen. After all, the baptismal issue was still bitterly
debated, and the electorate, the body of the lay saints, was successfully
opposing the Half-Way Covenant in most churches. It is more likely that
as the moderates returned to moderation, divisions reappeared in Massachusetts politics. In April 1665, commonwealth petitions came in
from Hadley and Northampton, centers of opposition to alterations in
church and state. Northampton urged the General Court to stand fast
against the commission and 'stand for, confirm, and maintain our
former and ancient rights, liberties and privileges, both in church and
commonwealth (which God himself has bestowed and Christ purchased
for us)'. Stung by criticisms in print and in speech, moderates mounted
a counterattack. In 1664, John Allin's *Animadversions on the Anti-
synodalia Americana* deprecated criticism of the Half-Way Covenant
by some clergymen and by Allin's own church at Dedham, while John
Norton's spirit (he had died in 1663) was resurrected when leading

Bostoners financed a new edition of his *Three choise and Profitable Sermons*, prefaced by John Wilson's ill-tempered poetic diatribe against the 'Corahs' who had made Norton's last years so unpleasant. In the spring of 1665, others, in Salem and Boston for instance, urged moderation on the imperial issue, and the General Court censured Hathorne for his rumor mongering against the commission. Constable Arthur Mason stood in danger of being charged with treason against the king by the General Court for a similar offense, but (ironically) the commissioners urged leniency.[99]

The General Court's tactics in the ensuing negotiations with the commissioners are difficult to identify with either a moderate or a commonwealth stance. The court's attitude was more temperate, and it treated the commissioners as civilly as it knew how, but it also settled down to some hard bargaining. The court seems to have taken the advice given it by several leading clergymen, and indeed by the town of Hadley, which was to strive to please both God and Charles II. It proved difficult to serve two masters well, and on some points the court took a position which was frivolous in the sense that it had chosen not to obey an order of the king and could offer only disingenuous arguments in defense.[100] In general, however, the court's arguments were skillfully arrayed, here unyielding, there conciliatory, but usually based on both the charter and the instructions to the commissioners, sometimes adding a pertinent phrase from one of the king's letters to the colony. Thus the magistrates finally took the full oath of allegiance, but most qualified it by swearing on the understanding that the oath was consistent with their obligations to His Majesty under the charter. The court accepted the commission's authority to examine territorial claims and colony's laws (which is not to say that the commissioners' decisions on these matters were accepted), but stubbornly defied the commission's power to sit as an appellate court. After all, the king had ordered them all to do nothing to infringe the charter, and he had specifically enjoined the commissioners against interrupting 'proceedings in justice, by . . . hearing & determining any particcular right betwixt party & party . . .'. Here the General Court quoted directly from Clarendon's public instructions. No doubt the commissioners were glad that the court had not seen the private instructions, which were even more cautious in this respect. To this, the court added that right reason dictated that the charter (which the king had confirmed and promised to protect) should convey to the magistrates very ample judicial powers, but not a general right of appeal, else how could local authority survive?[101]

It was a good question. Indeed the whole apologetical narrative, which runs to 116 pages in the printed colony *Records*, is full of good questions, precise, measured, and well documented. Religious rhetoric and biblical citations are conspicuously absent from the Court's self-defence. Scholars who argue that the secularization of Massachusetts political thought awaited a later generation in a later crisis would do well to consult the General Court's 'breife narrative' of 1665. What God made of this is beyond the historian's craft, but it was clear that the court's apologia angered the king of England. On 10 April 1666, Charles ordered Massachusetts to send agents to London, two of whom were to be Governor Richard Bellingham and Assistant William Hathorne, commanded on their allegiance to attend.[102] The response to this letter was as significant as the response to the commission.

The distinction between the king's sovereignty and his power to command was an important one, as (for instance) the army debates at Putney twenty years before had shown. What the Massachusetts General Court had done, in 1665, was to base its response to the commission on the same distinction. Only thus could the Court balance allegiance to the crown, adherence to the charter, and resistance to the royal commissioners. It also hewed to the only line it could follow if it wanted to achieve a consensus between moderates like Simon Bradstreet and commonwealthmen like Governor Bellingham. It is possible, too, that moderates actually thought the argument might convince the king. When the king's letter of 10 April 1666 proved otherwise, disagreements between commonwealthmen and moderates came much more into the open. Moderates, freemen and non-freemen, petitioned the General Court to comply with the royal command and send the agents. As the petitioners put the case, all the while protesting their loyalty to the colony government, the charter was a 'frail' ground upon which to base the 'transcendant' immunity implied by a refusal to obey a direct royal command (i.e.the 1666 letter, not the Royal Commission).[103]

A tantalizingly brief report of a debate over whether to obey the king helps us to fix into the context of seventeenth-century English politics and political thought the objectives of the Earl of Clarendon and the response of Massachusetts colonists. In Council, moderate magistrates (Bradstreet, Joseph Dudley, and William Stoughton) accepted that the colony's stand against the commission had been correct, but now argued that the king's direct command must be obeyed. 'I grant legal process in a course of law reach us not in an ordinary course', said Bradstreet, 'yet I think [the king's] prerogative gives him power to command our appearance'. Dudley made much the same point, and reminded his colleagues that 'the king's commands pass anywhere, Ireland, Calais, etc'. For the commonwealthmen (Bellingham, Hathorne, and Francis Willoughby), this was a sinister argument. Dunkirk and Calais were governed by commission, not charters; to grant the king similar powers over Massachusetts would be to give him leave to 'undoe all that he hath done'. In words strikingly similar to the Levellers' arguments at Putney, Willoughby asserted that 'if the king may send for me now, and another tomorrow, we are a miserable people'. For the moderates, Stoughton and Dudley answered as Cromwell and Ireton did at Putney. 'Prerogative is as necessary as law'. 'Corporations in England may lose their privileges, but yet not government, for they have still the laws of the land for their defense'. 'Though no appeal lies to his Majesty . . . yet the king may accept any complaint, and require an answer thereto, so that our absolute power to determine must not abate the king's prerogative'.[104]

* * *

In the end, the General Court sent not agents, but rather two 100-foot ship's masts and yet another loyal address. Writing to Clarendon, Massachusetts's old adversary Thomas Breedon reported the divisions provoked by the king's commands and urged resolute action, which, he said, would either bring the commonwealth faction to its senses or loosen its hold on the well-affected. Breedon claimed that even members of the faction 'were ashamed of theire actions'. He may well have been right. Captain John Pierce, who in 1660 had taken the regicides Goffe and Whalley to their New England refuge but who had already renamed his ship the Royal Exchange, now returned to England with the two masts, which Pierce christened 'the one Governor Bellingham, the other Major Hathorne'. Thus two masts served as types for the agents the crown had demanded. As Breedon pointed out, this was sacrifice rather than obedience, but Charles declared these symbolic submissions 'exceeding acceptable', and he was further pleased when Massachusetts sent supplies valued at £1,200 to victual the Royal Navy in the Caribbean. Thus encouraged, Massachusetts re-annexed the province of Maine, which the commissioners had put under separate government, and in 1668 sent the king twenty-four more masts valued at £1,600, again via the Royal Exchange. Clearly the masts were intended to mollify, and Breedon was right about the implied admission of wrongdoing.[105]

Whether the masts would have mollified Clarendon, by then deposed and in exile, is an unanswerable question. What is evident is that Massachusetts's resistance to the commission of 1664 had stymied the Lord Chancellor. Even in 1666, he could do nothing but call for the colony to send agents, but his objective remained, characteristically, a limited one. In London, the agents would learn 'how farr [the king] is from the least thought of invading or infringing, in the least degree, the royall charter' of Massachusetts. Writing privately to Richard Nicolls, Clarendon issued vague threats of what might happen should Massachusetts disobey, but he had shot his bolt. Never intending that Massachusetts should be governed in any way but by charter, Clarendon was desperately short of sanctions. His policy of restoration had been based on the assumption that there was a loyal party in Massachusetts which was ready to answer the king's invitation, and although he was probably right his commission failed to mobilize that party. Indeed, it did the reverse. Thus Clarendon's Massachusetts policy failed, but it may be more important that he persisted in applying to his most difficult case the same precepts that had governed his approach to the Restoration in England and elsewhere in America. The Lord Chancellor's conservative, contractual approach to government appealed to colonial elites and helped to restore royal sovereignty in America. However, he could win obedience neither from his friend Lord Willoughby in Barbados nor those 'moderates' he hoped to make his friends in Massachusetts. Clarendonian government was not working in England, either. The effects of that perception on English government would profoundly alter the Restoration settlement at home and in America.

CHAPTER SEVEN

The politics of management:
English government and the empire,
1667–1679

In 1667, one of the impeachment charges against Clarendon was that he had 'introduced an arbitrary government in the … plantations'. Restoration bills of impeachment are not notable for their accuracy, and this item has an almost surreal quality about it, but its underlying assumption is noteworthy. If Clarendon was to be guilty of autocracy in English politics, it stood to reason that he must be similarly guilty in imperial politics. Thus the House of Commons recognized, if a little crudely, connection and contingency between realm and empire. Sir Philip Warwick used the same idea when he vindicated expenditure on colonial defence during the second Dutch War. 'So connatural' were these dominions to England that the king 'as soule of the whole body was to provide for the outmost limbs'. Not all agreed that the imperial connection benefitted England, but most accepted that it was 'connatural'.[1] Colonists agreed. Governor Sir Thomas Modyford was but one of a number of colonial leaders who kept closely in touch with English politics. It was even rumored that Modyford moderated his treatment of Samuel Long, Speaker of the Jamaica Assembly, because 'poor Sam' enjoyed the luxury of a patronage connection with that rising star at court, Lord Arlington.[2]

Such beliefs were conventional, but they had been reinforced by events. Clarendon's imperial restoration gave them a reality which was clear even to men of short memory, including those who concocted the impeachment charges against him. For some years after Clarendon's fall, however, a disjunction appeared between English and imperial politics. The 'cabal' period (c.1668-1673) saw Charles II's most ambitious political offensive, a 'Grand Design' by which he aimed to escape from financial dependence upon parliament, rewrite the Restoration religious settlement, and perhaps to make himself absolute in England. Yet there was no imperial grand design which reflected the king's attempt to remake English politics. Not until after Charles abandoned his design and reverted to policies more pleasing to the political nation did the pace of imperial history pick up. This puzzle requires a solution in a study which alleges a close and continuing connection between the politics of realm and empire.

Part of the solution lies in the political framework which grew out of the ruins of the cabal period and the collapse of the 'Grand Design.' The architect was Sir Thomas Osborne, from 1673 Lord Treasurer and created Earl of Danby in 1674. However, we begin with the cabal years, when Osborne and some who would later be his bitter enemies served King Charles's grand design.

* * *

The disasters of the second Dutch War, the plague of 1665 and the Great Fire of London in 1666 left Charles II in a bad position. Far deeper in debt than he had been when the second Dutch war started, he now faced a parliament grown restive if not yet cursed with age. Parliament's committee of account and its insistence during the war on adding appropriation clauses to revenue Acts were ominous signs as, in truth, was the impeachment of Clarendon.[3] Evidently at a stand, the king promised yet another retrenchment of expenditure. Others, hoping to replace Clarendon as the king's chief minister, proposed less painful remedies which might induce parliament to open its purse. The Duke of Buckingham would build a new majority in parliament around a policy of toleration for protestant dissenters. The Earl of Arlington engineered a new foreign policy through the Triple Alliance with Holland and Sweden (1668) and a rapprochement with Spain first evidenced in the Anglo-Spanish treaty of 1667. Ashley and Lauderdale, among others, backed a plan for Anglo-Scottish union, thus increasing royal trade revenues and flooding parliament with docile Scottish MPs. However, parliament rebuffed Buckingham's project and would have no truck with the Scots. Arlington's 'protestant' foreign policy proved more popular,but Charles's aims lay in a different direction and had little to do with pleasing parliament.[4]

Charles looked to France to escape the constraints of English politics. The secret Treaty of Dover (May 1670) between Charles and Louis XIV committed England to join France in a war against Holland, to begin in 1672. Charles aimed to annex low country ports, to pursue a piratical naval strategy, to soak the Dutch for a war indemnity, and in the longer run to increase England's share of Europe's trade and thus his customs revenue. In the meanwhile, Charles could not go to war on his own resources, and parliament might not vote sufficient supply for a war which utterly reversed the popular foreign policy embodied in the Triple

Alliance. Moreover, Charles intended to reassert his religious supremacy and to establish toleration for protestant dissent and Catholic recusancy. This added to Charles's money problems, for the Cavalier Parliament had already used its financial leverage to frustrate the king's religious aims. Thus Charles sought and received a war subsidy from Louis. Charles's additional promise to Louis to declare his conversion to Rome would have provoked a political earthquake and drew from Louis an additional subsidy and, should Charles need it, the dispatch of French troops to England.

Whether or not Charles wished to make himself absolute, these aims amounted to an abandonment of the Restoration settlement.[5] We might therefore expect to find radical departures in imperial politics, but (save for the decision to separate the government of the Leeward Islands from Barbados) little happened before 1673 to disturb the outlines of Clarendon's imperial restoration. Yet there was no dichotomy between domestic and imperial politics. The grand design involved no direct assault on parliament or any other bastion of the political nation. It was, rather, a flanking maneuver. Charles intended to present parliament with accomplished facts: a successful war, improved finances, and an enlarged religious settlement. In the meanwhile, appearances mattered most. Thus Charles schemed for war against the Dutch while publicly pursuing an anti-French policy. Privately determined to secure toleration, Charles dropped Buckingham's project, acquiesced in a renewal of the Conventicles Act and promised renewed energy in enforcing the laws against recusancy. These public stances helped to obtain additional revenues from parliament. For a king whose main aim was to avoid going on his travels again, this was a considerable gamble, and it is understandable that he deceived parliament. Nor is it surprising that an important part of the policy of deceit was inaction. For all its plotting, the cabal period saw few dramatic political initiatives, at least until the beginning of 1672 when, with the Cavalier Parliament in the middle of its longest interval between sessions, Charles stopped payment on his debts, declared war against the Dutch and issued his Declaration of Indulgence. While the nation grew suspicious of the king's *bona fides*, the early stages of the grand design left the political landscape essentially untouched.

Thus a connection between English and imperial politics continued to operate. Certainly no cabal minister was willing to demonstrate a design to impose arbitrary government on the realm or the plantations. It is true that Arlington found himself facing just such charges after the collapse of the cabal, in 1674, when his enemies remembered that the Secretary of State, among other crimes against English liberties, had engineered the recall and arrest of Governor Modyford of Jamaica and thrown Modyford's son Charles into the Tower to insure the governor's appearance. However, Modyford's arrest had nothing to do with a design to impose arbitrary rule on Jamaica or England. Rather it occurred because Henry Morgan's Jamaican privateers had with Modyford's connivance attacked the Spanish town of Panama City. This put at risk the rapprochement with Spain which, along with the Triple Alliance, embodied Arlington's own insurance policy against the collapse of the grand design and a fall back position could he convince Charles to abandon the French affair. In 1670, Arlington's complicated game had reached a crisis. The Treaty of Madrid, by which Spain recognized England's right to Jamaica, had achieved the success promised in 1667. Meanwhile, the Triple Alliance remained popular, and Charles hoped to exploit it to gain further revenue. Yet Arlington had also acquiesced in the secret Treaty of Dover. Thus the privateers' bloody raid at once endangered Arlington and compromised the crown's public commitment to an anti-French European diplomacy. Once again, as at the Restoration, Thomas Modyford was guilty of nothing more than bad timing, but this time he paid more heavily for it because he had angered both the king and the Secretary of State.[6]

The circumstantial nature of Modyford's recall was underlined by its complex connections with the Restoration patronage system,[7] but it was proved by the experience of Modyford's successor, Sir Thomas Lynch. Lynch's instructions emphatically ordered him to leave the Spanish colonies in peace and to control the privateers. Lynch, long a spokesman for Jamaica's planters, endorsed both aims but received no support for his efforts to implement them. At one point he went fifteen months without receiving any communication from Arlington or even from the meanest clerk of the plantations council. Lynch owed his appointment and instructions to Arlington's fury against Modyford, but as the course of European politics lessened the importance of a rapprochement with Spain, Arlington lost interest in Jamaica. Lynch's problems became even more remote when with the collapse of the grand design Arlington faced not only loss of office but also impeachment. Meanwhile, Lynch prudently moved towards accommodation with the privateers; given recent history, there was no sense in burning bridges. Lynch's successor understood the lesson equally well. John Lord Vaughan, who went to Jamaica in the company of Sir Thomas Modyford and with the newly knighted Sir Henry Morgan as his deputy, was arguing for a flexible policy on privateering before he even cleared the Downs.[8]

Arlington's rage betrayed his vulnerability and reminds us that the cabal was not so much a government as a collection of courtiers ambitious for power and each suspicious of the other. Charles kept them in the dark by acting as his own chief minister. On the other hand, the king did not completely deceive his ministers. While only a few (just Clifford and Arlington of the five central figures in the cabal) knew of the king's aims as laid out in the secret treaty of May 1670, many more (including Buckingham, Ashley and Lauderdale) were privy to the less secret *traité simulé* of December. They did not know of the catholicity clause, but their complicity in the rest of the king's design placed them in a jeopardy best grasped by contrasting it with Clarendon's predicament during the second Dutch war. Clarendon acquiesced in that war as one sworn to obey the king and intent upon retaining his own position. While much the same could be said of the cabal ministers, they risked more than Clarendon had. The second Dutch war arose in an acceptable political context: the desire to make good the settlement of 1660. In projecting a third Dutch war, the king aimed at subverting that settlement. Charles thus had to sit tight, to wait for that fait accompli promised for 1672. His ministers were subject to similar constraints. They were unable to deflect the king from his course, if indeed they wished to try; but in their separate departments they continued to deal with the problems which had destroyed Clarendon and led the king into France's arms. While Charles aimed at political reconstruction, ministers engaged in housekeeping exercises. Their constitutionally innocuous reforms outlasted the grand design to shape the future of English and imperial politics.

Not all the chief figures of the cabal took part. Buckingham too much disliked hard work, while Lauderdale's Scottish responsibilities and Arlington's diplomatic role kept them otherwise engaged. The main contributors from the cabal were Lord Ashley and Sir Thomas Clifford, with assistance from minor figures like Sir William Coventry, Sir John Duncombe, Sir George Downing, and Sir Thomas Osborne, who would outlast them all. By 1667, several of them already had much administrative experience, and it was significant that they all had or came to have close connections with royal revenue or expenditure. Ashley's conduct as Chancellor of the Exchequer forecast later reforms. At the time of his appointment in 1661, Ashley began by memoing himself on 'the Authoritie of the Chaunceller'. He then expanded that authority beyond its traditional judicial role to include revenue policy and administration. His papers are full of schemes for change in these areas, and while it is dangerous to credit Ashley personally with any of them, we can assume his interest in most and his support for some.[9] Another improver was Sir George Downing, a Teller of the Exchequer and, like Ashley, an ex-Cromwellian. A characteristic Downing innovation was repayment of the king's debts in sequence, an administrative improvement which also, as Downing intended, encouraged men to lend to the crown.[10] However, revenue reform achieved sharper focus when, upon Lord

Treasurer Southampton's death in 1667, the Treasury was put under a commission of five: the Duke of Albemarle, perhaps as figurehead, Ashley, Duncombe, Clifford, and Coventry, with Downing as secretary.

The commissioners' main problem was the parlous financial situation they inherited. There was simply not enough money to go around. Thus the busybody Downing was indefatigable in pestering officials to forward money, make payments, and submit proper accounts. Such pressure was mainly intended to speed up existing procedures, but it implied more substantial changes which were not universally liked. When Downing demanded a list of fees charged by the under-officers of the Excise so that the Treasury might know how much per £1,000 of income was actually spent on the king's service, the under-officers balked. However, their defence (that they worked hard and honestly) missed the point, perhaps deliberately.[11] It was more common for such men to defend their territory on grounds of tradition and legal right. In 1661 Sir Robert Croke, Clerk of the Pipe by letters patent from Charles I, protested that reform endangered his rights, some dating 'from the time of King Stephen'. Sir Robert Long, Auditor of the Receipt, was 'ever afraid of innovation and unwilling to change ancient institutions', although the rights he defended dated only from 'Harry the 7th' and the '38th of Queen Elizabeth'. Long agreed to expedite a new process Ashley had suggested, but only after protesting that in the good old days chancellors had kept to their judicial functions and did not 'meddle' with revenue management. Naturally Croke and Long argued that the new ways were unsafe. The weight of their arguments, however, stressed property or patent rights. They would have agreed with another protestor that new Exchequer methods were 'injurious to the Tellers in their right, and illegall in procedure'.[12]

These complaints tell us much of the sort of government which had been restored in 1660, as did Clarendon's protests that the Treasury Commission of 1667 recalled the expedients of the Protectorate and that Ashley, Albemarle, and Downing, besides their service to the usurper, had between them little claim to governing status. Clarendon's goal had been to restore rather than to reform government, and patentees like Long and Croke were part of his success. However, while they might be efficient and honest, they might not be, and it was not easy to order them even to be venal. Governor Modyford's complaint that the patentees sent by the king to infest his Jamaican domain were 'proud, careless, and indiligent' must have struck a sympathetic chord of response among ministers in the home government.[13] About all that could be done, as Ashley suggested in 1664, was to see that the patentees did their work and submitted accounts promptly, although even that might be difficult to force upon them.[14] Complaints against patentees and their self-defence show that the pace and nature of reform were determined not only by financial necessity but also by the sheer contrariness of Restoration government. It was not surprising that those brought into the Treasury and Exchequer to keep a special eye on the king's money were, like Richard Sherwin and John Rushworth, commissioned rather than patent officers. And it was fitting that in 1671, when the greatest branch of the king's revenue, the customs, was taken out of farm and put into commission, Downing became one of the new commissioners and Sherwin was made secretary.[15]

Although it came as if by accident, the end of the customs farm was symptomatic of cabal period reforms. The negotiations over Charles's third Great Farm gave little hint that the system was in danger; given the king's predicament in 1670-71, the utility of farming as a means of raising credit strengthened its position. Farming, however, was held suspect on several grounds, and the 1660s produced an abundance of proposals to rid the crown of this 'dismal necessity'. Reflecting these suspicions, the Treasury Commission had surrounded the system with bureaucratic safeguards. In 1669 farmers were ordered to send enforcement officers to the colonies, a marked contrast to the 1664 'invitation' to do the same. In England, the Treasury preferred directly to commission customs officials who came to share functions with the farmers' men. This was not new in principle, but the Treasury extended it in practice, for instance by ordering that farmers' deputies could not discharge ships' bonds in the absence of commissioned royal officers.[16] The negotiations for a new farm gave the Treasury the chance to write into the contract formal provision for such supervision,[17] and it may have been partly for this reason, as well as the sharply increased rent demanded by the king, that the prospective farmers now sought substantial concessions. This eleventh-hour demand was the immediate cause of the end of the farm, yet there was more to it than circumstance. Both the decision and the task of the new commissioners were eased considerably by the experience of the Treasury and men like Downing in imposing checks on a method of revenue collection which, before 1671, they had been unable to dismantle.[18]

The end of the Great Farm removed an autonomous intermediary between the king and his money. It thus recalled the harassing of patent officers within the revenue departments and the circumvention of the Exchequer during the second Dutch war, when administration of prize moneys had been put under a commission headed by Lord Ashley. The Prize Commission, although not an unqualified success, demonstrated that money which flowed around rather than through the Exchequer evaded not only officers' delays and fees but also the grasp of creditors; it could thus be used to meet more pressing financial needs.[19] The Stop of the Exchequer in early 1672 more drastically expressed the same tendency. In the negotiations with France, Louis XIV had scaled down Charles's demand for a subsidy from £800,000 to only £200,000. Now, as the war approached, Charles was unable to find further credit from the bankers and unwilling to call parliament into session. Thus he stopped payment on most of his outstanding debt in order to liberate funds to put the fleet to sea. In the context of the grand design, the Stop was a desperate gamble on high stakes, but it was also an episode in English administrative history, recalling the Prize Commission and foreshadowing the Bank of England. By the Stop Charles stepped in not to liquidate but to seize control of his debt, postponing payments and setting interest rates on the new debts thus incurred.[20]

Besides meeting the financial needs of the grand design, then, cabal innovations addressed the bureaucratic problems of restoration government. These problems were clear enough; even Lord Treasurer Southampton had warned against cantonizing revenue administration,[21] and the logic had wider application. Farmers of the customs, patent officers in the exchequer, clamoring creditors, all alike interdicted Charles II's prerogative and limited his powers of command even within the government. Patent officers were a relatively minor but typical irritant, as successive Attorneys-General recognized in the 1670s. Asked whether parliament might tax office holding, Heneage Finch and William Jones advised that it might tax patentees but not commissioned officers. This led to a more significant distinction: 'A Commissioner hath only a Special Authority & no Interest, and if he be hindered in the Execution of his Authority 'tis an offence against the King not against him . . . he Differs from an Officer both in name & Nature'. The law officers' view was widely shared. In 1670 'most of the court party' backed a high assessment against patent offices in the subsidy of that year. After all, patentees were, like farmers, essentially ungovernable. 'By farmes in general the king looses . . . the title of Master to soe many persons as shall be by the farmers concerned in the mannagement' of royal revenues.[22] Farming periodically produced the spectacle of the king's customs collectors suing the king for shortfalls in his own revenue. Government by licence had apparently to operate in the licensees' interests. When it did not, as when patent officers were obstructed in their duty (often enough by other royal officers), they were left at law to sue the obstructor, whose offense, as the law officers pointed out, was not against the crown.[23]

It was no way to run a government which faced such massive problems as did Charles II's. That judgment was confirmed by contemporary critics of the system who echoed attacks made on Charles I's England by Thomas Hobbes and the Levellers. But these were more than echoes;

among the new generation's critics were John Locke and his patron Ashley (now the Earl of Shaftesbury), both identified as admirers of Hobbes. In his 'Advice to his Majesty', delivered in about 1672, Shaftesbury took 'for graunted' as his first principle,[24]

> That the Strength & glory of your Majestie and the wealth of your Kingdomes, depends not soe much on any thing . . . as on the multitude of your subjects, by whose mouthes and backes the fruits & commoditys of your lands may have a liberale consumption . . . & by whose hands, both your Majesties Crowne may be defended . . . & also the Manufactures of both your Native, and forreigne Commoditys improved, by which, Trade & your Majesties Revenue, must necessarily be encreased.

This recalled Sir Harbottle Grimston's homily of 1660 which likened merchants to bees bringing honey into the king's hive. But in 1660 the simile carried different implications for an administration inclined to conservative and corporatist thinking. For Clarendon, trade was a mystery upon which the state required advice, but trade involved also the fixed and settled interests of Englishmen. Customs farmers, trading companies, chartered boroughs and colonies, all were parts of a system to be restored; thus Clarendon's ideas about trade mirrored his view of government. Those who dealt with the problems Clarendon left them thought differently. Their idea that government must be made responsive to command implied also that it should be made responsive to changing circumstances. Years of experience toting up balance sheets of revenue and expenditure gave them a new perspective, and a new arithmetic. They would master the beehive by replacing a contractual calculus with the simpler tyranny of known numbers.

Their language was as expressive as their mathematics.[25] John Collins, mathematician, economist, Fellow of the Royal Society, and jobseeker, proposed a balance sheet of trade by which the government might better organize itself and the nation's trade. It was not necessary to consult merchants; numbers would speak for themselves and could be gathered by every collector of royal revenues from the villages to Whitehall. The only obstacle was getting collectors to make the reports, especially the farmers who, Collins complained, were always ready to show their books when they had a *prima facie* case for defalcations but withheld information during times of prosperity. Another indefatigable proposer, John Scott, argued that the way to profit and power might be mapped by anyone who would take 'the trouble to examine the Custome House bookes . . . and [view] the growing up of the great forrest of shipps now in being . . . &c, the numerous swarmes of Merchants, Cittizens, Artificers, Marriners, and other Industrious people of this nation, continually increasing both in number and Richesse'. Benjamin Worsley, secretary to the plantations councils of 1670 and 1672, developed the point further. Commerce, he declared in 1668, had 'in late years become an Expresse Affayre of State' because men recognized that nothing was more conducive to gaining or preventing 'universall monarchy'. Trade was too important to be left to the merchants. Commerce as an affair of state 'is widely different from the mercantile part of it . . . the whole of that Art or skill which is properly exercised by the merchant . . . is in every respect Comprehended, Having nothing more of mystery really further in it'. Worsley listed ten aims of economic policy and concluded that not one of them was within merchants' 'prospect or competence'.[26]

Such logic strengthens Worsley's claim to have authored the Navigation Act of 1651, and certainly he had accepted the Act's more revolutionary implications. He and others like him viewed the economy much as Adam Smith would a century later, the sum of private actions in pursuit of private ends. Neither Worsley nor other projectors, however, suggested leaving this economy to the ministrations of an invisible hand, nor would they cast the state in the supporting role of handmaid to prosperity. Rather commerce was to serve the state. So, too, were the merchants. Where Clarendon aimed to secure merchants' cooperation and to learn from them something of the arcana of trade, Worsley argued that by making trade its own business the state would guarantee merchants' 'loyalty and subjection'. This recalled the advice given in 1661 by another who claimed to be author of the Act of 1651, Thomas Violet, that the king who would 'be happie must alwaies rule the Merchants'. As for bankers, Locke argued that prosperity would lower their interest and lessen their importance.[27]

Clarendon's need for merchants' advice had been qualified by contempt for their social quality and suspicion of their good faith. Of course such attitudes persisted among England's rulers, but men like Worsley and Locke had better reasons than their patrons' sensibilities for devaluing the merchants. As *raison d'état* replaced contractualism as the organizing principle of commercial policy, mercantile and financial influence declined. This was illustrated by the changing membership of the councils for trade and plantations. Merchants, well represented on Clarendon's councils, scarcely appeared on those of 1668 and 1670, and Locke's 1672 list of possible members was drawn entirely from the Privy Council and parliament. In 1675, the process was completed when trade and plantations affairs were placed under a committee of the Privy Council.[28]

This shift away from the mercantile interest in the councils' membership raises the question of how these new ways of thinking about government and society affected the landed interest. Shaftesbury's decision to repent of his support for the 1665 act excluding Irish cattle from England is interesting here. By 1668, he reported that the Act had 'infinitely sunck' the customs and cost English commerce £400,000 yearly by diverting Irish trade to the continent. Prohibition also meant that England's feeding counties wanted stock while breeding counties had lost a market. Shaftesbury brought the same analysis to the projected union between Scotland and England. Scottish competition did not worry him; by increasing the total volume of the nation's trade, union would benefit all sections of the economy. Worsley could scarcely have put it better. Shaftesbury had abandoned the economic parochialism of his class, but knew its strength in parliament and supported the king's plan to achieve union by prerogative action.[29] Shaftesbury's view of the landed class in politics changed as he moved from government to opposition, but in economic terms landed gentlemen took their place beside the 'multitude of . . . subjects' upon whose production and consumption rested the health of the state.[30]

Many who thought in these ways about the economy and acted to reform government were veterans of the English revolution. Not a few favored other radical reforms, such as religious toleration, and Professor Appleby has suggested that such men can be thought of as a free trade lobby, anticipating Adam Smith. These connections are significant, but the pattern of thought should not be identified wholly with political radicalism or with the forces of progress. John Lord Berkeley was one old cavalier who moved from a downright old-fashioned social and economic analysis to endorse Shaftesbury's view that government's two main tasks were interconnected: to extend its power and to improve the wealth of its subjects. The commercial feudalism which had informed aspects of the Restoration settlement was still strong in England.[31]

* * *

Whichever side of this divide Charles II fell on, the connections men made between commerce and power aptly described his aim to make war on a trade rival in order to cast himself adrift from a landed parliament. England, Charles told his sister in 1668, could only be "considerable by our trade and power by sea." Charles weighed the power of France to help and the power of Holland to harm, and asked Louis XIV for enough money to smite the Dutch while protecting his trade routes. He warned Louis that inadequate naval preparations would enable the Dutch to 'cut off [one] of the best branches of His Majesty's revenue, viz., the customs valued at 500,000 sterling yearly'. Charles also worried about supplies of Baltic naval stores and 'the trade of our plantations'. When Louis cut the subsidy from £800,000 to £200,000, he forced Charles into absolute dependence upon the fortunes of a commercial war against Holland.[32]

We can appreciate Charles's reasons for not meeting parliament between April 1671 and February 1673, but the result was that he went to war on a shoestring, and because the war went badly he had to come to terms with parliament sooner than he wished. When parliament did meet, it announced that no money would be forthcoming unless Charles withdrew his Declaration of Indulgence, a revolutionary broadening of the religious settlement issued in the middle of parliament's recess. Shaftesbury urged Charles to stand firm: 'rather lose money than lose rights', the future whig advised, but it was advice Charles could not afford to follow. The price of the subsidy was not only the withdrawal of the Indulgence but its reversal, for Charles was forced to assent to the Test Act, and the cabal was in ruins. However, while Charles's ministers wisely looked to their defences, the king was safe enough. The Declaration of Indulgence had been his only open invasion of the territory held by the political nation; once it had been repulsed, parliament reverted to its traditional role. The subsidy underlined the point, for it was yet another of those special taxes laid by the Cavalier Parliament to meet the crown's emergent needs, and it came in the form of a land assessment.[33]

This set the context for another act of the February 1673 session, the Greenland and Eastland Trades Act, also known as the Plantations Act. After applying a land tax to the king's present needs, parliament gave its attention to securing an improvement in the king's ordinary revenue through the Plantations Act. Not that the Plantations Act was a revenue measure: as Lord Treasurer Danby pointed out in 1675, parliament laid duties on inter-colonial trade not to raise a revenue but better to enforce a previous trade measure, the enumeration clause of the 1660 Navigation Act.[34] Yet there can be no doubt that parliament intended to improve the king's revenue through the Act of 1673, on the assumption, as Danby put it, that regulatory measures would work to 'the further advantage of his Majesties Service and Revenue of his Customes in this Kingdome'.[35] This establishes a revenue context of the Act, for we have already seen that enforcement legislation, such as the Statute of Frauds, was a normal response of parliament to the monarchy's fiscal problems. Such Acts underlined parliament's belief that the king should live of his own, that his own should be enough, and that it should come mainly from the indirect taxes laid at the Restoration. New direct taxes were for emergent necessities or accumulated debts. Often both types of legislation passed at the same session. This was not surprising given the crown's persistent financial problems, but the distinction between them was clear and became clearer as parliament grew more suspicious of the king. Thus by the later 1670s a well-wisher to the crown could offer to make good the royal debt by special taxation, but reported that parliament would not 'upon any Termes' add to the ordinary revenues.[36] As a species of revenue legislation, the Plantations Act followed naturally the war subsidy of 1673.

However, there was more to it than a natural connection, for the Plantations Act was also a product of the political and administrative history of the cabal. The story begins with the previous parliamentary session of 1670-71. When the session opened in October 1670, Charles could not point out that he had added to his financial difficulties by allying with France. Instead, Charles wrapped himself in the Triple Alliance to tell parliament that he needed £800,000 (a resonating sum in these years) to set out the fleet in order to meet the French threat. Parliament resolved to meet this need as soon as it could devise an Act which would tax wealth generally and not just the land. Meanwhile, parliament moved to consider the accumulated debt. Here MPs generously volunteered additional duties to be laid for nine years on beer and law proceedings. Duties imposed on imported wine expressed anti-French feeling and were intended to be prohibitory; in compensation the Commons voted additional duties on colonial produce, notably tobacco and sugar. This was opposed in the House by a number of government spokesmen including Sir George Downing and his superior at the Treasury, Sir John Duncombe. 'Lay what you will', Downing told MPs, 'it will prejudice the customs and the farmers will not give'. The levies would discourage planters, encourage smugglers, and colonial products would be left to rot in the customs house. Down-ing did not prevail in the Commons, but his arguments were among those which moved the House of Lords to reduce the impost on sugar, an amendment which killed the bill by raising the constitutional issue of the House of Commons's sole right to initiate money measures.[37]

Downing was not heartbroken to see the additional impost fail on the constitutional issue, for he believed that better regulation, not higher imposts, would best increase revenues. Meanwhile, his own bill for 'preserving and improving the plantation trade' passed without trouble. His aim was to exclude Ireland from trading in enumerated colonial commodities. As Secretary to the Treasury he had already been involved with the question of Irish – colonial trade and with the problems of enforcing the Navigation Acts in the colonies.[38] The Commons saw a revenue connection, for it tacked an amendment limiting Downing's bill to nine years, the same period as that proposed for the additional imposts. In the same spirit, the House accepted Downing's provision that colonial governors should take an oath to enforce all relevant trade legislation.[39]

Downing carried these concerns through to the February 1673 session of parliament. In 1671, the Lords had deleted the provision in Downing's bill requiring an oath of colonial governors, possibly because it infringed the prerogative, possibly because William Lord Willoughby, Governor of the Caribbees, was a member of the Lords' committee which reported on the bill. However, the governors' oath was in 1673 a less relevant consideration for Downing, who was now one of the new Commissioners of the Customs. The 1673 Plantations Act repeated the concern of the 1671 act to close a loophole through which enumerated products might avoid paying English customs, but it employed a new enforcement mechanism. The Act bypassed the governors to charge the Customs Commissioners or their colonial deputies with issuing bonds to ships' captains to return enumerated goods to England or, if no bond were given, to collect the plantations duty. Thus parliament gave to colonial customs officers powers which did not depend upon, indeed were quite distinct from, the authority of all colonial governments, royal, proprietary, or corporate.[40] That authority momentously affected several colonies: for instance Virginia, where collector Giles Bland offended local authority and ultimately took part in Bacon's Rebellion; Massachusetts, where one Edward Randolph would play a vital political role; and Maryland, where a kinsman of Lord Baltimore would in exasperation murder a customs official.[41] This was not surprising. The direct commissioning of royal officers, based in the colonies and charged with the duty to regulate trade, marked a potentially revolutionary change in colonial government. In 1625, Charles I had grappled with the Virginia problem by trying to distinguish between matters of state and matters of trade and then, in effect, making the colony's government responsible for both. The Act of 1673 severed that connection.

It was appropriate that this change came during the cabal period. A government in crisis viewed as obstacles those aspects of the traditional order which Clarendon had cherished: contractualism, corporatism, rights of propriety. This was reflected by the preamble to the king's instructions to the 1670 council of trade and plantations, which based royal authority in America on the argument that the colonies had been settled 'by the Prudence of our Predecessors, and not without the great hazard, Charge, and Expence of these Nations . . . and being so setled are become the proper Right and Soverarine Posessions of us'. Here Charles invoked not the spirit of Breda but the rationale of the Commonwealth's Plantations Act of 1650.[42] In 1673, parliament proved its agreement with the crown by making direct use of an important cabal period innovation – the Customs Commission – to invade the autonomy of colonial governments and to assert clearly the supremacy in the empire of England's commercial and fiscal necessities. If we look beyond the sections of the 1673 Act which dealt directly with the colonies, we find that parliament also invaded the restrictive and monopoly practices which had characterized the Greenland and Eastland trades. This was a legislative endorsement of the king's instructions to the 1672 council of trade and plantations to consider 'of the several Advantages that may arise . . . by giving way . . . to a more open, and free trade then that of Companyes and Corporations'.[43] Taken together, the end of the Great Farm and the Act of 1673 embodied the idea that trade could be directly regulated by state power. They arose from the crises of the cabal period, but they owed much to the past, too, for now crown and parliament had come fully into line with the thinking and the actions of men like Downing, Worsley, and Collins, who themselves formed a link in ideas with the Commonwealth and the revolutionary potential of the colonial and trade legislation of 1650 and 1651. Coming in the very same session that parliament forced Charles II to abandon his Declaration of Indulgence, the Act of 1673 was a fitting, if ironic, capstone to the grand design.

It was just as well that it came at the end. In the curious politics of the cabal no new law nor administrative innovation could have a certain future. The 1670 and 1672 Councils of Trade furnish an example, for they used their compendious instructions rather timidly. They tended to follow lines of least resistance, to avoid confrontation and to deal with matters directly under their purview. It was partly for this reason that these councils failed to solve the Massachusetts problem. They considered sending commissioners with less power and more discretion than those Clarendon had dispatched in 1664. The Earl of Sandwich, council president until his death at the Battle of Sole Bay in 1673, proposed bombarding the Bay Colony with 'orthodox bookes, poetry, common Ballads', presumably as a softening up exercise. Indirection also characterized the council's advice that the king revive the Mason and Gorges claims to northern New England while cultivating the loyalty of Connecticut and Rhode Island. If it were surrounded by loyal governments, Massachusetts might come round. A letter drafted in December 1674 suggested a tougher approach, but it may never have been sent to Massachusetts.[44]

This caution reflected the view that Massachusetts was going to be a tough nut to crack, but it owed also to the councils' dependence on a government which lacked focus and direction in political matters. Charles had for several years adopted a distant attitude towards government, looked elsewhere for his solutions, and left ministers to tussle with specific problems in their specific spheres. From such origins had come the administrative reforms in the Treasury and the imperial reforms encapsulated in the Plantations Act. Now, with the collapse of his grand design, Charles was forced to mend his fences. For that task, he chose Sir Thomas Osborne. As Lord Treasurer and Earl of Danby, Osborne gave England its first real experience of party politics. It was no accident that he was also to give the colonies their first real taste of purposeful interference in local affairs. In his management of domestic and imperial government, Danby breathed political life into the bureaucratic innovations of the cabal period.

* * *

As Osborne moved from his appointment as Lord Treasurer in 1673 to the earldom of Danby, his political eminence also grew. By 1675 few could have doubted that he had become Charles's chief minister, endowed with sufficient power to give to government a sense of direction. For the first time since Clarendon it is possible to speak of government policy publicly and deliberately followed, even though King Charles still pursued French dreams and King Louis embarked on a complex game within English politics, bribing government and opposition leaders alike. These subterranean activities eventually contributed to Danby's downfall, but until late 1678 he remained in apparent control at the focal point of English politics. As a politician, Danby deployed considerable talents. Bishop Gilbert Burnet did not like Danby but acknowledged that he was a 'very plausible speaker... a positive and undertaking man'. Burnet also grudgingly admired Danby's perception of parliament. 'Those who were in the ministry before him ... had taken off the great and leading men: and left the herd as a despised company ... But Lord Danby reckoned that the major number was the surer game'. Thus Danby offered much of value to Charles, who now needed to regain the trust of parliament or, failing that, to get more money without conceding too much. Danby and his lieutenants like his brother-in-law the Earl of Lindsey took this political role seriously and kept in close touch with their clients in parliament, and indeed were well-informed about the voting proclivities of most members.[45]

Energy and attention to detail also marked Danby's administrative roles. Danby had already served as Navy Treasurer and then Treasury Commissioner during the cabal, and when the Duke of York was barred by the Test Act from exercising his duties as Lord High Admiral, Danby became one of the Admiralty Commissioners. His experience as Navy Treasurer stood him well, but just in case he kept with him a 'Generall Instruction' which reminded him of everything a Lord High Admiral should do, and he also kept sets of instructions to humbler Admiralty officers. These rule books stressed attention to detail,[46] and Danby followed the same precepts as Lord Treasurer. No matter seemed too small for him. Some of these small matters concerned eminent people applying directly to Danby for customs remissions. An elephant was no small problem, perhaps, but in any case George Lord Berkeley was to be reimbursed the customs he had paid on one, imported from 'some part of the East Indies'. Prince Rupert was reimbursed for customs paid on less surprising shipments, but the Countess of Cleveland was to pay customs on a large shipment she brought in on Charles's royal yacht. Another of the king's ladies, the Duchess of Portsmouth, won some remissions but had to pay full rate on twelve dozen pairs of gloves.

One must admire the humble collectors who forced these eminent persons to pay up in the first place, and so did Danby. He appreciated and rewarded subordinates' loyalty and initiative. He commended a collector's suggestion that some boats seized for illegal trading should be burned, not sold: 'a Publique Terror & Discouragement to the like Practice for the future', Danby thought. Giles Dunster's success in destroying £56 12s 11d worth of Gloucester-grown tobacco won from Danby an order to pay that exact sum to Dunster from the 'Accompt of Incidents'.[47] On the other hand, those who roused Danby's suspicion won his less welcome attention. Rumors of fraud in the Irish customs led to an investigation and to the extraordinary order that if the farm could not be voided in law the Lord Lieutenant should deal only through the 'trusted farmers'.[48] Others were luckier. Paul Badcock, dismissed as a tidesman for taking £2 unofficial compensation for goods he had seized, was restored to his post, Danby having satisfied himself that 'no fraud was intended' and that Badcock 'had otherwise demeaned himself well'.[49] One would like to know how the Lord Treasurer knew of a tidesman's demeanor, but there can be no doubt that Danby kept a sharp eye out for the sort of talent required by these minor but difficult jobs. A man who could uproot English farmers' home-grown tobacco would make a good searcher in the customs, and in due course the valiant Giles Dunster took up that post in nearby Bristol. Edward Randolph's similar attributes won him Danby's recommendation as a 'fit person in seizing prohibited and uncustomed goods' in the English customs service. When Danby's first choice as customs collector in Massachusetts did not turn up, Randolph got that job instead.[50]

Danby nevertheless recognized the limitations of zeal. Few politicians of the age understood better the politics of parliament. Upon this understanding, Danby built a base for a working majority of MPs which held together pretty well until it and Danby were swept away by the popish plot. It was a cavalier majority, and Danby knew the limits of its loyalty. Thus he tried to distance Charles from France, urged a rigidly Anglican course in religion, did his best to retrench expenditure, and brought William of Orange closer into the English royal family by marrying him to the Duke of York's daughter Mary.[51] Danby also knew that cavaliers' local loyalties could war with their devotion to the crown.

Gentlemen could not be relied on to support royal officials in the countryside. Everywhere Danby looked, he was pained to find the king's revenue obstructed not only by 'tumults of the people' but also by knights and gentlemen who imprisoned tax men or pursued them by 'sword and pistol'. Pained but not surprised: Danby knew that the Isle of Wight's acrimonious feud with Southampton customs officers was led by Sir Robert Dillingham and other gentlemen of the island. Danby even had to lecture the JPs of his home county, Yorkshire, for their eagerness to find loopholes in the Hearthmoney Act, and was not pleased by their reply. Disregarding Danby and the opinion of royal law officers, the keepers of the king's peace in Yorkshire declared that they were the 'final arbiters' of the Act's meaning. Other counties' gentry were not more cooperative. For every Dunster who loyally destroyed Gloucestershire tobacco, there seemed to be a Gloucestershire JP unmindful of his own duty in this 'matter of soe great importance not onely to his Majesties Customes but to the Trade & Navigation of this Kingdome'.[52]

With troubles like these in Gloucester, no wonder Danby worried that Edward Randolph might not advance the king's service in Boston. Should he prove 'obnoxious' to the people of Massachusetts, the Customs Commissioners were to find someone else. No wonder, either, that when queried about this, Randolph declared that many Massachusetts inhabitants would support him and, more than that, looked to the crown for release from the tyranny of the Massachusetts Bay government. So confident was he of his reception that he would take his family with him. The record is silent on the impact of this domestic detail, but clearly the issue of Randolph's acceptability in Massachusetts was deemed important enough for his appointment to be reviewed by the Privy Council. Neither his competence nor his courage would have gotten the issue that far. Nor did this care make Massachusetts unique; Danby sought the advice of leading inhabitants of English counties, and of Virginia and Maryland, before making similar appointments in those places.[53] During Danby's years in power, the colonies once again found their accustomed place as extensions of the English polity.

It was typical of Danby's government that in early 1675, just as he was consolidating his power, he settled colonial affairs in a Privy Council committee, the Lords of Trade and Plantations. This replaced the existing council and got rid of Shaftesbury, who had already lost his office of Lord Chancellor. It also saved money, as members of the old council had received salaries and had their own secretary.[54] These practical aims sufficiently explain the change, and the new committee's instructions tell us nothing of policy initiatives. Their lordships were to 'meet consistently at least once a Weeke' to consider all matters which had been under the cognizance of the old council.[55] Their lordships got right down to work. They ordered the old council's secretary, John Locke, to turn over his papers to Sir Robert Southwell, secretary to the new committee. They required royal governors to report on 'all things which have happened' during their terms of office.[56] Information was also needed on Massachusetts. Convinced that 'this is the Conjuncture to do some thing Effectuall for the better Regulation of that Government, or else all hopes of it may be hereafter lost', they were unsure of what that 'some thing' might be. Thus they sent Edward Randolph, ostensibly to look into the government and title to New Hampshire and Maine, but also to gather general intelligence about Massachusetts.[57] Information about enforcement of the navigation Acts was more readily accessible, and the commissioners of customs were asked to report on the subject. The commissioners did not know whether governors had taken the oaths to enforce the acts of trade, but oaths or not, few ships' bonds had been returned to England. The chartered colonies of Massachusetts and Maryland had returned some, but of the major staple-producing royal colonies only Virginia had returned any. This was information indeed, and it led to further inquiries and, in May 1676, a decision to require oaths of all governors. In February 1677 full sets of oaths and instructions were dispatched which could have left colonial governors in little doubt about their duties in trade matters.[58] Clearly the Lords of Trade and Plantation inherited that thirst for information which had characterized earlier councils, but they also took a lead from their most prominent member; a memo in Danby's papers urged the Lords of Trade and Plantations to follow the administrative precedents of the Admiralty Commission and stressed the importance of 'constant correspondence' with governors and other colonial officers.[59]

The two-year time lag between the first inquiries on the Acts of trade and the dispatch of new instructions was slow going, but it demonstrated a persistence of application which during these years was one of the hallmarks of the committee's work. It also reflected a persistent suspicion that the governors were not doing their job properly. The existence of 'good' governors like William Stapleton in the Leewards, who had enough sense to act as if he were obeying orders, made royal advisors readier to ride herd on bad governors like Sir Charles Wheeler, whom Stapleton had replaced. Bad governors had to be watched closely, had to be told what to do, could not be trusted to uphold the king's authority. The councils of 1670 and 1672 had also given much attention to royal governors, and in 1671 Sir Thomas Modyford contemplated these trends from his temporary apartments in the Tower of London and urged instead the practice of the Roman empire, whose governors had enjoyed vice-regal status. Modyford, of course, was an old imperial hand, but American experience was not necessary. Sir Jonathan Atkins and John Lord Vaughan grasped Modyford's point and protested similarly: Atkins before he was commissioned as Governor of Barbados, Vaughan before he left for his post at Jamaica. Take away our flexibility, governors warned, and we cannot be masters in our own houses.[60] However, those who now advised the crown on colonial matters were intent on making royal governors servants in the king's house.

Atkins repeatedly reinforced prevailing views on gubernatorial performance. In April 1675, shortly after his arrival in Barbados, he sent to England the colony's address against the acts of trade, the Royal African Company, and the $4^1/_2$ per cent revenue. Atkins conceived this to be his duty because, as he bluntly put it, the grievances were true. The Lords of Trade did not agree. They dealt quickly with the matters concerning the African Company and the $4^1/_2$ per cent revenue, neither as Atkins advised. Atkins did not get an early reply on the acts of trade; their lordships were still clarifying governors' duties here, and Atkins's position became another problem to take on board. However, when Atkins again presumed to air his views on the trade laws, the committee moved quickly. Within two weeks of receiving Atkins's second letter, in October 1676, several meetings had been held, and their lordships advised the king that for subjects to 'presume to petition your Majesty against Acts of Parliament . . . and call them Greivances' was of 'evill Consequence'. The committee placed the blame not on Barbadians ('your Subjects . . . would hardly presume to make any Addresse of this kind') but on Atkins, who was severely reprimanded for his 'Error and Mistake'.[61]

Atkins's opposition to the king's appointment of Francis Wyat as Clerk of the Market in Barbados fared no better. Atkins had already appointed a colonist to the post, and his claim of precedence drew from Secretary of State Sir Henry Coventry one of the starker statements of royal supremacy in the empire. That the king's Great Seal 'will not be controuled by any Seal in the Barbados' was the view of 'better Lawyers then I beleeve you have'. Not even the Lord Lieutenant of Ireland presumed precedence on such issues, 'and sure the Largeness, Riches, Ancientness and Establisht priviledges of that Kingdom, besides the quallities of the Inhabitants may pretend a little before Barbados'. The island assembly's support for Atkins also displeased Coventry, who warned that body 'not to be so insolent as to declare to the King who are fitt or not fit to serve him'. The king had not 'committed his Subjects so much to the Care of the Assembly, as not to make them worthy his own'. Coventry delivered these warnings in the same week that the Lords of Trade damned Atkins for his part in the assembly's petition against the navigation Acts.[62] There was a pecking order in Danby's empire, and governors and assemblies who challenged royal orders and parliamentary statutes stood pretty near the bottom of it. Once there, they found themselves in all sorts of trouble.

Men of an hierarchical cast of mind and with wide experience in English politics found it easy to blame governors and colonial elites for parochial resistance to central government. This predisposition helps to explain the rejection in April 1676 of Virginia's application for a royal charter. The crown's subsequent response to Bacon's Rebellion offered clearer evidence of the same tendency. Of course, raising rebellion against royal authority was a grave matter, no less so because this rebellion put at risk £100,000 of the king's revenue. However, it was more significant that the commanders sent to suppress the rebellion were also commissioned to examine Virginia's grievances. Even to suggest that a rebellion had causes which might be called grievances was a remarkable act for the Stuart crown. That, however, is exactly what happened. The commission took its brief from the analysis of the rebellion presented by Francis Moryson, one of the colony's agents sent to petition for a charter. The 'defection', as Moryson called the rebellion, was 'greater than is owned here' and had spread through the 'Major part of the Country'. So considerable a defection should be examined rather than put down by martial law, and an inquiry would more surely return the 'once Loyall country' to its wonted obedience. Delicately but definitely agent Moryson distanced himself from his fellow agents and abandoned Governor Berkeley to the results of the inquiry. Unnecessarily, Moryson closed his analysis by saying it was 'the last paper I shall write in this agency'; he must have known that by writing it he had insured his return to Virginia as one of the commissioners.[63]

In Virginia the commissioners made it plain that their list of legitimate grievances did not include the enumeration of tobacco and the king's grant of much of the colony's land to favored courtiers, even though anyone familiar with post-Restoration Virginia might have thought these among the more obvious causes of discontent. The commissioners proved far readier to entertain allegations about the sins of the colony government. Few inquiries can have had a more certain result than the Virginia Commission of 1676, and that was to blame the rising on Governor Berkeley and his Assembly. Virginia's grudging reception of the commissioners confirmed the prejudice. Berkeley's stubbornness particularly galled Secretary Coventry, who observed in May 1677 that 'the King hath very little hopes that the people of Virginia shall be brought to a right sense of their duty to obey their Governors when the Governors themselves will not obey the King'.[64] We are reminded of Danby's warnings to the fractious gentry of England's counties, whose obligation to keep the king's peace sat ill with their obstruction of the king's commands.

During the time that Whitehall was trying to bring Berkeley, Atkins, and their assemblies 'to a right sense of their duty', policy towards Jamaica was also under review. On 1 June 1676, a day after the king quashed Virginia's charter application, the Lords of Trade recommended that some laws recently sent from Jamaica were so objectionable that the amendments agreed in London should be "approved by the Governor, Council, and Assembly there without reenacting."[65] In July, Attorney General Sir William Jones reviewed a court case involving one of those laws which seemed to invade both the crown's admiralty jurisdiction and Royal African Company's charter, and to contradict Governor Lord Vaughan's commission and instructions. Worse, the Jamaica court had based its decision on a James I statute. To Jones this was nonsense. By the king's 'acquisition of that colony he is absolute sovereign, and may impose what form of constitution both of government and laws, he pleaseth, and the inhabitants are in no sort entitled to the laws of England . . . but by the mere grace and grant of the king'.[66] Finally, in April 1677, the Lords of Trade asked the Attorney General to draft a 'Bill (like Poynings Law in Ireland)' for Jamaica.[67] Henceforward, Jamaica's laws would be enacted in London and draw original legitimacy from the king's great seal; Jamaica's governor and assembly could only accept or reject them.

Jones's stark judgment suggests a redefinition of the colonies as essentially separate from the English polity. Indeed, the Poyning's Law episode has been seen as a doctrinaire attack on a colonial assembly, and as such a prelude to the more general assault on colonial autonomy which took place during the 1680s. However, it was not quite so simple. In other opinions on Jamaica matters, both Jones and admiralty lawyers made it clear that what was at issue was not whether English common law extended to Jamaica, but which statute laws and, more importantly, who chose which laws.[68] Clearly the choice could not be left to Jamaica's Assembly, whose legal redefinition of the colony's parish bounds had made 'the Sea, Land, and the Admiralty, Common pleas'.[69] But the assembly was not the only target of the Poyning's Law strategy, which attempted to solve other problems relating to Jamaica, particularly the role of the royal governor. From inception to outcome, the attempt to 'impose' Poyning's Law on Jamaica is best seen as a product of the political management which had characterized the Danby years, not as precedent for an absolutist imperialism.

The process began in 1674 with the appointment of Lord Vaughan as governor of Jamaica. Much was expected of Vaughan, MP for Carmarthen, son of the Earl of Carberry, and identified as one of Danby's court party. Vaughan's predecessor, Sir Thomas Lynch, was pleased that the crown had followed his advice to send a 'Lord Governor' who might both overawe islanders and stand on equal terms with Spanish governors. Besides managing the island's assembly, Vaughan was to mend the breach between privateers and planters which had bedevilled Jamaica. Thus Sir Henry Morgan was made Vaughan's deputy; how better to control the privateers than bring their old leader directly under royal command? Certainly Vaughan's early, probably premeditated decision to demote Morgan and return the Modyfords to power was not admired in London. "The King," Coventry warned Vaughan, 'doth not intend the Island shall be solely in the power of any one Family or party, and the King expecteth from your Lordship that you should balance the parties and factions'.[70] Thus instructed to emulate Danby's arts of political management, Vaughan restored Morgan to his offices; but he had made a resourceful enemy in Jamaica and damaged his reputation in England.

The laws produced by Vaughan's first assembly further damaged that reputation, despite Vaughan's apologetical gloss that the Assembly, while 'carefull to secure their Propertyes & Interestes', had been 'very tender' of the prerogative.[71] Morgan's different version had Vaughan scheming with the Assembly against the king's interest and honor. Sir Henry pointedly linked the 1675 revenue act, which appropriated money not to the king's but to the island's use, to Vaughan's refusal to allow Thomas Martyn, the Receiver of the King's Revenues in Jamaica, to exercise his office.[72] This insured that Poyning's Law would be aimed at the governor as much as at the assembly. The Earl of Carlisle, commissioned governor in 1677 and instructed to pass Poyning's Law through the Jamaica assembly, understood this; so did Lynch, in London, and Vaughan, still in Jamaica. As Vaughan put it, the 'Limits set down' by 'Commission and Instructions' reduced the governor's discretion and thus his power; a governor so bound would be at the mercy of disloyal councillors or of 'obstinate ... illiterate, & ... factiously bent' colonists who took 'high conceit in the title of Representative'. Carlisle protested in like vein and won some concessions, the most important being permission 'in case of invasion, rebellion, or some very urgent necessity' to 'pass an act or acts with the ... general assembly ... to raise money'. It was not enough leeway, however; he took to Jamaica a strict set of instructions and a frankly defeatist attitude. From Jamaica, Carlisle reminded Danby and the Lords of Trade that he had 'desired ... more power and scope to acomodate matters upon emergencys butt itt was denied, and I dout the kings service will suffer by itt'. In October 1679, stymied by colonial stubbornness, Carlisle concluded that he had 'mett with the difficulties here, I foresaw, but could neither avoyd, nor prevent, in England'.[73]

The Lords of Trade faced different difficulties. Their aim was to render governors and assemblies obedient by asserting the king's legislative power, but here they encountered unexplored territory. 'Wee doe not find', they reported on the eve of Carlisle's departure, 'since your Majestys happy Restoration, that any Law transmitted from your Majestys Plantations, has been confirmed by your Majesty . . . (the Act of $4^1/2$ per Cent in the Caribbee Islands only excepted)'. The historical record and the constraints of space and time suggested that Privy Council review of colonial legislation would be difficult and might be impossible. Thus the suggestion arose, in June 1676, during the review of Jamaica's 1675 legislation, that amendments agreed in London should be sent to the colony as laws incapable of further amendment by the governor and assembly.[74] The attempt to make Poyning's Law a rule of empire arose in part out of the desire to make practicable the king's theoretical powers over colonial lawmaking.

This, however, raised a serious problem. Before and after the adoption of the Poyning's strategy, Carlisle and other colonial governors good and bad argued that governors and assemblies must retain powers to make 'municipal' or 'bye-laws' to meet local necessities.[75] Their reasoning was simple. However the crown asserted its legislative power over America, the colonies required laws which fitted the demands of place and time in America. Such arguments were not accepted, but the Lords of Trade could not ignore the necessity to write useful and acceptable laws, not least because the centerpiece, Poyning's Law itself, had to be accepted by the assembly before it could become operative.[76] One solution, written into Carlisle's instructions, was to empower the governor and council to frame bills for Privy Council enactment, but the first laws had to be made in London, quickly; the breakdown of the old system meant that by 1678 Jamaica was technically without laws.[77] Their lordships' disarmingly simple response was to embark on another review of the laws sent by Governors Lynch and Vaughan, amend them where necessary, and thus send to the Jamaica assembly laws it had in substance already passed. In this, the Lords of Trade delighted to point out that under Lynch the assembly had already passed a perpetual revenue Act.[78] Once the laws had been sent to the Attorney General and Lord Chancellor and approved as congruent with the laws of England, the package was complete and, the Lords of Trade hoped, attractive.[79]

Jamaicans did not think so, and steadfastly refused to pass any of the laws.[80] In late 1678, Carlisle privately told Whitehall that there were only two ways out of the impasse. The king could relent, accept colonists' arguments, and modify his commission and instructions accordingly. Or he could give new powers to Carlisle to rule and legislate with the consent of the council only.[81] With this unwelcome advice came addresses against Poyning's Law from both Council and Assembly. These messages were discussed by the Lords of Trade and the full Privy Council in the spring of 1679, a time when there was little likelihood that their lordships would relent. They were even then dispatching Thomas Lord Culpeper to impose the same frame of government on Virginia. Moreover, they took ill Jamaicans' charge that they were infringing English law and the colonists' rights as Englishmen. The Lords of Trade had taken great care to insure that this was not the case, and the Spring of 1679 was no time for leading politicians to suffer such allegations lightly. The popish plot had reached its crisis, Danby had fallen to his enemies in the nascent Whig Party, and the exclusion controversy was gathering steam.[82] Amid these pressing diversions, Jamaica business was discussed first on 4 April and then in late May. Despite substantial changes in Privy Council membership on 22 April, the results were virtually identical. Jamaicans were taken to task for their contumacy, and for the first time the solution of directing Carlisle to govern by fiat was endorsed, in May, by the full Privy Council. The Lords of Trade watered this recommendation down when 'by reason of disagreement in their opinions' they refused to sign it. However, it was Charles himself who most diluted the advice when he gave Carlisle only the power to govern by his existing commission and instructions or by the advice of the island council. But as Carlisle had already pointed out, this was not sufficient to remake Jamaica's constitution unilaterally from London.[83] Unless the king gave Carlisle specified powers to rule autocratically, Jamaica's assembly still held the trump card; its assent was required.

The assembly knew it, too. In September 1679 it considered the Privy Council resolution and the king's milder letter and grasped the nettle. The assembly would 'submitt to weare which His Majesty shall please to order, but not give their consent to mak chaines for their posteri-tyes'.[84] Carlisle, too, had an important decision to make. He had never used the permission given to him to call an assembly to raise revenue for emergencies, but financial necessities were pressing. As early as January 1679 it was reported that Carlisle could 'hardly procure enough money to defray the charge of his Table'. Now the king's orders of May and the assembly's standpat response made it seem that such a situation would continue beyond the approaching termination of Lord Vaughan's last revenue Act. Thus Carlisle proposed an eighteen months' extension of the impost, which the assembly was glad to accept. Carlisle had given up, and proposed to the assembly that an agency be sent to London to beg a reformulation of Jamaica policy.[85]

Back in London, no one accepted the assembly's invitation to 'mak chaines' for the island. 'Upon the whole matter [the assembly] have reason to beg his Majesty's pardon for all their errors', was the mild response of the Lords of Trade. Secretary William Blathwayt, once a strong supporter of Poyning's, wrote that this 'craving pardon' would lead to 'an accommodation of the Differences' between crown and colony. The Lords of Trade again sought the law officers' advice; the question was 'what right the People of Jamaica have to The Laws & government of England & particularly whether they are not subject to the Laws which are beneficiall to the king as to others which are only of advantage to them'. Then their lordships considered 'the Politicall part whether it be convenient to continue on the present methods of government or direct a new one'.[86] Samuel Long's experience provided further evidence of London's pragmatism. Carlisle had sent Long home for trial as one of the chief opposers of Poyning's Law. The case was taken up in September 1680, but by late October Long had been discharged and transformed from defendant into expert witness. Now Lord Chief Justice North was consulting Long and other Jamaica 'gentlemen' on Jamaica's future.[87]

The 'Politicall' solution worked out in London during 1680 and 1681 was sent to Jamaica and achieved final success in 1683, with the London publication of *The Laws of Jamaica, passed by the Assembly, and Confirmed by his Majesty in Council* and a *Narrative* which included celebratory addresses of the assembly, its Speaker, and the Governor, now again Sir Thomas Lynch. Jamaica's assembly escaped Poyning's Law, but the crown achieved many of its original aims. Most of the laws sent out in 1678 were passed without substantial change, and Lynch achieved a twenty-one-year revenue: not a perpetual one, but then Lynch's private instructions conceded that a seven-year Act would be acceptable. In return, Jamaica accepted a twenty-one-year limit on its laws and greater responsibility for the support of its own government, which reduced the colony's drain on England's exchequer. The principle that the island's revenue should be appropriated to the king and not to Jamaica's government was enshrined not only in the words of the island's revenue act but also in the appointment of William Blathwayt as Surveyor and Auditor-General of the crown's American revenues. Not least by any means, the king confirmed in Council the Jamaican legislation of 1682, the first time that the principle of crown review of Jamaican law had actually been achieved in practice.[88] Governor Lynch explained the whole process in interesting terms.[89]

> Like ill Sculptures, some would have made the Head too big, as others the Members, neither of them considering that the perfection and beauty of the Figure consists in the symetry and due proportion of the parts: for it's in the Body Politick as in the Natural; if the Head attracts too much nourishment, the Members become debile and weak; if the Body does it, the Head will be rendered incapable of exercising the Divine Function lodg'd in it.

Lynch, in London for most of the period, knew better than most the hard work it had taken to achieve this symmetry.

* * *

There was a new imperial purposiveness best demonstrated by the English government's thirst for information. Those interested in imperial affairs had always desired information, but now gathering information about the colonies became almost routine, a far cry even from 1675 when the new Lords of Trade had asked each royal governor for a report on 'all that [had] happened' during his tenure. By 1680 governors, including those of chartered colonies, responded regularly to requests for information, as did colony secretaries and clerks of assemblies.[90] It is conceivable that by 1680 English government knew more about America than it had learned before 1670. More importantly, though, London also knew more about governing the empire. Used by such state servants as William Blathwayt, information became history and taught cumulative lessons to men who had the political will to use it. A good example was the Lords of Trade's 1678 'Report' on the Leeward Islands, a report which reviewed past decisions, calendared successes, regretted failures, and recommended new measures. The islands' defence, for instance, needed to be better provided for, 'not onely to preserve your Majesty's Soveraigntie but to quiet the minds of your Subjects who ought to live in the beliefe that they are in a state of Security'.[91] The Leewards report also demonstrated how information about one colony might influence decisions taken on another. During the 1670s examples of this sort of lateral thinking multiplied and offered evidence of a coherent imperial politics. Thus in November 1677 Secretary Coventry took time off from working on the drafting of the Poyning's law policy to tick off Barbados's governor for presuming higher precedence than the Lord Lieutenant of Ireland: surely a more than accidental linkage of act and thought.[92] In May 1681 Sir Thomas Lynch was sent to Jamaica as governor in his own right, not as a deputy, and among the grounds given was the experience of Lieutenant Governor Jeffreys in Virginia in 1677, when Governor Berkeley stood on his own commission to frustrate Jeffreys' authority.[93]

In 1625, Charles I had declared his intention to create a uniform course of government throughout his dominions. His vision of uniformity had been endorsed by successive American elites, for whom a contractual system of imperial government had proved ideal. This system had survived the Commonwealth and was then strengthened by Clarendon's Restoration settlement. Now, in the first few years of their existence, the Lords of Trade and Plantations had accomplished much to define and to realize a new vision of empire, a vision not so much based on the empire's form as on its governability. Their lordships deserve credit for this achievement, but one of their most active members was Lord Treasurer Danby. His private and Treasury papers demonstrate ample connections with colonial business. Colonial governors recognized his interest and power by writing to him. So, too, did lesser mortals like Edward Randolph and Robert Mason. As Lord Treasurer Danby was involved *ex officio* with a variety of colonial matters, especially those having to do with revenue and trade. And Danby paid more than passing attention to other colonial matters less directly under his ministerial purview; he was closely involved, not least, in the formulation of the Poyning's Law policy for Jamaica.[94]

Yet in the final balance Danby's personal contribution to the forging of an imperial government weighed little against the direction and purpose he and others brought to English government. The reforms of the cabal period and before were now turned to effect. An orderly and energetic Treasury which paid close attention to the fate of London tidewaiters and Yorkshire hearthmoney men was inclined to make similar commitments to those responsible for colonial revenues. A government bound and determined to manage parliament into a compliance with the crown would not quake at the prospect of pursuing a similar course for Jamaica or Virginia. Danby aimed to govern England, and he engaged in colonial government for the same end.

Thus when Danby fell from power there was no real break in the story. To be sure, Danby's fall caused concern. The articles of impeachment brought against him in the Commons charged him with having 'endeavoured to subvert the ancient and well-established form of government in this kingdom, and instead thereof to introduce an arbitrary and tyrannical way of government'. Doubtless, as in impeachment proceedings against Clarendon and Arlington, Danby's colonial actions would have been adduced in support of this proposition had the king not placed him in the relative safety of the Tower. Out in Jamaica, Governor Carlisle worried about the effects on him of Danby's fall, and Secretary Coventry conceded that a tree with roots like Danby's could not fall without disturbing the ground around it. But, Coventry advised Carlisle, government must go on; and indeed it did. Meeting on 4 April 1679, less than a week after Danby had gone to the Tower, the Lords of Trade reaffirmed their intention to press on with Poyning's.[95]

It is important to note in this regard that it was a Privy Council swollen in size by Charles II's politic addition of leaders of the whig opposition, including the Earl of Shaftesbury, which engaged in the crucial meetings of May 1679 on Jamaica's continued opposition to Poyning's Law. The whole Council strongly endorsed the policy, and it would be wrong to credit whig sensibilities with the plantations committee's failure to sign the recommendation that if Jamaica again rejected the new frame of government, Carlisle should be empowered to govern by fiat. The non-signers, whoever they were, nonetheless agreed that 'it was better to lose some planters than the allegiance of them all and that the Rebellion in Virginia was occasioned by the excessive power of the Assembly'. It is a reasonable guess that it was at this very meeting of the Council that Shaftesbury was remembered to have said that 'all plantations were of the King's making, and that he might at any time alter or dispose of them at his pleasure'.[96]

In 1679, 'whig' and 'tory' alike supported royal supremacy in the empire. Jamaicans' claim that their rights as Englishmen were threatened by a perpetual revenue and by the king's control of the colonial militia struck the whole Privy Council as insolent nonsense. Both, after all, had been essential features of the Restoration settlement in England, and Barbados and the Leewards already contributed a perpetual revenue to the king's government. During the few months of the 'whig' council, there was no reversal of the directions Danby had set. Massachusetts's claims to New Hampshire were unilaterally annulled and a separate royal government established there; preparations continued to send Culpeper to Virginia with Poyning's law in his pocket, and Governor Atkins received still more peremptory notice that his delayed and incomplete reports would no longer be tolerated.[97] In any case, the opposition councillors had little time to effect a reversal of policy even had they been inclined to do so. In October, Charles purged the Council and replaced it with a safely Tory ministry. It was under a tory aegis that the Lords of Trade began the formulation of the Jamaica compromise.

That 'Politicall' process was very much in Danby's style, and the time it took reminds us that what made the period of Danby's power important in imperial history was the belief, made clear in practice, that to govern the colonies was a hard and intricate task. Of course the crown would have been delighted had Poyning's Law worked in Jamaica, but 'the attack on representative institutions' that many see in the effort was at best peripheral to a policy which grew out of historical circumstance, not ideology. The time taken in devising it testified to its pragmatic origins and objectives. The possibility of failure was implicit in the process and made explicit by the settled intention that the new frame of government should first be accepted by the colonial assembly. Danby's government had not set out to remake the empire, rather to make the empire work. Neither the 'tory reaction' nor the short reign of James II had yet begun.

CHAPTER EIGHT

Routines of state and visions of the promised land: English politicians and America, 1660–1683

During the 1670s, English government took increasingly sure grip of itself. This owed mainly to necessity, the mother of invention in Restoration government, but an intellectual rationale was available, carried from the Interregnum by such as Sir George Downing and Benjamin Worsley to serve the monarchy. Whatever its sources, the government's growing ability to command its own resources was essential to the more purposeful colonial administration which characterized the 1670s. The Jamaica policy and the harrying of Massachusetts, which began in earnest in the late 1670s, required a sustained effort which would have been out of character in Clarendon's administration. Whether this assiduity entailed a new vision of empire is another question. It is certain that during the 1670s, greater and lesser officers of state learned more than Clarendon ever wished to know of the problems of imperial government. They articulated, indeed used ideas which might have overturned Clarendon's imperial restoration, but even their most extreme actions came in response to practical problems. Just as the Earl of Danby managed the Treasury and parliament, so he approached imperial problems with purpose but with limited aims. He would use Poyning's Law to bridle the governor and assembly of Jamaica, but he left them with the trump card of acceptance or rejection. His policy's pragmatic origins and objectives predictably led to a compromise which did not much alter the shape of the empire. Had Charles's Grand Design succeeded in England, the case might have been different, but the most we can say is that by the end of the 1670s the problems of the Restoration settlement had been grasped but not solved.

During the next decade more fundamental change would be imposed and resisted in England. The battle lines were drawn in the exclusion crisis. They would persist through the last years of Charles II and become sharper in the short reign of James II. Eventually, these fundamentally ideological conflicts provoked the Glorious Revolution of 1688 and reshaped English politics. In order to understand how they could also reshape the empire, it is necessary to look more closely than we have at the involvement of individual English politicians in imperial affairs. Such involvement was surprisingly wide and varied. What did it signify? Were politicians moved to take part by interest or ideology? Did patterns of patronage shape the empire? Such questions have assumed greater importance in recent years, especially with the publication of Stephen Saunders Webb's *The Governors-General*, which argues that a military connection increasingly governed imperial patronage and policy.

* * *

Restoration politicians' most obvious involvement with empire came with membership of one or more of the trades and plantations councils. We have noticed changing membership patterns in these councils, as merchants and planters, numerous early on, were gradually displaced by gentlemen and courtiers. This shift did not so much reflect suspicion of merchants' motives, which was constant, but a growing belief that government should be able to control trade without dependence upon the merchant community. But even in the 1660s, the view that government properly belonged to the political nation required the presence on the councils of trade of grandees like the Duke of Albemarle. His kinsman and Secretary of State Sir William Morrice sat on all five trade and plantations councils established between 1660 and his death in 1669. Sir William Coventry sat on four before he fell from favor in the same year. Other prominent members included Lord Robartes, the Earls of Sandwich, Shaftesbury, Lauderdale, and Arlington, and the Duke of Ormonde. Given such colleagues as these, no wonder John Evelyn delighted in the honor of his appointment to the 1670 council. Indeed, one reason for appointing great men was to provide the councils with dignity and power, a rationale at length perfectly manifested in the creation of the Lords of Trade.[1]

Appointments to these committees reflected other aims, too, both of the crown and of the appointees. Many who advised the crown on trade and colonies were interested parties. Early on, the councils included such men as Thomas Povey and James Drax, whom we have met, Richard Ford, a Lord Mayor of London and a leading merchant as well as an MP, and Sir John Shaw, a customs farmer. In due course, minor figures like Povey disappeared from the councils' membership, although we often find them as clerks or secretaries. However, the increasing eminence of council members did not sever the link between membership and interest. Except for William Penn and Lord Baltimore, each of the major colonial lords proprietors of the Restoration period appeared on at least one plantations committee, as did five governors of royal colonies: Francis Lord Willoughby, Sir William Berkeley, the Earl of Carlisle, Thomas Lord Culpeper, and the second Duke of Albemarle. Several courtiers served the crown as plantations councillors and their own interests in companies trading to America, notably the Royal African and Hudson's Bay. The crown noted one aspect of its own interests in colonies and commerce by appointing to the committees Lord Treasurers Southampton and Danby, most of the Treasury Commissioners of 1667-72 and 1679-85, several Customs Commissioners, and others from the Admiralty and Ordnance.

Parliament adopted similar criteria when it named committees to examine trade, colonial, or revenue bills. Of the men named above who sat as lords or commoners in parliament between 1660 and 1685, only Culpeper failed to serve on at least one such committee. The House of Commons often noted a connection between MPs' interest and involvement, as when the committee appointed to consider the Greenland and Eastland Trades bill included 'all the members of this House that are merchants, or serve for any port-town, and those that are of the council of trade, and the customs'. The House of Lords did not insult members by suggesting that they represented an interest, but some names appeared often enough to indicate a certain presumption. Shaftesbury was rarely left off, perhaps in recognition of his colonial interests as well as his Exchequer and Treasury offices. While he was in London on leave from Barbados Governor William Lord Willoughby was appointed to the Lords' committee on the 1670 bill to raise an additional revenue on sugar. No doubt he was a willing contributor to the resulting constitutional crisis which killed the bill.[2]

There was, then, an imperial connection in Restoration England which consisted of important politicians who served the crown on relevant committees or as officers of state and who were often personally involved in trade and colonization. It is, however, difficult to assess the significance of this connection for imperial history. Charles II's dependence on customs revenue may explain why he appointed four of his five Treasury Commissioners to the 1668 councils of trade and plantations: Shaftesbury, Albemarle, Sir William Coventry, and Sir Thomas Clifford. There they could advance or defend the crown's interests. Yet it is worth noting that one of the commissioners, Sir John Duncombe, was not appointed, that Clifford appeared only briefly, and that on one occasion when Clifford and Duncombe were both involved in a colonial revenue matter they disagreed sharply with one another.[3] Shaftesbury and Albemarle took their common interests as committee members, Treasury commissioners, and Carolina proprietors into several disagreements on colonial matters, notably on the question of policy towards Spanish

America, while Sir William Coventry differed from all his Treasury colleagues in his view that the colonies harmed England's economy.[4] At the other extreme from Coventry, the Earl of Craven, a confidant of the royal family, was extensively involved in colonial proprietorships and trading investments. Yet, despite Craven's membership of the Lords of Trade, one would not assign him a central role in imperial politics. Danby, on the other hand, had few personal interests in America but a very great deal to do with imperial government. Restoration politicians did not, then, always tread a clearly marked path from a common interest in the colonies to an agreed colonial policy.

The problem of assessing the connections between office, interest, and policy is further complicated because colonial business had some difficulty in establishing a bureaucratic home within government.The long series of short-lived committees and councils for the colonies may be regarded by historians as a series of experiments which led ultimately to the creation of the Lords of Trade and then the Board to Trade in 1696. It is as rational to suggest that it implied confusion, or government by accident, even that the colonies were not regarded as important in their own right.[5] For as long as the empire fell under the aegis of no one department of state, it fell to them all as each case warranted. Colonial matters of great and little moment, from the granting of a charter to the appointment of a collector of wine duties, passed through various offices of state on their way to and from the Privy Council.[6] Leading politicians might or might not be plantations councillors, colonial proprietors or trading company investors, but when they served as Lord Treasurer or Attorney General they dealt with colonial business *ex officio*. Clarendon's role in shaping the Restoration settlement would have given him great influence over imperial decisions whatever his office, but because he was Lord Chancellor he passed directly on charters,commissions, and patent offices. This was the stuff of patronage, itself an essential part of Stuart government. The empire fitted the system well, throwing up a number of posts and plums and thus providing temptations both for those who needed patronage and for those who would play the role of patron. Colonial correspondence was full of such business, as men sought (or expressed gratitude for help in finding) office or favor. Such correspondence increased in volume, for the number of colonial offices in London's gift grew during the late seventeenth century, especially after the creation of the colonial customs service in 1673 and, from the 1680s, with the vacation of several proprietary and corporate charters. Favors provided and sought ranged from office itself to material gifts to that simple but vital commodity, information.[7]

Patronage procedures were important. Besides providing fees and, no doubt, bribes vital to the well-being and *amour propre* of officers of state and their clerks, they ceremoniously linked crown and subject, reminding the latter that authority and privilege came from the prerogative. By the same token, patronage methods were resistant to change. Colonial patronage fitted into the routines of state, flowing along channels whose courses were set by history and the present necessities of English government. If the volume of business grew, there were never many colonial offices in absolute terms, let alone in relation to the number of patronage places available in England and Wales. These factors militated against the development of any particular set of reasons for seeking or of criteria for giving colonial patronage. Common sense suggests that a special link between patronage and colonial policy must be regarded as problematical.

A few examples may suffice to show why. The Royal Commission of 1664 was, as we have seen, one of the most important of Clarendon's colonial ventures, linked as it was with generous charters for Connecticut and Rhode Island and aimed at bringing Massachusetts to accept the main outlines of the English Restoration. Assuming that court patronage staffed the commission, we may identify Clarendon as Samuel Maverick's patron and the Duke of York as Richard Nicolls's. Sir Robert Carr enjoyed connections with Arlington and the Duke of Ormonde. If the fourth commissioner, George Cartwright, had a sponsor, could he have induced Arlington, Ormonde, and York to use their patronage to endorse Clarendon's conciliatory policy towards New England? One prefers Sir Joseph Williamson's contemporary judgment that the choice of commissioners was not only independent but also destructive of the commission's objectives. As for the new charters, themselves a form of patronage, it may be that Rhode Island's poverty and lack of court connections allowed Connecticut's agent to gain some territorial advantages for his colony. However, it is more significant that both colonies received charters. The money their agents spent did not determine Clarendon's policy, nor do we learn much about the policy from Clarendon's or his son's financial interests in New England.[8]

Because the commission of 1664 had military as well as political tasks to perform, three of the commissioners had military pasts. This was true of many appointees to colonial office and of most royal governors. Professor Webb's view that this marked a militaristic imperial policy is, however, misguided. Military experience was a criterion easily met by Restoration England's patronage system, and we should therefore be cautious in giving it a policy significance. The nobility and gentry were generally expected to have some acquaintance with the military arts in order, for instance, to take their accustomed places as Lords and Deputies-Lieutenant in the English counties. There was also a tradition of military service abroad, a potentially lucrative profession for younger sons and for gentlemen whose estates provided too little income or excitement. The social class from which governors would anyway be recruited was, then, likely to produce plenty of military men. This tendency was reinforced by the troubles of the Interregnum, which gave England an oversupply of gentlemen soldiers with real, recent military experience. Given the colonies' vulnerability to attack, it would have been irresponsible to appoint governors without military experience. Given the nature of Restoration English society, it would have been difficult to do so.[9]

Brief perusal of the state paper *Calendars* shows that this oversupply of military gentlemen affected all Restoration patronage, colonial and otherwise. Sir Richard Dutton would be governor of Barbados in 1680, but in 1660 he was plain Major Dutton and, like many civil war veterans, underemployed and in need of money or place. Not for Dutton the post of Gentleman in Ordinary to the Queen of Bohemia gained in 1660 by another soldier and future colonial governor, Edmund Andros. Dutton's Cheshire connections aimed him first at £300 as his share for finding money unlawfully concealed by the farmers of tithes for vacant parishes in neighboring Denbighshire. Then, in 1662, Dutton petitioned for the post of comptroller of the customs in Cardiff. Whatever the truth of the claim – supported by three MPs – that the incumbent was notoriously disloyal, Dutton did not become a comptroller until 1668, and then he shared the post. But by 1668 Dutton was again a major, of Sheerness, a post for which the second Dutch war may have made room. Other Restoration petitioners with military pasts and colonial futures included Lord Willoughby, Lord Windsor, Sir Charles Wheeler, and John Lord Vaughan. Their military experience seems not to have been the governing feature of their patronage careers, however. Willoughby was made governor of the Caribbees in lieu of his claim as lessee, and he and the rest of them spent as much time soliciting the crown for civilian favors as for military posts. Vaughan and his relations acquired a wealth of experience gathering up civilian posts and royal manors in South Wales where Vaughan's father, the Earl of Carberry, was Lord Lieutenant and ten of Carmarthenshire's thirty-two JPs were kinsmen. Nothing in the family pattern suggested Lord Vaughan's leap from Wales to the Jamaican governorship.[10] Inevitably, some petitioners ended up in colonial posts and, equally inevitably, most did not. The main reasons for this distribution were negative ones. There were fewer colonial plums to pick, and, in general, the English fruits of patronage were preferred. Certainly Richard Nicolls thought so, if after the fact; the experience of being Colonel-Governor of New York made Nicolls long for the comforts of being the Duke of York's 'domestick'.[11]

The catholic tastes of petitioners for office, to say nothing of the bribes offered by New England land speculators to some courtiers, remind us that pressure for patronage was generated as much by those who sought favor as by patrons. This points up a further difficulty in linking policy with patronage. The motives of office seekers were, like their numbers, legion. Simple greed always played its part and sometimes dominated. When in 1661 it became likely that the Barbadian settlement would include a permanent royal revenue, Thomas Povey petitioned to become the island's Receiver General at an annual salary of £100. A year later, men closer to the king secured the same office at the much higher salary of £400. Thus Thomas Chiffinch and Thomas Ross, respectively page and groom of the royal bedchamber, began their colonial careers. Ross and Chiffinch did not profit from their success, for Governor Lord Willoughby neglected to obey the king's orders to pay them their salary out of the $4^1/_2$ per cent revenue. However, they were unlikely to starve. Their combined annual salaries ran at £1,200 for their delicate bedchamber duties, Chiffinch's post as Comptroller of the Excise and Ross's as Keeper of the Royal Libraries.[12] Their story tells us something about the Restoration settlement in Barbados and about the state of official librarianship in the 1660s: but not much. It seems safe to conclude that in making these appointments the king saw no necessary link between patronage and policy, but insofar as any such link might have been perceived the bedchamber was perhaps a more important place than Thomas Povey's plantations council. New England's land speculators thought so; they made Chiffinch a partner in the Atherton Company, presumably to get his support for their claims, but did not pay Povey the same compliment.[13]

It is unlikely that any imperial vision led Ross and Chiffinch to seek colonial office, and the king's grant to them came from nothing more than his desire to reward loyal servants at no cost to his exchequer. Of course, office seekers and patrons often took a more instrumental view, as in the case of colonists who came to London to secure preferment and therefore to achieve prominence in their local bailiwicks. The rewards of power in America were considerable and might include (for instance) more direct access to the granting of land. Official salaries or fees and the esteem or envy of one's fellow colonists were also attractive, no doubt, but colonists often sought less mundane goals. Restoration patronage, for instance, helped to reduce Massachusetts's hegemonic influence in New England, while Sir William Berkeley used royal favor to press forward his blueprint for Virginia's economic salvation.[14] During the Restoration period colonists learned again, if they had ever forgotten, the lesson that local power and imperial dependence were closely related.

That colonists applied to the crown for office and favor helps us to measure the potential power of the king over colonial governments.

However, an accurate measure of royal power in America requires also a look at how English interests were served by the patronage system. The office of Provost Marshal in the West Indian islands had a military name but a civilian function which particularly concerned those who invested in or traded with the colonies. Its powers over the islands' civil courts attracted Englishmen who wished better results when they sued colonists for recovery of debt. We may assume that Thomas Lynch's success in gaining the good opinion of merchants on the plantations council during his visit to England in 1660-61 helped him to secure a life-time patent as Jamaica's Provost Marshal and embark on a colonial career which would bring him a good marriage, a knighthood, and the Jamaican governorship.[15] But Lynch was a colonist, a permanent settler; traders on the Exchange were doubtless happier with the appointment of Francis Cradocke, one of their own, to be Barbados's Provost Marshal. However, we should not casually accord the merchant connection too much power here. We have seen that the influence of the merchant group over West India policy was limited, and it is worth pointing out that Cradocke's first choice had been Clerk of the Bills in the London Customs House, a post his mercantile friends were unable to gain for him. It went instead to the papist and old cavalier Sir Samuel Tuke, who claimed it by right at the Restoration.[16]

Edwin Stede's 1670 appointment as Barbados's Provost Marshal was a clearer instance of purpose in patronage, even though he had first to buy his patent from yet another groom of the royal bedchamber, James Harrison. Clearly Stede expected to profit personally from the office; but he was also the Royal African Company's agent in Barbados, and might use his new office's powers better to secure the debts owed to the company by sugar planters. The African Company connection suggests also that Secretary of State Lord Arlington, a stockholder and assistant in the company, played more than a merely official part in Stede's appointment. There is no certain evidence for this, but we do know that Arlington was in 1670 intent on encouraging peaceful trade with the Spanish colonies, an objective in which the African Company figured prominently.[17] It is more likely still that Arlington secured the appointment of his friend Sir Charles Wheeler as Governor of the Leeward Islands. As an MP, Wheeler had supported Arlington in the impeachment of Clarendon. It was Wheeler who in debate particularly mentioned the arbitrary government of Clarendon's friend Francis Lord Willoughby in the Caribbees. Here, moreover, political friendship and policy worked together. The relationship between the Leewards and Barbados had never been happy, and the end of the Willoughby leasehold on the Caribbees in 1670 provided an opportunity which was not missed to give the Leewards a separate government, even though William Lord

Willoughby, Francis's heir, continued for a while as governor of Barbados. It was also a good time to do something about the $4^1/_2$ per cent revenue, for during the Willoughby tenure the crown's half of that revenue had come to naught. Now the crown accepted an offer of £8,000 annually for the farm of the revenue from a syndicate which included Wheeler, made Wheeler governor of the Leewards, and ordered that Wheeler's garrison should be paid out of the $4^1/_2$ per cent. Wheeler turned out to be an arbitrary and incompetent royal governor, but patronage, policy, and politics had worked together to make him one.[18]

A wise appointment and a well-meant one, however, do not add up to a pattern. Thomas Martyn's 1674 posting to Jamaica was more typical and suggests that if there was a pattern it was one of accidents. Martyn had no discernible interest or background in colonial office or policy. He was a merchant who had suffered losses from French privateers and petitioned the king for recompense from or letters of marque against the French. His claim seems to have been accepted as just, but in 1674 Charles II had no desire to ask King Louis to give money to someone else nor any wish to offend the French, and so Martyn became Secretary of Jamaica and, for good measure, collector of the island's wine duties. Martyn was appointed in preference to William Blathwayt, but only in hindsighted view of Blathwayt's later impact on imperial administration does that fact have any interest. In 1674 Blathwayt petitioned for the post largely on the ground that his uncle Richard Povey was the deceased incumbent. Given the circumstances, Martyn's appointment made more sense, but had little to do with colonial policy. Posts such as Martyn's had not yet assumed their role as essential links in the chain of command and information between crown and colony. Shortly after Martyn's arrival in Jamaica, he was thrown into jail for the crime of seeking to exercise his offices, but his pleas for help had little impact in London.[19]

The English patronage system got Martyn a colonial post he had not asked for and then served him ill. This was a common experience, but in general those with better connections than Martyn's fared better than he did. In 1661, as we have seen, Thomas Modyford avoided a far worse fate than had ever threatened Martyn by the grace of his cousin the Duke of Albemarle. Albemarle's influence helped, too, in securing Modyford a knighthood and the Jamaica governorship. Once established in Jamaica, however, Modyford fashioned a more complex relationship with England's patronage system. War with the Dutch and French increased the attractions of a *modus vivendi* with Jamaica's privateers, while Lord Arlington's complicated diplomacy required better relations with Spanish America and increased the risks of Modyford's deepening alliance with the privateers.[20] In these circumstances, Albemarle's anti-Spanish prejudices became as valuable as his kinship. Through letters and direct contact, Modyford, his brother James, and his son Charles cultivated the duke's Elizabethan phobias, but they also kept closely in touch with opposing forces at court, not least with Arlington and Joseph Williamson, Arlington's secretary. By playing Arlington off against Albemarle, Modyford escaped unscathed from the consequences of the privateers' raid on Porto Bello in 1668, and indeed seemed to have gained royal approval for it.[21] Albemarle's death in January 1670, news of which reached Jamaica in March, may have precipitated the decision to launch an attack on Cuba, a desperate gamble for success at court as well as in the Caribbean.[22] Just so, while wind and weather took Henry Morgan's fleet to Panama City instead of St. Iago, Modyford went shopping for a new patron, and thought he might find one in Shaftesbury, whom he begged for protection against his enemies at court. 'Judge you, my lord, in this exigent, what course could be more frugal, more prudential, more hopeful – the men volunteers, the ships, arms, ammunition their own, their victuals the enemy's, and such enemies as they have always beaten'. Shaftesbury probably was unsympathetic, but in the circumstances of 1670 it was unlikely that anyone could have saved Modyford from Arlington's ire.[23]

Patronage and policy undoubtedly came together when Arlington engineered both Modyford's recall under arrest and the appointment of his successor Sir Thomas Lynch. But the connection soon dissolved, leaving Lynch to work out his own *modus vivendi* with the privateers.[24] First Modyford and then Lynch discovered that the patronage system was an incidental rather than an integral part of imperial government. The colonial patronage system did, however, respond to changes in English government and politics. In the 1660s, Clarendon used colonial patronage rather as an end in itself than a political tool, for he aimed to restore government to its proper form and to those whose right it was. The men who replaced Clarendon were too many and too much at odds with one another to impose their will on the whole apparatus of government, but cabal ministers did use patronage effectively in their own bailiwicks, and also during this period the plantations council began to assert authority over some colonial office-holders, notably royal governors. Danby, as chief minister and Lord Treasurer, made better use of patronage to enhance control over both parliament and government, and his practice spread to the empire through the Lords of Trade and their minion William Blathwayt, patrons who expected those who gained from their favor at least to follow their orders. Those who did, like Sir William Stapleton in the Leewards, could win high praise and long tenure; those who did not were increasingly likely to lose office or, at the least, to get a severe ticking off.[25]

The consensus that the colonies were important led many Restoration era politicians to become involved in empire officially and privately. They had much in common, not only their belief in the importance of empire but also their interest in science and mathematics. Many of them were fellows – Charles II was patron and founder – of the new Royal Society. Besides curiosity in things American, like floating mosses from New England and Barbadian plants said to rejuvenate aged bulls, no doubt many came to share the view of humbler members like Worsley, Locke, and John Collins that statecraft itself was or could be made a manipulable science.[26] All of these commonalities, not least initial adherence to the Restoration settlement of 1660, had their certain effect on English and imperial politics and policy. It is equally apparent, however, that this consensus was not important enough of itself to shape imperial patronage or to give birth to a specifically imperial policy. The adherents to the imperial consensus were, after all, a pretty diverse lot who found it difficult enough to stick together on matters of domestic politics. A list of politicians who took a more than ordinary interest in the colonies and their trade would include, among others, such men as York, Shaftesbury, Danby, Arlington, Clarendon, and of course Charles II himself. We are reminded that Restoration politics made strange bedfellows but only rarely did it make for purposeful government. More than occasionally, some of these bedfellows would have gladly seen others hang. It seems safe to conclude that widespread involvement in imperial affairs owed to a mixed bag of motive and purpose: court fashion, conviction, patriotism, sheer self-interest, and doubtless others.

While the politicians bickered over how and, in a sense, whether England and the empire were to be governed, some of them had perforce to govern their American fiefs. These were the lords proprietors. Not all colonial proprietors gave much time or thought to their colonies, but historians are fortunate that two who stand out as active proprietors were also men of undoubted importance in English politics. By examining the colonial careers of James, Duke of York, and Anthony Ashley Cooper, Earl of Shaftesbury, we may better understand such connections as did exist between visions of empire and the politics of Restoration England.

* * *

Comparisons between York and Shaftesbury and their colonies of New York and Carolina are valuable because both adhered to the imperial consensus but came from opposite ends of the acceptable spectrum of restoration politics. Shaftesbury early showed his colors by taking parliament's side in the civil wars and then serving the Protectorate. By the 1660s, he was friend and patron of John Locke, and although he served Charles II well for over a decade, from 1673 he became estranged from the king. During the popish plot and exclusion crisis, 1678-81, he championed what might have been a parliamentary revolution, possibly a more radical one than the Glorious Revolution of 1688, which occurred five years after Shaftesbury's death in exile. The Duke of York professed a different politics. By inclination and experience a soldier rather than a politician, this younger son of the martyred Charles I distrusted parliaments and took an exalted view of kingship. He sealed his political identity by converting to Catholicism in 1668, a decision which eventually brought about the Glorious Revolution and James's exile. But it had more immediate implications, too. Charles's policies during the cabal years intensified the nation's historic fears of Roman religion and French politics, as did James's resignation of all his offices after the 1673 Test Act, which confirmed rumors of his conversion. As it became clear that Charles would not produce legitimate offspring, such fears focused on James as heir apparent. The popish plot hysteria thus led naturally to a clash between the king, intent on preserving the succession and the prerogative, and Shaftesbury, determined to exclude James from kingship.

These differences between York and Shaftesbury found obvious expression in their proprietaries. Carolina developed from the first in a parliamentary way, and after 1669, when Shaftesbury took over from the other seven proprietors the main responsibility for the colony, it seemed at times to be a laboratory of advanced 'whiggish' thinking. Not so New York. For nearly twenty years, the duke governed his colony without elected assemblies and by a court system and laws imposed by prerogative order. These contrasts strengthen the case that in America as in England York and Shaftesbury represented the ultimately incompatible extremes of the restoration consensus. Yet some caution and a closer look are required before we accept this *prima facie* case. The contrast it sets is insufficient because the differences between Carolina and New York ran deeper than those between autocratic and parliamentary forms of government to include radically opposed social and economic assumptions and aims. At the same time, however, these contrasts were by no means complete. Shaftesbury and York were strong proprietors whose common pursuit in America of effective government and prosperous economies reminds us that the political distance between them, if great, had once been comprehended by the restoration settlement of 1660. Leviathan lurked in both their courses and forecast the alternatives facing the empire and England in the last quarter of the seventeenth century. The early histories of New York and Carolina clearly exemplify the intimate connections between English and American politics.

Whatever James's politics, representative government was not on the cards for New York in 1664. Under Dutch rule, there had been no representative assembly, and the colony's status as a conquest left it by recognized principles of law at the conqueror's will. Charles II, the conqueror, gave it to his brother by a proprietorial charter which did not oblige James to call an assembly. There were, anyway, good reasons for not doing so. The only good parliament was a loyal one, and James had reason to doubt the loyalty of a population made up of a conquered Dutch majority and an English Puritan minority. Thus, although James's instructions to Governor Richard Nicolls do not survive, we may assume that by casting his government in a prerogative mould Nicolls pleased his master.[27]

Even so, Nicolls imposed autocracy cautiously. Moderate terms of surrender signed on 27 August 1664 accomplished this end for New York City itself, as did similar agreements with the Dutch at Albany and the polyglot outposts on the Delaware River.[28] Treaties of surrender, however, would not do for the Puritan English of Long Island. Recognizing this, Nicolls promised Long Islanders 'equall (if not greater Freedomes & Immunityes) than any of his Majestyes Colonyes in New England' and called for the election of deputies to meet at Hempstead in order to 'Settle good and knowne Laws . . . and to receive your best advice and information'. It sounded like an assembly, not least because Nicolls had already promised the Dutch burghers of New York City the right to choose deputies who would have 'free voices in all public affairs, as much as any other Deputies'.[29] Perhaps because they read too much into Nicolls's overtures and certainly because they did not place ducal government high on their list of preferences, several delegates arrived at Hempstead in February 1665 ready to press for political and economic guarantees, including taxation by consent only.[30] Nicolls was ready for them. He presented the meeting with his full authority from the king and the duke, a ready-made set of laws drawn largely from New England codes, and a demand for a penny rate to pay for the towns' government. Nicolls made it clear that it was the meeting's duty to submit to the 'Duke's Laws' rather than pass its own. The townsmen bridled, even forced amendments to some of the laws, but Nicolls conceded little. Hempstead was not a precedent for future assemblies, but a surrender to the duke's government and his governor. Almost all of the more than thirty delegates signed the required letter of submission.[31]

It is hard to see what else they could have done, but on returning to their towns several deputies felt their neighbors' anger at their surrender. This resentment continued. Long Islanders occasionally refused to pay the duke's taxes, and several towns neglected for a long time to take out the patents urged upon them by successive governors. It was not until 1676 that the last three towns symbolized their submission by asking Governor Edmund Andros to confirm their land patents. However, two of these towns, Southampton and Southold, had from 1667 submitted *de facto* by accepting the jurisdiction of the duke's courts. Southold did not hesitate to use the Duke's Law of "Possession" to advance its claim to Plum Island. Throughout Long Island, individuals as well as towns used the Duke's Laws and courts to sue and be sued, to sort out boundary disputes, to secure their Indian purchases. In doing so they submitted to the same logic which had swayed the Hempstead meeting and, twenty years previously, had forced New Hampshire and Maine settlements to succumb to the authority of the Massachusetts charter. Thus Jamaica, possibly the first of the Long Island towns to take out a new patent, immediately asked Nicolls's help in settling a local land dispute. Their affairs required a government, and they had but one. Legality and legitimacy belonged to the Duke of York, not to individual towns.[32] The imposition of prerogative government on Long Island was a considerable achievement, but it was not a surprising one.

It is also important to realize that New York's autocracy was limited. Their possession of legitimacy gave them an advantage they were not slow to use, but beyond requiring submission governors asked little of Long Islanders. The penny rate set at Hempstead raised but £200, country pay (about £100 sterling). It was, Nicolls told Clarendon, all the poor farmers could manage. Although Nicolls and his successors did eventually raise more, even that was not much. In 1680, the nineteen Long Island towns produced a tax revenue of just £517, country pay. Paid in kind, these taxes were hardly worth the trouble to collect. Indeed, Nicolls affected unconcern when several towns refused to pay his second rate. If they wished not to pay him, he said, they could meet the costs of government themselves, although of course Nicolls would continue to appoint local officers, who were part of his government however they were paid.[33] Apparently New York's governors had no grand design in mind for the Long Island towns.

The Duke of York did much to constrain his governors to a limited set of objectives. Even had they wished a more active autocracy, the duke deprecated such an objective in his periodic advice to use the colonists with all possible kindness and not ask too much of them.[34] However, the most significant limitation the duke imposed on his governors was probably unthinking. In June 1664, only days after Nicolls's fleet had set sail for America and thus before the conquest was his, James granted the lands between the Delaware and Hudson rivers to the courtiers John Lord Berkeley and Sir George Carteret, already part-proprietors of

Carolina.[35] Historians have offered various reasons for this munificent and misguided grant: James's inexperience, his impatience with the details of administration, even his rather demanding love life. It has also been noted that in comparison to other items of ducal income and expense New York was small beer; giving part of it away to two friends of the exile was at once the least James could do and not much. Taken together with James's failure to provide adequately for New York's financial needs and his placid acceptance of Governor Nicolls's decision not to press the disputed eastern boundary with Connecticut, the New Jersey grant to Berkeley and Carteret signalled a decidedly cavalier attitude on the duke's part towards his proprietary.[36] The duke's casual generosity was significant. The Jersey grant was a monarch's act, conveying both a large territory and rights of government to the recipients. As a grant by one subject to others it had no Restoration parallel and few precedents from before 1660.[37] Only the king's 1672 grant of much of Virginia to Lords Arlington and Culpeper matched James's gift to Berkeley and Carteret. These grants remind us that the Restoration empire was one in which the monarch's 'mere grace and motion' still ruled and tell us why the duke's own charter for New York placed few constraints upon him; he was a prince of the blood royal who might or might not govern colonists by prerogative means. To give away government was to possess sovereignty, a claim which no mere subject could safely make.[38] The New Jersey grant was also monarchical in its apparent unconcern for James's parochial interests as proprietor of what remained of New York.

However, James's governors had to live with the consequences. Nicolls, who quickly grasped New York's problems, protested frankly when he heard of the grant. He admired James's generosity but resented its destination, and he hoped that by redressing ducal ignorance ('great have beene the abuses of false reports') the grant might be withdrawn or changed. Later governors echoed his complaints. As a grant of government, the duke's gift denied New York port duties and customs on direct trades to New Jersey, offered a duty-free smugglers' route into New York, and diverted potential income from survey fees and quit rents. These revenue problems were to loom large, but it was also important that the loss of New Jersey helped to cast New York's government into a passive role. Colonial governments, as we have seen, grew vigorous from necessity, gaining function and muscle as well as revenue from overseeing new settlements and opening new trades. Doubtless Nicolls's claims about New Jersey's potential were inflated, but they mirrored New York's limited supply of attractive land; prospective farmers had to choose between living cheek by jowl with Dutchmen and Indians in the Hudson River valley or scrabbling a living from Long

Island's sandy soil. A hint of how things might have gone was provided by Nicolls's early success in organizing settlements by patent on the Hudson's west bank. The arrival of Captain Philip Carteret, the new governor of New Jersey and Sir George's nephew, at once removed from Nicolls's government these fruits of his labor and gave him less to do in future.[39]

Financially, the Jersey grant threw the duke's governors back on what was left, New York City itself, the Long Island towns, and the settlements along the Hudson up to Albany. The colony's revenue problems were worsened by James's financial dependence on the crown, then by the Dutch reconquest of New York in 1673, during the third Dutch war. In 1674, James's instructions to his new governor, Major Edmund Andros, sought a solution. Present levels of direct taxation were not to be raised, and quit-rents were to be imposed only on new land patents. Of course these revenues were to be reviewed to assess the 'probability of the increase or diminution thereof', but James and his advisors placed their main hopes on the customs. James took the calculated risk of lowering the *ad valorem* rates in order to attract more trade.[40] Presumably these instructions reflected the findings of James's Commission of Revenue, which reviewed New York's finances in 1674, but they were also significant concessions to the logic of colonization and to successive governors' advice that public and private prosperity depended utterly on new settlement and on 'constant supplyes of trade'. Governors Nicolls, Francis Lovelace, and Andros all supported local merchants' quest for a direct trade with Holland. Servants of a royal duke might wink at evasions of England's navigation laws,[41] and as head of a prerogative government James himself could raise or lower taxes as he wished, but the fiscal logic which required expanded or freer trade did not fit political realities in New York.

Forced from the first to depend mainly on trade revenues, James's governors talked free trade but built up a monopoly system based on New York City merchants and Albany fur *handlaers*. Despite complaints from Long Island towns, the list of city monopolies grew rapidly from Lovelace's first year in office to include such items as butchering all meat for export, control of the export trade in wheat, and an export monopoly on flour milling and packing. City merchants even won control of the river trade between New York and Albany, although the *handlaers* retained the direct trade with the Indians. Of course, the trend towards funnelling trade through the city owed partly to its superb harbor and its location. Governor Nicolls and his successors stressed these assets in urging the duke to resume control of New Jersey and to take control of western Connecticut.[42] But why go to such lengths to enforce on New York colony itself the city's natural monopoly? Here politics, not geography, proved crucial. A government which neither would nor could raise significant revenues from its outlying regions in the form of rates or quit-rents would not eagerly base its fiscal survival on collecting customs duties in the same places. Governor Andros did briefly allow ports of entry at the eastern end of Long Island, but he withdrew the privilege when it appeared that the duties were not being properly assessed or collected. Under strict instructions to 'lessen the chardge of the government without weakening it or hazarding it', Andros confessed the government's real weakness by falling back on the city's monopolies in order to enforce trade regulations and collect customs duties.[43]

From England, the duke's secretary Sir John Werden praised such schemes as 'not only secureing better the publique dutyes at New Yorke, but inriching the people thereof by giving them the opportunity of the first marketts'. Werden would not have been surprised to see the concurrent development of close political relationships between the governors and some New York City merchants. Monopoly regulations benefited both, the merchants for obvious reasons. For the governors, city monopolies made customs easier to collect and, by increasing trade within the city, added to the income of public officials and public facilities like the weigh house. Business and politics went together in other ways, too. Governors engaged in private trading ventures with city partners in order to supplement their meager salaries, while city merchants came to dominate the political institutions with which the duke's men had most to do, the city's Common Council and the colony's Council. Not surprisingly, governors generally turned a deaf ear to protests from Long Island towns against the city's stranglehold on trade.[44] This added political distance to the miles already between them, but could James's government maintain its hold on New York City itself?

The answer, eventually, was no. In the meanwhile, Governor Andros, like his predecessors, was thrown back on territorial expansion as a solution. Singing to a familiar tune, Andros lamented the loss of New Jersey and western Connecticut. Andros and the duke's English advisers looked further afield, even to Boston, with visions of trade and empire centered on New York City. The time seemed ripe. The new Lords of Trade were steamed up about New England, and the duke's obligations to the New Jersey proprietors weakened as Lord Berkeley sold his interests to Quakers and Sir George Carteret aged. In 1679 Sir John Werden restated the duke's right to the government of New Jersey. Meanwhile, in America, Andros stepped up pressure against his neighbors. He attempted to exercise authority at Saybrook in Connecticut while that colony was embroiled in King Philip's War, and he troubled both East and West New Jersey over trade and customs issues. With Carteret's death in January 1680 it must have seemed that New York's problems were soon to be solved by territorial and trade expansion based on the established pattern of channeling commerce through New York City's harbor and merchants.[45]

That solution was to be denied to the Duke of York. The exclusion crisis could not have helped, with James often absent from London and gossip incorrectly having him losing Charles's support. But this was not crucial. New York business continued to be dealt with at about the same pace as before. It even picked up a little when in July 1680 James referred his claim to West New Jersey to Sir William Jones's arbitration. Jones was a curious choice, for although he was an eminent lawyer he was also an exclusionist. In any case, Jones ruled that James had transferred his rights of government as well as of land and therefore had no standing in West New Jersey.[46] After Jones's decision, James again formally surrendered his claims to East New Jersey, and it may be that this, in turn, led James to acquiesce in the grant of Pennsylvania to William Penn and, in 1683, to assign to Penn his rights over the Delaware colony.[47] Events ultimately showed that James had not abandoned the idea of a consolidated government over the whole region, but in 1680 the territorial expansion of New York was well and truly arrested.

Meanwhile, New York's financial problems had worsened. Governor Andros's early optimism had given way to red balance sheets, and, worse for Andros, these continued despite reports (including his own) that trade had increased. Any suspicions that might have been roused by this seeming disparity were sharpened by complaints that Andros and his customs collector, William Dyer, were guilty of fraud and favoritism. James may have initially believed the charges, for he commissioned a merchant, James Lewin, to sail to New York and conduct a full investigation of the colony's trade and revenue system. As it happened, Andros and Dyer were exonerated, and their later preferments prove that James was ultimately convinced of their innocence. The real significance of the Lewin commission lies in its instructions, which effectively conceded that New York was not governable in the old style. Besides investigating Andros and Dyer, Lewin was to report on the system they administered. He was to 'find out whether the free trade of any of the inhabitants . . . now is or lately hath beene obstructed or hindered, and how such obstructions may be removed, and how and by what methods the trade and traders in those places may be encouraged and increased'. These were questions which advanced their own answers, for if James did not know whether or not his officers were honest, he well knew that New York's trade had been regulated through a place, not 'places' and by monopoly devices rather than 'free trade'. If he had forgotten, Lewin could tell him, for Lewin was one of a group of new merchants which found New York's restrictive atmosphere too stifling for comfort or prosperity.[48]

Radical changes in New York were now inevitable, but they were made urgent by a customs revolt in 1680-81. When Andros was recalled, neither he nor James had renewed the customs duties which by James's own instructions were to expire in November 1680. Caretaker governor Anthony Brockholls and collector Dyer went on collecting them anyway. In ordinary times, this might have passed without notice, but with Dyer already under the duke's suspicion city merchants dared to refuse to pay their dues and, when Dyer insisted, they brought him to trial charged with high treason.[49] They did not attempt to make the charge stick when Dyer was taken to London, but the episode demonstrated that the political foundations of James's government were as shaky as its finances. Both would have to be repaired by the materials at hand. Unable to soak enough revenue out of New York City's trade and resigned to operating from a narrowed territorial base, James turned to the colonists with the suggestion of an assembly.

Due credit has been given to New Yorkers for the part they played in forcing this change. The legislation produced by the first assembly, including the famed Charter of Liberties of 1683, proved that New Yorkers knew how to use their own troubled history, English constitutional precedent, and accepted practice elsewhere in America to earn 'the rights of Englishmen'.[50] However, they would have had to be very aggressively whiggish indeed to have demanded much more than James conceded to them, first in his instructions to James Lewin but more especially in his instructions to his new governor, Thomas Dongan. James was not one to do things by halves. His colony's parliament was to consist of eighteen deputies, elected by all the freeholders, and to have full liberty to debate 'all matters as shall be apprehended proper to be established for laws for the good government' of New York and to enact those laws. Dongan was to govern by the laws then in force until the assembly passed new ones, which put the Duke's Laws under the assembly's review. The only prerogative laws which were not to stand were those for revenue; Dongan was not 'upon any pretence or colour of law or other establishment' to levy any 'Customs or impost . . . until the same shalbe enacted and established by law'. James even accorded the assembly the right to appropriate money 'for the support of the Government or to such uses as the said law shall appoint', although his name had to appear first in the appropriation. James secured his interests and lord and proprietor of New York by retaining control over public and judicial appointments, the militia, new land grants and quit rents upon them. Nor could the assembly encroach on the governor's power to execute the laws. Still, James bound himself to assent to all the assembly's laws provided that they were manifestly for the public good and not detrimental to his rights.[51]

Anyone reading the instructions might reasonably guess that James would assent to all the laws passed by the assembly's first session. Even the laws making up the Charter of Liberties went beyond James's instructions in only a few particulars, notably in their attempt to give the gloss of English law and constitutional perpetuity to James's instructions. James did give preliminary approval to the charter, but before it reached the final stages he had become king,[52] and in 1685 he rejected the charter and allowed the assembly to lapse. Clearly, then, James had not converted to whiggery, but that is neither surprising nor interesting. The question which remains is this: why had this most autocratic of Stuarts conceded to his fledgling assembly a constitutional position in advance of that enjoyed by most other colonial legislatures? It is possible that James only fattened the fledgling preparatory to killing it off once it produced a golden egg, and the assembly did oblige with a 100 per cent increase in customs duties. Yet the legislative solution to New York's money problems had always been available. Edmund Andros suggested it in 1675, and if James had seen an assembly as nothing more than a short-cut to solvency he could have adopted the idea then or sooner.[53] He was a seventeenth-century Englishman who knew the usefulness of parliaments in granting revenues. But he was a prerogative man, too, suspicious of the 'Inconveniences' that attended legislatures. We may learn something more of James's reasons from a review of the colonial career of his arch enemy, the Earl of Shaftesbury.

* * *

Shaftesbury and his seven co-proprietors of Carolina began their colonial venture in 1663. Six of the eight were prominent courtiers (Clarendon, Albemarle, Shaftesbury, John Lord Berkeley, the Earl of Craven, and Sir George Carteret), two were colonists with court connections (Sir William Berkeley and Sir John Colleton). Although all adhered to the settlement of 1660, they were a diverse lot. During the period before 1669, when Shaftesbury effectively took sole direction of Carolina, proprietorial duties were shared, and it is doubtful whether any one of the eight could have imposed either ideological conformity or a particular colonial policy on the others. Rather they bowed to necessities which did not at first affect the Duke of York. Whereas he took over what was reputed to be a going concern, their territory was a wilderness. Whereas he was a royal duke who might rule his colony in a prerogative way, they were subjects and their charter required them to rule not only according to English law but also by consent. Thus the Carolina proprietors had to offer favorable terms of settlement. Had there been any doubt in the proprietors' minds on these points, they were quickly dispelled by two groups interested in Carolina settlement, the Cape Fear Company, made up of New Englanders and London merchants, and the Barbadian Adventurers.

Both groups warned that in going to Carolina they did not intend to leave behind them 'that freedome to our persons which [we] were borne with', nor would they sacrifice to the proprietors 'the full fruition of those fortunes we have made our own'. These prospective migrants demanded secure land titles, freedom of trade, and extensive political rights. To accept monopoly trade regulation would be, the Barbadians stated, to surrender to an 'Egyptian task-master', and they would have no part of it. The New Englanders planning to settle at Cape Fear required the continuation there of the privileges they had long enjoyed. Clearly both groups were familiar with their colonies' and England's recent history, but the Barbadians' demands were more explicit, perhaps because of their recent experience in trying to escape the toils of the Caribbee proprietary. In order to 'have the sole power of electing all delligates Governors and officers, and making Lawes, and governing amongst themselves', they asked to be incorporated by charter under the Carolina proprietary.

Unlike James, however, the Carolina proprietors could not resign to others the power of government conferred upon them by the crown. Thus they retained the power to appoint and dismiss governors and other officers. They also, of course, retained their interests over land and quit-rents.[54] Nevertheless, they made concessions. Settlers would have an assembly. Not only did the charter require it, but the proprietors (who did not wish to invest much money anyway) expected colonists to meet the costs of government. The proprietors consented to a generous headright system, laid down clear rules for land tenure and titles, turned over to the assembly responsibility for ordering the colony's trade, and in general made it clear that Carolina freeholders would share in the privileges conferred by the charter. These 'Concessions and Agreements'[55] were important precisely because they were unremarkable. They recalled the Virginia Company's Great Charter of 1618 and anticipated the Duke of York's 'concessions' of 1682 in their recognition of the necessities of colonization. This underlying logic continued to operate on Shaftesbury after he took over the direction of Carolina in 1669. He still aimed to entice settlers while retaining proprietorial sovereignty and sustaining the proprietors' economic stake. These objectives brought him troubles not strikingly different from those which almost killed the colony in the mid-1660s. Shaftesbury's significant accomplishment was to impart to Carolina a rationale which transcended the nuts-and-bolts character of the original Concessions and Agreements and gave the Carolina design a leading place in the political history of empire. The main vehicle of this transformation was the Fundamental Constitutions of 1669, a joint effort of Shaftesbury and his friend John Locke.

The Fundamental Constitutions is undeniably an odd document. The practical requirements it laid on the infant society were enormous and could not have been fulfilled in a life time. To create just one of its counties required patenting titles to 480,000 acres:12,000 acres to each of the eight proprietors; 48,000 acres to a major local noble, the landgrave; 24,000 acres to each of two minor nobles, or cassiques; and the remaining 288,000 acres to various ranks of freeholders, from lords of manors each holding between 3,000 and 12,000 acres down to 50-acre freeholders. That would have been only the beginning, for the huge estates of the proprietors, nobility, and manorial lords had to be peopled by dependents, African slaves and European leetmen. Even when all this had been accomplished, the single county could not hope to man the elaborate central government laid down in the Fundamentals. The 'Grand Council', an essential element in the government, was to have a membership of fifty drawn from various ranks but including the entire local nobility of at least seven counties.[56] Surely Shaftesbury and Locke did not seriously intend to implement this catalogue of impossibilities.[57]

Yet historians must take the thing seriously. As an intellectual set piece it was a base-eight numbers game used by a prominent politician and his philosopher friend to conceptualize an ideal social and political order. As a utopian fancy it had much in common with (and borrowed much from) James Harrington's *Oceana*. Even its daft vastness had significance; the Fundamentals was a grand gesture, a reminder that still, after six decades' practical experience of empire, Englishmen could think expansively about America as a *tabula rasa* on which they might write as they wished. Game or gesture, however, the Fundamental Constitutions represented an effort to solve a real problem. Shaftesbury had taken over a failed venture, and he and Locke meant to resurrect it. It was an earnest of serious intentions that Shaftesbury asked and the other proprietors agreed both to approve the document and to invest £500 each immediately and £200 each annually for four years. This was real money and a substantial increase on previous investment even if such sums were easy for some of the proprietors to find. Shaftesbury in-sisted that his plan was a working model for Carolina's development, and for some years after his death the other proprietors continued to regard it as such. Indeed, with appropriate modifications, Shaftesbury applied the Fundamentals to the Bahamas Islands, for which he and several of the Carolina proprietors received a charter in 1669.[58] Clearly, Shaftesbury and Locke perceived some link between theory and practice.

Underneath the document's utopian baroque decoration of offices, courts, and honors lay a theoretically simple and mathematically precise structure. Just as trade and customs statistics rendered the old mysteries of commerce irrelevant to the working statesman, so might numbers lay bare the mysteries of politics and provide a foundation for a stable social order. Thus the Fundamental Constitutions weighed up wealth and rank by acreages and apportioned power accordingly. Shaftesbury aimed to balance the colony government on this principle. Government was not, however, to be balanced within itself so that no one part of it dominated the rest, nor was balance intended to render government safe. Those eighteenth-century vogues were not Shaftesbury's purpose and were far from being his century's main political problem. Through the Fundamental Constitutions, as through most of his career as a leading English politician, Shaftesbury aimed to create a stable and effective state. Accordingly, the Fundamental Constitutions did not separate powers but gathered them. Power was to be lodged in an interlocking directorate of proprietors, local nobles, and manorial lords. Not until there were eight counties would the proprietors and nobility be balanced by commoners even in the colony parliament, and commoners would never attain parity in the proprietorial courts or on the Grand Council. To underline where power lay, Carolina's parliament was.like Ireland's, barred from initiating legislation.[59] Shaftesbury's balance was not within government but between government and society, and the balance mechanism was a virtual identity between state and society, between power and wealth.

This balance determined the relationship between central and local government, a serious problem in seventeenth-century English and colonial politics. In each county, local administration was dominated by those holding the most property: the landgrave, the two cassiques, and the manorial lords, with some help from substantial freemen. On their individual estates, moreover, nobles and manorial lords were to be virtually independent of external power and unambiguously supreme over their leetmen and slaves. On the other hand, the proprietors' collective wealth in each county was to be considerable but not dominant; their 96,000 acres precisely balanced the property holdings of the three local nobles, a balance then tipped in the locality's favor by the holdings of manorial lords and freemen. The proprietors' real power rested on their substantial landholdings in every county. From these bases they were to dominate every section of the central government and even to sit in the commons house of parliament. At the very center, supreme in wealth, rank and power, was the Palatine's Court, made up solely of the eight proprietors. Power radiated outward from this court to every agency of the central government and beyond to some aspects of local administration, but became more attenuated at each remove from the center. The proprietors had their finger in nearly every pie, but could grasp only a few – all of these agencies of central government – in the palms of their hands. One aim, then, of Shaftesbury's balance was to create a government in which the proprietors could not oppress local magnates within their counties nor, as Shaftesbury put it himself, even the 'meanest freeholder' on his 50 acres.[60] In Carolina, the Englishman's house was truly to be his castle, as long as it was his.

More than mere logic dictated the obvious corollary that the meanest freeholders ought not to be able to oppress proprietors and other men of wealth. Had the Fundamental Constitutions ever come fully into effect, ordinary freeholders would have had a hard time of that, but once in the early stages Shaftesbury, alarmed that they might succeed, withdrew his own 12,000-acre estate on the Edisto River from the colonial government's jurisdiction. It was worse than a state of war, he wrote, for those who had little or no estate to have power of making laws over those of great estate. For the most part, however, Shaftesbury feared the poor, if at all, as economic leeches who 'eate upon us'.[61] In the 1670s, the main threat to government seemed to come from jumped-up governors like Sir John Yeamans in Carolina and Hugh Wentworth in the Bahamas.

Given Shaftesbury's rapidly developing suspicions of Charles II, it is tempting to argue that his dim view of colonial governors grew out of his changing stance in English politics, but in terms of chronology the opposite case would be more logical. Trouble with Yeamans blew up in 1672 while Shaftesbury still loyally advised Charles against caving in to parliament as the grand design reached its climacteric. It was the logic of the Fundamentals which governed Shaftesbury's approach. The Fundamentals, indeed, had made Yeamans governor in the first place. He had both English and colonial rank, and Shaftesbury chose him over the perfectly competent John West simply because Yeamans was a landgrave, the only one in the colony.[62] But in a new society there were few men of substance, and Yeamans's combination of wealth, rank, and gubernatorial power could upset Shaftesbury's balance. Shaftesbury was ready to warn Yeamans when the governor's conduct seemed to warrant it. Shaftesbury had 'engaged my word that the people shall live safe there under the Protection of a faire and equall government'; people had gone to Carolina on that assurance and they were not to be oppressed. Had the Fundamentals been fully in operation, the situation should not have arisen, but in Carolina's embryonic state only the proprietors could balance a bad governor. In an extraordinary letter Shaftesbury not only informed Yeamans's council that he was looking for a new governor but also reminded proprietors' deputies on the council that they represented the proprietors' persons & therefore . . . ought not to deminish our right by makeing themselves but Cyphers & Submitting too much to the will of any Governor nay if . . . any of the Lords Proprietors should come upon the place our deputys ought to maintain our authority & share in the government according to the Fundamental Constitutions."[63]

By taking Yeamans down a peg, Shaftesbury underlined his intention to strengthen government by identifying it with the social order envisaged in the Fundamental Constitution. Yet there was never any doubt where, ultimately, power resided. When Governor Wentworth threatened the balance in the Bahamas by making common cause with the colonists against the proprietors, Shaftesbury 'would desire to know [of Wentworth] wether you hold your Place of Gouvernor as Chosen by the People or us; For if you hold it from the People, we shall quickly try how safe it will be under another'.[64] Already entitled by royal charter to name their governors, the lords proprietors intended the Fundamental Constitutions to insure that they and their properties would be the weightiest elements in the social and political balance. Shaftesbury's impatience with insubordination was strengthened by a lively sense that his personal dignity was involved. Perhaps a royal duke could take a more relaxed view of obstreperous colonists than the former Dorset baronet who, in 1672 risen to an earldom and the Lord Chancellorship of England, threatened that should Carolina fall by Sir John Yeamans's perversity

> the Indignation of haveing a designe of soe faire hopes & soe great Consequence upon which I had sett my minde ruined by his Covetousness or Ambition will make me endeavour to reach him & require Satisfaction in the remotest parts of the world for in this which is my darling and wherein I am entrusted alsoe by others I cannot suffer my selfe & them to be injured by anybody without great resentment.[65]

Nothing in the Duke of York's colonial correspondence breathes such fierce determination to command, but we cannot doubt that both proprietors aimed to govern authoritatively in America.

* * *

This is an important similarity between the proprietors, but had the Fundamental Constitutions come fully into operation, the contrast between colonies would have been very nearly absolute. The identity between government and society which was central to Shaftesbury's blueprint scarcely arose in New York. Until the duke ordained an assembly, his colonial government had an oddly disjointed relationship with its society. Indeed, early New York is better regarded as a regime than as a colony. Each area was governed differently. Long Island and Westchester, governed from the first by the Duke's Laws, were made up of distinct towns, each patented by the governor and governed by appointed magistrates and constables. Some outlying islands and a couple of other areas were autonomous manors, receiving authority from the governor but otherwise institutionally as remote from him as they were geographically distant. Albany and Schenectady were military outposts, the former enjoying and the latter trying to break into a monopoly over the fur trade. New York City enjoyed the most direct relationship with central government, as signified by the overlapping membership between the city and the colonial councils. Central institutions of government were, however, few and weak. In the profoundest sense, New York's government was unrepresentative, and the lack of an assembly was by no means the only reason for this.

New York was a strikingly old-fashioned regime. Trade was the government's lifeblood, but the government was too weak to pump life into the whole system. So it acted as a pacemaker, using monopoly as a simple and cheap method of regulation. The duke's commitment to maintain an autocratic political system over a large and diverse colony further isolated government from society. In these respects, James's colonial government calls to mind Charles I's England and its empire. Charles I, of course, had his problems, and so did his son run into difficulties in New York. Denied the opportunity to expand New York City's territorial sway, the duke could only aim to expand the colony's economy and tie it more closely to his favored New York City. There, however, monopoly regulation brought tension between new and old traders, similar to that between companies and interlopers in Charles I's London, and helped to bring about the Lewin commission and the customs revolt of 1680-81. And of course the monopoly system never served well in the colony's outlying areas. When the duke faced up to these problems he proved that he understood which half of the seventeenth century he lived in. Despite his preference for his father's ways, he abandoned autocracy and monopoly for forms of government and trade regulation which at once met colonists' preferences, satisfied his own fiscal needs, and promised to bring to an end a long period of political instability and weakness.

Shaftesbury's Fundamentals presents a striking contrast, for in it an assembly was but one expression of representativeness. Central government was to have had direct, identical links with every county. Conversely, every property-owning class in Carolina was to be represented in government in elaborate ways which included but were not comprehended by the assembly. Each gradation upwards in rank within county society produced a step upwards in public function. At the bottom of both ranks, the 50-acre freeman tended his farm and elected his Commons representative. Near the top, outranked only by the proprietors, was the overworked landgrave who sat by right in the assembly and, in addition, was likely to serve in one or more of the proprietorial courts, sit on the Grand Council, and play important public roles in his county. On his own estate he was supreme, owner of the soil, master of men, and magistrate through his manorial lordship. Indeed, save for the proprietors' Palatine Court, this manorial jurisdiction was the only autonomous public power in the Fundamental Constitutions.[66] Carolina, then, was to see a thorough symbiosis of property and power. More specifically, the connection was between landed property and power, and it is noteworthy that the Fundamental Constitutions gave little political weight to merchants or to trade. Of course, trade was vital; without it there could be no settlement, no quit rents for the proprietors, no revenue for the government. To meet this necessity, the Fundamental Constitutions required each county to have four conveniently located towns through which trade might flow, but each town was to be governed by the freeholders of its county, most if not all of whom were to have town lots by right. Not only that, each lot was to have river frontage and thus direct access to seaborne trade. There was to be no New York City in Carolina, no favored merchants, no monopolies.[67]

Whatever one might say of Shaftesbury's and Locke's sense of Carolina geography, theirs was a logical response to the realities of colonial production and trade and to the demands of those early settlers from Barbados and New England for 'free trade' and 'freedom of the river'. We are reminded again that Shaftesbury, possibly the leading mercantilist of his generation of English politicians, had never intended to give merchants much power even in England.[68] There was less reason to do so in his 'darling' Carolina. When New England ships' captains took advantage of Carolina's shallow and shifting inlets to interpose themselves between the planters and free access to Atlantic trade, Shaftesbury was disappointed. It was, he said, certain beggary to sell secondhand on a world market.[69] Thus he offered a rational assessment of the colony's dilemma and a hint of his fondest hopes for a productive, agricultural society in command of its economic as well as political fate. Carolina landowners, amongst whom the proprietors were pre-eminent, were to have freedom of trade and the power to regulate their own commercial affairs. Freedom and power went together in Carolina as surely as autocracy and monopoly went together in New York.

Shaftesbury's Fundamental Constitutions worked no better than James's autocracy: less well, measuring the distance between design and execution. That distance brought Shaftesbury much disappointment. Governors proved undependable, and the people themselves occasionally grew fractious. Shaftesbury himself did not always measure up; at one point, he claimed a monopoly of the Indian trade so that he might recoup the expense of peace negotiations with the Indians. On the whole, however, he remained true to his plan. If the huge land grants in the Fundamentals were unrealistic for the infant society, policy still required 'a right and equal distribution of land', so lesser amounts were to be granted in due proportion to men's rank. Even rank could be altered to fit realities; when too few qualified as landgraves and cassiques, the proprietors made ersatz nobles of their deputies. These half measures were devised to accord with the spirit of the Fundamental Constitutions and 'to order every ones condition as that all togeather make up a Quiet Equall and Lasting Government wherein every mans Right Property and Welfare may be soe fenc'd in and secured that the Preservation of the Government may be in every ones Interest'.[70] In 1678, in a tract designed to entice French Huguenots to settle in Carolina, Shaftesbury wrote that the colony was 'a sort of republic'.[71] This was not too wide of the mark. *Res publica* was the objective, a common good so inextricably identified with a hierarchy of landed wealth and power that no other and conflicting definition of the common good could possibly arise.

This perception marked out a line of consistency in a career which otherwise, as John Dryden was delighted to point out, was marked by abrupt shifts of allegiance. Shaftesbury could plausibly claim that in England as well as in Carolina he sought a balance and an identity between government and society. Thus in 1660 he could act for and in 1673 speak of the royal prerogative as that principle of government which bound together king and subject in their common interests; thus two years later, out of office and speaking in the House of Lords, he could warn the king, the commons, and the whole realm that their safety depended upon the maintenance of the privileges and powers of the aristocracy; and thus in 1679-81 he could organize in parliament and in the country a party which aimed to avoid the patent absurdity, as well as the danger, of fastening a Catholic king on a Protestant nation.[72]

* * *

This last episode put Shaftesbury and York firmly on opposite sides of an important political divide which, in imperial as well as English history, is where they belong. Yet they shared much in common. Both believed that commercial prosperity was crucial to the security and strength of the state, and this common commitment made them advocates and empire and supporters and practitioners of effective public administration. Such beliefs were unremarkable amongst men of their station, so conventional and so apparently logical that it would have required both bravado and foolishness for any courtier to think otherwise, but they were important. They define a consensus which helped bring about the restoration itself, the enactment of a comprehensive navigation code for overseas trade, and two wars with Holland. What this consensus failed to do was to give restoration England coherent, purposeful government, and certainly it failed to overcome the inconstancy and deviousness of the monarch, Charles II. The result, save for brief periods under Clarendon and Danby, was drift and indirection in domestic and imperial affairs.

It is this which gives the Duke of York and Shaftesbury their peculiar importance for historians. Over more than twenty years, they carried their commitment to the Restoration consensus to effect important reforms in their own departments of state, to participate in important trading ventures, and to become active proprietors of North American colonies. In England, such beliefs made both men loyal and effective servants of the crown until, in 1673, Shaftesbury fell from power and began his fateful move into opposition. As different as their colonial polities were, both aimed at Leviathan in America, too. Shaftesbury's Leviathan remained largely theoretical, but despite the curiosities of the Fundamental Constitutions it seemed more in line with American realities than James's old-fashioned, pinched autocracy. However, the power that James lacked as duke and proprietor was soon to be enhanced, first by the so-called 'tory reaction' of the early 1680s and then, more fully, when he became king in 1685. Then James would govern large areas of America and large numbers of colonists by the methods he had originally favored in New York. His success will remind us of the truth that as long as English government remained without clear direction, no officer of state could impose on the empire the sort of coherent policies that he and the Earl of Shaftesbury followed for their proprietorial domains. His ultimate failure may lead us to think that Shaftesbury's policy was the better conceived, for both English and American conditions.

CHAPTER NINE

Reaction and revolution:
the English empire at the end
of the seventeenth century

Ushered in by the Popish Plot and the Exclusion Crisis and climaxing with the Glorious Revolution, the century's end was a time of high political excitement in England. The plot roused old fears of Catholicism in the whole nation. Those we call whigs made the most of it, but their excesses forged an alliance between Charles II and those, now called tories, who had long claimed to be his best friends. Crown and tories set out to make safe the Stuart succession and the Anglican church, and soon the whigs were in deep trouble. Shaftesbury, unsuccessfully prosecuted for treason in 1681, thought of a Carolina exile but fled to Holland where he died in 1683. Those implicated in the 1683 Rye House plot to murder Charles and James were less lucky. The extent of tory triumph became clear at Charles's death; the Duke of York became James II in a remarkable political climate. In his 1685 parliament there were not forty members James could not trust; nor did many regret the bloody fate of those who joined rebellions raised by the Duke of Monmouth in the West Country and the Earl of Argyll in Scotland. The majority welcomed James warmly, and although there were some murmurings his 1685 parliament made James II the richest and the most secure of the Stuarts.[1] It was thus James's inheritance to see England's historic fear of popery and arbitrary government balanced by its dread of revolution, and he squandered it. His efforts to make England safe for Catholicism revived concern about the survival of parliament and local government, and produced the Revolution of 1688. The domestic reaction of the 1680s was accompanied by an imperial reaction during which most colonial governments lost autonomy and some ceased to exist. By 1688, all the colonies north of Pennsylvania were under the prerogative government of the Dominion of New England. The process might have gone further had not colonists been able to exploit both the event and the ideology of the Glorious Revolution in order to win back

[219]

some ground lost during the 1680s. Historians have given these developments in English and American politics much attention in recent years, creating a body of work which renders the task of this last chapter in some respects perfunctory.[2] There is an emergent consensus on a number of issues; but it leaves open some crucial questions. We are still not entirely sure why England invested so much energy in colonial government during the 1680s. Colonists' endorsement of the Glorious Revolution also raises hard questions, not least because colonies were so diverse amongst themselves and all from England. Most scholars accept that England's revolution for parliament, property, and protestantism was welcome to many on both sides of the Atlantic, but some argue that to see in its American variants more than opportunism or coincidence is to succumb to the whig (or neo-whig) fallacy.[3]

At the least, we can say that the coincidences which allowed opportunists in distant colonies take advantage of events in London showed that the empire had achieved a significant degree of political coherence. Indeed it had, but as we have seen this was no sudden achievement. Inheritors of a common political culture, Englishmen and colonists continued to face similar political problems. Their solutions were similar, too, and not only those which have been traditionally called 'whiggish'. To understand the state of imperial politics at the end of this century of revolution, we need to look beyond whiggism and to consider the 'toryish' elements of the English and colonial polities.

* * *

Underlying England's late seventeenth-century conflicts were widely shared ideas about government, a consensus apparent even at the height of the Exclusion controversy. This contest over the rights of the Catholic heir to the throne was also a struggle for control of a state which was meant to be powerful and stable. This was certainly true of the whigs, whose opportunism should not conceal the long-term commitment of leaders like Shaftesbury to strengthening the sinews of the state. One reason whigs sought to bar the Duke of York from his inheritance was their belief that the monarchy was and should be a vigorous institution, the repository with parliament of sovereign and effective power. Accordingly, whigs could not bear the thought of the crown in wrong hands. Nor did they like the idea that James might come to the throne with his powers limited by law. This would 'make the government a commonwealth', one said; while others worried that constitutional limitations would divide sovereignty and make the state prey to civil war. Whig sensibilities on these points explain not only the intensity of their election campaigns and their bravado at the Oxford Parliament of 1681 but also their behavior when Charles II called their bluff by dissolving parliament and refusing to call another. Left to choose between rebellion and retreat, most whigs chose the latter. Meanwhile, the tories pressed home their point that James's position as legitimate heir had to be preserved. Neither parliament nor people could share in his right – far less deny it – without weakening all law, property, and power.[4] However, tories' loyalty to the Stuart monarchy does not in itself qualify them as advocates of the powerful state. As Professor Western puts it, 'in the tory view of the state, the king was a proprietor, in that of the whigs he was a trustee'.[5] The proprietorial monarch was a rather old-fashioned idea, and there was in the tory an almost visceral desire to use politics to preserve, not to transform. Lurking here we may find important sources of the independent country opposition of Walpole's period, yet throughout the early 1680s tories demonstrated a commitment to a strong state in their persecution of whigs and dissenters, their celebration of the divine sanction of monarchy, and their elaboration of the doctrine of non-resistance.[6] Nor was ideology their only strong suit; when tories held power, they drove the state on towards more effective administration. During the 1680s the Treasury was again a center of energy, improving yields of most small revenues and, in 1683, putting the excise under commission. Throughout government, able administrators like Samuel Pepys and William Blathwayt, a rung or two safely down the political ladder, and Sidney Godolphin, on his way up, grew in influence.[7]

As Jamaicans had already learned, such concentrations of administrative power had a cumulative effect in imperial as well as in English government. Despite the waning influence during the 1680s of the Privy Council and the Lords of Trade, closer communications inside Whitehall and between England and America continued to strengthen the empire. William Blathwayt parlayed his offices of Secretary to the Lords of Trade and Receiver and Auditor General of American revenues into a formidable force, forging direct links with the Treasury and Customs in Whitehall, links which also bound governors and assemblies in America. By such simple means, mere bureaucrats assumed more power than ever Blathwayt's uncle, Thomas Povey, could have dreamed.[8] However, there was more to all this than administrative reform. The political will of the crown was important in itself, and in this James was more active than his brother. The point that colony governments were, after all, monarchical was best demonstrated when, in 1685, James acted upon Governor Lord Effingham's suggestion that the Virginia Assembly be dissolved by direct royal order.[9]

The Glorious Revolution deposed James, checked Effingham's colonial career and strangled in its infancy the Dominion of New England, the characteristic American offspring of Stuart policy, but there were important continuities in imperial as well as in domestic politics. In London, William Blathwayt and others stayed to serve William and Anne as well as they had served James, and for like ends. Similarly, those who had staffed the Dominion, Sir Edmund Andros, Francis Nicholson, Edward Randolph, even the colonists Joseph Dudley and William Dyer, all survived 1689 to play important parts in the decision to keep Massachusetts government under royal oversight through the new charter of 1691. Then they went on to take important posts in the post-revolution empire, Andros, Nicholson and Dudley as governors.[10] This continuity in personnel makes dubious the notion that 1688 signalled a whig triumph. Even more dubious, however, is the idea that a whig supremacy might have enhanced colonial autonomy. Shaftesbury's plans for his 'darling' Carolina forecast the refusal of the 'whig' Privy Council of 1679 to retreat from Danby's Poyning's Law policy in Jamaica and Virginia. It hardly matters whether the Privy Council took this decision because it believed 'that the Rebellion in Virginia was occasioned by the excessive power of the Assembly 'or because of Shaftesbury's advice that 'all plantations were of the king's making, and that he might at any time alter or dispose of them at his pleasure'.[11] Leading whigs of the 1690s who took part in imperial affairs seemed to feel the same way. Finally, it is important to note a constitutional lesson taught first by the Commonwealth Parliament in 1650 and 1651. Insofar as the Revolution of 1688 represented parliament's coming of age, it was unlikely to enhance colonial autonomy. In 1689, efforts in the Convention House of Commons to include the New England colonies in a bill for restoring corporation charters were killed by William's dissolution of parliament in early 1690, but the underlying principle would in 1701–5 and the 1720s be used in attempts to void all remaining colonial charters by legislative enactment. Parliament's new activism was reflected also in its attention to trade legislation. Here colonists sometimes profited from a more sophisticated approach than had characterized Restoration parliaments. James's 1685 parliament had hewed to the old line by raising new revenues from additional customs on enumerated colonial products. After 1688, however, in ways which would have pleased Sir George Downing, parliaments aimed as much at increasing the level of trade as at raising duties, notably in acts which increased customs rebates for re-exports of colonial products to Europe and ended the Royal African Company's monopoly. There were also new bounties for colonial goods which were thought important to England's security or prosperity. On the other hand, parliament produced the Navigation Act of 1696, which reiterated restrictive principles and provided for better enforcement of the trade laws, and the century ended with the first of a series of acts to discourage colonial manufactures.[12]

REACTION AND REVOLUTION

The Glorious Revolution put paid to the divine right of kings, but it did not reverse the growing power of government. After 1688, the conjunction between war and politics drove William and Mary, then Queen Anne, and their tory and whig ministries and parliaments to carry debts and raise taxes which would have been the envy of Charles or James. There was a continuum here, a growth of power and stability which led in time to the 'robinarchy' of Walpole but reached its seventeenth-century climax in the great recoinage, the founding of the Bank of England, and, in the same year as the Navigation Act of 1696, the king's creation of the Board of Trade. Eighteenth-century opposition politicians would regard the Bank of England and the national debt as symbols of national corruption; but in seventeenth-century perspective they stand in comparison to Ship Money and the Stop of the Exchequer as symbols of the state's growing competence. Thus the revolution which made William King of England was not inherently friendly to the growth of colonial autonomy. When in 1689 Massachusetts's agent, the Reverend Increase Mather, told King William that 'Your Majesty may... whenever You Please, become the Emperour of America', he did little more than turn a foregone conclusion into flattery. That he offered it on the 4th of July is ironic only in retrospect.[13]

* * *

That colonists did not seek independence in 1688-9 is one of the more significant – if obvious – truths of imperial history. At the same time, it is clear that many colonists expected to gain something from the Glorious Revolution. This owed partly to the opportunities of war, which gave added urgency to public affairs, created chances of profit and expansion, and made some colonists into imperial patriots.[14] More directly relevant to this study were colonial reactions to the Glorious Revolution itself. Echoing rebellions occurred in Massachusetts, Rhode Island, Connecticut, New York, and Maryland, and elsewhere colonists mobilized more peacefully to profit from the events and principles of 1688. We have seen this maneuvering for advantage during earlier English political crises – in 1649 and 1660, for instance. Then, colonists had proved to be aware of the benefits of autonomy, yet they had also demonstrated their local governments' dependence upon central authority. Thus colonists had conformed to and understood the rules of English politics. Their response to the Glorious Revolution was similarly ambivalent, similarly English. Yet the issues of 1688 were not those of 1649 or 1660, and colonists knew it. To understand how colonists' responses to this latest turn in English politics amounted also to a participatory role, it is necessary to confront an apparent discontinuity in seventeenth-century imperial history, the surprisingly intensive and corrosive attack on colonial autonomy which occurred during the 1680s.

Historians have long noted the coincidence between this imperial offensive and the reaction at home,[15] but most see it as little more than that; the tory reaction served as an occasion to implement long-standing imperial policies. However, it is difficult to demonstrate that these 'policies', mercantilist or militarist, were central to the decisions actually taken during the 1680s. Mercantilism had long been the orthodoxy of statecraft, but it had never led to the sustained activity which characterized imperial politics in the 1680s. Moreover, the argument that successive, failed attempts to make the navigation system work finally goaded the crown to act requires us to weigh up a lot of evidence only in the end to talk of straws and camels' backs. Nor does it fit the 1680s decade, when historic pressures which might have produced a mercantilist donnybrook actually eased as government debts fell and English trade waxed fat.[16] Much the same may be said of the idea that militarism had vaulted into the driver's seat after riding postillion to an essentially civilian policy. Perhaps so, but a decade in which England single-mindedly pursued peace in Europe was an odd occasion for such a change, and the crown's attention to lowering the costs of its American governments an odder way to put it into effect.[17] Finally, if mercantilism or militarism was the engine of empire during the 1680s, it needs to be explained why radical changes occurred only in the northern continental colonies. The New England colonies and New York were not generally regarded as more valuable or more vulnerable than Jamaica, Barbados, or Virginia, but they were the colonies which lost their charters and their separate identities to the Dominion of New England, and were denied a representative assembly. Such considerations lead the best study of New England's relationship with the crown to argue that the 'fundamental cause' of the Dominion lay in the politics of the tory reaction.[18]

Professor Johnson rightly sees the Dominion as the end product of an English chain of reaction, but his conclusion that the Dominion 'must be judged as much an anomaly as a consummation'[19] of 1680s colonial policy requires modification. By placing imperial politics in its English context, we can see first how intimately New England experienced the course of the English reaction and secondly how New England's treatment and that of other colonies were, if different, still part of the same process. We begin with Sir Keith Feiling's observation that while the toryism of the 1680s had a long gestation, its new-found and urgent sense of purpose were born of the political crises of 1678-81, when the tories were in trouble. Their weakness in the constituencies was measured by three defeats between 1679 and 1681 and by their failure to stop exclusion bills in the House of Commons. Whig views on the succession and the church intensified memories of the Great Rebellion and wakened old grievances that rebels and dissenters had done too well out of the 1660 settlement. Evidence that Charles had begun to see things their way encouraged tories to mount increasingly effective campaigns as the Exclusion Crisis wore on, and thus they were ready to move when Charles dissolved the Oxford parliament in October 1681. In 1683, the discovery of the Rye House plot to murder Charles and James intensified tory resolve to exorcise the ghosts of '41.

During the reaction, loyalty to the king, to the hereditary succession, and to the established church became important political tests, but they operated differently in different places. At court and in central government, the strength and security of the state was a particularly pressing concern, and this meant that tory loyalism would not be the *sine qua non* of royal approval. Cynical to the last, Charles took an instrumental view of his ministers, trusted no one, and retained his manipulative ways. Even men who had taken the wrong side in the exclusion crisis might return to favor were the king sure of their servility or effectiveness. The earls of Halifax and Sunderland exemplified of this kind of political survival. However, Charles did attack whigs where he could easily reach them, beginning with his October 1679 purge of the 'whig' Privy Council. Soon Charles made it clear that his bastard son Monmouth – touted by some whigs as a plausible successor – no longer enjoyed his favor, nor did his Protestant nephew and niece William and Mary. Courtiers who retained ties with these reversionary interests learned to be cautious about it. The crown also moved to insure loyalty in the higher judiciary. The 'twelve men in scarlet' had rarely been noted for their spirit of independence, but even so the crown's judicial appointments after 1679, not least that of Sir George Jeffreys in 1683, produced a more compliant bench than England had seen for some time. However, the tory reaction found fuller expression outside of Whitehall and the courts, in the counties and the borough corporations.

From 1679, recruitment of new faces at the center was accompanied by purges of county governments. With increasing purpose, the lieutenancies and the commissions of the peace were remade in a tory image as whigs and even the merely doubtful lost office or were surrounded by newly commissioned loyalists.[20] For much of the decade, these county purges enjoyed a degree of local support. They could also be quite extensive; it is estimated that by summer 1688 24 per cent of the deputy-lieutenants and JPs of England and Wales were Roman Catholics. At the same time, it is important to note some limitations on the process. Here and there, tory loyalists complained that the king had been too kind to some of his old servants; among notable survivors of local tory insurgencies was the Earl of Carlisle, who was not only Governor of Jamaica but also Lord Lieutenant of Cumberland and Westmorland. In other cases, the self-contained nature of county society and the class solidarity of the gentry kept individuals in place despite their lack of tory enthusiasm. Most significantly of all, the crown's attack on county government was generally limited to the exercise of patronage powers. However many new lords lieutenant or JPs held the king's commission, county institutions of government and the county parliamentary franchise remained untouched.[21]

It was not so with the chartered boroughs, where the reaction achieved more dramatic effects. This owed something to long-standing gentry suspicion of the boroughs, clearly stated by the Corporations Act of 1661 and now confirmed by the whigs' successes in towns during the Exclusion elections. Now, with Charles II on their side, the gentry achieved a unity of purpose which distinguished the 1680s from the 1660s and gave greater effect to the use of prerogative powers over town government. The motivation for political action in the boroughs was similar to that in the counties; to render boroughs safe by putting them under the control of safe men. However, in the towns neither the crown nor its local tory allies could easily proceed in the *ad hominem* way favored at court and in the counties. The charters stood in the way, bulwarks which in many cases had to be breached in order to purge the ill-affected. Thus it was the new charters and the 'regulations' of old charters which most clearly expressed the aims of crown and tories in the boroughs. Typical charter modifications of the 1680s included direct royal power to appoint or approve town officers and remove doubtful men from the freemanship. Parliamentary franchises were changed too, generally to reduce the number of electors. County justices were given jurisdiction within towns in answer to traditional complaints that justice was hard to obtain for outsiders or for crown officers. As before, new charters often brought new privileges, but the stick was more apparent than the carrot. Assuredly, resistance carried great risks. Against a writ of *quo warranto*, few towns could claim perfect adherence to their charters or depend on the sympathies of the king's new judges. Were they to defend their charters at law, boroughs had to consider the likelihood of failure and the certainties of expense and of offending the king. At its worst, resistance risked corporate extinction; this was to be the fate of the City of London and the Dorset borough of Poole.[22]

There were, then, important contrasts between counties and towns. Statute and custom inclined the crown to leave intact the structures of county government, the lieutenancy, the commission of the peace, the parliamentary franchise. The borough charters proved weaker reeds. But more was involved than structures. In dealing with the counties, the crown confronted loyalty to the idea of gentry rule and the self-contained character of county society. These constraints were apparent even during the early 1680s, but they assumed critical importance in 1687 and 1688. When King James placed Catholicism at the top of the agenda in the counties, local loyalty proved to be as strong amongst tory as amongst whig gentlemen, strong enough to shake even James II's resolve. However, urban society was more variegated and changeable than county society. This made the charters and those who held power under them vulnerable whether, as in the early 1680s, initiatives for new charters came from local insurgents, or as in 1685 when the desire to pack parliament brought many crown actions against borough charters. Even after James began to aim at creating very different political constituencies in the boroughs, he still found enough support (often from whigs and dissenters displaced by earlier charter regulations) to give credible hopes of success. In each successive case, local support for new charters proved urban society's capacity to produce new men so eager for power as to be immune to the parochial and class loyalties which protected county governments.

Such were the institutional and social variables which governed English politics in the 1680s. Not all of them transferred to imperial politics. The desire to secure a compliant English House of Commons, so important in 1685 and again in 1687 and 1688, could not have motivated the assertion of control over colonial governments. In the navigation system, on the other hand, the crown possessed a plausible rationale for imperial centralization which did not directly apply to its attacks on English local government. Yet there were similarities in policy towards English and American local government. The chief American casualty of the period was that redoubt of the dissenting interest, the chartered colony of Massachusetts. In due course the Bay and its neighbors, most of them chartered colonies, also lost their representative and town institutions, and throughout the decade the Pennsylvania, Maryland, and Carolina proprietaries accepted significant royal oversight of their activities.[23] Meanwhile, despite a crop of authoritarian governors who were not slow to remove obstreperous individuals from office, the royal colonies retained their main institutional characteristics, including their representative assemblies and their local court systems.

* * *

The evolving relationship between the crown and Massachusetts proves that these connections were fundamental, not accidental. Here a critical role was played by Edward Randolph, royal customs collector in Boston. Most historians cast Randolph as an indefatigable servant of mercantile imperialism, from his first visit consistent in his aims to bring profit to himself, favor to his Mason relations, and imperial power to the king.[24]

However, a reconsideration of Randolph's confrontation with New England suggests that he, like Thomas Povey in the 1650s and 1660s, was important not so much for his pursuit of policy goals as for his conformity to the rules of English politics. In the end, he failed to achieve his preferred aims because at a critical juncture, English politics changed so abruptly as to leave him in the lurch, but that was not until late 1684.

Until then, Randolph's behavior was patterned by the fact that he divided his time between New England and Whitehall. In America, he encountered obstacles which provoked fevers of frustration. From Boston, or immediately on one of his returns to London, he typically urged drastic action against the Bay: a naval blockade, a *quo warranto*, a governor-general. In both 1677 and 1681 he returned from tours of duty in New England breathing fire which failed to ignite anyone else. On the first occasion, despite Randolph's offer to include Danby's son in the spoils of victory, the Lord Treasurer worried that the customs collector had made himself obnoxious to the colonists, while Sir Robert Southwell urged that Randolph's program be put on ice 'least his Majesties intentions should bee foiled for the want of Authority in Mr Randolph to support them'. In 1681 Randolph's advice was again rejected, by both the tory Attorney General Sir Robert Sawyer and the customs commissioners, who warned that some of Randolph's proposals went beyond the law, beyond English practice, and indeed beyond all human power. On both occasions, Randolph learned that the crown preferred less extreme measures. Thus before the end of his first London visit, Randolph entered into negotiations with William Stoughton, one of the colony's agents, about the future shape of Bay Colony government and moved from recommending a frontal attack on the charter to the advocacy of lesser changes, for instance in the colony freemanship. After his second visit, Randolph returned to Boston without a writ and aware that the crown still aimed to solve the Massachusetts problem within the context of charter government.[25]

This suggests continuity with the aims of the Royal Commission of 1664, but there were more pertinent reasons, including, ironically, Randolph's own reports, which though unsparing in their denunciation of Massachusetts's Puritan 'faction' also discovered in the colony a loyal party which waited only on royal support to take its rightful place in government. In 1681 Randolph confidently asserted that had Lord Culpeper been ordered to regulate the Bay's charter during his visit to Boston he would have succeeded, and Culpeper (now a shareholder in the Atherton Company) confirmed that Massachusetts had enough loyal men to staff the sort of government it deserved.[26] Such reports encouraged London to think that in New England as in English towns there were loyalists of sufficient weight and number to cooperate on the matter of regulation and then to govern under modified corporate charters. This assumption, reinforced by tory success in remodelling English borough charters, was implicit in the 1681 decision to reject Randolph's advice to institute legal proceedings and instead to require Massachusetts to send agents.[27] Randolph conformed to this emergent parallel between English and imperial politics. On his return to Boston in 1682, he played more assiduously on what had been for him a minor theme, the strength of New England moderates. He cultivated leading men like Assistant Joseph Dudley and Governor Simon Bradstreet of Massachusetts and Plymouth's Governor Thomas Hinckley. Some he identified as loyal; others, like Dudley, would be useful because they had their fortunes to make; still others feared the consequences of offending the king. These consequences, Randolph thought, had been made clearer by his own strengthened commission, by the appointment of a royal governor for New Hampshire, and news from England of the prosecution of whigs; all had 'shaken the faction' and encouraged the moderates. In 1683 Randolph even drew comfort from Gove's rebellion in New Hampshire. It had horrified 'the whole province' and moved the Reverend Joshua Moody, although a stalwart of the 'faction' in New Hampshire, to preach against rebellion using the fifth commandment as his text and the anniversary of Charles I's execution as his occasion.[28]

The imperial gadfly had become a political agent of the crown whose job it was to identify and encourage the king's friends as well as to spite the king's enemies. It was a role worth playing, and the script was already written. In faraway Boston, Randolph emulated courtiers and royal officers in England who orchestrated loyal parties, brought them to power in such towns as Lancaster, York, and Norwich, and as a part or a result of that process, secured new or regulated charters. New Hampshire's new royal governor, the rapacious Edward Cranfield, acted his part by trying to displace Randolph in Boston (as the moderates' friend) and in London (as the officer best able to raise an effective loyal party). 'If there be any ungrateful office to be done' in Massachusetts, Cranfield wrote shortly after his arrival, 'let Mr. Randolph (who is sufficiently disgusting to them already) be Imployed, that I may scape a business so unsuitable to my Genius, & be the better capable' of securing the king's ends. Massachusetts loyalists, Cranfield assured William Blathwayt, already knew that 'you & I may be capable of doing them good offices'.[29]

Whether there was a 'moderate party' worth writing home about is an interesting question,[30] but it is important to note that Randolph's and Cranfield's approach to New England politics was determined as much by the English context as by what they actually found in America. In turn, both men used this context better to explain things to London and to help themselves understand what it was all about. In 1682, Randolph explained verdicts against the crown in New England navigation cases by reference to the 'Arbitrary and Successfull verdict of the Lord Shaftesburys Jury at the Old Baily (now become a leading President to the factious here),' labelled the 'factious' as a 'great branch of the Gang' of the king's English enemies, and named Cranfield as a dupe of the 'Gang'. Just as effortlessly, Cranfield turned to English events to explain his success in securing a treason verdict against the rebel Gove. He had now the power to impanel juries, 'for want of which we lost the Ketch as his Majestie did my Lord Shaftesberry'. And, when the situation warranted it, Cranfield dropped his claim that Randolph had alienated local support to charge that Randolph trucked with the factious.[31]

This name-calling was more than mere opportunism. The sharpness of the political climate made it into a pervasive mode of analysis and a guide to behavior. When, in Jamaica, some of the council styled themselves the 'Loyal Club', Governor Lynch saw their intention to brand him as a whig and defended himself accordingly. In Maryland, Lord Baltimore rebutted charges that he obstructed the work of royal customs collectors by calling the collectors notorious whigs who said in public that the witnesses appearing against Shaftesbury were 'stout sinners and Irish blades'. In 1683, the president *pro tempore* of Barbados's council reported that his local opponents were either under Shaftesbury's 'care' or the worst sort of 'trimmers'.[32] Imperial decisions in London followed a similar pattern. On 2 July 1681, the Lords of Trade advised disallowance of a Virginia statute authorizing the assembly to appoint sheriffs. On the same day, their lordships in Privy Council ordered Shaftesbury's arrest on treason charges, and they knew that only a week before London's freemen had elected whigs to the city's shrievalty. In Virginia and England sheriffs impanelled juries, and there was more than coincidence in their lordships' decision to keep the selection of Virginia's sheriffs within the prerogative, as it was in England's shires. The City of London had best look to its defences. So, too, Maryland, where the murder of a customs collector by one of Baltimore's kinsmen drew from a Royal Navy captain the appropriate warning: 'now my Lords Charter was not worth a pinn . . . there were a greate many of hungry Courtiers that would jump . . . [to] doe my Lords business with the King'. From Dublin, in early 1684, Nathaniel Mather could see that Massachusetts was also in trouble; was not the Bay more 'whiggish' than its 'toryish' and more compliant southern neighbor, Connecticut?[33]

If it was not a good time for the whiggish, it was not much better for Massachusetts's toryish elements, the moderates, who failed to deliver what the crown wanted and Randolph worked for, the regulation of the charter. The Bay's repeated failure to send agents empowered to accept regulation tested the crown's commitment to this strategy and in late 1682 provoked the Lords of Trade to urge that further delay should lead to legal process. Randolph was summoned home to attend the matter, and on 4 and 12 June 1683 he submitted bills of particulars against the colony. On the 26th, a *quo warranto* ordered the colony to appear within three months to defend its charter. Still, there was no sense of urgency. Randolph had to wait until September to sail, and the writ lapsed while he was in mid Atlantic. Further politicking was necessary before there could be a legal confrontation.[34] Perhaps anticipating this necessity, Randolph negotiated with Joseph Dudley a plan for New England government under which each colony would retain its corporate identity while being subjected to a royally appointed governor and a council selected by the king from the colonial magistracies.[35] Whether or not the Randolph – Dudley plan was known to the crown, Whitehall must have thought that some similar settlement would be acceptable in Massachusetts. Otherwise the decisions and delays of summer 1683 can only be explained in terms of inefficiency and oversight. There was much of both, no doubt, but in the Summer of 1683 what most encouraged the crown to think that Massachusetts might yet voluntarily submit were developments in English politics. For this summer saw the apparent triumph of the campaign to regulate the greatest charter of them all, that of the City of London. A writ had been issued against London's charter, and on 12 June the judges decided in the crown's favor. Upon Attorney-General Sawyer's motion, however, judgment was deferred; the city was to be allowed to submit voluntarily to royal regulation of its charter. This strategy seemed to work. On 14 June, the Aldermanic Council begged royal pardon for the city's past sins, and on the 20th the Common Council decided in principle to proceed to a surrender. Informed observers concluded that if judgment against the great city could move it to a surrender, boroughs which had held back would now submit. It was also thought that the discovery of the Rye House Plot would move boroughs to surrender hurriedly, to prove their loyalty in extremity. As if to confirm these predictions, loyal messages of outrage and horror poured in from English towns and, indeed, from Connecticut and Rhode Island.[36]

All this gave some weight to the message Randolph carried to Massachusetts in September 1683: a regulated charter would be better and cheaper than whatever government the crown might impose after the inevitable issue of legal proceedings. Randolph continued in his efforts to encourage the moderates, perhaps even to speak to fears expressed by hard-liners like Thomas Danforth. The Randolph – Dudley plan addressed such concerns, as did Randolph's successful request to Lord Keeper Guilford to secure from Charles II a declaration promising the people the retention of their 'liberties and proprieties'.[37] The same case was put to the General Court, which met between October and December 1683. Early on, perhaps buoyed up by moderate petitions from some towns and clergymen, Randolph seemed confident of success. He warned Governor Thomas Hinckley that Plymouth should be 'very carefull to improve the present opportunity; for . . . what regulation is made here will passe through all New England'. He convinced a majority of Massachusetts magistrates that the colony should not 'Contend with his Majestie in a Course of Law' but make 'an humble submission' 'according to his Majesties . . . Declaration'. The magistrates had sadly to report, however, that 'by no meanes can wee at present obteyne the Consent of the deputy Representatives of the people whereby it might become an Act of the Corporation'.[38]

This letter of December 1683 makes clear the magistrates' perfect understanding of Randolph's message. Surrender by 'an Act of the Corporation' was necessary to save the corporation, and they bitterly confessed their failure to meet the crown's objectives. The General Court's decision to defend the charter seemed to confirm Peter Bulkeley's earlier fears that by '(ape-like) overfondness, wee are hugging our privileges and franchises to death, and preferre the disolution of our Body politique, rather then to suffer Amputation in any of its limbs'. The moderates did not, however, abandon all hope. Throughout 1684, Randolph and the moderates continued to press their case as best they could in London and Massachusetts. News of the Boston town meeting's intemperate resolutions of January 1684 was balanced with better tidings from Watertown and one or two other places, while Randolph (again back in London) sweetened reports of the moderates' poor showing in the 1684 elections with remarks on the size and social weight of the procession which escorted the defeated Joseph Dudley to his home. For his part, Dudley wrote to the Secretary of State that he hoped for a good settlement even though he was resigned to the 'severity of the law'. Governor Bradstreet and the remaining moderate magistrates thought it worth informing London of continued efforts to bring the people to a better understanding of their plight. Little wonder that throughout 1684 Cranfield and William Dyer signalled growing distrust of Randolph and the moderates. Cranfield charged that Randolph had accepted bribes to keep the old magistrates in place; by October he 'saw reason' to disown Randolph as his agent in London. Dyer expressed his suspicions less moderately, as was his wont.[39]

Whether or not bribery was involved, Randolph had become one of Massachusetts's leading moderates, and he knew it. Not surprisingly, when it became apparent that a final decision on Massachusetts was imminent, Randolph was distraught at being sent into Holland to snoop out New England ships trading there. Once he might have welcomed the task, but it was no time for a man ambitious for self and friends to be away from Whitehall. Randolph made the best of a bad situation; before leaving he asked to be made recorder and secretary of New England.[40] But in what sort of government? From the first, royal government had been a possibility, but Randolph had frequently been forced to abandon that objective in favor of regulation, and the plan he concocted with Joseph Dudley in 1683 contained elements of both royal and corporate rule. As late as the summer of 1684 the leave given for Massachusetts to surrender voluntarily suggested that some kind of corporate status remained a possible outcome.[41] So did Randolph's petition of late October, for the place of recorder was associated particularly with corporate government. Now, suddenly, the crown ruled out a new charter. Only two days after Randolph was made recorder and secretary, it was decided to establish a new royal colony which would include not only Massachusetts but also Maine, New Hampshire, and Plymouth. The governor was to be a career military man, Colonel Percy Kirke.

It remained unclear what sort of royal colony this was to be. Lord Keeper Guilford, who on 23 October had entered judgment against the Massachusetts charter, was quick to recommend that the new province should have an assembly and that martial law (in contrast to other royal governors' commissions) should extend only to soldiers in pay. Apparently Guilford thought that Massachusetts's past chartered status still carried some privileges. Whether or not his fellow Lords of Trade shared his view, they were concerned enough on 17 November to ask the king directly whether the colony would have an assembly. Five days later came the answer; no mention was to be made of an assembly in Kirke's commission; he was to govern with an appointed council. Now the Lords of Trade conveyed to the king, through Guilford, another question. Would Kirke's government raise new taxes or simply continue old ones? No public answer was immediately forthcoming, but by December it was clear that Kirke and his council were to have power to make laws and to raise new revenues. The crown had decided upon a form of royal government so new as to surprise some at least of the Lords of Trade.[42]

This surprising fate[43] owed partly to Massachusetts's persistent refusal to accept regulation of its charter. Sooner or later, the crown would have to conclude that a loyal constituency for a remodelled corporation simply did not exist. Yet by the same token it had been a long time, and this begs the question of why it was in 1684 that royal patience finally ran short. The crown acted drastically in 1684 because of two further twists in the politics of reaction. The first involved London, whose fate had already been linked to Massachusetts's in political rhetoric and temporal coincidence. In 1683, when London apparently bowed to the decision against its charter, it was decided to offer Massachusetts another chance to surrender. Randolph sailed for Boston in September; had he delayed longer, he could better have illustrated the consequences of refusal. When on 2 October London's Common Council reversed its decision to surrender the charter, the crown's response was swift. On the 4th, judgment was entered, and the king decided to rule London from Whitehall. The Common Council ceased to exist, and the king appointed, during pleasure, leading City officials. These decisions successfully destroyed London's corporate identity, broke the whigs, and extended crown influence into the City's guilds and companies. They also offered a precedent to apply when in 1684 Massachusetts emulated London by refusing to submit after judgment had been given, but not entered, against its charter.[44]

However, Guilford's querulous reaction to the crown's decisions on Massachusetts suggests that the London precedent was not automatically applied. More significant was the dissent entered by the Marquis of Halifax, a most unlikely champion of colonial rights. Although in 1678-81 he had supported limitations on a popish king, he detested Shaftesbury, opposed exclusion, and stayed in government to serve the tory reaction, latterly as one of the royal commissioners appointed to oversee London. Nor was he a friend to protestant dissenters, although later he proved adept at courting them. On the other hand, Halifax was no high tory, and during 1683 he had signalled his view that the tory reaction had gone far enough. He attempted to effect a reconciliation between Charles and the Duke of Monmouth, showed public sympathy for some victims of the Rye House prosecutions, and continued his efforts to keep the Duke of York out of English politics and out of England. Halifax's aims were to have a new parliament, to prevent the abrogation of the penal laws and the release of the remaining Popish Plot prisoners, and to cast England's lot in Europe with the Prince of Orange and against France. In mid 1684, William Blathwayt singled out Halifax (and Guilford, it is worth noting) as hostile to the high-flyers at court, and at about the same time Halifax was successful in displacing two of his court rivals.[45]

Whether or not Halifax was close to real power in the autumn of 1684, he played for high stakes, and from his point of view there were many disturbing straws in the wind. His efforts to isolate James were not successful, rather the reverse. Soon James returned to London and, in May 1684, to the effective exercise of his office as Lord High Admiral despite the Test Act. In early 1684, Halifax's Yorkshire friend Sir John Reresby had it on good authority that reaction was in the saddle: 'no Parliament was near, and . . . some near the King were designing other measures than those of Parliaments'. There were sinister stirrings in

Ireland, where Richard Talbot, a Catholic who had absented himself during the Popish Plot, had returned and now plotted with London to weaken Lord Lieutenant Ormonde's hold on the Irish army. Then in October came the news that Ormonde himself, that prince of cavaliers, was to be replaced by Halifax's enemy the Earl of Rochester. As much as Halifax might have liked to see Rochester in Dublin, he could not have liked the reasoning behind it. 'I find it absolutely necessary', the king told Ormonde, 'that very many, and almost general alterations should be made in Ireland'. Thus Charles confirmed rumors of an 'almost total change in all the changeable parts of the Government of [Ireland]'.[46]

Halifax's defence of Massachusetts rested on his belief that its fate owed to a new pattern in English politics. That he was not alone was made clear by the French ambassador, Barillon, who recorded Halifax as saying in Privy Council on 28 November 1684 that

> there could be no doubt but that the same laws, which are in force in England, should also be established in a country inhabited by Englishmen... an absolute government is neither so happy nor so safe, as that which sets bounds to the authority of the prince. He exaggerated the inconveniences of a sovereign power and plainly declared that he could not make up his mind to live under a King who should have it in his power to take whenever he thought proper the money he has in his pocket.

Barillon minimized the importance of the episode, perhaps because Halifax was speaking about a distant colony, but Louis XIV, the Duke of York, and Lord Chief Justice Jeffreys knew better. Louis concluded that Halifax 'hardly merits the confidence that the King of England has in him' and was 'not surprised that the Duke of York remarked on the consequences [of Halifax's views] to the King his brother'. As for Jeffreys, Halifax recorded bitterly that 'I argue[d] for the liberty of the people, [Jeffreys] replyed that whosoever capitulateth, rebelleth. This at the Cabinet Councell'.[47] If even to enumerate the powers of the crown was to rebel, then Halifax's arguments were in vain.

Halifax elaborated his concerns in a private appeal to the king, the famous *Character of a Trimmer*. The manuscript was probably written after the council debate of 28 November; certainly it advanced similar arguments. In one respect, however, the Trimmer retreated from the position he had taken on New England. Halifax had based that argument on 'rights', but he did not like absolutes in politics (he later asserted that the only political fundamental was that 'every supreme power must be arbitrary'.)[48] The Trimmer advanced the more circumspect argument that the king who elects to act arbitrarily acts foolishly. He rested his case not on abstractions but on history. England's constitution, when it was successful, avoided arbitrary foolishness by inviting the crown to assent and adhere to the law and, when the law proved an ass, to alter law through parliament. The crown was not obliged to act thus, but it should. Defending Massachusetts, Halifax stated that no sensible Englishmen would elect to live where the king could pick his pocket. Defending English liberties, the Trimmer argued that no sensible king would require his subjects to make such a judgment. However, if the king forced it, that 'judgment will come, though we know neither the day nor the hour'. If Halifax had the king in mind as the victim of that judgment, he knew better than to say so, but he did offer judgment on the crown's advisers who 'out of guilt or interest, are afraid to throw themselves upon their country, knowing how scurvily they have used it'. Such 'insolent bunglers' would force the people 'whether [they] will or no to be valiant' and 'lead men into a short way of arguing that admitteth no distinction, and from the foundation of self-defense they will draw inferences that will have miserable effects upon the quiet of a government'.[49]

This combination of personal bile and portentous warning, so alien to the character the Trimmer gave himself, speaks to the sting of defeat Halifax felt late in 1684 and to his belief that Massachusetts had lost its representative assembly for reasons other than its refusal to accept charter regulation. Massachusetts was the victim of another turn of the screw as the Stuart reaction replaced the tory reaction. William Blathwayt, writing soon after the crucial cabinet meeting to Lord Effingham, sensed the new direction and vented a grandiose notion of what increased royal authority in America might mean. Not only had Massachusetts fallen; others would follow, for the duke was 'ready to surrender the Government of New York to the King', and writs would soon challenge all remaining colonial charters. Such measures would 'bring about that Necessary union of all the English Colonies in America which will make the King great & extend his reall Empire in those parts'. Blathwayt hinted that Effingham might extend his own government by looking to his proprietary neighbors Maryland and Carolina. Effingham, who shared his predecessors' interest in annexing Maryland, was 'extreamly Joyed to find that the name of a Proprietor will in due time be extinct'.[50] In distant Virginia Effingham understood that a sea change in English politics had affected the fate of the English colonies. As for Halifax, soon after James's accession to the throne he was 'kicked upstairs' and then, in October 1685, kicked out.

* * *

The Trimmer had warned that to provoke the people to self-defence was dangerous, for 'when the Leviathan is roused it moveth like an angry creature'. But it was also 'preposterous', for the people were naturally inclined to 'suffer anything rather than resist'.[51] No doubt he had the English in mind, but the observation was applicable to colonial political behavior, too. Once colonists were 'roused', as they were in several places during these years, 'the streame of popular resolution', as Fitz-John Winthrop of Connecticut put it in 1689, was not to be easily diverted, far less dammed up. For the most part of the 1680s, however, colonists showed a preference for slumber. Even in Massachusetts, where a majority of the electorate resisted compromise on the issue of charter regulation, a substantial body of men took the opposite view, and, in the issue, the 'faction' acquiesced quietly. Such bravado as there was melted away in 1684 and 1685, and Samuel Sewall's resigned attitude at the end of the last session of the Massachusetts General Court, in May 1686, was typical: 'This day New England begins to die'. Indeed it was so. Massachusetts's neighbors resisted the Dominion only halfheartedly. 'We must tell you', wrote the Connecticut General Court, that 'we love our own things, if wee may injoy them'. In due course Connecticut surrendered by default. The legend that the Connecticut charter was hidden in a venerable oak tree, as if for later use, is rendered dubious by the ceremonial welcome laid on for Sir Edmund Andros when he came to settle Dominion government in Hartford. Moreover, leading Connecticut gentlemen emulated their fellows in Massachusetts by taking important civil and military commissions from Andros.[52] Some of these colonial servants of the Dominion used their influence to protect local interests, and some important dissents were registered even on Andros's royal council.[53] Still, open resistance was rare; those who dared it, such as the Massachusetts clergyman John Wise, suffered their penalties and nursed their grievances against not only Andros and his imperial henchmen but also their fellow colonists who served the Dominion. A more interesting, possibly more significant form of resistance was entirely passive; few in Essex County, at least, trusted the Dominion's civil courts well enough to use them.[54]

These were common patterns of behavior. In Virginia, some leading planters, like Robert Beverly, stoutly opposed high-handed governors, and the tobacco-cutting riots of 1682 may be seen as popular protests against the colony's economic subordination to empire; but the Virginia Assembly had its wings clipped nonetheless. True, in 1680 the assembly successfully resisted Lord Culpeper on the Poyning's Law issue, but it paid a higher price than had Jamaica, notably a permanent revenue on exported tobacco. Soon, the dispatch to the colony of Governor Lord Effingham made some long for Culpeper's return. Besides imperious governors, aggression from England continued. In May 1684, dismayed by the king's direct disallowance of an old law, the burgesses politely asked why the king's ancient and lucrative colony should not be treated as well as English borough corporations. Sixteen eighty-four was not the best year to suggest that analogy, but the burgesses also appealed to Charles to continue the 'Antient usage . . . that such Lawes . . . as by the Authority of your Majesties Governor Council and Burgesses . . . shall be ordained for the welfare Advantage and Good Government of this your dominion . . . May have the force of Lawe until they shall be declared voyd, and Repealed by the same Authority'. If that could not be, the burgesses begged the king not to repeal laws unilaterally 'at least untill' the assembly presented a case for their continuance. This was hardly defiance, for as the burgesses later recognized they had effectively conceded that the king could repeal existing laws if he had a mind to do so. Yet Effingham and his councillors, most of them Virginia planters, refused to join in the petition on the ground that it was presumptuous![55] In this context it may be said that when Effingham assured Blathwayt that he could deal with any local difficulty with only twenty soldiers, he was making a political, not a military point. On the other hand, during the tobacco-cutting riots, with no royal governor in the colony, Virginia councillors had put the military requirements for stability a good deal higher, thus confessing their own dependence upon the crown in the face of popular unrest.[56]

Virginia offers the salutary reminder that while royal colonies survived the reactionary 1680s with their local institutions more or less intact, they did not get off lightly. As in English counties pressure fell as much on individuals as on institutions. Members of royal councils found that opposition to commands from governors, the crown, or bureaucrats like Blathwayt could lead to dismissal from lucrative and prestigious offices.[57] The use of patronage in the service of empire forced councillors to toe the line politically, too. In their disputes with Effingham, Virginia's burgesses failed almost without exception to gain the support of councillors. One exception, Councillor Philip Ludwell, proved the rule by being cast into a political wilderness from which he was rescued by the fortuitous coincidence between his and William of Orange's arrival in England in 1688. Encouraged by Ludwell's example, Virginians like William Byrd, Nathaniel Bacon, Sr, and Nicholas Spencer operated as loyal adjutants to governors in their political roles and to the crown in such offices as surveyor, secretary, and auditor of revenues. However, royal councillors were not alone in feeling the heat. Effingham emulated his royal masters, both Charles and James, by removing obstreperous burgesses from patronage employments or by 'razing' them from their counties' commissions of the peace.[58]

Thus 1680s politics contrasted sharply with Virginia's earlier history, when Governor Berkeley's Green Spring circle had dominated council and burgesses, forming a united front which attempted to reform

Virginia's economy, led the quest for a charter in 1675, and resisted challenges put to its continued dominance first by Bacon's rebels and then by the royal commissioners of 1677. Similar changes occurred in the royal colonies of the West Indies. In Jamaica, in the late 1670s, an emergent planter class had led the opposition to Poyning's law in both council and assembly and then under Sir Thomas Lynch had settled the constitutional issue and displaced the privateers from power. James's Governor, the Duke of Albemarle, broke into this circle and seemed set fair to break the planter class in government and society by giving favor to small planters and even buccaneers. Albemarle added injury to insult by advancing the interests of Royal African Company, as did Governor Sir Edwin Stede – a former employee of the Company – in Barbados. Albemarle and his fellow island governors of the late 1680s also worked to bring Catholics and Protestant dissenters into office, thus following James's policies in England and replicating their effect by disturbing local elites. As if such governors were not enough, London issued sharp reminders to both assemblies and office-holders of their duty to obey the crown.[59] Yet resistance was rare and generally passive. It was during this period of imperial reaction, Professor Dunn suggests, that Barbadian planters began to succumb to the attractions of absentee ownership. In Jamaica, Albemarle's timely death after a drinking bout offered some relief, but in all the islands it was William of Orange's descent upon England which returned to the planter class their political spurs and made timely the publication of Edward Littleton's *The Groans of the Plantations*.[60]

In this colonists did not differ much from Englishmen like Sir John Reresby, men who as Halifax sensed and historians have since accepted, would go to great lengths to accommodate even James's version of kingship. A Yorkshire MP, justice of the peace, and military governor of York Castle, Reresby disapproved of such signs of the times as the presence on the county bench of papist justices, but he took great pleasure in the king's favor and resolved to obey 'so good a master' in all that he could. In Ireland, Lord Lieutenant Clarendon reacted similarly to the insertion of large numbers of Catholics into his administration. He complained only a little and concluded that if 'the King like it so, it is all well'. Similarly, James's campaign of 1687-88 to secure support for his religious programme from the county gentry provoked more unhappiness than defiance. In a manner reminiscent of the assemblies of Jamaica, Virginia, and Massachusetts, Englishmen told their king that they would obey such laws as he and his parliament might pass, but they could not promise either to vote that way themselves or to elect only those who would.[61] So it was that many otherwise loyal subjects elected to sit on their hands rather than take up arms when they heard of the impending Dutch invasion, then were relieved when James fled the country, effectively leaving his subjects in the care of his nephew and daughter. Such parities or similarities in political behavior between colonists and Englishmen help to define the politics of empire at the end of the seventeenth century.

* * *

Students of seventeenth-century American politics have generally stressed colonial resistance to English authority. Whether they have celebrated or deprecated this resistance, they have provided a context for colonists' eighteenth-century quest for power and their ultimate resistance of 1776. Yet in a seventeenth-century context, acceptance of English rule was as deeply rooted in the colonial experience as was resistance. During the early decades of settlement, fragile social orders gave to colonial elites a sense of isolation and vulnerability which weighed heavily even in New England. However much colonists in government wished to keep English authority at arm's length, it was nice to know it was there and sometimes they needed to grasp it. Colonial reactions to the civil wars and the Restoration demonstrated this tension between dependence and autonomy and its varied social, economic, and political roots.[62] Colonists' passive behavior during the reactionary years of the 1680s suggests that dependence was still a powerful force, At the same time, it has been amply shown that colonists chafed under the new imperialism and gave voice to "whiggish" principles. They cherished their rights and liberties as Englishmen, believed that their local governments' powers were vital to protect these rights, and on these bases often perceived a conflict of interests between themselves and an aggressive imperial authority. Thus they constructed the rationale which would enable them, without too much embarrassment or hypocrisy, to endorse and take ready advantage of England's Glorious Revolution.[63]

Colonists' response to the crises of the 1680s shows that by the century's end the colonial tension between dependence and autonomy had not so much weakened as it had changed. This owed much to a changing social context. The older colonies, especially, were no longer fragile beachheads in the wilderness but settled, permanent, even comfortable places. The New England through which Sarah Knight travelled in 1704 was a going concern. Five months on the road, from Boston to New York and back, she suffered occasionally from bad lodgings and worse food, but she found good roads and bridges among the bad and as much good as rude entertainment. She saw a complicated social structure, yet one where even the very 'picture of poverty' included a 'Hutt and its Inhabitance . . . very clean and tydee'. Raw nature frightened her, or at least she said it did, but in one wilderness stretch of the journey, the moonlight filled her 'Imagination with the pleasent delusion of a Sumpteous citty, fill'd with famous Buildings and churches, with their spiring steeples, Balconies, Galleries and I know not what'. In 1697 Boston's Samuel Sewall noted that Mary Browne, the first-born of Newbury, still lived, but more than that her many children and grandchildren had spread out across the landscape 'to begin other Plantations'. There seemed no reason it should not go on 'as long as Nature shall not grow Old and dote; but shall constantly remember to give the rows of Indian Corn their education, by Pairs'.[64] Granted, Sewall's was an exercise in religious prophesy, not political analysis, but it came less than four decades after John Norton's warning that left to its own devices New England would become a dry and withered, a shrivelled thing. A spirit of independence was not yet abroad, but Norton's dim view of New England's self-sufficiency had been replaced by a sturdy provinciality, in which men not only desired but could afford to emulate metropolitan styles of dress, discourse, and architecture.[65]

Of course, New England was in some respects exceptional, but not in this one. Everywhere societies had taken root and branched out. The new colony of Pennsylvania, first settled in 1682, quickly attained a substantial prosperity which cannot be explained entirely as a happy coincidence between climate, geography, and the Quaker settlers' devotion to both meeting house and counting house. Plainly, Englishmen were getting better at living in America. Even in the West Indies the fine townhouses of Bridgetown and, before the 1692 earthquake, Port Royal, served merchants' businesses and their egos, while new plantation houses were grand enough to make surprising their owners' increasing absenteeism. In the 1680s, Barbadians marked the funeral of Lady Willoughby, the discovery of the Rye House Plot, the birth of the Prince of Wales, and the accession of William and Mary in ways which displayed their society's coming of age, at least its adolescence. Their apologies that as poor sugar farmers they could not do justice to one occasion were belied when, during another, 'the crowd of coaches' caused disputes over the order of march. Later, two baronets were told off for queue jumping; one stormed out of the council chamber, but the other apologized and punished his coachman. We hardly need the famous census of 1680 to sense that this was a complex society.[66] In Virginia, there were not so many baronets, but in the older sections of the colony and the upper reaches of the social order, the phenomenon of natural population growth was producing a large creole elite. The founders of several notable eighteenth-century dynasties, among them the Fitzhughs and Byrds, had already begun to live in the style to which their progeny would be accustomed. They had their portraits painted, their coats of arms engraved, built fine houses, and engaged in gentlemanly correspondence among themselves and in business with an impressive range of English and colonial merchants.[67]

As colonial societies began to produce that 'compleat polity' which earlier generations of colonists had longed for, colonial politics grew more complex in both the imperial and local contexts. An important feature of this development was a shift in ideal prescriptions for colonial government. In general, seventeenth-century colonists had sought either to obtain or keep corporate, chartered status. The attractions of charter government were, as we have seen, considerable. In the imperial context, this traditional model for English local government and economic regulation benefited colonists in ways perfectly, if negatively, defined first by fears that Charles I might impose monopoly trade regulation, then by the Commonwealth's Plantations Act of 1650, and after the Restoration by Charles II's casual gifts of American real estate – much of it already settled – to court favorites. No wonder, then, that at several times between the 1640s and 1670s, Barbados, Virginia, and some other colonies sought their own contractual relationship with the English state. However, corporate government also made sense in the colonial context, where elites felt all the strains of being beleaguered minorities in unstable wilderness societies. When in 1646 Robert Child protested that the Massachusetts charter government denied him his English rights, the authorities not only admitted the charge; they accused Child of deluding the people of New England and of maligning 'the wisdom of the state of England' which had granted the 'liberties and privileges of our charter . . . only to such as the governor and company shall think fit to receive'. Colonial elites' quest for corporate status in imperial politics replicated their political behavior 'at home', as they used their direct hold on public power to secure their private interests and to restrict the privileges and freedoms of others.

However, the climate was changing, as can be seen by reconsidering the efforts of Governor Berkeley and his Green Spring faction to pursue corporate schemes for Virginia's economy and, in 1675, to secure a charter from the crown. Whether well-meant or statesmanlike or merely self-interested, these objectives roused resentment from the 'poor, discontented, mutinous, and armed' majority of Virginians. Bacon's Rebellion exposed another weakness of the system, its inability to incorporate immigrant gentlemen like Nathaniel Bacon and home-grown, ambitious planters from the colony's expanding frontier regions. Thus Berkeley's corporate paternalism gave way not only because of its frailty in the face of an aggressive imperium but because (as the Commissioners of Customs noted in the 1680s) its historic ends and means now provoked serious discord in Virginia.[68] As John Rainbolt and

Edmund Morgan make clear, the colony's expanding gentry class was beginning to work out its own salvation through a combination of slavery, economic diversification, and better control over the marketing of tobacco. 'Our Estates here depend altogether upon Contingencyes', wrote Virginia's William Fitzhugh to an English friend in 1687, '& to prepare against that, causes me to exceed my inclinations in worldly affairs'. It had, as we have seen, ever been thus in America, for the pressures of a market economy had been particularly acute in new wilderness settlements; but now the contingencies had become much more complicated. Fitzhugh's worldly affairs brought him into a series of different relationships with his neighbors and English merchants, as a planter, commission merchant, storekeeper for imported goods, creditor, and lawyer. And still he schemed to gain even better advantage in the market.[69] Men like Fitzhugh, who despite his wealth played only a minor role in Virginia politics, had no wish to surrender their ambitions or interests to a closed elite and its Virginia blueprint, however attractive it might seem. It might be suggested that even by 1676 Virginia's elite was too large, and if not too heterogeneous then too spatially diffused to operate as a corporate polity. By the century's end the claim of Virginia's gentlemen burgesses to represent a wider commons of other gentlemen and substantial freeholders, indeed to represent their neighborhoods, their county communities, was not only more plausible than it had been before, but a good deal safer.[70]

Colonists' changing political self-regard was replicated in England, where the corporate and contractual forms of colonial government and trade regulation now lost those historic attractions which made them so dominant a part of Charles I's empire. In 1660, to be sure, Clarendon tried to restore such forms, but the crown's rejection of Virginia's quest for a charter in 1676 and the strong – if unsuccessful – opposition from within the government to the Pennsylvania charter of 1681 suggest that the traditional ideas had lost force and that the idea of royal government was now in the ascendant. It is, however, essential to note that this model was not necessarily an autocratic one. Even the governors charged with putting the Poyning's Law policy in operation had argued that some local legislative initiative should be retained. The Dudley – Randolph plan for New England, put forward in 1683, adhered to similar principles, and in 1681, Lord Culpeper advised Charles II to make the colonies into little Englands whose parliaments would surely confer upon the crown a better inheritance than it enjoyed from the navigation system and the revenue settlement of 1660. As Halifax and Guilford proved in late 1684 by their querulous dissent from the New England policy, a parliamentary model for American royal governments was much in men's minds.[71]

Ignoring such possibilities during a decade of reaction, the crown instead imposed autocratic rule in New England as if the colonies were still little more than species of English local government. Just so, in England James's campaign of 1687-88 enjoyed its best success in the chartered boroughs. In the issue, these polities proved too weak to resist autocracy and too isolated to sustain it, and when James encountered stronger constituencies in the county communities, his attempt to pack parliament foundered. Together with Prince William's crucial intervention, this resistance culminated in the preservation of parliament and gentry, Anglican rule. Colonists' own experience pointed towards similar conclusions and helped to insure that the crisis of the 1680s would be resolved similarly in England and in America. Jamaicans' celebration of the settlement of the Poyning's Law dispute set the stage by asserting a symmetry between their own and England's national political institutions, king, lords, and commons. We can read much of colonists' later enthusiasm for the professed principles of the Glorious Revolution in these Jamaican speeches, and another symmetry, too, for a revolution to secure parliament, property, and protestantism made sense within the American context. The Jamaica assembly's successful struggle against the Poyning's Law policy marked also the political coming of age of a nascent planter class, its victory over other social groups in the island. In rapidly expanding societies which were beginning to display some of the lineaments of pluralism, men of property and standing found parliamentary government a surer route to power and stability, a better guarantor of rights, than the old corporate forms. The Glorious Revolution insured that, as Halifax had done in defending New England's rights, colonists would abandon the corporate model in favor of analogies between English and colonial political institutions and processes which saw colonies not as species of English local government but as fully-fledged polities, parallel with England if still subordinate to it.[72]

New England provided the most fully studied model of the shift from corporatism. There the waning power of corporate ideals was accompanied by the rise of the group which most clearly challenged the old ways, that elusive 'moderate faction' which in the 1680s gathered around the unlikely figure of Edward Randolph: land speculators eager for personal advantage, dissidents from the New England way, merchants impatient of their society's parochialism, a few outright royalists, and undoubtedly (in men like Simon Bradstreet, William Pynchon, and Peter Bulkeley)[73] representatives of that conservative strain in Puritanism which had so enlivened Massachusetts politics in the 1660s. They were, of course, members of an elite, sometimes painfully self-conscious about it, yet it is important to recognize that they were not a small, unified, or well defined group; nor were they alone, nor would they have things their own way. In country towns, social articulation had proceeded at a slower rate than in the port towns of Boston, Salem, and Charlestown, but it proceeded nevertheless, and as it did it further weakened the force of the corporate ideal. One hears less of covenants in town politics, and in many towns the focus of power moved from the selectmen to the town meeting, as if the smaller body could no longer function as fathers of the towns. Where balance or consensus could not be reached, towns split apart, new selectmen were elected, proprietors and townsmen fell out over divisions of land.[74]

For many Massachusetts towns, the rebellion of 1689 not only presented a chance to escape the exactions of Andros's Dominion but radically to alter the basis of corporate rule. Historians have stressed the debate between those who would immediately resume the old charter governments and those who wished to wait for further word from England. That division was typical of the colonies' seventeenth-century past. It was perhaps more significant for their eighteenth-century future that whether they pressed for action or delay, many towns insisted on calling meetings of all the inhabitants, then included in their petitions requests for a wider voting franchise than had been the case under the old charter.[75] Towns called for a freeholder rather than a saintly electorate as if in recognition that New England now required a government which would represent men's interests rather than their souls. Massachusetts's new royal charter of 1691 was by no means universally popular, but it enjoyed significant support from groups and individuals who, on many other issues, had been and would be at odds with each other. In this sense it both symbolized the failure to restore corporate rule and fit with long-term trends in both Massachusetts and English politics.[76]

It would be wrong to suggest that such transitions as these were complete or even close to consummation by the 1680s and 1690s. Yet they were undoubtedly underway. In this situation, it was not only the corporate ideal which was anachronistic. So, too, was James's attempt to impose autocracy on the colonies. This is not to say that it was bound to fail. Colonists, like Englishmen, had every reason to cling to legitimate authority, and had the crown possessed a more realistic sense of the requirements of autocratic rule in the American context it might have succeeded. But in lieu of more soldiers, more money, and a larger and more pervasive bureaucracy, the colonial autocracies of the 1680s were as feeble as Duke James's New York government had been, more a throwback to his father's time than a child of his own. If the Stuart imperium of the 1680s was not doomed to failure, it was weak. So said a succession of royal officials, from governors like Carlisle to functionaries like Edward Randolph, and in this they echoed the advice of Edmund

Andros who, when governor of New York, had suggested to James that a representative assembly would do much to secure the power of imperial rule in America. Historians have concluded much the same thing about the prospects for Stuart absolutism in England. In both England and America, governments had not only to be powerful, but to have powerful constituencies. James did not succeed in building such constituencies, and the collapse of his schemes in 1688 meant that in England and in the colonies these constituencies would be found in existing class structures and traditional institutions, not in new civilian bureaucracies or in military rule.

Given colonists' situation, it was just as well that England's Glorious Revolution provided a workable imperial context. Had members of colonial elites been forced really to determine their own political fate within the confines of local institutions and local mores, they might have quailed at the attempt. Had they been forced to deal with their rivals or their inferiors within the same constraints, they might have imposed despotisms far more draconian than those imposed by James II. The savage repression visited upon Bacon's rebels in 1676 by Virginia's elite is worthy of note here, as is the conduct of Massachusetts's lay and clerical leaders during the witchcraft episode of 1692. We must also remember the important contributions made by human slavery to the emergent social and political stability of the Chesapeake and West Indian colonies. Indeed, it has been suggested that in Virginia racism and slavery divided the underclass and created a situation in which members of the elite could rule securely through the relatively benign institutions of a representative system.[77] Glorious Revolution principles were 'popular' in America not only because they promised to roll back Stuart autocracy but also because they provided legitimation for America's evolving polities. We must not casually assume that colonists used the principles of 1688 simply to achieve greater autonomy.

* * *

The creation of a framework within which local and imperial authorities could function together amicably was, perhaps, ultimately an impossible goal. The American Revolution stands witness to that. But it is not without significance that in the imperial crisis of 1763-76 many colonists looked back longingly to the Revolution of 1688 and argued not only that they might do it again but that it was the British crown and parliament which had forsaken its principles.[78] Those principles, indeed, promised much to create a stable relationship between imperial and colonial government, to solve a problem which had bedevilled colonists and kings, America and England, ever since 1625 when Charles I had declared his intention to put his empire in one frame and course of government. Very considerable difficulties stood in the way of that objective, but a number of factors, not least the colonies' rapid social development, insured that they had not been substantially different for the colonies or the realm. Stability, perhaps, had been the main aim, and stability required a legitimate, widely acceptable locus of authority. But in pursuit of stability Englishmen confronted the problems presented by rapid social and economic change, and thus learned to like the idea of powerful, positive governments, governments which could act to secure the interests of dominant social groups. In England and the colonies it was found that this objective could not be obtained without securing the place and power of local governments and local elites. Failure to recognize this was King James's fundamental error in 1685-88, just as it had been Duke James's fundamental error with New York in 1664-81. It certainly had been Thomas Hobbes's oversight, if not his error. In his philosopher's haste to make the sovereign into Leviathan he forgot society, or viewed it as an obstacle to political order and authority.

Even so, Leviathan was what England got in 1688. As if to celebrate, England fought a series of foreign and imperial wars which would have bankrupted its late tyrants. All the while, the country engaged in a virulent party politics which, only a decade previously, would have been viewed as presaging civil war, but which now accomplished transitions not only of ministries but also of dynasties. When England's Leviathan came and survived, it confounded Hobbes by virtue of uniting the state and society, viewing them as contiguous. Locke and Shaftesbury had employed this insight in their Fundamental Constitutions, and in 1691 the surviving Lords Proprietors of Carolina endorsed the principle and demonstrated their understanding of it; we have, they wrote, 'kept on bounding our own power and extending that of the people to the end that your strength and security might be increased'.[79] That this vision of the state left out the poor and many others as well was not the least of its attractions on either side of the Atlantic. The Glorious Revolution made sovereignty and legitimacy the joint possession of crown and parliament, and in this sense united state and ruling class in what we might call Locke's Leviathan. In the extension of this model to the colonies and the acceptance of it by American social elites we see that English politics remained the engine of empire at the end as it had been throughout the century of revolution.

ABBREVIATIONS

AHR.	*American Historical Review.*
APCC.	*Acts of the Privy Council, Colonial Series.*
Bath Coventry Mss.	The Coventry Papers of the Marquess of Bath, Library of Congress Microfilm.
BL.	British Library, London.
Bodl.	Bodleian Library, Oxford University.
BPCW.	Blathwayt Papers of Colonial Williamsburg.
CHSC.	Connecticut Historical Society *Collections.*
CSPC.	*Calendar of State Papers, Colonial Series: America and West Indies.*
CSPD.	*Calendar of State Papers, Domestic.*
CTB.	*Calendar of Treasury Books.*
CTP.	*Calendar of Treasury Papers.*
DNB.	*Dictionary of National Biography.*
EHR.	*English Historical Review.*
JAH.	*Journal of American History.*
JSocH.	*Journal of Social History.*
MHSC.	Massachusetts Historical Society Collections.
NEQ.	*New England Quarterly.*
NYHSC.	New York Historical Society *Collections.*
P&P.	*Past and Present.*
PRO.	Public Record Office, London.
SRO.	Scottish Record Office, Edinburgh.
VMHB.	*Virginia Magazine of History and Biography.*
WMQ.	*William and Mary Quarterly.*

NOTES

Chapter 1

1 John J. McCusker and Russell R. Menard, *The Economy of British America, 1607-1789* (Chapel Hill, 1985), 212-34; David S. Lovejoy, *The Glorious Revolution in America* (New York and London, 1972), xii-xvi; Theodore B. Lewis, 'A Revolutionary Tradition, 1689-1774: "There was a Revolution here as well as in England"', *NEQ* 46 (1973), 424-38.

2 Lawrence Stone, 'The Results of the English Revolutions of the Seventeenth Century', in J. G. A. Pocock (ed.), *Three British Revolutions: 1641, 1688, 1776* (Princeton, 1980), 23-108.

3 Jack P. Greene (ed.), *Great Britain and the American Colonies, 1606-1763* (New York, 1970), xiii.

4 Compare C. M. Andrews, *The Colonial Period of American History*, 4 vols (New Haven, 1934-1938), vol. IV, *England's Commercial and Colonial System* to Webb's *The Governors-General: the English Army and the Definition of the Empire, 1569-1681* (Chapel Hill, 1979). See also Richard R. Johnson, 'Charles McLean Andrews and the Invention of American Colonial History', *WMQ* 3rd ser. 43 (1986), 519-41, and, in the same volume, a debate between Johnson ('The Imperial Webb . . . ') and Webb ('The Data and Theory of Restoration Empire'), 408-59.

5 Compare J. M. Sosin, *English America and the Revolution of 1688: Royal Administration and the Structure of Provincial Government* (Lincoln, 1982) to Lovejoy's *The Glorious Revolution in America*. Sosin plainly identifies the differing traditions and aligns his interpretation of imperial politics with the approach inspired by Bernard Bailyn's 'Politics and Social Structure in Virginia', in James Morton Smith (ed.), *Seventeenth-Century America* (Chapel Hill, 1959).

6 The quotes come from Andrews, *Colonial Period*, III, 1; Thomas C. Barrow, *Trade and Empire: The British Customs Service in Colonial America* (Cambridge, Mass., 1967), 5; George L. Beer, *The Old Colonial System. . . 1660-1688* (2 vols, Gloucester, Mass., 1958), I, 2; and Greene (ed.), *Great Britain and the American Colonies*, xi.

7 A classic statement of this view is in Andrews, *Colonial Period*, III, pp. xi-xiii.

8 See Sosin's *English America and the Restoration Monarchy of Charles II* (Lincoln, 1980) and Webb's *1676: The End of American Independence* (New York, 1984). Webb's general thesis is briefly outlined in *The Governors General*, xv-xvii. Sosin summarizes his views in *English America and the Revolution of 1688*, 1-17, 262.

9 See the editors' introductory essay in Jack P. Greene and J. R. Pole (eds.), *Colonial British America: Essays in the New History of the Early Modern Era* (Baltimore and London, 1984), 1-17, and see Greene's *Pursuits of Happiness: The Social Development of Early Modern British Colonies and the Formation of American Culture* (Chapel Hill, 1988).

10 Timothy Breen, 'Persistent Localism: English Social Change and the Shaping of New England Institutions', *WMQ* 3rd ser., 30 (1973), 3-28.

11 See below, Chapter 8.

12 Charles Wilson, *England's Apprenticeship, 1603-1763* (London, 1965), 63; R. W. K. Hinton, *The Eastland Trade and the Common Weal in the Seventeenth Century* (Cambridge, 1959). See also below, Chapter 3.

13 This theme has been substantially explored in the revision of later Stuart and early Hanoverian history undertaken by Sir John Plumb and others. See Plumb's *The Growth of Political Stability: England, 1675-1725* (New York, 1967) and J. R. Western, *Monarchy and Revolution: The English State in the 1680s* (London, 1972). The relevance of such works to colonial history is established by Richard Johnson's

Adjustment to Empire: The New England Colonies, 1675-1715 (New Brunswick and Leicester, 1981) and his review article 'Politics Redefined: An Assessment of Recent Writings on the Late Stuart Period of English History, 1660-1714', *WMQ* 3rd ser., 35 (1978), 691-732.

14 David Grayson Allen, *In English Ways: The Movement of Societies and the Transferal of English Local Law and Custom to Massachusetts Bay in the Seventeenth Century* (Chapel Hill, 1981); Darrett B. and Anita H. Rutman, '"Now-Wives and Sons-in-Law": Parental Death in a Seventeenth-Century Virginia County', in Thad W. Tate and David L. Ammerman (eds.), *The Chesapeake in the Seventeenth Century: Essays on Anglo-American Society* (Chapel Hill, 1979); and Bernard Sheehan, *Savagism and Civility: Indians and Englishmen in Colonial Virginia* (Cambridge, 1980).

15 See Russell Menard, 'From Servant to Freeholder: Status Mobility and Property Accumulation in Seventeenth-Century Maryland', *WMQ*, 3rd ser., 30 (1973), 37-64, and Richard S. Dunn, *Sugar and Slaves: The Rise of the Planter Class in the English West Indies, 1624-1713* (Chapel Hill, 1972). Northern colonies' social structures were less subject to such early hardening, but in farming villages opportunity declined with succeeding generations. See Philip J. Greven, Jr, *Four Generations: Population, Land, and Family in Colonial Andover, Massachusetts* (Ithaca, 1970), 39-40, 123-24, 211-14 and James Henretta, 'Towards a Morphology of New England Society in the Colonial Period', *Journal of Interdisciplinary History* 2 (1972), 379-98.

16 Similarities between colonial and English political discourse in the late seventeenth and early eighteenth centuries are noted by David Lovejoy, *The Glorious Revolution in America*, and Timothy Breen, *The Character of the Good Ruler: Puritan Political Ideas in New England, 1630-1730* (New Haven, 1970), especially Chapters 5-7.

17 Any discussion of this period in England's imperial history must acknowledge the work of David Beers Quinn. Here I depend on Quinn's *England and the Discovery of America, 1481-1620* (London, 1974) and on K. R. Andrews, *Trade, Plunder and Settlement: Maritime Enterprise and the Genesis of the British Empire, 1480-1630* (Cambridge, 1984). See also Edmund Morgan's imaginative treatment of the 'Virginia vision' in *American Slavery, American Freedom: The Ordeal of Colonial Virginia* (New York, 1975), 3-107.

18 Nicholas P. Canny, 'The Ideology of English Colonization: From Ireland to America', *WMQ*, 3rd ser., XXX, no. 4 (1973), 575-98.

19 Sheehan, *Savagism and Civility*, especially Chapter 1, 'Paradise', 9-37. Thomas Morton took a roseate view of Indian life in order to make an unfavorable comparison with the English: *New English Canaan . . . an Abstract of New England* (London, 1632), reprinted in Peter Force, (ed.), *Tracts and Other Papers . . .* (4 vols, Washington, D. C., 1836-1846) II, no. V, 38-40.

20 Gillian T. Cell, *English Enterprise in Newfoundland, 1577-1660* (Toronto, 1969), 44-7, 53-61; Morgan, *American Slavery, American Freedom*, 3-70; Sheehan, *Savagism and Civility*, 89-116.

21 Quinn, *England and the Discovery of America*, for instance 236-42, 258, 265-6, 270-1, 289, 297-8, 302-5.

22 'The problem which was not faced or solved in practice by the Virginia companies ... was how to exploit these military men productively ... it was hard to expect them ... to become laborers, craftsmen, merchants and administrators. ' Quinn, *England and the Discovery of America*, 486. K. R. Andrews sees *Trade, Plunder and Settlement* as much more closely linked, but concludes (p. 356) that 'one reason why the British Empire took such an unconscionable time getting born is that the English put colonization well below trade and plunder in their priorities'.

23 Andrews, *Colonial Period*, I, 78-149, offers a sufficient guide here. But see also Theodore K. Rabb, *Enterprise and Empire* (Cambridge, 1967).

24 The Plymouth Company could not even claim credit for the settlement in 1620 of the Pilgrims at New Plymouth, which was undertaken under licence from the Virginia Company. See George Langdon, Jr, *Pilgrim Colony: a History of New Plymouth, 1620-1691* (New Haven, 1966), 8-11, 17.

25 Dale's 'Articles, Lawes, and Orders, Divine, Politique, and Martiall . . . ', are in Force,

Tracts III, no. 2. Virginia's charter revision of 1612 is summarized in Andrews, *Colonial Period* I, 103n, 116-18. The Somers Islands Company charter of 1615 also directly linked investment shares with voting rights: J. H. Lefroy, *Memorials of the Bermudas* (2 vols, London, 1877-1879), I, 90-91.

26 Andrews, *Colonial Period*, I, 150-85. For this and the following two paragraphs, see Morgan, *American Slavery, American Freedom*, 71-107 and 'The Labor Problem at Jamestown, 1607-1618', *AHR* 76 (1971), 595-611; Sigmund Diamond, 'From Organization to Society: Virginia in the Seventeenth Century', *American Journal of Sociology*, LXIII (1958), 457-75; and Wesley Frank Craven, *The Dissolution of the Virginia Company: The Failure of a Colonial Experiment* (reprint, Gloucester, Mass., 1964), esp. 47-104.

27 The 'Great Charter' is in Susan M. Kingsbury (ed.), *Records of the Virginia Company of London* (4 vols, Washington, D. C., 1906-35), I, 98-109.

28 See *Virginia Records* I, 98-109, 448, 468. These aims were underlined in the company's deliberations of 1619; see *ibid.*, I, 212, 215-6, 218-9, 231-2, 234-5. In 1620, Sandys pursued the point by announcing plans to involve the king in the colony's legislative process, 'itt beinge not fitt that his Majestys subjects should be governed by any other lawes then by such as shall receive influence of life from his Majesty . . . ', *ibid.*, I, 333. The Somers Island Company also imposed 'the forme[s] used in England' on its colony; see Lefroy, *Memorials of Bermuda*, I, 152-3.

29 *A Declaration of the State of the Colonie and Affaires in Virginia . . .* (London, 1620), Force, (ed.), *Tracts* III, no. 5, 5.

30 *Virginia Records* I, 235-7, 240, 272-3, 293-4, 303; II, 325; Craven, Dissolution, 112-17.

31 *Virginia Records* I, 256-7, 262, 265-8.

32 Leo F. Stock (ed.), *Proceedings and Debates of the British Parliaments Respecting North America* (5 vols, Washington, D. C., 1924-1941), I, 64-6.

33 One damaging report came from the Governor of Bermuda, Nathaniel Butler, an associate of Smith's. His 'Unmasked face of Our Colony in Virginia', presented to the Privy Council in April 1623, is in *Virginia Records*, II, 374-6.

34 The fullest account is in Craven, *The Dissolution of the Virginia Company*, 81-291. The process of events between April and July 1623 can be followed in *APCC* I, nos. 98, 100-4, and 107.

35 The decision was probably made by 31 July 1623: *Virginia Records* IV, 253-6.

36 *APCC* I, no. 109.

37 For the commissions to Mandeville and Wyat, see Ebenezer Hazard, *Historical Collections: Consisting of State Papers . . .* (reprint,Freeport, N. Y., 1969) I, 183-92. Legal proceedings are recorded at *Virginia Records* IV, 358-98.

38 Below, Chapter 2.

39 *APCC* I, no. 109. James repeatedly promised to preserve the interests 'in parson or purse' of both adventurers and planters. See *Virginia Records* IV, 255-6; *APCC* I, no. 112.

40 Besides the terms of the declaration of October 1623, agreement on the general point between the crown, the crown's lawyers, and both main company factions is evident from *Virginia Records* I, 325, 348-62, 350, 353, 358-9. See also *Virginia Records* IV, 124-6, 255-6.

41 Francis Bacon, 'Of Plantations' (1625), in Jack P. Greene (ed.), *Settlements to Society, 1584-1763* (New York, 1966) 9-11.

42 See for instance *A Declaration of the State of the Colonie and Affaires in Virginia...* (London, 1620), Force, *Tracts* III, no. 5, and 'An Account of the colony of the Lord Baron of Baltimore, 1633', in C. C. Hall (ed.), *Narratives of Early Maryland, 1633-1684* (reprint, New York, 1967), 5-10.

43 David S. Lovejoy, *Religious Enthusiasm in the New World: Heresy to Revolution* (Cambridge, Mass., and London, 1985), 6-8.

Chapter 2

1 Charles Carlton, *Charles I: the Personal Monarch* (London, 1983), 151. A. B. Keith, *A Constitutional History of the British Empire* (Oxford, 1930), 46-7, offers a classic dismissal of Charles's policies, recently endorsed in Jack Greene, *Peripheries and Center: Constitutional Development in the Extended Polities of the British Empire and the United States, 1607-1788* (Athens, 1986), 11-3.

2 Derek Hirst sums up judiciously in *Authority and Conflict: England 1603-1658* (London, 1986), 136-87. See also Conrad Russell, *Parliament and English Politics, 1621-1629* (Oxford, 1979), 53-4, 417-33 and B. W. Quintrell, 'The Making of Charles I's Book of Orders', *EHR* 95 (1980), 553-72.

3 *APCC* I, no. 142. It was rumored in the spring of 1625 that Sandys was to become Secretary of State. Russell, *Parliaments and English Politics*, 33, 149, 151, 177-8, 200.

4 The 'Discourse of the Old Company' is in *Virginia Records* IV, 519-51 and *VMHB* I (1893-94), 155-63, 287-309.

5 Clarence S. Brigham (ed.), *British Royal Proclamations Relating to America, 1603-1763*, American Antiquarian Society *Transactions and Collections* XII (Worcester, Mass., 1911), 52-5.

6 Excepting Charles's abortive civil war commissions, for which see below, Chapters 3 and 4.

7 'Discourse', *Virginia Records*, IV, 520-2. See also the company's 1623 'Relation of the late proceedinges . . .', *Virginia Records* II, 353, 358, and its 1624 petition to the House of Commons which asserted that its business was 'not simply matter of trade, butt of a higher nature'. Stock, *Proceedings*, I, 65.

8 *Virginia Records* III, 637-8; IV, 22-6, 37-9, 64-72, 253-6.

9 'Discourse of the Old Company', *Virginia Records*, IV, 521-2. Bacon, 'Of Plantations' (1625), in Greene (ed.), *Settlements to Society*, 9-11. Winthrop's judgment was shared by others in the Massachusetts Bay Company. See Massachusetts Historical Society, *Winthrop Papers* (5 vols, Boston, 1929-1947), II, 106-49, *passim*.

10 For these efforts, which persisted through the 1630s, see Andrews, *Colonial Period* I, 200-2; and Beer, *Origins*, 312. On the early Stuarts' predilection for monopoly regulation, see Robert Ashton, *The City and the Court, 1603-1643* (Cambridge, 1979), 12-13, 18-24, 83-156 and C. G. A. Clay, *Economic Expansion and Social Change: England, 1500-1700* (2 vols., Cambridge, 1984), II, 204-5, 210-1, 252-63.

11 Sandys was not the parliamentary hero as cast by early historians of Virginia, but a comparison between his colonial and parliamentary careers suggests a consistency of principle based on relatively modern attitudes towards government and society. See Russell, *Parliaments and English Politics*, 170; Noel Malcolm, 'Hobbes, Sandys, and the Virginia Company', *HJ* 24 (1981), 297-324; Raab, *Enterprise and Empire*, 5-7, 38n, 40. 95; and compare Sandys's speech to the Virginia Company General Court, 17 November 1619, *Virginia Records* I, 267-8 and his 1623 draft reply to the Privy Council, *Virginia Records* II, 325.

12 Edmund S. Morgan, 'The First American Boom: Virginia, 1618-1630', *WMQ* 3rd ser., XXVIII, no. 2 (1971), 169-98. For awareness of the 'mischeife' which resulted from the 'profuse throwinge out libertie, amongst the planters' and from the greed of those in government, see John Bargrave to Lord Treasurer Middlesex, 10 June 1623, *AHR* XXVII (1922), 508-14; *Virginia Records* I, 456, 480-1; III, 637-8, IV, 22-6, 37-9; 58-62, 106-11, 535-40.

13 The leaders of the Sandys faction remained adamant on this point. See J. Mills Thornton, 'The Thrusting Out of Governor Harvey: A Seventeenth-Century Rebellion', *VMHB* 75 (1967), 14-16.

14 Pory to Carleton, 30 September 1619, Aspinwall Papers, *MHSC*, 4th ser., IX, 4-30. The Virginia government's assertion of power was immediate, for instance over the 'private plantations' like Martin's Hundred. The high death rate produced an early assertion of widows' property rights; 'in a newe plantation it is not knowen whether

man or woman be most necessary'. H. R. McIlwaine (ed.), *Journals of the Virginia House of Burgesses, 1619-1659/60* (Richmond, 1915), 4-9.

15 For early colonial reactions to the charter crisis, see McIlwaine (ed.), *Journals... 1619-1659/60*, 21-7 and Virginia Council to Viscount Mandeville, 30 March 1623, *Virginia Records* IV, 69-70. See also *Virginia Records* IV, 562-7, 571-4; and H. R. McIlwaine (ed.), *Minutes of the Council and General Court of Virginia, 1622-1632*, 1670-1676 (Richmond, 1924), 45, 65, 70, 72-3, 103.

16 Lefroy, *Memorials* I, 160-1, 232-3, 379-84. John Smith reported that under the company Bermudans feared that they would have no 'preferment... nor... any land at all of their owne', but would live 'as tenants, or as other mens poore servants'. *History of Virginia*, in *ibid.*, 147.

17 Here the king endorsed Sir George Calvert's vehement views on the subject. Russell, *Parliaments and English Politics*, 94; Malcolm, 'Hobbes, Sandys, and the Virginia Company', 303.

18 See again the proclamation of 13 May 1625, Brigham, ed., *British Royal Proclamations*, 52-5.

19 Russell, *Parliaments and English Politics*, 53-5, argues that at this time Charles had no doctrinaire objection to parliaments in general. For the 1628 assembly, see *CSPC 1574-1660*, 89-90 and McIlwaine, *Journals. . . 1619-1659/60*, 45-51.

20 Bacon, 'Of Plantations', *loc. cit.* .

21 Andrews catalogues some proprietary charters from this period in *Colonial Period* II, 222-5. For texts see Lord Baltimore's Maryland charter in Merrill M. Jensen (ed.), *English Historical Documents*, IX (London, 1969), 84-93, and the virtually identical Heath patent for 'Carolana' in W. Keith Kavanagh (ed.), *Foundations of Colonial America: a Documentary History* (3 vols, New York, 1973), III, 1724-31. The Gorges patent for Maine is in O. G. Libby (ed.), *Province and Court Records of Maine*, I (Portland, 1928), 9-29. For trading regulations under the Carlisle patent, see Williamson, *The Caribbee Islands Under the Proprietary Patents* (London, 1926), 40-1, 46-7, and Appendix I. Carlisle's personal trading privileges were removed in the second patent of 1628.

In these charters, 'free trade' meant not freedom to trade anywhere but the absence of monopoly regulations which unduly favored one group or individual against others. The Gorges patent limited this freedom only to inhabitants of the province and any others who might be licensed by the Lord Proprietor.

22 Whether proprietary charter rights *could* include monopoly powers had been raised, interestingly enough, by the Bishop of Durham during debates over the Monopolies Bill in 1621. Lord Bishop Neile had then been assured that the bill would not affect his privileges, and the inclusion of monopoly rights in the first Carlisle proprietary suggests that Charles I agreed. See Russell, *English Parliaments*, 190-1.

23 Andrews, *Colonial Period*, II, 197-222, points out affinities between the proprietaries and contemporary ideas about society and government, but then (282-4, 297-9) stresses the Maryland charter's archaism. Baltimore, although undoubtedly an authoritarian and a conservative, made no attempt to recreate medieval Durham in America, and later stated that the charter conveyed to him 'all Royall jurisdiction', possibly an anachronistic statement when he made it, in August 1649, but not in 1632 when he received the charter. See W. H. Browne, et al (eds.), *Archives of Maryland* (65 vols, in progress, Baltimore, 1883-), I, 262-72. Similar points were made by Attorney General Bankes in the 1630s (Bodl. Ms. Bankes 8/10) and by *The Lord Baltamore's Case. . .* (London, 1653), in C. C. Hall (ed.), *Narratives of Early Maryland* (New York, 1910), 173-5.

24 In 1622, the West Country propagandist for New England settlement, the Reverend John White, noted the importance of learning from Virginia's mistakes: Samuel Eliot Morison, *Builders of the Bay Colony* (Boston, 1930), 44. His advice was followed by the organizers of the Massachusetts Bay settlement: *Winthrop Papers* II, 106-52.

25 N. B. Shurtleff (ed.), *Records of the Governor and Company of the Massachusetts Bay in New England* (4 vols in 5 parts, Boston, 1853-1854), I, 23-69, *passim*. See pp. 48-51 and *Winthrop Papers*, II, 151-2, for the decision to transfer the government to New

England.

26 See John Winthrop's address to the Massachusetts Bay Court meeting, 1 December 1629, *Winthrop Papers* II, 174-7.

27 Andrews, *Colonial Period*, I, 366-74. John E. Pomfret and Floyd M. Shumway, *Founding the American Colonies, 1583-1660* (New York, 1970), 151-5.

28 See William Shepheard, *Of Corporations, Fraternities, and Guilds . . . The Learning of the Law touching Bodies-Politique . . .* (London, 1659), 18-20. The Merchant Adventurers' General Court was resident outside England, but the company's court in London was the dominant power. E. Lipson, *The Economic History of England*, II, *The Age of Mercantilism* (London, 1956), 215, 249-62. Hinton, *Eastland Trade*, pp. 56-8, 71-83, demonstrates the importance of these issues to the Eastland Company. In parliament, 'free trade' agitation was often concerned with the location of trading company government or the ease of access to company privileges. Ashton, *The City and the Court, 1603-1642*, 85-7, 106-20; B. E. Supple, *Commercial Crisis and Change in England, 1600-1642* (Cambridge, 1964), 30-31, 68-71.

29 There is no evidence that the company considered the possibility of moving its charter government to America until August 1629, and not all were reconciled to the idea in December. *Winthrop Papers* II, 151-2, 174-9.

30 A. P. Newton, *The Colonizing Activities of the English Puritans* (1914), 105-11.

31 C. M. Andrews, *British Committees, Commissions, and Councils of Trade and Plantations, 1622-1675* (Baltimore, 1908), 10-11, 13-20.

32 Andrews, *Colonial Period* II, 279-80. See also Bodl. Ms. Bankes, 8/3, 'List of the Charges made by the Virginia Company against Sir John Harvey and Against Lord Baltimore's deputies', c. 1635, and Petition of the Virginia Planters to the Privy Council, c. 1635, Bodl. Ms. Bankes, 8/4; *APCC* I, nos. 315, 317.

33 The New England Council's patent is in Hazard, *State Papers* I, 103-18. See also *APCC* I, no. 74 and Andrews, *Colonial Period* I, 322-6. Attorney General Sir John Bankes applied similar reasoning in cases concerning the powers of the old councils and Laud's new committee over individual colonial ventures; see Bodl. Ms. Bankes, 7/7, 7/10, 8/5, 8/10, 8/11, 8/12, 8/16.

34 *Virginia Records* IV, 491-2 and *APCC* I, nos. 112, 142, 154, and 336. Several of these royal letters (and the 1625 proclamation) were cited in the mid-1630s to prove that settlers' and stockholders' rights were not affected by the judgment against the company's charter; Ms. Bodl. Bankes, 8/4.

35 Andrews, *Colonial Period*, I, 192-205; Wesley Frank Craven, *The Southern Colonies in the Seventeenth Century* (Baton Rouge, 1949) 149-77; Morgan, *American Slavery, American Freedom*, 142-5, 158-79.

36 Craven, *Southern Colonies*, 160.

37 Thornton, 'The Thrusting Out of Governor Harvey', 11-26, is the most complete account.

38 Captain Thomas Yong to Sir Toby Mathew, 1634, and Governor Leonard Calvert to Lord Baltimore, 25 April 1638, in Hall, (ed.), *Narratives of Early Maryland*, 53-61, 150-9.

39 McIlwaine (ed.), *Journals . . . 1619—1659/60*, 45-51; McIlwaine, (ed.), *Minutes of the Council . . . 1622-1631, 1670-1676*, 168.

40 *CSPC* 1574-1660, 151. *APCC* I, no. 314.

41 Thornton, 'Governor Harvey', overdraws the attractiveness of the Company to Virginians during Harvey's first tenure as governor. By the decisions of 1624, company property was to have been used for the support of the royal government, and its whereabouts became a major bone of contention between the crown, the company, and local politicians. (See for instance *Virginia Records*, IV, 559-70.) Much of this property was held by those opposing Harvey, and it is doubtful that they would have welcomed a reimposition of company government. For those who held the property, see Morgan, 'The First American Boom', 188-93.

42 The instructions of 1638 and 1642 are at *VMHB* II (1894), 281-88, and XI (1903-1904), 50-57. 'The Act against the Company' is in W. W. Hening, *The Statutes at Large; Being a Collection of All the Laws of Virginia, from . . . 1619* (13 vols, Richmond and

Philadelphia, 1819-1823), I, 230-35, and see also McIlwaine (ed.), *Journals . . . 1619-1659/60,* 69-70.

43 Compare Sir Edwin Sandys's speech to the Company Court of 4 November 1620, *Virginia Records* I, 413 with McIlwaine (ed.), *Journals . . . 1619-1659/60,* 57-65, 126-7; *CSPC 1574-1660,* 190, 250-1.

44 Governor Henry Ashton to Sir James and Archibald Hay, 24 December 1642, Scottish Record Office, Hay of Haystoun Mss. (SRO GD 34)/923. See also Bailyn, *The New England Merchants in the Seventeenth Century* (New York, 1964), 45-74, and McCusker and Menard, *The Economy of British America,* 71-2, 93-101, 117-23, 148-56.

45 Rev. Francis Higginson to [his friends in Leicester], July 1629, Everett Emerson (ed.), *Letters from New England: the Massachusetts Bay Colony, 1629-1638* (Amherst, 1976), 25-7. In part, of course, such language was used to attract new settlers, but there can be no doubt that early colonial economies did offer a good deal of opportunity. See Russell R. Menard, Lois Green Carr, and Lorena S. Walsh, 'A Small Planter's Profits: The Cole Estate and the Growth of the Early Chesapeake Economy,' *WMQ,* 3rd ser., 40 (1983), 171-96, esp. 180, 191.

46 *New Englands Plantation . . .* (London, 1630), in Force (ed.), Tracts I, no. 12, 11; *An Abstract of the Lawes of New England . . .* (London, 1641), in *ibid.* III, no. 9, 6.

47 Morgan, *American Slavery, American Freedom,* 129. Two works on the West Indies confirm Morgan's bleak picture of early plantation societies: see Dunn, *Sugar and Slaves* and Carl and Roberta Bridenbaugh, *No Peace Beyond the Line: the English in the Caribbean* (New York, 1972).

48 For Virginia, see Secretary Richard Kemp to Sir Francis Windebanke, 6 April 1638, McIlwaine, *Journals . . . 1619-1659/60,* 126-27. See also Governor Ashton (Antigua) to the Earl of Carlisle, 8 February 1642, SRO GD 34/933, and papers relating to St. Christopher, including 'The agreivances of the Inhabitants', 8 February 1642, SRO GD/34/26/939, A - D and [Sir Thomas Warner?] to Sir James and Archibald Hay, 24 December 1642, SRO GD 34/26/923. For New England, John White to Winthrop, 1636 and 1637 (two letters), *Winthrop Papers* III, 321-3, 335-7.

49 For Winthrop see *Journal* II, 49; for Harvey, see McIlwaine (ed.), *Minutes of the Council . . . of Virginia, 1622-1632, 1670-1676,* 482, 496-98. See also letters from English correspondents to John Winthrop and John Winthrop, Jr, 1637-45, *Winthrop Papers* III, 377-80; IV, 91-2, 248-9; V, 28; Bailyn, *New England Merchants,* 61-71.

50 SRO GD 34/955 ('A Breif of the Patent and its Conveyance') and GD 34/921 ('Instruction by the late Earl. . . to Peter Hay [1636]').

51 Peter Hay to Sir James and Archibald Hay, 25 [?] 1636, 29 May 1637, and Peter Hay's 'demands' to the Governor and Council of Barbados, 1637, SRO GD 34/923; Peter Hay to Archibald Hay, 11 August 1638 and 24 May 1639, SRO GD 34/924.

52 See warrant, 1 March 1641; Peter Hay to Archibald Hay, 29 September 1640; James Hay to Archibald Hay, 6 October 1640; William Powry to Archibald Hay, 18 November 1640; and James Hay to the Earl of Carlisle, 24 February 1641: all in SRO GD 34/922 and 34/923. For previous losers in politics, see V. T. Harlow, *A History of Barbados, 1625-1685* (Oxford, 1926), 10-15.

53 *CSPC 1574-1660,* 281, 287-8; *VMHB* XI (1903-1904), 56. But in 1642 Governor Berkeley was given leave to grant exemptions to the requirement (*VMHB* II (1894-1895), 286); this left the decision in the colony government's hands and doubtless enhanced its power. Virginia's governors and councillors were generally more favorable than burgesses to regulatory restrictions. For an earlier attempt by the Governor and Council to establish restrictive trade regulations, see McIlwaine (ed.), *Minutes of the Council . . . 1622-1632, 1670-1676,* 113-14, 121.

54 The Governor's Answer to the Ipswich Letter', July 1643, *Hutchinson Papers* (2 vols, Albany, 1865), I, 136-7. See also *ibid.,* 127-49, and Winthrop's *Journal,* II, 107-16.

55 See above, Chapter 1.

56 Compare Bailyn, 'Politics and Social Structure in Virginia'; Morgan, *American Slavery, American Freedom,* 118-28, 143-6, 166-77; Dunn, *Sugar and Slaves,* 49-59; and Timothy Breen and Stephen Foster, 'The Puritans' Greatest Achievement: A Study

of Social Cohesion in Seventeenth-Century Massachusetts', *JAH* 60 (1973-4), 5-22. This contrast between New England and the plantation societies is not universally accepted; see for instance Jon Kukla 'Order and Chaos in Early America: Political and Social Stability in Pre-Restoration Virginia', *AHR* 90 (1985) 275-98. See also John [?] Pond to William Pond, 15 March 1631, Emerson, *Letters*, 65. See also below, Chapter 4.

57 Harro Hopfl and Martyn P. Thompson, 'History of Contract as a Motif in Political Thought', *AHR* 84 (1979), 936-41; Michael McGiffert, 'God's Controversy with Jacobean England', *AHR* 88 (1983), 1151-74; and William Lamont, *Godly Rule, 1603-1660* (London, 1969).

58 Dunn, *Sugar and Slaves*, 51-9, 118-21; Gary A. Puckrein, *Little England: Plantation Society and Anglo-Barbadian Politics, 1627-1700* (New York, 1984), 11-3, 24-30, 39; Morgan, *American Slavery, American Freedom*, 116-34.

59 It is not necessary to debate here the social background or religious motivation of the New England migrants. Present purposes are served well enough by the entirely safe assertion that New Englanders were to a significant degree 'more' equal and 'more' religiously motivated than their fellows in Virginia and the West Indies.

60 For Winthrop's 'Modell' see E. S. Morgan (ed.), *Puritan Political Ideas, 1558-1774* (Indianapolis, 1965), 75-93. The following give a sense of the range of New England towns' early social structures: R. H. Akagi, *The Town Proprietors of the New England Colonies* (Gloucester, Mass., 1963), 17-21, 32-4, 44-52; Allen, *In English Ways*, 31-2, 65, 78-80, 127-9, 134-6; Greven, *Four Generations*, 41-66; Kenneth Lockridge, *A New England Town: The First Hundred Years* (New York, 1970), 8-10, 57-78; Stephen Innes, 'Land Tenancy and the Social Order in Springfield, Massachusetts, 1652 to 1702', *WMQ* 3rd ser., 35 (1978), 33-56; and Rutman, *Winthrop's Boston*, 72-88.

61 John J. Waters, 'Hingham, Massachusetts, 1631-1661: An East Anglian Oligarchy in the New World', *J. Soc.* 1 (1968), 351-70; Allen, *In English Ways*, 30-40, 82, 109-12, 115-6; Watertown Historical Society, *Watertown Records* (vols 1 & 2, Watertown, 1894-1900), I, 2-4, 10-2; Lockridge, *A New England Town*, 3-16. For the 'relation', see *Winthrop Papers* III, 215-7, 231; Edmund S. Morgan, *Visible Saints: the History of a Puritan Idea* (Ithaca, 1965), 65-106; David D. Hall, *The Faithful Shepherd: a History of the New England Ministry in the Seventeenth Century* (Chapel Hill, 1972), 96-8.

62 In 1636 Richard Mather explained that such changes would keep churches from proceeding 'at random or blindfolded', Emerson, *Letters*, 201-8. Boston church's new covenant was preceded by a town ordinance restricting new allotments of land to 'such as may be likely to be received members of the congregation': J. B. Felt, *Ecclesiastical History of New England* (2 vols, Boston, 1855) I, 236. See also Richard D. Pierce (ed.), *The Records of the First Church of Boston, 1630-1868* (3 vols., Boston, 1961), I, 12 and *Winthrop Papers* III, 171-72, 223-25, 244-45. For events outside Boston, see B. R. Burg, *Richard Mather of Dorchester* (Lexington, 1976), 29-33, 46-9; Richard P. Gildrie, *Salem, Massachusetts, 1626-1683: A Covenant Community* (Charlottesville, 1975), 51-4; Lockridge, *A New England Town*, 23-30.

63 David Hall, (ed.), 'John Cotton's Letter to Samuel Skelton', *WMQ* 3d ser., 22 (1965), 480-85; Richard Saltonstall (the younger) to Emmanuel Downing, 4 February 1632, Emerson, *Letters*, 91-3; Emmanuel Downing to John Winthrop, [August 1645], *Winthrop Papers* V, 38-9; and 'Certain proposals made by Lord Say, Lord Brooke, and other persons of quality, as conditions of their removing to New-England, with the answers thereto' [by John Cotton], 1636, reprinted in Morgan, *Puritan Political Ideas*, 161-73.

64 Saye and Sele to John Winthrop, 9 July 1640, *Winthrop Papers* IV, 263-8.

65 Nathaniel Ward to John Winthrop, 22 October 1639, and Edward Winslow to same, 10 October 1640, *Winthrop Papers* IV, 162-3, 291-2. See also N. B. Shurtleff (ed.), *Records of the Governor and Company of the Massachusetts Bay in New England* (5 vols., Boston, 1853-1854) I, 115-7, 137, 167, 168, 196; and *Winthrop Papers* III, 231. On the general issue, see Breen, 'Persistent Localism', 3-28; Allen, *In English Ways*, passim; Perry Miller, *Orthodoxy in Massachusetts* (Cambridge, 1933), 148-91; David T. Konig, *Law and Society in Early Massachusetts: Essex County, 1629-1692* (Chapel Hill, 1979), 18-29, 33-4.

66 Ward to John Winthrop, Jr., 24 December 1635, *Winthrop Papers* III, 215-7; G. A. Schofield (ed.), *Ancient Records of the Town of Ipswich . . . 1634-1650* (Ipswich, 1899), 6; John Eliot to Sir Simonds D'Ewes, 18 September 1633, Emerson, *Letters*, 104-09; Stephen Foster, *Their Solitary Way: the Puritan Social Ethic in the First Century of Settlement in New England* (New Haven, 1971), 25-37, 114-20.

67 D. G. Hill (ed.), *The Early Records of . . . Dedham* (6 vols., Dedham, 1886-1936), III, 2-3, 20, 26, 34-5. *Watertown Records* I, 2, 6. Cambridge, or Newtown, had more experience than most towns of settlers moving on (*The Records of the Town of Cambridge, Massachusetts, 1630-1703 . . . Town Meetings*, I, 2-64 *passim*, II, 17, 18-9, 24, 32-3, 125-6), and made a series of interesting efforts to balance the right to sell land with the towns' interests in insuring the suitability of the purchasers.

68 Hugh Peter and Emmanuel Downing to John Winthrop, 13 November 1640, and John Endecott to same, 28 January 1641, *Winthrop Papers* IV, 304-5, 311-2; *Town Records of Salem, Essex Institute Historical Collections* IX (1869), 27-8. Marblehead's later disputes over land divisions and common land testified to the relative shortage of both: W. H. Bowden, 'Marblehead Town Records, 1648-1683', *Essex Institute Historical Collections* 69 (1933), 207-9, 210-1. Gildrie, *Salem*, 47-9, 56, 68-70, 105-54, shows how such stresses and strains diluted communalism. For the importance towns attached to attracting or keeping particular individuals, see for instance *Winthrop Papers* III, 241-2, 432-3; and IV, 94-5.

69 The general issue is discussed below in Chapter 4.

70 Thomas Hutchinson, *History of the Colony and Province of Massachusetts Bay* (L. S. Mayo (ed.), 3 vols, Cambridge, 1936), I, 422.

71 Edmund S. Morgan, *The Puritan Dilemma: the Story of John Winthrop* (Boston, 1958), 115-54; Philip F. Gura, *A Glimpse of Sion's Glory: Puritan Radicalism in New England, 1620-1660* (Middletown, 1984), 31-92, *passim*; Lovejoy, *Religious Enthusiasm in the New World*, 62-86; and Stephen Foster, 'New England and the Challenge of Heresy, 1630-1660: the Puritan Crisis in Transatlantic Perspective', *WMQ* 3rd ser., 38 (1981), 624-60.

72 A letter of August 1637 from Gorges to the Governor and Council of Massachusetts suggests little more than the '"conciliar' schemes earlier used by James I and Charles himself: *Winthrop Papers* III, 492-3.

73 George Chalmers, *An Introduction to the History of the Revolt of the American Colonies* (2 vols in one, Boston, 1845), I, 67-8.

Chapter 3

1 Russell, *Parliaments and English Politics, 1621-1629*, 94.

2 Here Sir Keith Feiling's views have been generally confirmed by later works: *The History of the Tory Party, 1640-1713* (Oxford, 1924), 14-17, 37-41, 68-73. On parliament's initial conservatism and the importance of localism, see Hirst, *Authority and Conflict*, 37-8, 42, 188, 194-212, 221-34 and John Morrill, *The Revolt of the Provinces: Conservatives and Radicals in the English Civil Wars, 1630-1650* (Harlow, 1980).

3 See Stock, *Proceedings*, I, 97-139, *passim*, for colonial business heard in the Short Parliament and in the Long Parliament to January 1643. For Virginia, see pp. 123-8 and below, Chapter 4.

4 For the Book of Rates, see Beer, *Origins*, 341-2. The New England ordinance was preceded by a resolution that New Englanders should enjoy customs privileges 'granted by their charter; and for so long a time as is granted by the same charter'. Probably on the discovery that the charter granted such exemptions for seven years only, the ordinance then extended these privileges to run 'until the House of Commons shall take further order'. See Stock, *Proceedings*, I, 140-2; Massachusetts *Records* II, 34; Winthrop, *Journal* II, 297.

5 Stock, *Proceedings*, I, 119, 121, 133-4, 145; C. H. Firth and R. S. Rait, *Acts and Ordinances of the Interregnum, 1642-1660* (3 vols., London, 1911), I, 202-14; Beer, *Origins*, 215-9, 342; Neville Williams, 'England's Tobacco Trade in the Reign of

Charles I', *VMHB* LXV (1957), 403-49; and Warwick to Governor and Council of Barbados, [c. 1639], and Sir Archibald Hay to Peter Hay, 8 November 1639, SRO GD 34/955 and 34/922.

6 Firth and Rait, *Acts and Ordinances* I, 331-3; Stock, *Proceeding,,* I, 146-9.

7 Alison Gilbert Olson offers a range of plausible explanations for the committee's decisions in *Anglo-American Politics, 1660-1775...* (Oxford, 1973), 15-22. See also BL Stowe 184, ff. 123-4; Wesley Frank Craven, *The Southern Colonies in the Seventeenth Century* (Baton Rouge, 1970), 224-46; Winthrop, *Journal,* II, 387-90; and Robert Emmet Wall, Jr., *Massachusetts Bay: The Crucial Decade, 1640-1650* (New Haven, 1972), 121-224. In the case of Bermuda, the committee awaited petitions from both company and colonists before deciding to grant the company the right to export goods to the islands free of duty and to grant the islanders freedom of worship. See Stock, *Proceedings,* I, 169-70, and Lefroy, *Memorials,* I, 600-602.

8 Carlisle blamed the evil influence on the king of some 'great Lords'; meanwhile the (royalist) creditors were early assured that 'parliament doth not intend to prejudice us in our Right'. See Carlisle to Governor Philip Bell, 5 January 1644 and 10 March [1644?], Hay Mss, SRO GD 34/941 and 34/26/940; and J. H. Bennett, 'The English Caribbees in the Period of the Civil War, 1642-1646', *W&MQ* 3rd ser., XXIV (1967), 370-71.

9 See Stock, *Proceedings,* I, 146-9: 'there beinge lately procured from the kinge severall grantes for governors . . . '

10 William Powry to Archibald Hay, 10 September 1645 and 3 October 1646, SRO GD 34/26/945; Philip Bell et al. to the Earl of Warwick [1646], and William Hay to Archibald Hay, 5 July 1645, SRO GD 34/924; Philip Bell to Archibald Hay, 21 July 1645, SRO GD 34/945. Warwick's letters to the islands are at BL Stowe 184, ff. 122, 124-5.

11 Stock, *Proceedings* I, 153, 155; Craven, *Southern Colonies,* 234. A 1645 report in *Mercurius Civicus* charged that in Virginia Berkeley and his minions had forced a royalist oath on the people and had 'mark't out' those who refused for future punishment. Joseph Frank (ed.), "News from Virginny, 1644," *VMHB* 65 (1957), 84-7.

12 Stock, *Proceedings* I, 146-9. Warwick (BL Stowe 184, 122-5, *passim*) made clear his desire to preserve internal harmony in the colonies, advising one colony government to 'take care of your liberties . . . in such a way as you shall find most prudential, and having pitch't upon it walk with all possible unitedness'.

13 See parliament's act for the 'Safety . . . of his Majesty's person, the Parliament, and the Kingdom'. Firth and Rait, *Acts and Ordinances,* I, 1. See also Warwick to Samuel Mathews, n. d., BL Stowe 184, f. 124. Massachusetts's act of neutrality used the same rationale. *MassachusettsRecords,* II, 69.

14 Christopher Hill, *The World Turned Upside Down* (London, 1975) and David Underdown, *Revel, Riot and Rebellion: Popular Politics and Culture in England, 1603-1660* (Oxford, 1987) testify to the breadth of these attacks and their diversity of origin.

15 Edward Hyde, Earl of Clarendon, T*he History of the Rebellion and Civil Wars in England . . .* (ed. by W. Dunn Macray, 6 vols, Oxford, 1888), I, 1-4.

16 Underdown, *Revel, Riot and Rebellion,* 1-43, reviews an extensive literature and reminds us that instability was not pervasive. See also Robert L. Brenner, 'The Civil War Politics of London's Merchant Community', *P&P* 58 (1973), 53-107; A. L. Beier, *Masterless Men: The Vagrancy Problem in England, 1560-1640* (London, 1985), 1-48, 146-75; and Peter Clark and Paul Slack, (eds.), *Crisis and Order in English Towns, 1500-1700* (London, 1972), especially Clark's 'Introduction', 10-16, and 'The Migrant in Kentish Towns, 1580-1640', 117-54.

17 See Joyce Appleby, *Economic Thought and Ideology in Seventeenth-Century England* (Princeton, 1978), Chapter 2, for an interesting discussion of this process.

18 For Milton, see William Haller, *Tracts on Liberty in the Puritan Revolution* (3 vols, New York, 1965) I, 64-94. On the general point, see Hill, *World Turned Upside Down,* 98-101; G. E. Aylmer, *Rebellion or Revolution: England from Civil War to Restoration* (Oxford, 1987), 66-8.

19 C. B. Macpherson, *The Political Theory of Possessive Individualism: Hobbes to Locke* (Oxford, 1964), especially 1-4, 89-95, 141, 154-6. Macpherson's views on the extent to which Levellers wished to widen the suffrage have aroused controversy; here we need

only accept that the Levellers wished to extend the suffrage radically enough to make it rather inclusive than exclusive.

20 Thomas Hobbes, *Leviathan* (1651); I have used the 'Everyman' edition, London, 1914. See especially Chapter X. Among many Leveller statements on this point, see the Agreement(s) of the People, 1647 and 1649, in S. R. Gardiner (ed.), *Constitutional Documents of the Puritan Revolution, 1625-1660* (3d edn, London, 1912), 333-5, 368-9. Richard Overton put it well in *An Appeal from the Commons to the Free People* (1647), in A. S. P. Woodhouse, *Puritanism and Liberty* (London, 1938), 326.

21 Hobbes, *Leviathan*, Chapter xxii, 122-4; Chapter xxix, 171. In Chapter xxix, Hobbes objected to other forms of government by license, such as farms of the public revenue and parliament's claim to original jurisdiction. In Chapter x, he argued that distinctions given to individuals (e. g. offices and peerages) might, for similar reasons, weaken the strength of the sovereign.

22 Agreement of the People, Gardiner (ed.), *Constitutional Documents*, 359-71. Hobbes wrote that 'the Liberty of the Subject, lyeth therefore only in those things, which in regulating their actions, the Sovereign hath praetermitted: such as the liberty to buy, and sell, and otherwise contract with one another' (*Leviathan*, Chapter xxi, 112). Of course Hobbes said 'only', but as Macpherson points out, acceptance of the market as a fair determinant of men's status, power, and freedom was important to the thought of both Hobbes and the Levellers: *Possessive Individualism*, pp. 53-87, 137-54.

23 Overton, *A Remonstrance of Many Thousand Citizens*, Haller (ed.), *Tracts on Liberty*, III, part 2, 356-63. For Wildman, see Woodhouse, *Puritanism and Liberty*, 66.

24 Winstanley quoted in Hill, *The World Turned Upside Down*, 138-9.

25 Woodhouse, *Puritanism and Liberty*, 7-10, 31. Cromwell's clearest statement came before the suffrage had become the center of attention.

26 Woodhouse, *Puritanism and Liberty*, 26-7, 53-4, 72.

27 Levellers did not concentrate on what, once in power, they might actually do by way of changing England, but we must remember that their situation put them on the defensive. Fearing both king and parliament, they dwelt at length on the limitations which should be put on public power. See the so-called Leveller petitions of January 1648 in Don M. Wolfe (ed.), *Leveller Manifestoes of the Puritan Revolution* (New York, 1944), 263-72.

28 Ireton's warnings were repeated often, or anticipated, in America. See the Reverend Thomas Harrison to John Winthrop, 10 April 1644, *Winthrop Papers* V, 212-13, a letter which Winthrop could have used for his 1645 speech on the Hingham Militia affair, *Journal*, II, 238-9.

29 Woodhouse, *Puritanism and Liberty*, 123-4.

30 For the Diggers, see Hill, *World Turned Upside Down*, Chapter 7, NB 137, 147, 149.

31 The act of 1651 has spawned a contradictory literature. For a selection, see Andrews, *Colonial Period*, III, 1-12, and IV, 14-49; J. E. Farnell, 'The Navigation Act of 1651, the First Dutch War, and the London Merchant Community', *Economic History Review*, 2nd ser., XV (1964), 439-54; Hinton, *Eastland Trade*, ix, 84-94; Charles Wilson, *Profit and Power. A Study of England and the Dutch Wars* (London, 1957), 48-60; L. A. Harper, *The English Navigation Laws* (New York, 1939), 39-49; and Brenner, 'London's Merchant Community'. Of these, Farnell and Brenner give most weight to the contribution of interlopers and a 'free trade' ideology to the Act's passage.

32 Two men who later claimed a role in drafting the Act of 1651 had differing views on regulating trade through chartered companies. See [Benjamin Worsley], *The Advocate* (London, 1652); B[enjamin] W[orsley], *Free Ports, the Nature and Necessity of them stated* (London, 1652); and Henry Robinson, *Briefe Considerations, Concerning the advancement of Trade and Navigation . . .* (London, 1649). The Act remains its own best evidence. It is widely reprinted, but see Gardiner, *Constitutional Documents*, 468-71.

33 For examples of company petitions, see *CSPD, 1649-1650*, 11-12, 64-5; *CSPD 1650*, 21, 72, 460; and Hinton, *Eastland Trade*, 187-94.

34 Stock, *Proceedings*, I, 214, 217-18. Andrews, *British Committees* 24-30 and, for the instructions to the Council of Trade, 115-16. The ninth instruction is directly critical

of the companies, while instructions 2, 4, 5, and 10 note the evils of monopoly and other restrictive regulation.

35 David Underdown (in Pride's Purge: Politics in the Puritan Revolution (Oxford, 1971), 284) notes that the Rump failed to act positively 'in the interests of the small traders, or provincial clothiers, or the outports'. However, it is wrong to conclude from this that there was 'no doctrinaire hostility to chartered companies' (J. P. Cooper, 'Social and Economic Policies under the Commonwealth', in G. E. Aylmer (ed.), The Interregnum: the Quest for a Settlement (London, 1974), 132). The companies did not get what they wanted, the instructions to and activities of the Councils of State and Trade suggest such hostility, as does the radical expansion of economic freedom implied by the Act. Brenner's argument ('London's Merchant Community', 54-5, 68-9, 77-82, 84-101) that corporate interests were weakened politically by their apparent support for the 'presbyterian' or 'peace' parties in 1648 is worth noting here, as is his view that interlopers' radicalism put them in a strong position after 1649. However, it is somewhat difficult to identify interlopers. Maurice Thompson was not the only London merchant who was at once an interloper and a member of a major trading company.

36 Wilson, England's Apprenticeship, 63. Hinton, Eastland Trade, 84-94 and 138-66, offers a sustained argument that the growth of state power was a necessary corollary of the navigation system.

37 See Chapter 2, above.

38 Gardiner, Constitutional Documents, 388.

39 See, for instance Nicholas Foster's A breife Relation of the late Horrid Rebellion Acted in the Island of Barbados . . . (London, 1650), 4-7.

40 Firth and Rait, Acts and Ordinances, II, 425-9; Stock, Proceedings, I, 208, 211-12, 214-15, 218-19.

41 Stock, Proceedings, I, 218-23. Brigham, British Royal Proclamations, 52. VMHB, I, 79.

42 The statute is at Massachusetts Records III, 224. The petitions to Laud and to the Rump Parliament can be directly compared in Hutchinson, History, I, 421-2 and 428-30.

43 The Virginia and Barbados resolves are in VMHB, I, 78-81, and R. Schomburgk, History of Barbados (London, 1848), Appendix X. See also William Arnold to Governor of Massachusetts, 1651, Hutchinson Papers, I, 238.

44 These points are discussed in Chapter 4, but note that as late as 1659 a Barbadian petition asked for the repeal of the Act of 1650 but made no mention of the Act of 1651. BL Egerton 2395, f. 182.

45 The articles of surrender and other relevant documents may be found in Hening, Statutes, I, 363-8; N. Darnell Davis, The Cavaliers and Roundheads of Barbados (Georgetown, British Guiana, 1887). 250-55; Stock, Proceedings, I, 228-32; and Hall, Narratives of Early Maryland, 167-71, 206-17.

46 Maurice Ashley, Financial and Commercial Policy under the Cromwellian Protectorate (London, 1934); G. E. Aylmer, The State's Servants: the Civil Service of the English Republic, 1648-1660 (London, 1973); Max Savelle, The European Origins of American Diplomacy (London, 1967), 51-5, 62-3, 69-70, 74-6, 89-91; Charles P. Korr, Cromwell and the New Model Foreign Policy: England's Policy towards France, 1649-1658 (London, 1975), 114-16, 138-47; Karen Ordahl Kupperman, 'Errand to the Indies: Puritan Colonization from Providence Island through the Western Design', WMQ 3rd ser., 45 (1988), 70-99; and Beer, Origins, 360-424. The troubled sojourn of the Jamaica fleet at Barbados is nicely summarized by Harlow, A History of Barbados 106-16.

47 Davis, Cavaliers and Roundheads, 217-19. For social conditions in the island at mid-century, see Dunn, Sugar and Slaves, esp. Chapter 1.

48 Edward Winslow to Secretary Thurloe, 16 March 1655, and Governor Daniel Searle to Cromwell, 1 June 1655, Thurloe State Papers, III, 249-52, 499-500. Harlow, Barbados, 105-17. And see Thomas Modyford's 'protestation', BL Add. Mss. 35251, f. 39.

49 Worsley to [Lady Clarendon?], 8 November 1661, F. J. Routledge, (ed.), Calendar of the Clarendon State Papers Preserved in the Bodleian Library, vol.V, 1660–1726 (Oxford, 1970), 154. Chapters 7 and 8, below, further discuss Worsley and Cooper (later Baron

Ashley and then then Earl of Shaftesbury).

50 Povey to Daniel Searle and Noell to Governor and Council of Virginia, BL Add Mss 11411, ff. 19-20, 41-3. In 1642, Povey advanced the view that by truly considering their private interests men would add to the public good, (J. A. W. Gunn, *Politics and Public Interest in the Seventeenth Century* (London and Toronto, 1969), 46-7)). For Justinian Povey, see G. E. Aylmer, *The King's Servants* (London, 1961), 390, and *CSPC 1574-1660*, 254.

51 'An Essaie or overture for regulating the Affaires of his Highness in the West Indies', BL Add. Mss. 11411, ff. 11-12. Povey struck a similar pose in his 'The State of the Difference as it is pressed between the Merchants and the Planters in relation to free Trade and the Charibee Islands . . . ', *Ibid.*, ff. 4-6.

52 Such frustrations surface frequently in Povey's papers for the later 1650s, but see his letters to Jamaica's Governor Edward D'Oyley, Searle, Mathews, and his brother Richard in early 1658 for the matters mentioned here. BL Add. Mss. 11411, ff. 53-5, 58-62, 67-72.

53 BL Egerton 2395, ff. 89-90, 99, 100. Many of Povey's papers from this critical period are undated drafts, but important variations between proposals suggest a definite sequence, and Povey's use of tell-tale words or phrases like 'His Highness', 'His Majesty', 'the state', 'commonwealth', and 'kingdom' suggests a chronological order. Povey's dated correspondence from *c.* 1658-61 offers some clues, too. For the various company and council proposals, see BL Egerton 2395, ff. 87-111, 202-37, and 270-75.

54 BL Egerton 2395, ff. 87-8, 90-92, 103-4, and the more elaborate 'Act for incorporating a Company for the Trade of America', ff. 202-37, all date from this period. There are minor variations from one to the other. The proposal at ff. 87-8 is probably the first and would seem to date from September 1659: see a letter from Povey at BL Add. Mss. 11411, ff. 90-94.

55 BL Egerton 2395, ff. 103-4.

56 Povey to Richard Povey, n. d. but probably late 1659, and to Thomas Temple, 3 April 1660, BL Add. Mss. 11411, ff. 17-18, 27-28.

57 Povey's papers are to be found principally in BL Add. Mss. 11410 and 11411 and BL Egerton 2395. Andrews's initial enthusiasm about Povey is illustrated well in *British Committees*, 38-60; the later and more balanced judgment is in *Colonial Period*, III, 37-40.

58 BL Add. Mss. 11411, ff. 7-8, 60.

59 I accept Povey's self-assessment that he was a 'Journey Man' in the patronage market, with 'little power' but (undeniably) 'greater industrie'. (The quotes are from Povey's letters to General William Brayne, 7 April 1657, and Governor William D'Oyley, 28 March 1658, BL Add. Mss. 11411, ff. 15-16, 61.) These skills made his insights more important than his influence.

Chapter 4

1 For the view from the Chesapeake, see *Maryland Archives* III, 144; Hening, *Statutes* I, 296, 519; and McIlwaine (ed.), *Minutes of the Council . . . 494.* In 1657, Boston's John Hull noted that "as yet, our chief supply, in respect of clothes, is from England. ""The Diaries of John Hull," *Transactions and Collections of the American Antiquarian Society*, III (1857), 180. On the importance of regular credit and supply, see Bailyn, *The New England Merchants*, 32-9.

2 Hening, *Statutes* I, 240-82; Billings, 'Growth of Political Institutions in Virginia', 229; Kukla, 'Order and Chaos in Early America', 287-89; 'The Massachusetts Body of Liberties' (1641), in Morgan (ed.), *Puritan Political Ideas*, 177-203; Max Farrand (ed.), *The Laws and Liberties of Massachusetts . . . 1648 . . .* (Cambridge, 1929); Konig, *Law and Society*, 21-6, 35-7.

3 Benjamin Gostlin to John Winthrop, 8 May 1640, and Winslow to same, 7 July 1640, *Winthrop Papers*, IV, 237-8, 262. 'A Remonstrance of the Grand Assembly [of Virginia]', July 1642, McIlwaine (ed.), *Journals . . . 1619-1659/60*, 69-70.

4 Johnson to Sir James and Archibald Hay, 24 December 1642, Hay Mss., SRO GD 34/26/923; Warner to same and to Carlisle (copies), 1 April 1642, SRO GD 34/26/939B & C; Ashton to Carlisle, 8 February 1642, Hay Mss., SRO GD 34/26/933.

5 John Haynes to John Winthrop, 1 December 1643, *Winthrop Papers* IV, 418-19; Winthrop, *Journal*, II, 72. Richard S. Dunn, *Puritans and Yankees: the Winthrop Dynasty in New England, 1630-1717* (Princeton, 1962), 40-43. For a later 'neutrality' proclamation, see Massachusetts Archives CVI, f. 26.

6 Steven D. Crow, '"Your Majesty's Good Subjects": A Reconsideration of Royalism in Virginia, 1642-1652', *VMHB* 87 (1979), 158-69. Susie M. Ames (ed.), *County Court Records of Accomack-Northampton, Virginia, 1640-1645* (Charlottesville, 1973), 297, 301. See also Hening, *Statutes* I, 240-82, statutes I, III, XIV, XVII, LI, LXIV, LXV-LXIX, LXIII, but note that Kukla, 'Order and Chaos in Early America', 288-9, identifies some of these as revisions from earlier sessions. For Harrison, see *Winthrop Papers* V, 197-9, 212-13, 273-4 and Edward D. Neill, *Virginia Carolorum: The Colony under the Rule of Charles the First and Second, AD 1625-AD 1685* (Albany, 1886), 195-203.

7 Russell R. Menard, 'Maryland's "Time of Troubles": Sources of Political Disorder in Early St. Mary's', *Maryland Historical Magazine* 76 (1981), 124-8, 135-8; Craven, *Southern Colonies* 233-4; John Hammond, *Leah and Rachel, Or, the Two Fruitful Sisters Virginia, and Mary-land . . .* (London, 1656) in Force (ed.), *Tracts*, III, no. 14, 21-4.

8 Bennett, 'English Caribbees', 364-7; 'The agreivances of the Inhabitants [of St. Christopher]', 8 February 1642, and William Johnson to Sir James and Archibald Hay, 24 December 1642, SRO GD 34/26/939 B and 923.

9 See Chapter 3, above.

10 The Hays' loyalty may be inferred from their offices and because they were present at court through most of the civil war period. Hay Mss., SRO GD 34/26, *passim*. For Carlisle and Warwick, see Williamson, *The Caribbees under the Proprietary Patents*, 109-10, 113-22.

11 Philip Bell to Archibald Hay, 21 July 1645, SRO GD 34/26/945; William Hay to Archibald Hay, 5 July 1645, SRO GD 34/26/924; Bennett, 'The English Caribbees', 371.

12 Carlisle to Bell, 5 January 1644, SRO GD 34/26/941; Bell to Archibald Hay, 21 July 1645, SRO GD 34/26/945; Bell et al. to Warwick, c. 1646, SRO GD 34/26/924; A. B., *A breife Relation . . .* (London, 1651), in BL Egerton 2395, ff. 48-53.

13 Bennett, 'English Caribbees', 373, states that Barbados had thus achieved 'virtual independence of King, Parliament, and proprietor'. Gary Puckrein entitles Chapter 6 of his *Little England* 'A precarious independence'.

14 Bell to Warwick, 1646, SRO GD 34/924; Bell to John Winthrop, 18 September 1643, Felt, *Ecclesiastical History*, I, 491; Richard Ligon, *A True & Exact History Of the Iland of Barbados . . .* (London, 1657), 22, 34, 38-40, 44-6, 57-8, 94-6; James Parker to John Winthrop, 24 June 1646, *Hutchinson Papers*, I, 175-8.

15 Francis Jennings, *The Invasion of America: Indians, Colonialism, and the Cant of Conquest*(Chapel Hill, 1975), 233-8, 244-9.

16 Norton, *The Answer to the Whole Set of Questions of the Celebrated Mr. William Appolonius. . .* (London, 1648), composed in or before 1645. See 27-43, 88, 115-16. Cotton's *Keyes* is reprinted in Larzer Ziff (ed.), *John Cotton on the Churches of New England* (Cambridge, Mass., 1968), 70-164. Bulkeley's *Gospel Covenant* was published in London in 1646.

17 Cotton, *Keyes*, 101-12.

18 Norton, *Answer*, 86-7; Cotton, *Keyes*, 130-35.

19 See letters of 1645 from Stephen Winthrop, Thomas Goodwin, Hugh Peter, and George Downing to both the elder and younger John Winthrop, *Winthrop Papers* V, 13, 23-5, 30-31, 42-5. See also Foster, 'The Challenge of Heresy'; Gura, *A Glimpse of Sion's Glory*, esp. chapters 6-8; Hall, *The Faithful Shepherd*, esp. Chapters 5 and 7.

20 Perry Miller, *Errand into the Wilderness* (New York, 1964), title essay; Theodore Dwight Bozeman, 'The Puritan "Errand into the Wilderness" Reconsidered', *NEQ* 59 (1986), 246-51; David Cressy, *Coming Over: Migration and Communication between England and New England in the Seventeenth Century* (Cambridge, 1987), 191-212;

and Andrew Delbanco, 'Looking Homeward, Going Home: The Lure of England for the Founders of New England', *NEQ* 59 (1986), 358-86. For Sewall, see the extract from his *Phaenomenon Quaedam Apocalyptica*... (Boston, 1697) in Perry Miller and Thomas Johnson (eds.), *The Puritans* (2 vols, New York, 1963), I, 376-7.

21 Ward, *The Simple Cobler of Aggawam, in America*... (London, 1647, ed. P. M. Zail, Lincoln, 1969), 7-25; Gura, *Glimpse of Sion's Glory*, 24; Thomas Shepard, *New Englands Lamentations for Old Englands Present Errours*... (London, 1645), quoted in Gura, '"The Contagion of Corrupt Opinions" in Puritan Massachusetts...', *WMQ* 3rd ser., 39 (1982), 469.

22 For Ward, Morison, *Builders of the Bay Colony*, 241-3, and Stephen Winthrop to John Winthrop, 29 July 1647, *Winthrop Papers* V, 174-5. For Plymouth, Edward Winslow to John Winthrop, 23 November 1645, *Hutchinson Papers* II, 172-5. For Parker and Noyes, James Noyes, *The Temple Measured*... (London, 1647), and its prefatory letter. Bulkeley to Cotton, 4 April 1650, is reprinted in Lemuel Shattuck, *A History of the Town of Concord... to 1832*... (Boston, 1835), 155-6, but should be amended as suggested by Charles Walcott, *Concord in the Colonial Period... 1635-1689* (Boston, 1884), 43n.

23 Norton, *Abel being Dead yet Speaketh* (London, 1658), 7-8, 31, 34-7; John Cotton to John Winthrop [1648], *Winthrop Papers* IV, 192-4; a letter from Cotton, dated 20 September 1652, used as preface in Norton's *The Orthodox Evangelist* (London, 1657). See also Increase Mather, *First Principles of New England* (Cambridge, 1675), 5-8, 28, and Larzer Ziff, *The Career of John Cotton: Puritanism and the American Experience* (Princeton, 1962), 208-9, 227-9, 244-5.

24 'Papers Relating to the Controversy in the Church at Hartford, 1656-1659', Connecticut Historical Society *Collections* II, 51-126. The letter, dated 4 August 1656, is at 59-63.

25 *MassachusettsRecords*, IV, part 1, 277-9, 308-9, 321, 345-7; Felt, *Ecclesiastical History*, II, 203-5; George Bishop, *New-England Judged by the Spirit of the Lord* (London, 1703 edn), 100-03. Even John Davenport regretted that Massachusetts had not taken a more merciful and less troublesome course: Davenport to John Winthrop, Jr., 6 December 1659, I. M. Calder (ed.), *Letters of John Davenport, Puritan Divine* (New Haven, 1937), 146-50.

26 The General Court's apologia for the death sentences passed in 1659 on the Quakers Marmaduke Stephenson, William Robinson, and Mary Dyer appears in *Massachusetts Records* IV, part 1, 385-90, and was substantially repeated in broadsides published in Boston and London. I have used the London (1660) edition of Norton, *The Heart of New-England Rent at the Blasphemies of the Present Generation*.

27 *Heart of New-England Rent*, 24, 41-8, 53-4, 65, 78-80.

28 *Heart of New-England Rent*, 65, 81-5.

29 The 'Remonstrance', signed by Child, Samuel Maverick and five others and probably the work of William Vassall, is at *Hutchinson Papers* I, 214-23. See also Wall, *Massachusetts Bay... 1640-1650*, 140-48, 159-64; W. G. McLoughlin, *New England Dissent, 1630-1833: The Baptists and the Separation of Church and State* (2 vols, Cambridge, Mass., 1971), I, 6-48; Hall, *The Faithful Shepherd*, 98-9; John Clarke, *Ill Newes from New England* (London 1651); and Robert F. Scholz, "Clerical Consociation in Massachusetts Bay: Reassessing the New England Way and its Origins," *WMQ* 3rd ser., 29 (1972), 409-14.

30 *Hutchinson Papers* I, 226-7, 237. See *Winthrop Papers* IV, 467-82; Winthrop, *Journal* II, 296-305; John Childe, *New Englands Jonas Cast up at London*... (London, 1647), in Force, *Tracts* IV, no. 4, 8-16; and Wall, *Massachusetts Bay... 1640-1650*, 93-233.

31 Nathaniel Bourton, et al. (eds.), *Documents and Records Relating to the Province of New Hampshire* (40 vols., Concord, 1867-1943), I, 126-34, 168, 170-71; XVII, 501; Winthrop, *Journal*, II, 38-9, 165-7; *Winthrop Papers* IV, 143-4, 176-9. 285-8, 316-17; *Massachusetts Records* I, 326, 332, 342-3; II, 37, 43-5, 71-2. C. H. Bell (ed.), *John Wheelwright: His Writings*... (Prince Society *Publications*, IX, Albany, 1876), 37-56; D. E. Van Deventer, *The Emergence of Provincial New Hampshire, 1623-1641* (Baltimore and London, 1976), 1-15.

32 See Winthrop, *Journal*, II, 266-7 and *Winthrop Papers* vols. IV and V, for instance IV, 420-21, 429-31, 433-4, 436-8, 440-41; V, 14-16, 33, 37-8, 39-41, 57, 62, 66-7, 75-7.

33 *Winthrop Papers* V, 173-4, 259-60; Winthrop, *Journal*, II, 266-7; Libby, (ed.), *Province and Court Records of Maine* I, 133; Maine Historical Society *Collections* I, 385-9, and 2nd ser., IV (1889), 28-31, 35-7, and 156-9.

34 *Early Records of the Town of Portsmouth, 1639-1697*, (Providence, 1901), 1.

35 Roger Williams to John Winthrop, 27 May 1638 and September 1638, The *Complete Writings of Roger Williams* (7 vols, New York, 1963), VI, 95-6, 120-25. William Coddington to John Winthrop, 22 May 1640, *Winthrop Papers*, IV, 245-8.

36 *Massachusetts Records* II, 26-7. Samuel Gorton, *Simplicities Defense against Seven-headed policy . . .*, (London, 1646), in Force, *Tracts*, IV, no. 6, For Arnold, see *Winthrop Papers* V, 246-8, and *Hutchinson Papers* I, 267-9.

37 Williams's struggles to give government to Rhode Island were only beginning, and can be followed through J. R. Bartlett (ed.), *Records of the Colony of Rhode Island and Providence Plantations in New England* (10 vols, Providence, 1856-65), I, 27-31, 143-50, 233-5, 248-9, 259-62; Williams, *Complete Writings*, VI, 149-51, 166, 170, 206-9, 231-3, 253-9, 262-76; and Winthrop, *Journal*, II, 198.

38 For the Fundamental Orders, see J. H. Trumbull and C. J. Hoadly (eds.), *Public Records of the Colony of Connecticut* (17 vols, Hartford, 1850-1890), I, 20-22. Winthrop's comments are in his *Journal*, I, 287-91, and see also his correspondence in *Winthrop Papers* III, 274; IV, 18-20, 23-4, 36-7, 53-4, 74-84, 98-100, 254.

39 The text of the United Colonies' agreement is in Winthrop's *Journal*, II, 100-105: note the preamble and articles 3, 6, and 9. See also Andrews, *Colonial Period*, II, 128n, 164-5; Isabel M. Calder, *The New Haven Colony* (New Haven, 1934), 116-24, 210-11; Benjamin Thompson, *A History of Long Island* (3 vols, New York, 1918) I, 225-34, 467-72, 476-7; James T. Adams, *History of the Town of Southampton* (New York, 1918), 55; *Records of the Town of East-Hampton, Long Island* (5 vols, Sag Harbor, 1887-1895), I, 53, 59, 78, 140; John L. Gardiner, 'Notes and Observations on the Town of East Hampton . . . 1798', New York Historical Society *Collections*, vol. II (1869), 237-8; and Felt, *Ecclesiastical History* I, 563.

40 *Massachusetts Records*, IV, part 2, 238-9, 265-70; Maine Historical Society *Collections*, I, 385-9. See also Chapter 6, below.

41 J. Baxter (ed.), *Documentary History of the State of Maine*, vol. II (Portland, 1889), 137-41.

42 The quote is from a 1647 declaration by the Governor, Council, and Burgesses of Virginia, McIlwaine, *Journals. . . 1619-1658/59*, 74. For Bermuda, see Lefroy, *Memorials* I, 576-651, *passim*, esp. 622-4, 630-1, 641, 647-51; and for Barbados, see *A Declaration Set Forth by the Lord Lieutenant Generall the Gentlemen of the Counsell & assembly [of Barbados]* (The Hague, 1651), 3.

43 *Archives of Maryland*, I, 238-43, 259, 262-72, 312-20; II, 243-4. See also Andrews, *Colonial Period*, II, 310-15, and Craven, *Southern Colonies*, 233-6.

44 *Archives of Maryland*, I, 320, 327-9, 331.

45 William Reyner and Rev. Peter Copeland to John Winthrop, 31 March and 21 August 1646, *Winthrop Papers* V, 71-3, 96-7; Lefroy. *Memorials*, I, 593-9, 626-7, 642-54, 700-702, 712-3.

46 Hening, *Statutes* I, 359-61; Craven, *Southern Colonies*, 227; *VMHB* V, 134-41. The agency legend has been variously attributed to Lee and Colonel Henry Norwood. See R. L. Morton (*Colonial Virginia* (2 vols., Chapel Hill, 1960), I, 167); Andrews, *Colonial Period* II, 255; and Henry Norwood, *Voyage to Virginia* (c. 1650), Force (ed.), *Tracts* III, no. 10, 50. Lee did travel to Europe in 1650 or 1651: see Francis Lord Willoughby to Lady Willoughby, 9 August 1651, Bodl. Tanner 54, ff. 147-9.

47 Harlow, *Barbados*, 46-55. Puckrein, *Little England*, 105-11, sees the matter differently.

48 Willoughby arrived in Carlisle Bay before 3 May 1650, but kept his presence a secret until 5 May. Harlow, *Barbados*, 57-61; Puckrein, *Little England*, 111-13. See also BL Egerton 2395, ff. 48-53, and Foster, *A breife Relation . . . 23-37, 51-6, 59-62, 82-3, 109-10.

49 The correspondence between Willoughby and St. Christophers, June 1650-January 1651, is in Bodl. Tanner 56, ff. 209a, 209b, 211, 240b. 'An Essay Evenly Discussing the Present Condition & Interest of Barbados. . . ', n. d., Newberry Library, Ayer Mss., gives news of Willoughby's 'moderate' stance and could have been written by the agent he sent to London. Even Nicholas Foster's *A breife Relation* . . . (esp. 82-83) accepts that there was a 'moderate' constituency. See also Davis, *Cavaliers and Roundheads* 17-75, and Harlow, *Barbados*, 59-61.

50 A. B. [probably Thomas Modyford], *A Breif Relation*, BL Egerton 2395, ff. 48-54 and 'A letter from Barbados. . . ',9 August 1651, Bodl. Tanner 54, ff. 153-4. See also Philip Bell to Martin Noell, 15 February 1651, SRO GD 34/952.

51. Lord Willoughby wrote to 'his lady' that England 'wilbee a friend, or that wee make them so by tyring them out, either their sea men by the teadious Voyages, or the State by the great expenses they must bee at'. Bodl. Tanner 54, ff. 247-9. See also BL Egerton 2395, ff. 48-54 and, for Virginia, Craven's judgment in *Southern Colonies*, 254-5.

52 See the 'Declaration . . . of . . . Barbados' in Schomburgk, *Barbados*, 706-8; McIlwaine (ed.), *Journals . . . 1619-1658/9*, 75-8.

53 Something of Ayscue's qualities can be gleaned from Ayscue to Lord President, 26 February 1652, Bodl. Tanner Mss. 55, ff. 141-2.

54 The articles are in Hening, *Statutes* I, 363-8, and Davis, *Cavaliers and Roundheads*, 250-55. The Barbadian articles effectively confirmed the old 'treaty' between royalist and parliamentarian planters. 'The main and chief cause of our late troubles . . . has grown by loose, base, and uncivil language', and the island's assembly was to pass strict laws against 'reviling speeches of what nature soever'.

55 Puckrein, *Little England*, 91-8, and Chapter 6, below.

56. Davis, *Cavaliers and Roundheads*, 199; *VMHB* I, 76. Consider also the terminology used earlier by a royalist to discredit the Barbadian planter - merchant James Drax: 'a factor for the Rebells in England, and here . . . to vent his trade of disloyalty, Rebellion, and Ruine'. Foster, *A breife Relation* . . ., 27.

57 The seventh article of the Virginia treaty stated 'that the people of Virginia have free trade as the people of England doe enjoy to all places and with all nations according to the laws of [that Commonwealth] *and that Virginia shall enjoy all privileges equal with any English plantations in America*'. Parliament modified the words in brackets to 'the Commonwealth of England' and disallowed the italicized phrase, possibly because under it Virginia tobacco might have claimed duty-free status on the New England precedent. The ninth Barbadian article stated 'that all port-towns and cities under the Parliament's power shall be open to the inhabitants of this island in as great a freedom as ever, and that no companies be placed over them, nor the commodities of the island be ingrossed in private men's hands; and that all trade be free with all nations that do trade and are in amity with England'. The Navigation Act, only passed in October 1651, was not significant in these negotiations nor was it the object of these articles, as their language makes perfectly plain.

58 Harlow, *Barbados*, 86-7; Searle to Council of State, 8 October 1652, *CSPC 1574-1660*, 390-91; Edward Winslow to Secretary of State John Thurloe, 15 March 1655, *Thurloe State Papers* III, 249-52; Hening, *Statutes* I, 469, 535-7.

59 BL Egerton 2395, f. 182.

60 Warren M. Billings, 'Some Acts Not in Hening's *Statutes*: The Acts of Assembly, April 1652, November 1652, and July 1653', *VMHB* 83 (1975), 22-76; Hening, *Statutes* I, 371-3.

61 For relevant lists of councillors and burgesses, see Hening, *Statutes* I, 235-6, 238-9, 282-3, 358-9, 369-71, 373-4, 379, 386-7, 506-7. See also Billings, 'Some Acts not in Hening's S*tatutes*', 27-8, and Kukla, 'Order and Chaos in Early America', 286-90, 292, 296-7.

62 Hening, *Statutes* I, 371-2.

63 Stock, *Proceedings* I, 230-32 and notes. Hening, *Statutes* I, 365; *Thurloe State Papers* I, 197-8.

64 As an instance of the assembly's caution, see Hening, *Statutes* I, 431. In early 1654, Virginia did receive from the Lord President advice to carry on under the articles of

1652 until the Protector's pleasure should be known (*CSPC 1574-1660*, 412-3), and Cromwell did warn Virginia to let Maryland alone. See Wilbur C. Abbott (ed.), *The Writings and Speeches of Oliver Cromwell* (4 vols, New York, 1970 reprint), III, 833, 842-3, and *Thurloe State Papers* III, 590-91, 596.

65 For documents relating to the dispatch of the agency, see Hening, *Statutes* I, 426; McIlwaine, *Journals . . . 1619-1658/59*, 105; Virginia Assembly to Thurloe, 15 October 1656, *Thurloe State Papers* V, 497-8; and see *ibid.*, V, 80-81 for an undated but relevant petition concerning Virginia.

66 BL Add. Mss. 11411, ff. 19-20; BL Egerton 2395, f. 147.

67 Hening, *Statutes* I, 496-505. There were other problems; in May, the Council wondered whether, 'New Commission not having come', the governor could grant a warrant for an execution. McIlwaine (ed.), *Minutes of the Council . . .*, 506.

68 Hening, *Statutes* I, 500-5.

69 Hening, *Statutes* I, 505-11.

70 Hening, *Statutes*, I, 511-2.

71 What Virginians might have known in March is suggested by an April letter from John Davenport in New Haven colony: Calder (ed.), *Letters of John Davenport* 159-61. See also Morton, *Colonial Virginia* I, 184-5. Berkeley's speech is extensively quoted in Thomas J. Wertenbaker, *Virginia under the Stuarts* (reprint, New York, 1959), 111-13.

72 For the most important legislation of March 1660, see Hening, *Statutes* I, 530-41. The act 'for the Peace of this Collony' is at 531-2.

73 Edward D. Neill, *Virginia Carolorum*, 352-3, notes. See also the October 1660 'Act for makinge and Addresse to Sir William Berkeley to intercede for a gennerall pardon' in Kukla (ed.), 'Some Acts not in Hening's *Statutes*', 87-8.

74 *CSPC 1574-1660*, 481, 486.

75 Two of the commissioners, Bennett and Claiborne, had personal and historic reasons to wish to subvert Baltimore's rule. Hall (ed.), *Narratives of Early Maryland*, 50, 164, 167-77.

76 Cromwell first confirmed Baltimore's rights in 1655, but a settlement in Maryland was delayed two years. See Bodl. Rawlinson A43, ff. 101, 103; *Archives of Maryland* II, 311-13, 324-7, 332-4; Olson, *Anglo-American Politics*, x, 34-6; Craven, *Southern Colonies*, 296-9.

77 *Archives of Maryland* I, 388-91; II, 387, 391-3; III, 387-8.

78 George Alsop to T. B., 20 February 1661, in Hall (ed.), *Narratives of Early Maryland*, 380. See also Andrews, *Colonial Period* II, 317-24; Craven, *Southern Colonies*, 197-8; *Archives of Maryland*, II, 387, 391-3; and below, Chapter 6.

79 For interesting documents on these events, see Bodl. Rawlinson A29, ff. 376-409. The quotations in this and preceding paragraphs are from ff. 378, 380, 407. Kaynell's commission is at ff. 394-5. It seems that Kaynell had abandoned his post once before the 'uprising' in August; in June, he was warned by the commissioners with the Western Design fleet to return to his post. Bodl. Rawlinson A29, f. 385.

80 Communications of any sort were important; see the use made of the proclamation of the Protectorate by the Barbados council, 14 March 1654, Bodl. Rawlinson A40, 362. See also *CSPC 1574-1660*, 404.

81 For example, Prize Commissioners to Admiralty Commissioners, 5 June 1655, *CSPC 1675-1676, Addenda*, no. 216; Edward Winslow to Thurloe, 16 March 1655, and Searle to Cromwell, 1 June 1655, *Thurloe State Papers* III, 249-52, 499-500. Harlow, *Barbados*, 105-15.

82 BL Egerton 2395, f. 182.

83 See for instance David Underdown, *Somerset in the Civil War and Interregnum* (Newton Abbot, 1973) Chapters 9 and 10, and 'Settlement in the Counties, 1653-1658' in G. E. Aylmer (ed.), *The Interregnum*, 165-82; Peter Clark, *English Provincial Society from the Reformation to the Revolution: Religion, Politics, and Society in Kent, 1500-1640* (Hassocks, 1977), 394-7; and Anthony Fletcher, *A County Community in Peace and War: Sussex, 1600-1660* (London, 1975), 294-311.

84 Harlow, *Barbados*, 115-16.

85 Much of the relevant correspondence is in Povey's papers, BL Add. Mss. 11411, ff. 51-

60. See also *CSPC 1574-1660*, 456.

86 Thomas Povey to William Povey, 25 April 1659; Povey and Noell to Searle, 30 April 1659; and Povey to Searle, 8 June 1659; BL Add. Mss. 11411, ff. 78. 83-6, 89.

87 *CSPC 1675-1676, Addenda*, no. 322; BL Egerton 2395, f. 182.

88 BL Egerton 2395, ff. 184, 238, 245. See also Povey to Searle, 20 September 1659 [with an October postscript], BL Add. Mss. 11411, ff. 90-94.

89 BL Egerton 2395, f. 245.

90. See above, this chapter; Bodl. Rawlinson A29, ff. 378-80, 402-09; and Wertenbaker, *Virginia Under the Stuarts*, 113.

91 Povey to Sir Thomas Temple, 3 April 1660, BL Add. Mss. 11411, ff. 27-8; and see below, Chapter 6.

92 Nathaniel Ward, *The Simple Cobler of Aggawam*, especially 45-63.

Chapter 5

1 See Sosin, *English America and the Restoration Monarchy*, esp. 2-4, 31-2, 39-45, 125.

2 Hening, *Statutes* I, 526-9.

3 David Ogg's fine phrase, in *England in the Reign of Charles II* (2 vols, Oxford, 1956), I, 17. The following depends also on Godfrey Davies, *The Restoration of Charles II, 1658-1660* (London, 1955); A. H. Woolrych, 'Last Quests for a Settlement, 1657-1660' in Aylmer (ed.), *The Interregnum*, pp. 183-204; and Ronald Hutton, *The Restoration: A Political and Religious History of England and Wales, 1658-1667* (Oxford, 1985), pp. 3-154. Recent work is summarized in Robert M. Bliss, *Restoration England, 1660-1688: Politics and Government* (London, 1985), 4-13.

4 Cobbett's *Parliamentary History of England . . . to the year 1803* (London, 1808) IV, 34.

5 Clarendon, *History*, VI, 197.

6 For the Declaration and the letters, see Clarendon, *History*, VI, 202-10.

7 Charles to the House of Commons, 4 April 1660. So attractive was the letter that the House quoted it in its reply. Clarendon, *History*, VI, 204, 218.

8 BL Egerton 2543, ff. 105-12.

9 C. D. Chandaman, *The English Public Revenue, 1660-1688* (Oxford, 1975), 202-9, offers an excellent summary. For early evidence of dissatisfaction amongst the king's advisers, see Shaftesbury Papers (PRO 30/24): PRO 30/24/3, f. 90, and PRO 30/24/7, ff. 479-81, and BL Add. Mss. 10119, ff. 15-18.

10 The estimate was based on Charles I's last peacetime revenue, but also enjoyed close precedents in the amounts offered to Cromwell by Barebone's Parliament in 1654 and by the Humble Petition and Advice in 1657. See Gardiner, (ed.), *Documents of the Puritan Revolution*, 414, 431, 444-45, 452-53.

11 Chandaman, *Public Revenue*, 348-63.

12 Chandaman, *Public Revenue*, 138, 140-45.

13 Chandaman, *Public Revenue*, 37-43.

14 Cobbett, *Parl. Hist.* IV, 146-8. That a hereditary revenue could be regulated remained a dubious proposition, as Barbadians were to find in the case of the 4 1/2 per cent revenue they voted Charles II in 1663. See below, Chapter 6.

15 Arthur Annesley spoke against the compensatory excise but only a week later, on 27 November, moved that the House should consider itself obliged to make up the excise to whatever was needed. Cobbett, *Parl. Hist.* IV, 147, 151-2. Mercantile interests in the Convention opposed the excise precisely because it shifted a tax burden from land to trade. See J. H. Sacret, 'Restoration Government and Municipal Corporations', *EHR* 45 (1930), 246.

16 For these points, see the Humble Petition and Advice (1657) in Gardiner (ed.), *Constitutional Documents*, 453; Ashley, *Financial and Commercial Policy under the Cromwellian Protectorate*, 44-5, 107-8; Wilson, *Profit and Power*, 9-10, 22-4, 43-60; Korr, *Cromwell and the New Model Foreign Policy*, 138-45.

17 Stock, *Proceedings* I, 277-9; PRO 30/24/3, part 1, f. 90; T. H. Lister, *Life and*

Administration of . . . Clarendon (3 vols, Oxford, 1838), III, 504-8; and Wilson, *England's Apprenticeship*, 167-9. In November, Shaw became officer in charge of enforcing the Navigation Act at £600 p. a. : *CTB* I, 87.

18 Ashley estimated the marginal value of the Convention's non-fiscal legislation at £125,000, of which about £100,000 can be attributed to the Navigation Act. PRO 30/24/36, no. 25, f. 84. See also *CTB* I, 117, 250, and K. H. D. Haley, *The First Earl of Shaftesbury* (Oxford, 1968), 236.

19 PRO 30/24/36, part 25, f. 84; Stock, *Proceedings*, I, 283, 283n.

20 Stock, *Proceedings*, I, 277-8, 295-6, 301-2, 304-7. BL Stowe 326, ff. 110-12. PRO 30/24/30, f. 20. Sir Edward Turner to Lord Treasurer Southampton, 20 July 1661, *CTB* I, 266.

21 See for instance Charles's addresses to parliament of 1663 in Cobbett, *Parl. Hist.* IV, 264-9.

22 Chandaman, *Public Revenue*, 13-14.

23 Stock, *Proceedings*, I, 281-2.

24 The Book of Rates is 12 Car. II c. 4. See also Chandaman, *Public Revenue*, 10-14, and Stock, *Proceedings* I, 272-7.

25 The long range importance of these matters is discussed by Harold Perkin, 'The Social Causes of the Industrial Revolution', *Transactions of the Royal Historical Society*, 18 (1968), 123-43. See also Christopher Hill, *Reformation to Industrial Revolution* (London, 1967), 146-7, 149-50. Chandaman, *Public Revenue*, 43-4, 55, 83-5, 171-4. Seymour quoted by Feiling, *Tory Party*, 142-3.

26 Grimston's speech (Cobbett, *Parl. Hist.* IV, 111-12) bears marked similarity to the advice given the king in 1660 by the old royalist Duke of Newcastle: Thomas P. Slaughter (ed.), *Ideology and Politics on the Eve of Restoration: Newcastle's Advice to Charles II* (Philadelphia, 1984), 35-8. See Cobbett, *op. cit.*, IV, 289-91 for similar views in a 1664 speech by the king. The Customs Farmers chimed in on the same note (BL Stowe 326, ff. 110-12), and parliament's attitudes may be distilled from Stock, *Proceedings* I, 277, 294-308.

27 Clarendon, *The History of the Rebellion . . . also his Life Written by Himself* [hereafter *Life and Continuation*] (Oxford, 1843 edn), 1084; Cobbett, *Parl. Hist.* IV, 123-30, 247-53, 266-9; Somers *Tracts* VII, 549, 552-4; Stock, *Proceedings* I, 282.

28 The text of the 1660 Act is in *Statutes of the Realm* V, 246-60. For Downing, see his letter to Clarendon from The Hague, c. 1664, Bodl. Clarendon 108, ff. 132-3. For the companies' approaches to king and parliament, see for instance *CTB* I, 140-41, 247; *CSPD 1660-1661*, pp. 204, 372; and Wilson, *Profit and Power*, 97-8. Hinton, *Eastland Trade*, 138-45, 153, argues that the Act of 1660 was another nail in the companies' coffin despite Restoration conservativism.

29 BL Egerton 2543, ff. 137-9. See also Wilson, *England's Apprenticeship*, 137-8, 170-76.

30 Charles II to the Lord Mayor, Aldermen, and Common Council of London, 4 April 1660, Clarendon, *History*, VI, 209-10. See also Reginald R. Sharpe, *London and the Kingdom* (3 vols, London, 1894), II, 394-8.

31 *CSPD*, *CTB*, and *CSPC* testify to the level of this sort of activity in 1660-1661. Ogg, *Charles II*, I, 167-8, sketches its variety. John Evelyn, *Diary* (E. S. de Beer, ed. , London, 1959) regarded the crush of office seekers as 'intollerable . . . unexpressable'; but he joined in. See entry for 4 June 1660.

32 See below, Chapter 6, and Stock, *Proceedings*, I, 288.

33 There are good sketches of Clarendon in Feiling, *Tory Party*, 68-71, and Ogg, *Charles II* I, 149-51.

34 Clarendon, *Life and Continuation*, 1093-95, 1114-16; Feiling, *Tory Party*, 101-2; Cobbett, *Parl. Hist.* IV, 289-91.

35 For which, unfortunately, I must credit J. K. Galbraith.

36 A. P. Thornton, *West India Policy under the Restoration* (Oxford, 1956), 8-14; Clarendon, *Life and Continuation*, 1102-3. Newcastle's advice to Charles II caught perfectly this ambivalence between dependence upon and disdain for merchants. Slaughter (ed.), *Ideology and Politics*, 36-8.

37 Clarendon's views on government may be canvassed in Ogg, *Charles II*, I, 149-51, 189-97; J. R. Jones (ed.), *The Restored Monarchy, 1660-1688* (London, 1979), 12-13, 105-7.

For Povey's much-cited (but undated) memorandum on the plantation councils' lack of power, see BL Egerton 2395, f. 276.

38 Cobbett, *Parl. Hist.* IV, 88, 181-92. See also Hutton, *Restoration*, 159-62, 166-71, 174-80; I. M. Green, *The Re-Establishment of the Church of England, 1660-1663* (Oxford, 1978), 3-36 and *passim*.

39 *Statutes of the Realm*, V, 321-3. My discussion of the Corporations Act depends on Sacret, 'The Restoration Government and Municipal Corporations'; M. Mullett, The Crown and the Corporations, 1660-1689 (Cambridge U. M. Litt., 1972); and John Miller, 'The Crown and the Borough Charters during the Reign of Charles II', *EHR* 100 (1985), 53-84.

40 See below, Chapter 6.

41 *Calendar of Clarendon State Papers* V, 149, 170. *CSPD 1661-1662*, 179; Sharpe, *London and the Kingdom* II, 394-8, 403; Hutton, *Restoration*, 158-61.

42 The chief evidence that Charles preferred the Lords' version (that a Lords' committee discussed the legislation at the Duke of York's lodgings) is not very convincing. It is as rational to endorse Andrew Marvell's view that the amendments were designed to wreck a Commons bill which had passed by only six votes, and which threatened to dilute the royal prerogative in the granting of charters. See Andrew Marvell to the Corporation of Hull, 17 June 1661, in H. M. Margoliouth (ed.), *The Poems and Letters of Andrew Marvell* (3rd edn, 2 vols, Oxford, 1971), II, 32.

43 For evidence that the crown's approach was determined by other criteria than those laid down in either the Corporations Act or the Lords' amendments, see M. Mullett, 'Conflict, Politics, and Elections in Lancaster, 1660-1688', *Northern History* 19 (1983), 65-67, and 'The Politics of Liverpool, 1660-1688', *Transactions of the Historic Society of Lancashire and Cheshire* 124 (1972), 45; J. T. Evans, *Seventeenth-Century Norwich* (Oxford, 1979), 237-8; and Miller, 'The Crown and the Borough Charters,' 56-67.

44. Of course, a new charter was not necessary. Bristol spent over £800 for the privilege of retaining its old charter, while both Massachusetts and the cavalier town of Norwich made creative use of royal letters to uphold their old and avoid having to seek new charters. See Hinton, *Eastland Trade*, 138; Alfred C. Wood, *A History of the Levant Company* (London, 1935), 95; Hutton, *Restoration*, 158-61; Evans, *Seventeenth-Century Norwich*, 229-45; Miller, 'Crown and Borough Charters', 64-7; Mullett, The Crown and the Corporations, 1-64; and below, Chapter 6, for Massachusetts.

45 See for instance Secretary of State Nicholas's papers at BL Egerton 2543, ff. 24-32; *CTB* I, 184; Evelyn, *Diary*, 5 January 1661.

46 Ogg, *Charles II*, I, 154-5, 197-9; Clarendon, *Life and Continuation*, 1031-3; Feiling, *Tory Party*, 108-9; Hutton, *Restoration*, 161-80.

47 Andrew Browning (ed.), *English Historical Documents VIII, 1660-1714* (London, 1966), 371-4. This was not strictly speaking a declaration of indulgence, but 'His Majesty's Declaration to his Loving Subjects'.

48 Ogg, *Charles II*, I, 200-04; J. P. Kenyon, *The Stuart Constitution, 1603-1688* (Cambridge, 1966), 363-4, 401-6; Robert S. Bosher, *The Making of the Restoration Settlement: The Influence of the Laudians, 1649-1662* (London, 1957), 252-3, 260-70.

49 See below, Chapter 6.

50 Clarendon, *Life and Continuation*, 1114-16; Hutton, *Restoration*, 196-214.

51 PRO 30/24/7, ff. 479-81. Chandaman, *English Public Revenue*, 303-63.

52 The retrenchment scheme is at BL Egerton 2543, ff. 129-34. See also Chandaman, *Public Revenue*, 43-4, 83-5, 204-9; Hutton, *Restoration*, 198-201.

53 S. B. Baxter, *The Development of the Treasury, 1660-1702* (Cambridge, Mass., 1957), 9-11, 127, 260; Ogg, *Charles II*, I, 149-51; Chandaman, *Public Revenue*, 213; Feiling, *Tory Party*, 114-15. See also *CTB* I, 59, and Ormonde's 'proposals concerning Ireland', c. 1670, Bodl. Rawlinson 255A, ff 132-5. For Downing and Shaftesbury, see below, Chapters 7 and 8.

54 BL Stowe 326, ff. 53-112, *passim*, esp. 100-4; *CTB* I, 132-3; and Chandaman, *Public Revenue*, 21-9, 50-58.

55 For the suspicion with which farming was regarded, see BL Add. Mss. 28089, ff. 41-6; Add. Mss. 28079, ff. 126-30, 137-44, 197-8, and BL Egerton 3351, ff. 10-17, 77, 136. The

Shaftesbury papers also contain much; see especially PRO 30/24/36/25. Coventry is quoted by Maurice Lee, Jr., *The Cabal* (Urbana, 1965), 134.

56 Henry Roseveare, *The Treasury: the Evolution of a British Institution* (London, 1969), 65-6; Chandaman, *Public Revenue*, 22-5, 52-8.

57 Bodl. Clarendon 84, ff. 96-105.

58 Andrews, *Colonial Period* IV, 129-30. Webb, *The Governors-General*, 103-7, draws a different lesson from the Isle of Wight episode.

59 E. B. O'Callaghan and Berthold Fernow (eds.), *Documents Relative to the Colonial History of the State of New York (NYCD)* (15 vols., Albany, 1853-1887), III, 45-6, 48-50; *APCC* I, no. 618. The customs farmers' commitment to colonial enforcement was suspect. Sir John Shaw, one of the farmers, already held a patented post at £600 per annum to see to the enforcement of the navigation laws. There is no evidence that he or his deputy ever did more than to collect the salary, which the deputy's *executors* continued to do as late as 1687. CTB I, 87, 232; Harper, *English Navigation Laws*, 82n.

60 The general problems of enforcing policy on JPs are summarized by Anthony Fletcher, *Reform in the Provinces: the Government of Stuart England* (London, 1986), see especially Chapters 2, 3, and 6. See also John Kenyon, *The Popish Plot* (London, 1984 edn), 6-9, L. K. J. Glassey, *Politics and the Appointment of Justices of the Peace, 1675-1720* (Oxford, 1979), and John Miller, *Popery and Politics in England, 1660-1688* (Cambridge, 1973).

61 Fletcher, *Reform in the Provinces*, 15-21, 32-4, 43-5, 357-60, finds the Deputy Lieutenants and justices 'firmly' in control of their shires by the 1660s. See also Sir Robert Hyde to Clarendon, 30 July 1664, Bodl. Clarendon 82, f. 44.

62 On Virginia, see letters from Thomas Ludwell and Governor Berkeley, Bodl. Clarendon 84, ff. 228-31; ‚85, ff. 68-9; and *CSPC 1661-1668*, no. 1037. For Jamaica, see Modyford's letters to the Duke of Albemarle and Secretary of State Lord Arlington, *CSPC 1661-1668*, nos. 942, 979, 1142, 1147, 1537; *CSPC 1669-1674*, nos. 103, 103. I, and to Clarendon, 5 March 1666, Bodl. Clarendon 84, ff. 80-81.

63. *CSPC 1661-1668*, nos. 1017, 1018, 1036, 1057, 1151, 1152; Clarendon to Willoughby, 13 April 1666, Bodl. Clarendon 84, ff. 126-8. The articles of impeachment against Clarendon are in Browning (ed.), *EHD* VIII, 193-4.

64 For the offer, see the first article of the instructions to the Commission of 1664, *NYCD* III, 51.

65 PRO CO 31/1. ff. 29-30; *CSPC 1661-1668*, no. 158; *APCCI*, no. 598.

66 Joan de Lourdes Leonard, 'Operation Checkmate: The Birth and Death of a Virginia Blueprint for Progress', *W&MQ* 3rd ser., 24 (1967), 44-74; John Rainbolt, *From Prescription to Persuasion: Manipulation of the Seventeenth-Century Virginia Economy* (Port Washington, NY, 1974), 14-70; and Morgan, *American Slavery, American Freedom*, 186-95.

67 Francis Moryson to Clarendon (1665), *NYHSC* (1869), 109-12. See also William L. Saunders (ed.), *Colonial Records of North Carolina* (10 vols., Raleigh, 1886-1890), I, 144 and Bodl. Clarendon 84, ff. 230-31.

68 A translation of Jamaica's motto is 'either [or any] of the islands serves the whole'. See also Harlow, *Barbados*, 105-16. *CSPC 1661-1668*, nos. 681, 739, 784, 1664. *CSPC 1669-1674*, no. 604. Clarendon to Willoughby, 13 April 1666, Bodl. Clarendon 84, ff. 126-8.

69 Ogg, *Charles II*, I, 205-6; Haley, *Shaftesbury*, 159-71; Hutton, *Restoration*, 191-4, 201-03.

70 Elizabeth Donnan (ed.), *Documents Illustrative of the Slave Trade to America* (4 vols, reprint, New York, 1965), I, 156-65, 168-9 has some correspondence. See also *CSPC 1661-1668*, nos. 583-5, 414-15, 504.

71 K. G. Davies, *The Royal African Company* (London, 1957), 40-45, 63-74. See also *CTB* I, 107, 234 and Haley, *Shaftesbury*, 208-9, 227-30.

72 Charles Wilson, *Profit and Power*, remains the best general study. Ashley's speech on the third Dutch war ('Delenda est Carthago') is more succinct. See PRO 30/24/4, part 3, no. 238.

73 The annual customs loss was reckoned at one-half the cost of the expedition itself, and

would certainly have paid for some at least of the 'retrenchment' imposed in 1663. See *NYCD* III, 43-7; *NYHSC* (1869), 3-4, 11-12, 19-22, 27; BL Egerton 2543, ff. 129-34.

74 Charles II to Henriette-Anne, Duchess of Orleans, 2 June 1664, in Arthur Bryant (ed.), *The Letters . . . of King Charles II* (London, 1935), 159. 'I will', he wrote to his sister on 14 July, 'have full satisfaction, one way or another'. *Ibid.*, 161. An early intimation of the commercial arguments for war may be found in Sir George Downing's paper on the king's revenue, dated The Hague, 16/26 August 1661, Bodl. Clarendon 104, ff. 252-8. See also Clarendon, *Life and Continuation*, 1116-21, and in a paper by Sir Richard Ford, 1664 [?], Bodl. Clarendon 83, ff. 373-4.

75 Clarendon, who opposed the war, poured scorn on this idea in his *Life and Continuation*, 1099. For Charles's public rationale, see Stock, *Proceedings*, I, 228-32.

76 The Irish Parliament clearly expressed the widely held view that increased duties would necessarily decrease trade, and the English parliament would later apply the principle in order to reduce the level of trade with France. See Stock, *Proceedings*, I, 462-4; Wilson, *Profit and Power*, 155; Chandaman, *Public Revenue*, 14-19.

77 Hutton, *Restoration*, 262, 279-81; Ogg, *Charles II* I, 316-21.

78 Charles II to Cooper, quoted in Haley, *Shaftesbury*, 89; Charles II to the House of Peers and the Declaration of Breda, 4 April 1660, Clarendon, *History*, VI, 206, 208

Chapter 6

1 The Convention's bill to annex Jamaica and Dunkirk to the crown was revived by the Cavalier Commons in 1661 and lost in the Lords: Stock, *Proceedings* I, 278, 281, 283, 284; *APCC* I, nos. 299-303; Clarendon, *Life and Continuation*, 1038. During the winter of 1661-62, Clarendon ignored advice that New England should be annexed to the crown by Act of Parliament. *NYHSC* (1869), 35-7.

2 Appleby, *Economic Thought and Ideology in Seventeenth-Century England*, especially 52-128; Carl Bridenbaugh, *Fat Mutton and Liberty of Conscience: Society in Rhode Island, 1636-1690* (Providence, 1974), 63-5, 70; and Sydney V. James, 'Colonial Rhode Island and the Beginnings of the Liberal Rationalized State', in Melvin Richter (ed.), *Essays in Theory and History: An Approach to the Social Sciences* (Cambridge, Mass., 1970), but note that James sees this development occurring later in the colonial period.

3 Williams to John Winthrop, Jr, 8 September 1660, *Complete Writings* VI, 310-13. For Jenks, see Massachusetts Archives, CVI, ff. 29-35. For the condemnation of Eliot's book see *Massachusetts Records* IV, part 2, 6.

4 Davenport to John Winthrop, Jr, 6 December 1659 and 1 August 1660, and Rev. William Hooke to same, 16 April 1658 and 30 March 1659, *MHSC*, 4th ser., VII, 507-11, 515-17, 587-93; *Massachusetts Records* IV, part 1, 417-18; John Hull, "Diaries", 194-5.

5 Dunn, *Puritans and Yankees*, 110-11; Andrews, *Colonial Period* II, 37-8; *Rhode Island Records* I, 433-5; and Williams, *Complete Writings* VI, 308, 310, 313, 314-17.

6 Rhode Island had reacted quickly, too, to the changes in English politics following Oliver Cromwell's death: *Rhode Island Records*, I, 414-16, 423, 432.

7 *Connecticut Records* I, 361-2, 367-8; Leete to Winthrop, 6 August 1661, *MHSC* 4th ser., VII, 548-50; *Rhode Island Records* I, 515-16.

8 *Rhode Island Records* I, 509-11.

9 *Connecticut Records* I, 388, 437-8; and see Pope, *Half-Way Covenant*, 76-8, 87-95. Lucas, *Valley of Discord*, 59-86, gives little weight to the new charter.

10 See *New Hampshire Records* XVII, 506-13; *Province and Court Records of Maine* II, 111-13, 134-5, 138-43, 151; and *MHSC* 2nd ser. IV, 148-54.

11 Leete to Winthrop, 11 April and 6 August 1661, *MHSC* 4th ser., VII, 546-50; C. J. Hoadly, ed., *Records of the Colony or Jurisdiction of New Haven, from May, 1653, to the Union* (Hartford, 1858) 402-3, 418-23; Calder, *The New Haven Colony*, 217-30.

12 Calder (ed.), *Letters of John Davenport*, 224-40. See also Calder, *The New Haven Colony*, 230-52 and Dunn, *Puritans and Yankees*, 138-41, 144-6, 150.

13 Hening, *Statutes* II, 24-5, 33-148 and Kukla (ed.), "Some Acts not in Hening's *Statutes*", 87-88.

14 *NYCD* II, 118; *Maryland Archives* III, 391-8; and Hall (ed.), *Early Narratives of Maryland*, 380-82.

15 Bailyn, 'Politics and Social Structure in Virginia'; Rainbolt, *From Prescription to Persuasion*, 11-54; David W. Jordan, *Foundations of Representative Government in Maryland, 1632-1715* (Cambridge, 1987), 55-9, 97-100; Pope, *Half-Way Covenant*, 87-8; John Davenport to John Leverett, 24 June 1665, Calder (ed.), *Letters of John Davenport*, 248-53.

16 *Connecticut Records* II, 3-12; and *Rhode Island Records* II, 1-21. See also Dunn, *Puritans and Yankees*, 117-42, and Robert C. Black, *The Younger John Winthrop* (New York, 1966), 206-45.

17 See above, Chapter 3.

18 See above, Chapter 3, and BL Egerton 2395, ff. 270-75. Of the lay members of the 1660 council, only Edward Digges and Governor Sir William Berkeley, both of Virginia, stood outside the West Indian circle. Andrews, *British Committees*, 67-8; Beer, *Colonial System*, I, 232-3.

19 PRO CO 324/1. ff. 148, 159. These observations probably date from early 1661.

20 The new charters of the 1660s included those for New York, Surinam, Carolina, the Bahamas, Connecticut and Rhode Island. Sir Thomas Temple's commission for Nova Scotia's government was an exception which proved the rule, for it was issued for his life in recognition of his proprietary rights to the colony, In this sense, it was similar to the solution applied to the Caribbee proprietary in Lord Willoughby's favor. For Willoughby's grant, see below, this chapter. For Temple, see *CSPC 1661-1668*, nos. 240-42, 271, 273.

21 See BL Egerton 2395, ff. 272-3 and BL Egerton 2543, ff. 120, 125, for good examples of the genre. See also *CSPC 1661-1668*, nos. 3, 5.

22 Savelle, *Origins of American Diplomacy* 62-5; Stock, *Proceedings* I, 288; Earl of Lauderdale to Lord Cassilis, January 1662, Ailsa Mss., SRO GD 25/9, box 30.

23 The decision to commission D'Oyley was taken on 17 October 1660, but there was a delay before the commission actually issued. In the meanwhile, decisions were taken to reject Spain's *de jure* claims to the island and to send a supply to the garrison. *APCC* I, nos. 491, 500, 501; *CSPC 1574-1660*, 485, 490-92; *CSPC 1661-1668*, nos. 20, 22. See also *The Diary of John Evelyn*, entry for 27 September 1660.

24 See for instance D'Oyley to Commissioners for the Admiralty, 26 July 1660, *CSPC 1574-1660*, 485.

25 *CSPC 1661-1668*, no. 56; *CSPC 1675-1676, Addenda*, no. 364; PRO 30/24/49, ff. 31-3 (undated paper from 1660 or 1661), and Cassilis to Lauderdale, 28 December 1660, Ailsa Mss., SRO GD 25/9, box 30.

26 BL Egerton 2395, ff. 289-90; and see above, Chapter 3.

27 Captain Thomas Lynch's proposal of January 1661 at BL Egerton 2395, ff. 283-6 and Povey's memo, *ibid.* f. 291, formed the basis of a group of schemes which can be traced through *CSPC 1661-1668*, nos. 5, 12, 15, 54, 56, and *CTB* I, 267, 303.

28 See below, Chapter 7.

29 Povey argued in the same memorandum that it would endanger the safety of the realm to return Jamaica's garrison to England. Captain Thomas Lynch, one of the garrison's officers, thought that the men went to Jamaica because they would not work in England. See PRO CO 324/1, f. 162; BL Egerton 2395, ff. 283-6; Cobbett, *Parl. Hist.* IV, 124.

30 Brigham, (ed.), *British Royal Proclamations*, 112-14. For Cromwell's guarantees, see *ibid.* 96-100. Instructions to Governors Lord Windsor (1662) and Modyford (1664) are at CO 324/1, ff. 37-65 and Bodl. Rawlinson A255, ff. 1-5. See also Lauderdale to Cassilis, January 1662, SRO GD 25/9, box 30.

31 See PRO 30/24/49, ff. 31-3; Bodl. Rawlinson A347, ff. 32-5; *CSPC 1574-1660*, 491. See also Stock, *Proceedings* I, 293, and Clarendon, *Life and Continuation*, 1084.

32 *CSPC 1661-1668*, nos. 135, 615, 656; BL Egerton 3351, f. 351; BL Egerton 2395, ff. 283-6, 289-90; *CTB* I, 362, 589; *APCC* I, no. 593; Bodl. Rawlinson A255, ff. 1-5, 7-10. Dunkirk and Tangier were a good deal more expensive, and Charles sold Dunkirk in 1662 and abandoned Tangier twenty years later. See Chandaman, *Public Revenue*, 130-32; Hutton, *Restoration*, 190; PRO 30/24/3, f. 90.

33 Windsor's instructions, PRO CO 324/1. ff. 327-65. Modyford's instructions clearly state the purpose of the tax on liquor, which followed advice from Thomas Lynch and Edward D'Oyley that drink was a more virulent killer than the climate. See Bodl. Rawlinson A255, ff. 1-5; Bodl. Rawlinson A347, ff. 32-5; BL Egerton 2395, ff. 283-6.

34 Initial confusion on these matters was finally cleared up by Article 12 of Modyford's instructions. *CSPC 1661-1668*, nos. 107, 118, 307, 1003, 1165; PRO CO 324/1, f. 47; BL Egerton 2395, ff. 301-2; Bodl. Rawlinson A255, ff. 1-5.

35 Stock, *Proceedings*, I, 293. See also above, Chapter 5.

36 See Webb, *The Governors-General*, 196-249, *passim*, for an interpretation along these lines.

37 PRO CO 324/1, ff. 42, 45, 47, 51, and Bodl. Rawlinson A255, ff. 1-5.

38 See D'Oyley and Lyttleton to Clarendon, Bodl. Rawlinson A347,ff. 32-8; Windsor to Williamson, 17 January 1664, *CSPC 1661-1668*, no. 638; reports by Lyttelton at *ibid.* nos. 812, 815. See also Richard Povey to Lyttleton, 10 December 1664, Bodl. Clarendon 84, ff. 253-8; and Modyford to Arlington, 16 November 1665, *CSPC 1661-1668*, no. 1085 and to Clarendon, 5 March 1666, Bodl. Clarendon 84, f. 80.

39 'A Journal Kept by William Beeston, from his first coming to Jamaica', in *Interesting Tracts, Relating to the Island of Jamaica . . . down to the year 1702* (St. Jago de la Vega, 1800), 274-80, 282-4.

40 A Barbadian petition to the king of 4 July 1661 included the phrase 'wee growing poorer and our ground every day decaying', in PRO CO 31/1, ff. 53-4. Such reports were not believed; see Clarendon on Barbadians' 'incredible' wealth in his History, V, 262-3.

41 Willoughby's instructions are at *APCC* I, no. 598. See also *ibid.* no. 599. Another indication of interest in Barbadian wealth was the land bank proposal of Francis Cradocke, accepted on condition that the promoters would pay 25% of their profits to the king. *CSPC 1661-1668*, nos. 183, 194, 265; *APCC* I, no. 557.

42 BL Egerton 2395, f. 267; Harlow, *Barbados*, 128.

43 Willoughby to Charles II, May 1660, Bodl. Clarendon 72, ff. 439-40; Feiling, *Tory Party*, 88.

44 See PRO CO 31/1, ff. 15-21, where we also find that Modyford published the Act of Indemnity on 1 August. The record may have been altered by Peter Watson, Modyford's agent in London. Neither Act had been passed by 1 August, and Nevis did not hear of the former until December 1660. *CSPC 1675-1676, Addenda* no. 354. Harlow, *Barbados*, 76-8, 98-100, 107-08, 113-14, and 119-26 conveys a sense of Modyford's political flexibility.

45 PRO CO 31/1. ff. 23-6.

46 See Modyford's speech of 1 August 1660 and his 'Reasons given . . . ', 15 August,PRO CO 31/1, ff. 18, 28-9. See also above, Chapters 2-4 for Barbadians' historic concerns about English merchant control of their trade.

47 PRO CO 31/1, ff. 28-9. Puckrein, *Little England*, 137-8; and see above, Chapter 4.

48 PRO CO 31/1, ff. 28-30. Clearly the assembly had reason to distrust Modyford, yet within two years he would be speaker.

49 *CSPC 1574-1660*, 492, 494, 496; PRO CO 31/1. ff. 31-3.

50 Harlow, *Barbados*, 133-4; *CSPC 1661-1668*, nos. 1, 6, 11, 24, 60; *APCC* I, no. 509; PRO CO 31/1. ff. 38-41; Bodl. Clarendon Mss. 72, f. 408. One of Modyford's judges was Daniel Searle, who had accepted commissions from both both Commonwealth and Protectorate and who may have been a little worried himself. In 1660 we find him trying to buy land on Long Island. *MHSC* 4th ser., VII, 64-5.

51 Harlow, *Barbados*, 128-36, 144, is generally accurate here, and see also Williamson, *The Caribbee Islands under the Proprietary Patents*, 20-63 and 200-217. However, note that the merchant group was divided within itself, and that individuals changed their tune from time to time in 1660 and 1661. See BL Add. Mss. 11411, ff. 31-4; BL

Egerton 2395, ff. 270-71, 303-4; *CSPC 1574-1660*, 485-7; *CSPC 1661-1668*, nos. 34, 36, 37, 39, 60, 80, 83, 304; *APCC* I, nos. 485, 506, 507, 509.

52 *APCC* I, no. 509. Lord Treasurer Southampton was concerned to avoid all such obligations to the Carlisle creditors. See *CTB* I, 101. See also PRO CO 1/15, f. 87.

53 *CSPC 1661-1668*, nos. 39, 40, 60, 80, 83, 180-81.

54 Walrond, the Council, and the Assembly agreed at several points that some compensation would have to be paid in order to secure land titles, and had remembered that 'two and fower per Cent' duties had once been voted in compensation for the proprietor's land rights. See PRO CO 31/1. ff. 42-3, 56-62, 76-7.

55 See Willoughby's letters to Barbados, Montserrat, and Nevis, September 1660 - February 1661 and some responses at BL Add. Mss. 11411, ff. 28-32 and BL Egerton 2395, ff. 287, 288, 305-6, 329. See also PRO CO 31/1, f. 29 and above, Chapter 4.

56 The Leewards' Acts are at PRO CO 324/1, ff. 285-330. That Nevis and St. Christopher understood the nature of the transaction is made clear by *CSPC 1661-1668*, no. 732 and *CSPC 1685-1668, Addenda*, no. 2021. The Barbadian Act is at PRO CO 29/1, ff. 47-50.

57 PRO CO 29/1, ff, 47-50; *APCC* I, no. 598. Harlow, *Barbados*, 146, quotes the appropriation clause out of context and gives a different impression.

58 *CSPC 1661-1668*, no. 981; Chandaman, *Public Revenue*, 127, 352-60.

59 Willoughby's success in keeping Surinam perhaps owed something to his decision to take on Laurence Hyde, Clarendon's second son, as partner. See *CSPC 1574-1660*, 484; *CSPC 1661-1668* nos. 83, 451; *APCC* I, no. 485; BL Egeton 2543, f. 120.

60 For Cradocke's appointment, and its background, see above, Chapter 2-4, and *CSPC 1574-1660*, 487; *CSPC 1661-1668*, no. 265; BL Egerton 2395, ff. 270-71, 303-4; BL Add. Mss. 11411, ff. 41, 45, 51-3. The Barbadian Council's attempt at debt evasion, the assembly's response, and that of London merchants, can be followed through *CSPC 1661-1668*, nos. 458, 459, 462; PRO CO 31/1, ff. 54-55, 62; *APCC* I, no. 595.

61 *CSPC 1661-1668*, no. 40; Willoughby's similar assessment is at *ibid.*, no. 764.

62 Thornton, *West India Policy under the Restoration*, 8-14. For confirmation, see *CSPC 1661-1668*, no. 5; BL Egerton 2395, f. 276.

63 Clarendon, *Life and Continuation*, 1264-8, presents a detailed explanation of these proceedings which carries authority even though written as a defence against the bill of impeachment against him.

64 See *CSPC 1661-1668*, nos. 3, 45, 46, 49, 50, 64, 75, 80, 87, 89, 90; Breedon to the Council for Plantations, 11 March 1661, Maverick to Clarendon, n. d. (three letters), and [?] to Clarendon, n. d., *NYHSC* (1869), 16-32; *Hutchinson Papers* II, 43-51; and Hutchinson, *History* I, 179-92. Venner was called 'diabolical' by the Massachusetts General Court: 'He went from us because he was not of us', the Court truthfully declared. *Massachusetts Records* IV, part 2, 32-3.

65 BL Egerton 2395, ff. 299-300.

66 Most of Maverick's correspondence with Clarendon is undated but the editors have the sequence about right. See *NYHSC* (1869), especially 16-28, 35-43, 48-50, 52-6. See also *CSPC 1661-1668*, nos. 248, 271, 274; and Massachusetts Archives CVI, ff. 26a, 56.

67 *CSPC 1661-1668*, nos. 26, 28-30 (the royal letter of 15 February is better consulted at PRO CO 5/903, ff. 15-16); *CTB* I, 206-7; *APCC* I, no. 504.

68 *APCC* I, no. 513.

69 For examples of alarmist reports, see Calder (ed.), *Letters of John Davenport*, 176-79; 'The Mather Papers', *MHSC* 4th ser., VIII, 166-207, and Hull, "Diaries", 195-6.

70 Hull, "Diaries," 201, was encouraged by the royal letter of February, as was the General Court, *Massachusetts Records* IV, part ii, 20; but see also *ibid.* 24-7 and Charles II to the Governors of New England, 9 September 1661, *CSPC 1661-1668*, no. 168.

71 For the sequence of events and the debate over the agency see *Massachusetts Records* IV, part 2, 32, 34, 35, 37, 39-40; *Hutchinson Papers* II, 57-93; Massachusetts Archives, CVI, ff. 37-48; and Felt, *Ecclesiastical History*, II, 284.

72 The Bill for Uniformity was going through parliament as negotiations with the agents commenced. See Hutton, *Restoration*, 174-6. See also John Winthrop, Jr, to Samuel Willys, 17 February 1662, in Robert C. Black, III (ed.), 'Honored Sir: A Recently Discovered Letter . . . ' Connecticut Historical Society *Bulletin* 48 (1983), 169-73.

73 See letters from Temple and 'J. Curwine' (probably Boston merchant John Corwin), Massachusetts Archives CVI, ff. 26a, 56; *APCC* I, no. 521. Temple succeeded in discrediting Thomas Breedon, whose grant of Nova Scotia, the king declared, had been obtained by 'surprise' and was to revert to Temple. *CSPC 1661-1668*, nos. 248, 271, 274.

74 *Hutchinson Papers* II, 68, 70, 77, and (for the king's letter to the colony), 100-104; Hull, "Diaries," 205-6, noted some problems which the king's letter would cause.

75 Charles II to Governor and Company of Massachusetts, 28 June 1662, *Hutchinson Papers* II, 100-104.

76 Much later, Cotton Mather remembered that on his return Norton 'imagined, that his best Friends began . . . to *look awry* on him', *Magnalia Christi Americana* (Boston, 1702), Book III, 37-8. For fears (and some hopes) in 1660-63 that popery (or the Book of Common Prayer) waited in the wings, see Massachusetts Archives CVI, ff. 58-64; *Massachusetts Records* IV, part 2, 60; Calder (ed.), *Letters of John Davenport*, 198-201, 204, 204n. See also John Allin, *Animadversions on the anti-synodalia Americana* (Cambridge, 1664), Preface and 5-6, 7, 10; Norton's *Three Choise . . . Sermons*, 2, where note the tone of John Wilson's dedicatory poem; and Felt, *Ecclesiastical History* II, 224, 299-300, 306. For divisions over the suffrage issue, see *ibid.* II, 197; Hull, "Diaries", 207; Massachusetts Archives CVI, ff. 66, 79; *Massachusetts Records* IV, part 2, 117-28.

The best study of the connections between internal religious conflict and the imperial issue is Richard C. Simmons, 'The Founding of the Third Church in Boston', *WMQ* 3rd ser., 26 (1969), 241-52, but see also Bailyn *The New England Merchants*, 105-26; Dunn, *Puritans and Yankees*, 119-24, 152-63, 212-28; and Paul Lucas, 'Colony or Commonwealth: Massachusetts Bay, 1661-1666', *WMQ* 3rd ser., 24 (1967), 88-107.

77 Lucas, 'Colony or Commonwealth', 96, says the vote was not carried, but see Massachusetts Archives CVI, ff. 52, 52a, 58-64.

78 *Massachusetts Records* IV, part 2, pp. 58-9, 69-70, 74-5. See also Temple to Clarendon, 21 and 22 August 1663, (1869), 52-6.

79 *Massachusetts Records* IV, part 2, 58, 60, 73-4, 86-7. 99; Hull, *Diary*, 207; Humphrey Davies to John Davenport, October 1662, *MHSC* 4th ser., VIII, 204; Pope, *Half-Way Covenant*, esp. Chapter 6; and above, note 76.

80 Endecott's letter was apparently not addressed to the king, but it was intended to reach him and it did. See *MHSC* 2nd ser., VIII, 47-8.

81 *Massachusetts Records* IV, part 2, 73-4; *APCC* I, no. 589.

82 Charles told Massachusetts in 1664 that Norton and Bradstreet knew of his intention to send commissioners to settle boundaries, which would explain the flurry of negotiations Massachusetts set in train with its neighbors in 1663. *NYCD* III, 62; Massachusetts Archives CVI, 67-71a. For other early intimations of the Commission, see Maverick to Clarendon, 28 March 1662, Bodl. Clarendon 102, f. 5f; *APCC* I, no. 576; *CSPC 1661-1668*, no. 706; and Massachusetts Archives CVI, ff. 26a, 56.

83 For the commission and public and private instructions, see *NYCD* III, 51-65; the quotation is from the private instructions, 57.

84 *NYCD* III, 46; *APCC* I, no. 585. Years later, Sir Robert Southwell acknowledged that the Commission had been Clarendon's project: *CSPC 1677-1680*, no. 801. This is supported by 'Considerations in order to the establishing of his Majesty's interests in New England', *CSPC 1661-1668*, no. 706, attributed to Clarendon and almost certainly dating from 1662. See also article one of the private instructions, *NYCD* III, 57, and Sosin, *English America and the Restoration Monarchy*, 110 and notes.

85 See Andrews, *Colonial Period* III, 67-8. Dunn, *Puritans and Yankees*, 151-2, sees this possibility as a part of a set of not necessarily complementary motives.

86 See above, Chapter 5, and *NYCD* III, 54, 59-60. The commissioners were instructed to attend congregational church services, and in their private services their chaplain was not to wear the surplice.

87 See above, Chapter 5, and *NYCD* III, 59-60.

88 Endecott's 'concessions' (*MHSC* 2nd ser., VIII, 47-8) were a more likely source for this agenda than Thomas Povey's 'Important points for the Settlement of New England', [1664?], BL Egerton 2395, f. 396. See private instructions, articles 4, 5, 6, and 8, and

public instructions for Massachusetts, articles 4 and 11, *NYCD* III, 52, 54, 58-60; *Massachusetts Records* IV, part 2, 31-2; and Sir John Wolstenholme to Massachusetts Secretary Edward Rawson, 18 February 1664, *Hutchinson Papers* II, 108-9.

89 Articles 3 and 8 of the private instructions, *NYCD* III, 58, 60.

90 *NYCD* III, 58, 62.

91 Public instructions for Massachusetts, *NYCD* III, 51.

92 Temple offered to bet his life on the existence of a majority 'loyal' party in Massachusetts. Massachusetts Archives, CVI, f. 56.

93 Massachusetts Archives CVI, ff. 78-81, 92-8; *Massachusetts Records* IV, part 2, 117-33.

94 The king's letter is at *NYCD* III, 90-91 and *Hutchinson Papers* II, 115-17. It arrived on 13 May, with magistrates and deputies already sitting and in negotiations with the commissioners. For a different interpretation, see Lucas, 'Colony or Commonwealth', 102-5. The average electoral turnover was calculated by comparing rosters of deputies at succeeding May sessions between 1655 and 1665.

95 *Massachusetts Records* IV, part 2, 157, 168.

96 Lucas's identification of Johnson as a moderate led him to read his petition differently: 'Colony or Commonwealth', 100-01. The petition is at Massachusetts Archives CVI, f. 80. And see Hull, 'Diaries', 213, 217. The disparity between the commission and the king's accompanying letter may be assessed at *NYCD* III, 61-5.

97 The whole 'transaction' between the commissioners and the Massachusetts General Court is at *Massachusetts Records* IV, part 2, 157-273; for the quoted passage, see 168.

98 Maverick to Nicolls, 4 February 1665, *NYCD* III, 88-9; Massachusetts Archives CVI, ff. 101-02.

99 Allin's tract (Boston, 1664) was written to counter Charles Chauncy's *Antisynodalia Americana*. For the various petitions of April 1665, see Massachusetts Archives CVI, 103-11; for the case of Constable Mason, see Hutchinson, *History*, I, 218-19. Hathorne's apology is at *Massachusetts Records* IV, part 2, 149.

100 See the court's argument that the liberty of Christians to form particular congregations met the king's demands for full ecclesiastical rights for Anglicans. *Massachusetts Records* IV, 220-21.

101 *Massachusetts Records* IV, part 2, 223-8.

102 On the secularization of political rhetoric, see Breen, *Character of the Good Ruler*, 134-202. See also Charles II to Massachusetts, 10 April 1666, Hutchinson, *History*, I, Appendix, 453-4.

103 *CSPC 1661-1668*, no. 1301; Massachusetts Archives CVI, ff. 106, 167, 169, 170, 176, 178, 188, 189. For petitions from Ipswich, Newbury, Salem and Boston, see *MHSC* 2nd ser., VIII, 103-7. *Massachusetts Records* IV, part 2, 317-18 identifies seven men as the chief movers of these petitions and states that they were 'all save one freemen of this colony & members of churches'. Eleven of the twenty-six Boston signatories appear on freemen lists between 1642 and 1666.

104 *MHSC* 2nd ser., VIII, 99-101, 103. And see above, Chapter 3.

105 Breedon to Clarendon, 22 October 1666, Bodl. Clarendon 84, f. 329; *CSPC 1661-1668*, nos. 1648, 1797, 1798; *CSPC 1669-1774*, no. 58; *Massachusetts Records* IV, part 2, 368-9.

Chapter 7

1 Stock, *Proceedings*, I, 340-41; Caroline Robbins (ed.), *The Diary of John Milward. . .* (Cambridge, 1938), 100, 115; PRO 30/24/30, f. 41; BL Sloane 3828, ff. 205-10.

2 Richard Povey to Lyttelton, 10 December 1664, Bodl. Clarendon 82, ff. 253-8.

3 BL Egerton 2543, ff. 186-9; *CTB* II, xxxvi - lxxxvi (Introduction by Dr. W. A. Shaw). John Milward noted but disapproved of parliament's increasing tendency to link grievances with revenue; see Milward, *Diary*, 35, 195, 212-13.

4 Lee, *The Cabal*, 172-8; BL Add. Mss. 10119, f. 19; BL Egerton 2543, f. 209; Henry

Roseveare, *The Treasury, 1660-1870: the Foundations of Control* (London, 1973), 120-24; Bryant, *Letters of Charles II*, 217.

5 Lee, *The Cabal*, 5-7, 17, 102-14 and Ogg, *Charles II*, 332-50. See also John Miller, 'The Potential for "Absolutism" in Later Stuart England', *History* 69 (1984), 187-207, for a general consideration of Charles's motivation and prospects.

6 Lee, *The Cabal*, 83-91, 95-7, 107, 114-16; Stock, *Proceedings*, I, 361, 401-4. Correspondence relevant to the raid and Modyford's recall is at *CSPC 1669-1674*, nos. 162, 172, 216, 227, 237, 293, 310, 504, 608. Modyford's defence of his actions ([June 1671?], BL Egerton 3340, ff. 110-15) is also useful.

7 See below, Chapter 8.

8 *CSPC 1669-1674*, nos. 729, 787, 885, 1082; Lynch to [Sir Henry Coventry?], 23 September 1674, Bath (Longleat) Coventry Mss., 74, ff. 19-20. Vaughan to [Coventry?], 28 December 1674, Bath Coventry 74, f. 22.

9 Haley, *Shaftesbury*, 152-3. For a sampling of 'reform' papers, see PRO 30/24/36/25, *passim* and *CTB* I, 272-3. The undated memo on the Chancellor's authority is at PRO 30/24/30, f. 60.

10 Chandaman, *Public Revenue*, 295-7.

11 *CTB* II, 544, 631, 634. Sir Robert Long to [Sir Thomas Osborne?], BL Egerton 3351, ff. 61-2. See also illustrative documents in Roseveare, *The Treasury, 1660-1870*, 113-15, 118, 120-24, 127-30, 134-6.

12 Croke to Southampton, 2 July 1661, *CTB* I, 148-9. Long to Ashley, 7 July 1668, PRO 30/24/4, part 2, f. 167; and see also PRO 30/24/7, ff. 454-53 (reverse folios). In 1672 Ashley (now Earl of Shaftesbury) admitted to Long's charge and urged his successor at the Exchequer to do the same. PRO 30/24/5, 242/2 (printed pamphlet).

13 'Sir Thomas Modyford's reasons for the inconveniences of settling . . . places for life and by patent', *CSPC 1685-1688, Addenda*, no. #2049.

14 PRO 30/24/3. part 3, ff. 105-7.

15 Sherwin and Rushworth can be followed through the indices of *CTB* I, II, and III. The rationale for Rushworth's office is given at PRO 30/24/46c/45. See also Baxter, *Treasury*, 146-49, 241; Chandaman, Public Revenue, 27-30.

16 See above, Chapter 5, and *APCC* I, nos. 827, 828; *CSPC 1669-1674*, nos. 6, 104; and PRO T 11/1, f. 28.

17 *CTB* III, 796-7.

18 For a different view, see Chandaman, *Public Revenue*, 26-9. See also Haley, *Shaftesbury*, 293-4.

19 Haley, *Shaftesbury*, 173-6.

20 Shaftesbury opposed the Stop, but it may have set him to thinking on banking. His papers from this period contain two proposals for a bank: 'Observations . . . for . . . the Imaginary payment of the Publique debts . . . ', c. 1672, PRO 30/24/46c, ff. 18-20; and Thomas Newcomb, *An Humble Proposal* (London, 1674), printed pamphlet in PRO 30/24/5/1, no. 274.

21 *CTB* I, 219.

22 Finch's opinion (1673) and Jones's (1678) are in BL Add. Mss. 30218, ff. 60-61, 73. See also Maurice Bond (ed.), *The Diaries and Papers of Sir Edward Dering* (London, 1976), 39-40, 57 and 'Ten short queries concerning farmeing of his Majesties Revenue', n. d., PRO 30/24/7, f. 519.

23 Patent officers' problems in the colonies were legion and typically involved conflict with royal governors. The trying times of the Barbadian Provost Marshals may be followed through the careers of two incumbents; follow references for 'Cradocke, Francis' and 'Stede, Edwin' in *CSPC 1661-1668* and *CSPC 1669-1674*.

24 Aubrey to Locke, PRO 30/24/7, f. 493; PRO 30/24/49, ff. 88-9.

25 Barbara Shapiro, *Probability and Certainty in Seventeenth-Century England* (Princeton, 1983), esp. 227-66.

26 Collins to Lord Ashley, November 1667, and same to Charles II, n. d., PRO 30/24/3, part 1, f. 160, and 30/24/30, f. 8; Scott, 'Description of the English Colonies', c. 1670, BL Sloane 3662, ff. 78b-49b (reverse folios); Worsley, 'Some Considerations about the Commission for Trade', c. 1668, PRO 30/24/49, ff. 90-93. At about the same time,

Worsley wrote similarly to Arlington: Bodl. Rawlinson A478, ff. 48-50 and, at ff. 65-72, an extended version.

27 For Locke, see William Letwin, *The Origins of Scientific Economics: English Economic Thought, 1660-1776* (London, 1963), 159-62; Violet is quoted in Cooper, 'Social and Economic Policies under the Commonwealth', 122.

28 For Locke's list, see PRO 30/24/49, f. 114. See also Thornton, *West-India Policy*, 145-7; Hinton, *Eastland Trade*, 154; Andrews, *British Committees*, 89, 96-9.

29 Ashley's memo, c. 1669, on the Cattle Act is at PRO 30/24/30, f. 65. The Irish government had similar views: Bodl. Clarendon 85, ff. 59-62, 158-61. For the projected union, see Haley, *Shaftesbury*, 187-92, and Lee, *The Cabal*, 52, 63.

30 The 'Advice' is at PRO 30/24/49, ff. 88-9.

31 Appleby, 'Ideology and Theory: the Tension between Political and Economic Liberalism in Seventeenth-Century England', *AHR* 81 (1976), 499-515, and *Economic Thought and Ideology in Seventeenth-Century England*. But see 'A Treatise about Government writ by John Lord Berkeley', BL Sloane 3828, ff. 81-91.

32 Charles II to 'Madame', 2 September 1668, and 'Statement of position . . . ', 24 January 1670, in Bryant (ed.), *Letters . . . of King Charles II*, 224, 242-3.

33 Lee, *The Cabal*, 192-7, 216-51; Ogg, *Charles II*, I, 354-6, 365-71; Dering, *Diary*, 114-18, 128-9, 138-61.

34 *CTB* III, 705. See also William Blathwayt's similar remark in 1692, *CSPC 1689-1692*, no. 2065.

35 Andrews, *Colonial Period*, IV, 121; Beer, *Old Colonial System* I, 83; Barrow, *Trade and Empire*, 9-10, 13; BL Add. Mss. 28089, ff. 30-35. For retrospective recognitions of the revenue potential of the Act, see PRO T1/1, ff. 145-6, and *CTB* IX, 1965.

36 Sir Thomas Neale to Lord Treasurer Danby, c. 1678, BL Add. Mss. 28079, ff. 90-96.

37 Stock (ed.), *Proceedings*, I, 361-97; Cobbett, *Parl. Hist.* IV, 480-96; Margoliouth, (ed.), *The Poems and Letters of Andrew Marvell*, II, 109-10, 112-13, 119, 121, 134-41.

38 *CTB* II, 41, 43, 46; III, 461, 463; PRO T11/1, ff. 49-51; *CSPC 1669-1674*, no. 6; and Downing to the Law Officers and the Farmers of the Customs, as quoted in Andrews, *Colonial Period* IV, 127n.

39 Stock, *Proceedings* I, 380, 391, 395, 396-7.

40 Stock, *Proceedings* I, 380, 391, 395, 396-97.

41 Barrow, *Trade and Empire*, 11-13, 20-38; Lovejoy, *Glorious Revolution*, 10-17, 46, 93-6. The Act did not create the colonial customs service. The king's instructions to the pioneer (Virginia) collector, November 1671, are at PRO 30/32/41, ff. 3-4.

42 The instructions are in Andrews, *British Committees*, Appendix, 117. See also a draft latter to New England, 18 December 1674, BL Egerton 2395, ff. 497-8.

43 Andrews, *British Committees*, Appendix III, 127-32; Hinton, *Eastland Trade*, 153-5.

44 Frank R. Harris, *Life of . . . Sandwich* (2 vols, London, 1912), II, 214-22 and Appendix K, 337-41; Evelyn, *Diary*, 26 May 1671; *CSPC 1669-1674*, nos. 512, 566, 598, 652, 860, 1247. BL Egerton 2395, ff. 497-8.

45 Gilbert Burnet, *History of His Own Time* II, 12-13, 71. Andrew Browning, *Thomas Osborne, earl of Danby* (3 vols, Glasgow, 1944-1951), remains standard. Ogg, *Charles II*, II, 524-58, offers a dependable survey of the Danby years, subject to Browning's caution about the extent to which Danby actually controlled a court party.

46 These bound booklets are in the Danby Papers, PRO 30/32/1. Some date from the 1690s, others from the 1670s.

47 These incidents are all taken from PRO 30/32/34, ff. 27-8, 30, 44-5, 53, 65, 70, 74.

48 PRO 30/32/34, ff. 9-10, 24-6, 29-30, 34-5.

49 *CTB* V, part 1, 785.

50 PRO 30/32/38, ff. 95-8, 151, 198, 222; PRO 30/32/39, ff. 27, 35.

51 See Danby's memoranda for the king of April and June 1677, extensively quoted in Feiling, *Tory Party*, 162-4.

52 Danby to the Judges of the Northern Circuit, 26 July 1675, PRO 30/32/51, ff. 147-8; PRO 30/32/38, ff. 47, 100, 161, 177; Danby to Yorkshire JPs and Yorkshire JPs to Danby, March and May 1676, PRO 30/32/51, ff. 259-60, 357-8; see also ff. 96-7, 100-01, 114-15, 121-2, 173.

53 PRO 30/32/38, ff. 151, 198, 222; PRO 30/32/39, ff. 27, 35. *APCC* I, no. 1218; PRO 30/32/51, ff. 138, 142.

54 Andrews, *Colonial Period*, IV, 58-9, and Thornton, *West India Policy*, 157-8. See also Evelyn, *Diary*, 23 June 1673; PRO 30/24/49, ff. 100-104; BL Egerton 3340, ff. 148-9; and *NYCD* III, 228.

55 *APCC* I, no. 1021.

56 *NYCD* III, 229-32; *APCC* I, no. 1021.

57 Randolph's commission is in A. N. Toppan (ed.), *Edward Randolph . . . His Letters and Official Papers* (7 vols, Boston, 1898-1909), II, 192-201. Edward Cranfield, who was also to have much to do with New England in the 1680s, had previously been ordered to gather information on Massachusetts: *CSPC 1675-1676*, nos. 457, 545, 721, 746, 813.

58 *APCC* I, nos. 1046, 1080, 1123; *CSPC 1675-1676*, nos. 568, 679, 694, 695, 728, 747, 814, 872-75, 905.

59 BL Egerton 3340, ff. 148-9.

60 See Thornton, *West India Policy*, 145-7, 153, 155-6; Leonard W. Labaree (ed.), *Royal Instructions to British Colonial Governors, 1670-1776* (2 vols, New York, 1967 repr.), *passim* and I, xi. Typical correspondence on these points may be found in *CSPC 1669-1674* nos. 578, 1044, 1183, 1184; *CSPC 1675-1676*, no. 973; Vaughan to Danby, 28 December 1674, BL Egerton 3340, ff. 124-5; Vaughan to Coventry, 28 May 1677, Bath Coventry Mss. LXXV, ff. 180-81; William Lord Willoughby to Thomas Povey, December 1672, BL Egerton 2395, ff. 484-6.

61 *CSPC 1675-1676*, nos. 526, 714, 841, 911, 973, 1084, 1096, 1106, 1116, 1125, 1179; *APCC* I, nos. 1044, 1102; Atkins to Coventry, 20/30 April 1675, Bath Coventry Mss., LXXVI, f. 343; Atkins to Danby, 10 January 1676, BL Egerton 3340, f. 151. The revenue matters were referred to the Lord Treasurer; Danby's papers on the 4 1/2 per cent revenue are at BL Add. Mss. 28089, ff. 141-6.

62 See above, note 61, and Coventry to Atkins, 31 July and 21 November 1676 and 21 November 1677 BL Add. Mss. 25120, ff. 90-91, 96-8, 120-22; and same to same, 16 September 1676, *CSPC 1675-1676*, no. 1033.

63 Lovejoy, *Glorious Revolution in America*, 37-42, 45-9. Moryson's letter (to Sir William Jones, ca. October 1676) is at PRO CO 5/1371, ff. 8-13. See also Coventry to Berkeley, 14 July and 15 November 1676, BL Add. Mss. 25120, ff. 88-9, 94-5, and *CSPC 1675-1676*, nos. 1098, 1123.

64 Coventry to Berkeley, 15 May 1677, CSPC 1677-1680, no. 245. See also nos. 34-8, 67, 239, 242, 244, 247; PRO CO 5/1371, ff. 32-3, 35-51.

65 Vaughan to Coventry. 4 and 29 April 1675, and Lt. Gov. Sir Henry Morgan to Coventry, April 1675 and 6 April 1676, Bath Coventry Mss. LXXIV, ff. 230, 234, 241-2, 269; Coventry to Vaughan, 31 July 1676, BL Add. Mss. 25120, ff. 84-5. *CSPC 1675-1676*, nos. 926, 927.

66 *CSPC 1675-1676*, nos. 916, 957, 958, 966, 972, 976, 987, 988, 994. APCC I, nos. 1089, 1090. Admiralty lawyers also reviewed the case.

67 CSPC 1677-1680, nos. 195, 200, 201, 226, 306, show that the 'great affair' was long in gestation.

68 See note 67 and Vaughan to Coventry, Bath Coventry Mss. LXXIV, ff. 195-203; Vaughan to Sir Robert Southwell, 30 October 1676, *CSPC 1675-1676*, no. 1094. For interpretations of the Poyning's Law episode, see Richard S. Dunn, 'Imperial Pressures on Massachusetts and Jamaica, 1675-1700', in A. G. Olson and R. M. Brown (eds.), *Anglo-American Political Relations, 1660-1775* (New Brunswick, 1970), 52-75 and Lovejoy, *Glorious Revolution in America*, 22-3, 55-7. Webb, *The Governors-General*, 279, argues that troops were sent with Carlisle to 'help him impose . . . the new law code', but it has to be pointed out that Carlisle did not think that he had the power to 'impose' Poyning's Law. See Carlisle to Coventry, 30 June 1679, Bath Coventry Mss. LXXV, ff 314-15. See also Richard Johnson's well-taken caution in *Adjustment to Empire*, 35n.

69 Coventry to Vaughan, 31 July 1676, BL Add. Mss. 25120, ff. 84-5. The law itself is at Bath Coventry Mss. LXXIV, f. 41.

70 *EHD* VIII, 249; and Browning, *Danby*, III, 39, 71, 90, 114; Coventry to Vaughan, 30 July 1675, BL Add. Mss. 25120, ff. 51-4. See also Vaughan to Coventry, 18 May 1675, and Morgan to Coventry, 28 June and 20 September 1675, Bath Coventry Mss. LXXIV, ff. 60, 72, 110-11. Vaughan to Danby, 18 May 1675, BL Egerton 3340, f. 127.

71 Vaughan to Coventry, May 1675, Bath Coventry Mss. LXXIV, f. 60; and Vaughan to Danby, 18 May and 16 August 1675, BL Egerton 3340, ff. 127, 137. Webb's view of the events of the session is hampered by his need to place Vaughan as a parliamentarian. See *The Governors-General*, 265-9.

72 Morgan to Coventry, 6 April 1676, Bath Coventry Mss. LXXIV, ff. 241-2. Martyn's case is copiously documented. See the relevant volumes of *CSPC* (1669-1680) and *APCC* (vol. I), s. v. Martyn, Thomas, and Bath Coventry Mss. LXXIV, ff. 185, 256, 298; LXXV, ff. 239, 264; and BL Egerton 3340, ff. 120-22. For Morgan's inconsistency in these matters, see his letters in Bath Coventry Mss. LXXV, ff. 231-2, 239, 243-4.

73 *CSPC 1677-1680*, nos. 6, 307, 457, 465, 474, 569, 575, 641; Vaughan to Coventry, 28 May 1677, and Carlisle to Lords of Trade, 24 October 1679, Bath Coventry Mss. LXXV, ff. 180-81, 281; Vaughan to Danby, BL Egerton 3340, f. 177. For the crucial parts of Carlisle's instructions, see Labaree (ed.), *Royal Instructions*, I, 45, 52-3, 63, 89-90, 125-26.

74 *APCC* I, no. 1201; *CSPC 1669-1674* no. 1206; Vaughan to Coventry, 3 May 1676 and 6 March 1677, Bath Coventry Mss. LXXV, f. 281, and LXXIV, f. 158.

75 See for instance *CSPC 1669-1674*, no. 1130; *CSPC 1675-1676*, no. 801; Vaughan to Coventry, 3 December 1677, and Carlisle to Coventry, 24 October 1678 and 28 April 1679, Bath Coventry Mss. LXXV, ff. 225, 281, 309.

76 *CSPC 1677-1680*, nos. 720, 1074, 1079; 'Report [of the Lords of Trade] to the king', 4 July 1679, BL Egerton 2395, ff. 583-6; Coventry to Atkins, 25 July 1679, BL Add. Mss. 25120, f. 143.

77 Labaree (ed.), *Royal Instructions*, I, 125. Morgan to Coventry, 8 April 1678, Bath Coventry Mss. LXXV, f. 237.

78 *CSPC 1677-1680*, nos. 206, 485.

79 *CSPC 1677-1680*, nos. 200, 306, 412, 423, 425, 486, 569, 596, 647. The Commissioners of the Customs were also consulted: PRO 30/32/38, f. 227; PRO 30/32/39, f. 2.

80 Dunn offers a different interpretation of Carlisle's role in 'Imperial Pressures on Massachusetts and Jamaica, 1675-1700', 60-61. But the whole body of Carlisle's correspondence over the period suggests that he genuinely tried to get the laws through, at least until late 1679. See for instance Carlisle to Coventry, November 1679, Bath Coventry Mss. LXXV, ff. 336-7.

81 See Carlisle to Coventry, 24 and 29 October 1678, and Carlisle to [?], n. d., Bath Coventry Mss. LXXV, ff. 276, 279-81. The undated letter, in Carlisle's own hand, contains the suggestion for additional powers and asked that 'it be not owned to aris from my advis'.

82 For Virginia, see Lovejoy, *Glorious Revolution*, 53-5.

83 *CSPC 1677-1680*, nos. 1118, 1188, 1199, 1344; Bath Coventry Mss. LXXV, ff. 274, 276. Coventry had already told Carlisle that his commission and instructions enabled him to govern without an assembly. BL Add. Mss. 25120. f. 138.

84 Carlisle to Coventry, 15 September 1679, Bath Coventry Mss. LXXV, ff. 328-30.

85 Thomas Martyn to Coventry, 12 August 1678 and 28 January 1679, Bath Coventry Mss. ff 264, 293; *CSPC 1677-1680*, nos. 1096-8 and 1103-1105. Jamaica's petitions to the king, October and November 1679, are at Bath Coventry Mss. LXXV, ff. 277, 344-51.

86 See letters from Blathwayt to Carlisle, 2 October and 22 December 1679 and 14 January and 5 March 1680, BPCW XXII. The deliberations of the Privy Council and the Lords of Trade are at *CSPC 1677-1680*, nos. 1182, 1227, 1228, 1234, 1238-40, 1259-60, and 1315.

87 The sheer number of citations possible is in itself significant. See for instance Blathwayt to Carlisle, 14 January 1680, BPCW XXII, and *CSPC 1677-1680* nos. 1234, 1227, 1228, 1239, 1259, 1319, 1503, 1509, 1511, 1512, 1538, 1540, 1559, 1561, 1550, 1566.

88 A judgment of the law officers in 1724 confirms this reading of the Jamaica settlement of 1680-1683. See George Chalmers, *Opinions of Eminent Lawyers. . .* (2 vols, London, 1814), I, 204-24. See also *APCC* I, nos. 1277, 1287; *CSPC 1677-1680*, nos. 1016, 1242, 1243, 1258, 1569-72; *CSPC 1681-1685*, no. 227; Blathwayt to Carlisle, 2 September 1680, BPCW XVII, and same to same, 4 July 1680, BPCW XXII.

89 I have used the version of Lynch's speech in the *Narrative of Affairs . . . Jamaica* (London, 1683). See p. 5 for the quoted passage.

90 See Sir Robert Southwell to William Blathwayt, 15 January 1680, on the importance attached to information from any source. *CSPC 1677-1680*, no. 1266. Blathwayt's papers show how seriously he took the advice. See BPCW *passim*, but BPCW XXII has an especially good letter to Carlisle, 4 July 1680, on the importance of information gathering.

91 'A Report to His Majesty from the Lords of the Comittee of Trade touching the Leward Islands, Anno 1677', Bodl. Rawlinson A295, ff. 45-58. Internal evidence fixes the true date in 1678, which is confirmed by *CSPC 1677-1680*, nos. 679. 700-02, and by *APCC* I, no. 1145.

92 See Coventry to Vaughan, 31 July and 21 November 1676, and to Atkins, 21 November 1677, BL Add. Mss. 25120 ff. 90-1 and 120-22.

93 *CSPC 1681-1685*, no. 125.

94 See Carlisle to Danby, 31 July and 12 August 1678, BL Egerton 3340, ff. 175, 177.

95 For the political situation in England, see J. R. Jones, *The First Whigs: the Politics of the Exclusion Crisis, 1678-1683* (London, 1961), 26-37, 48-67. The articles of impeachment are in Browning, (ed.), *EHD* VIII, 198-9; see also Stock (ed.), *Proceedings* I, 401-4. For Carlisle and Coventry, see their letters of 1678 and 1679, particularly in Bath Coventry Mss. LXXV, ff. 274, 328-30, and BL Add. Mss. 25120, f. 138.

96 *CSPC 1681-1685*, no. 1087; Blathwayt to Carlisle, 31 May 1679, BPCW XXII.

97 See for instance *CSPC 1677-1680*, nos. 1028, 1034, 1050, 1074.

Chapter 8

1 Evelyn, *Diary*, 28 February 1671. For information in this and following paragraphs on officeholders' interests in colonization and trade I am indebted to a table compiled by John Rainbolt, late Professor of History at the University of Missouri, when John was a post-graduate student at the University of Wisconsin. Professor David Lovejoy passed the table on to me; I have checked Rainbolt's table against other sources, notably the relevant *Calendars* of state papers, especially *CSPC, CSPD*, and *APCC*, the *DNB*, and company histories such as K. G. Davies, *The Royal African Company*.

2 Stock, *Proceedings* I, 277, 280, 281, 295, 312, 316, 350, 377, 380-82, 398 suggest the pervasiveness of this pattern.

3 Duncombe and Clifford fell out over the revenue bill of 1670. See Stock, *Proceedings* I, 363, 364, 373, and above, Chapter 7.

4 For Shaftesbury and Albemarle, see Haley, *Shaftesbury*, 251-2. For Coventry, see BL Add. Mss. 3828, ff. 105-10.

5 Andrews, *British Committees*, established the convention that there was something like the experimental method involved in setting up means of administration and enforcement, an idea which he extended in other works, most notably the fourth volume of *The Colonial Period*. See also Lawrence Harper's *The English Navigation Laws: A Seventeenth-Century Experiment in Social Engineering*. For a recent corrective, see Sosin, *English America and the Restoration Monarchy of Charles II*.

6 For the route, see the fees and gifts paid by the Carolina proprietors for their first and second charters of 1663 and 1665: South Carolina Historical Society *Collections* V, 55-6. C. M. Andrews, *Guide to the Materials for American History, to 1783, in the Public Record office of Great Britain* (2 vols., Washington, DC, 1912-1914), I, 241-2, lays out the process in more detail.

7 William Blathwayt's correspondence with Virginia provides a sense of how individuals acted as both patron and client. See for instance Blathwayt to Culpeper, 5 April 1680,

BPCW XVII; Blathwayt to Effingham, 3 April and 9 December 1684, BPCW XIV; Blathwayt to Henry Chichely, 30 October 1680, and to Nathaniel Bacon, 22 October 1681 and 4 February 1684, BPCW XIII; Moryson to Blathwayt, *c.* 1680, *CSPC 1677-1680*, no. 1372; and William Byrd I to Blathwayt, 30 December 1687, 21 June 1688, 12 July 1689, and 22 October 1689: Marion Tinling (ed.), *The Correspondence of the Three William Byrds . . . 1684-1776* (2 vols), Charlottesville, 1977), I, 74, 84, 109-10, 112.

8 On the general points, see above, Chapter 6. For the attributions of sponsorship, Maverick's letters in *NYHSC* (1869), 19-57, passim., Evelyn, *Diary*, 5 May 1664, Feiling, *Tory Party*, 140, and Browning (ed.), *EHD* VIII, 242.

9 Webb's *The Governors-General* has generated a good deal of controversy. For a recent re-run, see Richard R. Johnson, 'The Imperial Webb: The Thesis of Garrison Government in Early America Reconsidered' and Webb, 'The Data and Theory of Restoration Empire', *WMQ* 3rd ser., 43 (1986), 408-59.

10 The petitioning careers of several major and minor colonial office-holders have been followed through the indices of the relevant volumes of *CSPC, CSPD,* and *CTB*. Webb, *The Governors-General*, gives governors' military pasts in detail but tends to ignore their civilian experience. For citations concerning Andros, Dutton, and Vaughan, see *CTB* I, 24, 101, 176, 256, 318, 334, 376, 396; *CTB* II, 206, 218, 277, 481, 632, 516; *CTB* III, 211, 248, 1166, 1365; *DNB* I, 411; *DNB* XX, 171-4. See also Fletcher, *Reform in the Provinces*, 20.

11 *NYHSC* (1869), 74-7.

12 *CSPC 1661-1668*, nos. 99, 100, 376, 435, 487, 488 and *CTB* I, 35, 40, 61, 116, 184, 220, 354, 384, 519, 521, 541; see also (for Ross) *DNB* 278-9. Chiffinch's brother Will had a more interesting bedchamber career but apparently minimal connections with the empire: *DNB* IV, 237-9.

13 *CSPC 1661-1668*, nos. 494, 497, 967; *NYCD* III, 47-8.

14 See above, Chapter 6.

15 *DNB* XII, 337-8; BL Egerton 2395, ff. 273-6.

16 *CTB* I, 2; *APCC* I, nos. 557, 558; *CSPC 1574-1660*, 487. See also above, Chapter 6.

17 For Stede, *CSPC 1669-1674*, nos. 187, 189, 634, 840, 927, 948, 1167, 1177, 1238 and, in summary, 1281. For Arlington, Davies, *The Royal African Company*, 63-6.

18 *APCC* I, nos. 878, 881, 977, 978; Cobbett, *Parl. Hist.* IV, 382-3; *CTB* III, 472, 627, 1217; Chandaman, *English Public Revenue*, 352-3. For Wheeler's governorship, see C. S. S. Higham, *The Development of the Leeward Islands under the Restoration, 1660-1688: A Study of the Foundations of the Old Colonial System* (Cambridge, 1921).

19 *APCC* I, nos. 908, 912, 914, 1017, 1086; *CSPC 1669-1674* nos. 1204, 1260. For Martyn's unhappy Jamaica career, see Bath Coventry Mss. LXXIV, ff. 185, 256, 298; ff. LXXV, 239, 264; and BL Egerton 3340, ff. 120-22.

20 Modyford's alliance with the privateers can be traced through *CSPC 1661-1668*, nos. 629-35, 664, 739, 767, 786, 942, 976, 1085, 1264, 1838, 1863. Webb, *Governors-General*, 235-5, takes a different view. For a suggestive alternative, see Nuala Zahedia, 'Trade, Plunder, and Economic Development in Early Jamaica, 1655-1689', *Economic History Review* 2nd ser., 39 (1986), 205-22.

21 Modyford brazenly summarized his strategy in his letter to the Spanish ambassador in London, 15 June 1669, *CSPC 1669-1674*, no. 74; see also *ibid.,* 103, 114, 129, and *CSPC 1661-1668*, nos. 1652, 1850, 1851. In October 1668, HMS Oxford arrived in Jamaica, 'sent by the king to countenance the war with the Spaniards'. William Beeston's Journal, in *Interesting Tracts*, 286.

22 Sir James Modyford[?] to Thomas Lynch, 18 March 1670, *CSPC 1669-1674*, no. 162. See also ibid., nos. 172, 227, 237, 293, 310, 504, 608; BL Egerton 3340, ff. 110-15.

23 See Modyford to Shaftesbury, 6 July 1670, *CSPC 1669-1674*, no. 216. For Shaftesbury's attitudes, see a 1667 memo at PRO 30/24/49, ff. 31-3; and Haley, *Shaftesbury*, 251-2, 284.

24 See above, Chapter 7.

25 See above Chapter 7.

26 Dunn, *Puritans and Yankees*, 130-31 and Sir Peter Colleton to John Locke, 12 August 1673, PRO CO 30/24/49, ff. 14-15. The Royal Society connection deserves fuller study.

27 For the charter, see *NYCD* II, 295-8. See also *NYCD* III, 215-18 and Andrews, *Colonial Period* II, 92-107.

28 *NYCD* II, 250-53; III, 67-71; XIV, 559.

29 *NYCD* XIV, 564-5. Five mainly Dutch towns at the western end of Long Island were also asked to send deputies.

30 *NYCD* II, 252; XIV, 564. See also John Cox, Jr, *Oyster Bay Town Records* (8 vols, New York, 1916-1940), I, 39, for an earlier proclamation from the royal commissioners.

31 Robert C. Ritchie, *The Duke's Province* (Chapel Hill, 1977), 33-8; *NYCD* III, 91; XIV, 564-6; *CSPC 1661-1668*, no. 951. The Duke's Laws are in *The Colonial Laws of New York from the Year 1664* . . . (5 vols., Albany, 1894-6), I, 6-71. For later amendments and an important 'Explication' by Nicolls, see *ibid*., I, 73-82, 88-9.

32 Ritchie, *The Duke's Province*, 50-51. See also *NYCD* III, 230-31, and XIV, 560, 562, 568, 570-72, 582, 588-9, 600-602, 681-5; Josephine C. Frost (ed.), *Records of the Town of Jamaica* . . . *1656-1751* (3 vols, Brooklyn, 1914) I, 37-8; J. W. Case (ed.), *Southold Town Records* (2 vols, Southold, 1882-84), I, 246-7. For Maine and New Hampshire during the Interregnum, see above, Chapter 4.

33 Nicolls to Clarendon, 30 July 1665, *NYHSC* (1869), 74-7; Ritchie, *The Duke's Province*, 52-3; *NYCD* III, 585-6, 590; XIV, 758-61.

34 The instructions for and correspondence with Edmund Andros, governor from 1674 to 1680, provide good examples of this sort of direction. See *NYCD* III, 216, 218, 230-31, 233, 237.

35 Andrews, *Colonial Period*, III, 138-40.

36 On the Duke's motives see Andrews, *Colonial Period* III, 96-7; Ritchie, *The Duke's Province*, 48-9; F. C. Turner, *James II* (London, 1948), 60-64. Also useful is John C. Miller, *James II: A Study in Kingship* (Hove, 1978). BL Egerton 3340, f. 108 and Beer, *Old Colonial System* I, 119, show that New York's financial difficulties were not entirely James's fault. On the Connecticut boundary, see *NYCD* III, 106; XIV, 561.

37 The New England Council of the 1620s made grants of territory and government, but it had been commissioned to do so by James I. In 1643 the Warwick Committee was given similar powers by parliament, but exercised them with great caution. See above, Chapters 2 and 3.

38 See Andrews, *Colonial Period*, III, 138-9 and note for a discussion of the legal point. Charles confirmed the political aspect of the grant in a letter to Sir John Berry, 9 December 1672, BL Harleian 7001, f. 199.

39 NYHS *Collections* (1869), 74-7; *NYCD* III, 104-6; *New Jersey Archives* I, 14-19, 43-6.

40 Ritchie, *The Duke's Province*, 100-107; *NYCD* III, 216-19, and XIV, 758-61.

41 On New York's trade problems generally, see *NYCD* III, 69-70, 91, 104-5, 167-8. For governors' attitudes towards the navigation system, see *ibid*. 163-7, 175-8, 236-8; V. H. Paltsits (ed.), *Minutes of the Executive Council of New York* (2 vols, Albany, 1910), I, 194-5; and Ritchie, *The Duke's Province*, 60-66.

42 *NYCD* III, 105, 114; XIV, 631-2; Ritchie, *The Duke's Province*, 98-100; Lawrence Leder, *Robert Livingston, 1654-1728, and the Politics of Colonial New York* (Chapel Hill, 1961), 37-8.

43 Ritchie, *The Duke's Province*, 104; *NYCD* III, 219.

44 Werden to Andros, 31 January 1676, *NYCD* III, 238. Lovelace and his Council thought it 'not equitable [that] any small creek or cove should have greater privileges than the head city of the Government': *NYCD* XIV, 631-2.

45 *NYCD* III, 236, 239, 240; Sir John Werden to [Sir Henry Coventry?], *Docs. Col. New Jersey*, I, 289-91; Andros to William Blathwayt, 18 May 1680, BPCW III; and *Connecticut Records* II, 569-74, 578-86.

46 In 1680, Jones was being weaned from the radical exclusionists; Jones, *The First Whigs*, 151-2. See also Ritchie, *The Duke's Province*, 166-7; *NYCD* III, 284-7.

47 See official and private correspondence in Richard S. Dunn and Mary Maples Dunn, (eds.), *Papers of William Penn*, (4 vols, in progress, Philadelphia, 1981-87) II, 43, 44, 115-17; *NYCD* III, 284-7. See also Andrews, *Colonial Period* III, 279-85, 292-6.

48 *NYCD* III, 282; Ritchie, *The Duke's Province*, 115, 122-3; Lewin was also connected with Boston merchants Wait Winthrop and Thomas Deane: *CSPC 1677-1680* no. 1537.

49 *NYCD* III, 246, 287-9; *NYHSC* (1912), 8-15.

50 Lovejoy, *Glorious Revolution in America*, 107-12, 115-19.

51 Instructions for Governor Dongan, 27 January 1683, *NYCD* III, 331-4. James's instructions to customs collector Lucas Santen are also useful: *ibid*. 335-6.

52 Lovejoy, *Glorious Revolution*, 171-2, and Ritchie, *The Duke's Province*, 177-9. See also 'Observations on the Charter of New York' and Duke of York to Dongan, 26 August 1684, *NYCD* III, 348-9, 357-9; *CSPC 1681-1685*, no. 1885.

53 Werden wrote that the duke intended to grant the colony 'equall priviledges, in chooseing an Assembly &c as the other English plantations in America have ... upon the supposition that the Inhabitants will agree to rayse money ...' Werden to Brockholls, 11 February 1682. See also William Penn to Blathwayt, 21 November 1682, BPCW VII and *PWP* II, 311. For evidence that previous governors were aware of the usefulness of assemblies in this respect, see *NYCD* II, 583-4; III, 188, 230-31, 235; XIV, 574, 580-81.

54 'Proposals of Severall Gentlemen of Barbados', [Duke of Albemarle?] to Sir Thomas Modyford, August and September 1663, and Lords Proprietors to [the Barbadian Adventurers?], 11 January 1665, *SCHSC* V, 10-12, 16-18, 53; *North Carolina Records*, I, 36-42, 46-8, 58-9; Samuel Farmer et al. to the Carolina Proprietors, 20 March 1665, PRO 30/24/49, ff. 8-9.

55 E. E. Parker (ed.), *North Carolina Charters and Constitutions* (Raleigh, 1963), 109-27.

56 For these requirements of the Fundamental Constitutions, see especially articles 3, 9, 28, 29, 35, 38, 39, 41, 43, 44, and 45. I have used the copy reproducing the original editing in the *Thirty-third Report* of the Deputy Keeper of the PRO (London, 1857), 258-69.

57 Andrews, *Colonial Perio*d III, 194-206, 212-20. M. Eugene Sirmans, Colonial *South Carolina: a Political History, 1663-1763* (Chapel Hill, 1966), 9-17, and Converse D. Clowse, *Economic Beginnings in Colonial South Carolina,*19-22, have useful discussions of the Fundamentals, despite Clowse's insistence on seeing the document as 'feudalistic'.

58 For references to the Fundamentals as a guide to action, see for instance *CSPC 1669-1674*, no. 86; *CSPC 1685-1688*, no. 1162. On investment, see *CSPC 1669-1674*, nos. 54, 55; PRO 30/24/48, f. 13; Haley, *Shaftesbury*, 228-35.

59. Fundamental Constitutions, articles 28, 29, 30, 50, 51, 71.

60 It is important that not all the proprietors' powers under the Fundamentals were to transfer to their heirs, unless the latter removed to the colony. Shaftesbury's concern that the Fundamentals should protect the smallholder is made clear in his letters to the colony in 1670, 1671, and 1672, PRO 30/24/48, pt. 2, ff. 141, 176-7, 192-3.

61 Shaftesbury to the Governor and Council at Charles Town, 10 June 1675, PRO 30/24/48, pt. 2, ff. 215-16. For the poor, see correspondence between Shaftesbury and John West on the subject of the proprietors' store house arrangements, *loc. cit., passim.*

62 Shaftesbury to West, 16 December 1671, *North Carolina Records* I, 211.

63 Shaftesbury to Yeamans and same to the Council, both dated 20 June 1672, PRO 30/24/48, pt. 2, ff. 192-5. See also PRO 30/24/48, pt. 3, f. 11.

64 Shaftesbury to Wentworth, 17 May 1675, PRO 30/24/49, f. 62.

65 Shaftesbury to Sir Peter Colleton, 1672, PRO 30/24/48, pt. 2, ff. 198-9.

66 Fundamental Constitutions, articles 11, 13, 15, 20. Manorial independence was limited only by the magistrates' obligation to follow English law and by the manorial title's connection with the land itself. Once the property relationship was dissolved the manorial satrapy ceased utterly to exist. Yeamans and others objected to the fragility of manorial inheritances under this system, and it was subsequently modified, at least for landgraves. See Shaftesbury to Yeamans, 10 April 1671, PRO 30/24/48, pt. 2, ff. 176-7.

67 The Palatine and other proprietorial courts had considerable powers over towns, including the appointment of mayors. See Fundamental Constitutions, articles 41, 44, 92; *CSPC 1669-1674*, nos. 86, 89, 514; Shaftesbury to Yeamans, 18 September 1671, PRO 30/24/48, pt. 2, ff. 185-7; *North Carolina Records* I, 36-9; PRO 30/24/49, ff. 8-9.

68 Above, Chapters 2, 4, and 7. See also E. E. Rich, 'The First Earl of Shaftesbury's Colonial

Policy', *Transactions of the Royal Historical Society* 5th ser., 7 (1957), 47-70.
69 Instructions to the governor and council of Albemarle County, 21 November 1676, *North Carolina Records* I, 230-31.
70 Shaftesbury to Yeamans, 10 April 1671, PRO 30/24/48, pt. 2, ff. 176-7; Temporary Laws of Carolina, 1671-1672, W. K. Kavenagh, (ed.), *Foundations of Colonial America* (3 vols, New York, 1973), III, 1924-30; *CSPC 1669-1674*, nos. 94, 140, 515, 1307; Shaftesbury to West, 16 December 1671, *North Carolina Records* I, 211.
71 *Description du Pays nomme Carolina* (London[?], 1678), printed pamphlet in PRO 30/24/48, pt. 2, ff. 192-5.
72 See Lord Chancellor Shaftesbury's speech in the Exchequer investing Baron Thurland, 24 January 1673, printed pamphlet at PRO 30/24/5/242/2. Shaftesbury's speech in the Lords on the case of *Shirley v. Fagg* is quoted extensively in Haley, *Shaftesbury*, 393-6. For Shaftesbury's role in the Exclusion crisis, see especially Jones, *The First Whigs, passim*, and Haley, *Shaftesbury*, 498-683.

Chapter 9

1 David Ogg, *England in the Reigns of James II and William III* (Oxford, 1963, 143-62; Chandaman, *English Public Revenue*, 20-1, 48, 155-6, 256-61, 360-61.
2 See especially Johnson, *Adjustment to Empire*; J. R. Jones, *The First Whigs* and *The Revolution of 1688 in England* (London, 1972); Lovejoy, *Glorious Revolution*; Miller, *Popery and Politics in England, 1660-1688*; Plumb, *Origins of Political Stability*; Sosin, *English America and the Revolution of 1688*; G. S. Holmes, *British Politics in the Age of Anne* (London, 1967); and Western, *Monarchy and Revolution*.
3 Among such historians, see Sosin's *English America and the Revolution of 1688*; Lois Green Carr and David William Jordan, *Maryland's Revolution of Government, 1689-1692* (Ithaca, 1974); and Thomas J. Archdeacon, *New York City, 1664-1710: Conquest and Change* (Ithaca, 1976). Historians have yet to take account of Ian K. Steele's reconstruction of what colonists knew of events in England in 1688-89, and when they knew it: *The English Atlantic, 1675-1740: an Exploration of Communication and Community* (Oxford, 1986), 94-110; see especially his remarks at 108-10.
4 Jones, *The First Whigs*, 183-217; Western, *Monarchy and Revolution*, 19-41.
5 Western, *Monarchy and Revolution*, 31.
6 Olson, 'William Penn, Parliament, and Proprietary Government', 183-95; Feiling, *Tory Party*, 482, 492-3; Tim Harris, *London Crowds in the Reign of Charles II: Propaganda and Politics from the Restoration until the Exclusion Crisis* (Cambridge, 1987), 65-8, 130-55.
7 Plumb, *Origins of Political Stability*, 11-14. See also Chandaman, *English Public Revenue*, 69-76, 118-19, 128; Stephen S. Webb, 'William Blathwayt, Imperial Fixer: From Popish Plot to Glorious Revolution', *WMQ* 3rd ser., 25 (1968), 3-21, and 'William Blathwayt, Imperial Fixer: Muddling Through to Empire, 1689-1717', *WMQ* 3rd ser., 26, (1969), 373-415.
8 Webb, 'William Blathwayt, Imperial Fixer', *passim*.
9 *CSPC 1685-1688*, nos. 563, 800, 822, 1143. Wertenbaker, *Virginia under the Stuarts*, 248-50, offers a different conclusion.
10 Johnson, *Adjustment to Empire*, 165-241.
11 On these points, see above, Chapters 7 and 8. See also *CSPC 1669-1674*, nos. 692, 712; *CSPC 1675-1676*, no. 987; *CSPC 1681-1685*, no. 1087; Blathwayt to Carlisle, 31 May 1679, BPCW XXII; and Lovejoy, *Glorious Revolution in America*, 166-9.
12 Andrews, *Colonial Period* IV, 338-67; Colin Brooks, 'Projecting, Political Arithmetic, and the Act of 1695', *EHR* 97 (1982), 31-53; R. Davis, 'The Rise of Protection in England, 1669-1786', *Economic History Review* 2nd ser., 19 (1966), 306-17; Peter Laslett, 'John Locke, The Great Recoinage, and the Origins of the Board of Trade, 1695-1698', and

Michael G. Hall, 'The House of Lords, Edward Randolph, and the Navigation Act of 1696', *WMQ* 3rd ser., 14 (1957), 370-402 and 494-515.

13 Cotton Mather, *Parentator: Memoirs of . . . Increase Mather . . .* (Boston, 1724), in *Andros Tracts* III, 154.

14 G. M. Waller, *Samuel Vetch, Colonial Enterpriser* (Chapel Hill, 1960); Johnson, *Adjustment to Empire*, 312, 375-9.

15 P. S. Haffenden, 'The Crown and the Colonial Charters, 1675-1688', parts 1 and 2, *WMQ* 3d ser., 15 (1958), 397-411, 452-66. Western states the case succinctly in *Monarchy and Revolution*, 154-5.

16 Chandaman, *English Public Revenue*, 247-55, 357-63.

17 Western, *Monarchy and Revolution*, 102-5, 242-5; for the colonies, see Beer, *Old Colonial System* I, 205-23.

18 Johnson, *Adjustment to Empire*, esp. 22-36, 50-2.

19 Johnson, *Adjustment to Empire*, 64.

20 Glassey, *Justices of the Peace*, 32-62. See also Western, *Monarchy and Revolution*, 48-61; J. P. Kenyon, *Robert Spencer, Earl of Sunderland, 1641-1702* (London, 1958), 74-110; and G. W. Keeton, *Lord Chancellor Jeffreys and the Stuart Cause* (London, 1965), 186-248.

21 Miller, *Popery and Politics*, 209, 218-19; Western, *Monarchy and Revolution*, 48-54, 79-81, 210-25; Jones, *Revolution of 1668*, 137; Glassey, *Justices of the Peace, 1675-1720*, 32-99; Ogg, *James II and William III*, 122-32.

22 Western, *Monarchy and Revolution*, 69-77; John Miller, 'The Crown and the Borough Charters in the Reign of Charles II'; M. A. Mullett, '"To Dwell together in Unity": The Search for Agreement in Preston Politics, 1660-1690' and 'The Politics of Liverpool, 1660-1688', *Transactions of the Historic Society of Lancashire and Cheshire* 124 (1973), 31-56, and 125 (1975), 61-81.

23 It is difficult to assess the significance of the fact that several of the colonial proprietors, including William Penn, enjoyed good personal or political relations with James. For Penn, see J. R. Jones's interesting 'A Representative of the Alternative Society of Restoration England?', in Mary Maples Dunn and Richard S. Dunn, *The World of William Penn* (Philadelphia, 1986), 55-69. Even so, the proprietaries were under pressure during these years. The Carolina proprietors, for instance, anxiously assured King James that 'all ill men are put out of office' in their colony. *CSPC 1685-1688*, no. 1457.

24 The standard account is Michael G. Hall, *Edward Randolph and the American Colonies, 1676-1703* (Chapel Hill, 1961).

25 For the first visit, see *Randolph Papers*, II, 268-70, 273-4, 280-84, 292; III, 2-5, 19-31, 38-43; VI, 75-7; Randolph to Danby, 5 March 1676, BL Egerton 3340, f. 155; and *APCC* I, no. 1143. For the second visit, in 1681-82, see *Randolph Papers* III, 70-76, 89-91, 95-9, 109-10; VI, 84-94, 99-112.

26 Randolph to Secretary of State Jenkins, 30 April 1681, *Randolph Papers* VI, 89-94; *CSPC 1681-1685*, nos. 82, 88. As early as 1676, Randolph urged the king to act firmly because he would find support in New England: *Randolph Papers* II, 225-59.

27 Western, *Monarchy and Revolution*, 72-5; Mullett, *Crown and Corporations*, 44, 45n, 46, 48-50; Evans, *Seventeenth-Century Norwich*, 269-89. See also Johnson, Adjustment to Empire, 31-2 and note 52 and *Randolph Papers* III, 110-13.

28 Randolph's June 1682 letters to Secretary Jenkins and the second Earl of Clarendon are typical: *Randolph Papers* III, 154-63. See also Randolph to Bradstreet, 21 September 1682, *CSPC 1681-1685*, no. 698; Randolph to Blathwayt, 3 February 1683, *Randolph Papers* VI, 135-6; and, for a different view of Moody's sermon, Robert Mason to Blathwayt, 22 March 1683, BPCW XII.

29 Western, *Monarchy and Revolution*, 47-52, 72-6; Jones, *Revolution of 1688*, 40-50, 138-46; Glassey, *Justices of the Peace*, 57-62; Evans, *Seventeenth-Century Norwich*, 287-91; Mullett, 'Preston Politics, 71-6 and 'Conflicts, Politics, and Elections in Lancaster, 1660-1668', *Northern History* 19 (1983), 73-4; Sir John Reresby, *Memoirs* (London, 1875), 255; Cranfield to Blathwayt, 1 December 1682 and 10 January 1683, *Randolph Papers* VI, 120-24, 130-33.

30 For the 'moderates', see above, Chapter 6, and Dunn, *Puritans and Yankees*, 212-28; Bailyn, *New England Merchants*, 92-111, 154-67; Lewis, 'Land Speculation and the Dudley Council of 1686'; and Foster, *Their Solitary Way*, Appendices C and D.

31 Cranfield to Blathwayt, 20 February and 19 June 1683, BPCW I, 20 October 1684, BPCW II, and 16 January 1684, *Randolph Papers* VI, 153-5; Randolph to Blathwayt, 14 September 1682, *ibid*. VI, 127-8; Randolph to Commissioners of Customs, 30 December 1682, *ibid*. III, 216-19.

32 *CSPC 1681-1685*, nos. 128, 129, 312, 313, 1177; *CSPC 1689-1692, Addenda*, no. 2077; *APCC* II, no. 64.

33 Narcissus Luttrell, *A Brief Historical Relation of State Affairs . . .* (6 vols., Oxford, 1847) I, 83-4, 87-8, 96-8, 102-3, 105-9; Sharpe, *London and the Kingdom* II, 472-6; Jennifer Levin, *The Charter Controversy in the City of London, 1660-1688, and its Consequences* (London, 1969), 20-6; *CSPC 1681-1685*, no. 161; Nathaniel Mather to Increase Mather, 26 March 1684, *MHSC* 4th ser., VIII, 55; *Maryland Archives* XVII, 334.

34 *Randolph Papers* III, 236-50, especially the king's Declaration of 20 July 1683. See also Randolph's letters of early 1683 to governors Hinckley and Bradstreet, *ibid*., 220-27. His bills are at *CSPC 1681-85*, nos. 1101, 1121.

35 M. G. Hall, 'Randolph, Dudley, and the Massachusetts Moderates of 1683', *NEQ* 29 (1956), 513-16; Randolph to Southwell, 19 August 1683, *Randolph Papers* III, 262-5; and *CSPC 1685-1688, Addenda*, no. 2127.

36 Levin, *The Charter Controversy in . . . London*, 21-30; Sharpe, *London and the Kingdom* II, 494-500; Luttrell, *Historical Relation* I, 261-2, 276-7; Reresby, *Memoirs*, 254-5; Western, *Monarchy and Revolution*, 74-6.

37 *Randolph Papers* III, 227-8, 248-9 and VI, 146-8, for Thomas Danforth to Randolph, 2 April 1683, Randolph to Sir Leoline Jenkins, 26 July 1683, and Randolph to Blathwayt, 3 September 1683; Randolph to Lord Keeper, 11 July 1683, *CSPC 1681-1685* no. 1145.

38 Randolph to Hinckley, 29 October 1683, and to Jenkins, 14 February 1684, and Governor and Magistrates of Massachusetts to Jenkins, 7 December 1683, *Randolph Papers* III, 265-7, 271-9; *Massachusetts Records* V, 420-25.

39 Dudley to Blathwayt, 9 December 1683 and Bulkeley to same, 7 December 1683, BPCW IV; *Randolph Papers* III, 273-4, 283-5, 309-11; Dudley to Jenkins, 7 May 1684, *CSPC 1681-1685*, no. 1670; Cranfield to Blathwayt, 16 January 1684, *Randolph Papers* VI, 153-5; same to same, 20 October 1684, BPCW XII; Dyer to Blathwayt, 17 September 1684 and 5 March 1685, BPCW IV.

40 *Randolph Papers* VI, 156-60, 162-3.

41 *Randolph Papers* III, 297-9, 307. On 21 June 1684, Attorney General Sawyer moved to set aside execution should the colony submit by Michaelmas term.

42 These events may be followed through *Randolph Papers* III, 324-6, 332-5; VI, 156-60, 162-3; and *CSPC 1681-1685*, no. 2026.

43 That this decision represented a drastic shift in English thinking is recognized by both Johnson, *Adjustment to Empire*, 47-50, 52-4, 63, and by Lovejoy, *Glorious Revolution in America*, 169-70, although both err in assuming that royal government had been the crown's aim for some time before late 1684.

44 See above, notes 33 and 36, and Keeton, *Lord Chancellor Jeffreys*, 205-7.

45 Helen C. Foxcroft, *The Life and Letters of Sir George Savile, First Marquis of Halifax* (2 vols, London, 1898), I. 233-435, passim. See also Blathwayt to Lord Effingham, 28 July 1684, and Halifax's 'Letter to a Dissenter (c. 1687), in J. P. Kenyon (ed.), *Halifax: Complete Works* (London, 1969), 105-17.

46 Foxcroft, *Halifax*, I, 420-27; Reresby, *Memoirs*, 265-6, 268-72, 275-6, 285-7, 289, 293-4, 308-9; S. W. Singer, (ed.), *The Correspondence of Henry Hyde, Earl of Clarendon, and . . . Laurence Hyde, Earl of Rochester . . .* (2 vols, London, 1828), I, 96-103; and Burnet, *History*, II, 445, 459-61.

47 Blathwayt's letters to Effingham, 28 July and 9 December 1684, BPCW XIV; Barillon to Louis XIV, 28 November 1684, and Louis to Barillon, 3 December 1684, in Charles James Fox, *A History of the Early Part of the Reign of James the Second . . .* (London, 1808), Appendix, vii-ix; Foxcroft, *Halifax*, I, 428 and note.

48 Political thoughts and reflections (n. d.), In *Halifax: Complete Works*, 198.
49 *Trimmer, Complete Works*, 51-3, 62-3, 66, 100-101.
50 Blathwayt to Effingham, 9 December 1684, and Effingham to Blathwayt, 20 March 1685, BPCW XIV.
51 *Trimmer, Complete Works*, 100.
52 Governor and Council of Connecticut to President and Council of New England, 4 August 1686, *Connecticut Records* III, 364-5; Gershom Bulkeley, *The Peoples Right to Election* . . . (Philadelphia, 1689, reprinted in *Andros Tracts* III), 85-109; Gershom Bulkeley, 'Will and Doom . . . ', printed in *CHSC* III, 69-269. For the political behavior of the 'moderates' during the Dominion period, see Lovejoy, *Glorious Revolution*, 181-95; Dunn, *Puritans and Yankees*, 238-52.
53 See especially the efforts of John Allyn, late Secretary of Connecticut under the charter regime: *Connecticut Records* III, especially 395-8, 436-47, 422-35.
54 Konig, *Law and Society in Puritan Massachusetts*, 159-65.
55 McIlwaine (ed.), *Journals . . . 1659/60-1693*, 228-30, 243, 270, 277-8; Lovejoy, *Glorious Revolution*, 63-4.
56 Effingham to Blathwayt, 13 May 1685, BPCW XIV; Nathaniel Bacon to Blathwayt, 26 August 1682, BPCW XIII; and Nicholas Spencer to Sir Leoline Jenkins, 12 August 1682, *CSPC 1681-1685*, no. 652.
57 For an idea of what these posts might be worth, see William Fitzhugh to Lord Culpeper, 8 January 1683, and same to Captain Henry Fitzhugh, 5 April 1687, *William Fitzhugh and His Chesapeake World, 1676-1701*, ed. R. B. Davis (Chapel Hill, 1963), 134-5, 215-16.
58 Ludwell may be followed through the indices of *CSPC 1681-1685, 1685-1688*, and *1689-1692*. For his harassment of Effingham after 1689, see Stock, (ed.), *Proceedings* II, 5-6, 5n, and *CSPC 1689-1692* nos. 164, 168, 232, 412, 447, 460, 462, 578, 604.
59 For instance *CSPC 1685-1688*, nos. 742, 783, 1260, 1278, 1404, 1527, 1528 and Blathwayt to [Nathaniel Bacon, Sr. ?], 17 October 1682, BPCW; Lovejoy, *Glorious Revolution*, 53-69; Webb, *The Governors-General*, 359-435; and Rainbolt, *From Prescription to Persuasion*, 110-41.
60 Dunn, *Sugar and Slaves*, 101-3.
61 Reresby, *Memoirs*, 348-50, 368, 377, 386-9, 392-3, 398-400. See also *Clarendon Correspondence* I, 575-6.
62 For these points, see above, Chapters 2, 4, and 6.
63 Lovejoy, *Glorious Revolution*, must be regarded as definitive on this point.
64 *The Journal of Madame Knight*, ed. Malcolm Freiburg (Boston, 1971), *passim* and 8, 13; Samuel Sewall, *Phaenomenon quaedam apocalyptica* (Boston, 1697), in Miller and Johnson, eds., *The Puritans*, I, 376-7.
65 For good portraits of this sort of provincialism, see Perry Miller, *From Colony to Province*; Dunn, *Puritans and Yankees*, 191-211; and Breen, *The Character of the Good Ruler*, 180-239.
66 Dunn, *Sugar and Slaves*, 98-116, 287-99; *CSPC 1681-1685*, no. 1292; *CSPC 1685-1688*, no. 679, 1876. III; *CSPC 1689-1692*, no. 158. C. and R. Bridenbaugh, *No Peace Beyond the Line*, 371, note that the 'most impressive developments in [West Indian] architecture took place in Jamaica after 1700'.
67 David W. Jordan, 'Political Stability and the Emergence of a Native Elite in Maryland', and Carole Shammas, 'English-Born and Creole Elites in Turn-of-the-Century Virginia', both in Tate and Ammerman (eds.), *The Chesapeake in the Seventeenth Century*, 243-96; John Rainbolt, 'The Alteration in the Relationship between Leadership and Constituents in Virginia, 1660 to 1720', *WMQ* 3rd ser., 27 (1970), 428-34; Morgan, *American Slavery, American Freedom*, 271-362; and Alan Kulikoff, *Tobacco and Slaves: The Development of Southern Cultures in the Chesapeake, 1680-1800* (Chapel Hill, 1986) 30-44.
68 Customs Commissioners to Lords of Trade and Plantations, 10 January 1681, *CSPC 1681-1685*, no. 3; Nicholas Spencer to Secretary of State Sir Leoline Jenkins, 25 March 1683, *CSPC 1681-1685*, no. 1018.
69 Davis (ed.), *William Fitzhugh*, 12-39 and *passim*, especially Fitzhugh to Nicholas

Hayward, 30 January 1687, 201-08; William Byrd I's letters to his merchant contacts are also useful; Tinling (ed.), *The Correspondence of the Three William Byrds*, I, 8-163, *passim*.

70 Rainbolt, 'Leadership and Constituents', 411-34, and *From Prescription to Persuasion*, 117-24; Morgan, *American Slavery, American Freedom*, 338-87.
71 See letters by Lords Vaughan and Carlisle, BL Egerton 3340, f. 177, and Bath Coventry Mss. LXXIV, f. 60; LXXV, ff. 225, 279-80; *CSPC 1677-1680*, no. 815; 'Memorial concerning the Plantation trade from Lord Culpeper', BL Add. Mss. 28079, ff. 84-5; and Hall, 'Edward Randolph, Joseph Dudley, and the Massachusetts Moderates'.
72 See for instance Governor Kendall (of Barbados) to the Lords of Trade and Plantations, 4 April and 4 July 1691, *CSPC 1689-1692*, no. 1384, 1621.
73 For Pynchon, see Stephen Innes's provocative discussion of the implications of the 1680s in *Labor in a New Land*, 151-70.
74 Kenneth A. Lockridge and Alan Kreider, 'The Evolution of Massachusetts Town Government, 1640-1740', *WMQ* 3rd ser., 23 (1966), 549-74; Michael Zuckerman, 'The Social Context of Democracy in Massachusetts', *WMQ* 3rd ser., 25 (1968), 523-44.
75 Petitions from Lynn, Watertown, Newbury, Cambridge, Dunstable, Andover, Dorchester, Beverly, and Boxford (sic) all declared explicitly for widening the suffrage. Other towns, whether for or against reassumption of the charter, did not deliver a clear opinion on the matter. See Mass. Arch. CVII, ff. 8, 8a, 14, 14a, 15, 16, 17, 17a, 19, 20, 24b, 37, 37b, 38a, 39a, 39b, 40a, 41, 43, 43a, 43b, 44, 44b, 45, 45a, 46a, 47, 49, 49a, 50. At f. 52 *et seq.* there is a census of the towns' views.
76 The question of whether 1689 and after saw radical changes in leadership *personnel* is a difficult one. See Innes, *Labor in a New Land*, 157-8 and Johnson, *Adjustment to Empire*, 102-3, 114-16, for the gist of disagreement on this matter.
77 Morgan, *American Slavery, American Freedom* and, more particularly, 'Slavery and Freedom: The American Paradox', *JAH* 39 (1973).
78 Lewis, 'A Revolutionary Tradition, 1689-1774', 424-38; David S. Lovejoy, 'Two American Revolutions, 1689 and 1776', in Pocock (ed.), *Three British Revolutions*, 244-62; Jack P. Greene, *The Quest for Power: The Lower Houses of Assembly in the Southern Royal Colonies, 1689-1776* (Chapel Hill, 1963).
79 Lords Proprietors to the Grand Council of South Carolina, 14 May 1691, *CSPC 1689-1692*, no. 1499.

INDEX

Admiralty Commission, 176, 179
African Company, Royal, 112, 127-8, 180, 192, 197, 222, 239
agriculture, *see under economy*
Albany, 202, 205, 215
Albemarle, Christopher Monck, second Duke, 192, 239
Albemarle, George Monck, first Duke, 129, 144, 191, 198-9
   Carolina proprietor, 125, 209
   patronage and, 143-4, 198-9
   Restoration and, 104-5
   Treasury Commissioner, 166
Allin, John, *Animadversions on the Antisynodalia Americana*, 156-7
America, 5, 7
   English views of, 8-10, 15-16
Anabaptists, 82
Andrews, C. M., 2, 70
Andros, Sir Edmund, 195, 205-9, 222, 237, 245-6
Anglesey, Arthur Annesley, Earl of, 104, 148
Anne, Queen, 222, 223
Antiqua, *see* Leeward Islands
Appleby, Joyce, 171
architecture, 1, 241-2
Arlington, Sir Henry Bennett, Earl of, 113, 128-9, 161-5, 188, 204
   Jamaica and, 163-4, 198-9
   patronage and, 191, 194, 197, 198-9
army, in England, 45
   empire and, 3, 9-11, 21, 139-41, 191, 194-5, 197, 224, 238
army debates, *see* Putney debates
Ashley, Baron, *see* Shaftesbury, first Earl of
Ashton, Henry, 75
assemblies, colonial, 11-12, 23, 24, 29, 74, 93-5, 180-7, 189, 202, 208-9, 209 n. 53, 212, 214-16, 233-6, 238, 239, 242-4
   see also government *and under separate colonies*
assessments, *see* revenue and taxation
Atherton Company, 134, 196, 228
Atkins, Sir Jonathan, 180-1, 189
autocracy, limitations of, 17-8, 203, 215, 218, 245-6
autonomy and dependence, 2, 4, 18, 28, 73-5, 83-6, 89-92, 98-102, 124-5, 130-1,

134-5, 223-4, 240-6
Ayscue, Sir George, 89, 97-8

Bacon Sir Francis, 15, 21, 24
Bacon, Nathaniel, 239, 242
Bacon, Nathaniel, Sr., 238
Bacon's Rebellion, *see* Virginia
Badcock, Paul, 177
Badcocke, Nicholas, 122
Bahamas, 103, 137, 211
Baltimore, Cecilius Calvert, second Baron, 76, 86-7, 96-7, 126, 191
   English civil war and, 49-50, 76, 87
   Restoration and, 97, 136-7
   see also Maryland
Baltimore, Charles Calvert, third Baron, 174, 191, 230
   see also Maryland
Baltimore, Sir George Calvert, first Baron, 16, 29, 46
   see also Maryland
Bank of England, 168, 223
Barbados, 33-4, 36, 65-6, 68, 86-91, 97, 98-100, 124-6, 180-1, 187, 197, 224, 239, 241
   census of 1680, 241
   English civil war and, 49-50, 60, 63-6, 73-8
   4$^{1}/_{2}$ per cent revenue in, 145-7, 180
   rebellion in (1650), 60-1, 86-91
   regicide and, 86-91
   Restoration in, 133, 142-6, 160
   social structure in, 36, 241
   see also Caribbees *and* Leeward Islands
Barillon, Paul, 235
Bell, Philip, 77-8
Bellingham, Richard, 158-9
Bennett, Richard, 76, 92, 95
Berkeley, George Lord, and elephant, 177
Berkeley, John Lord, 139, 171
   proprietor of Carolina, 209
   proprietor of New Jersey, 203-4, 206
Berkeley, Sir William, 30, 47, 61, 92, 94-7, 125, 181-2, 187, 192, 238-9, 242
   on Act of 1650, 28-7, 90
   Bacon's Rebellion and, 181, 238-9, 242
   Carolina proprietor, 209
   English civil war and, 49, 51, 76
   rebellion of 1650 and, 86-7
   Restoration and, 133, 136

INDEX